Summe...

To Karen with much
appreciation for the
book you have made
for me of our long
dreamed of trip with
Dad to his home, our family.

Elise

FRUITS IN COOKING

A SELECTION OF
UNUSUAL AND
CLASSIC
FRUIT RECIPES

FRUITS IN COOKING

Robert Ackart

Illustrations by Marjorie Zaum

MACMILLAN PUBLISHING CO., INC.
New York

LIBRARY OF CONGRESS CATALOGING IN PUBLICATION DATA

Ackart, Robert C
    Fruits in cooking.

    1. Cookery (Fruit) I. Title.
TX811.A26 1974   641.6'4   72-12452
ISBN 0-02-500150-7

Macmillan Publishing Co., Inc.
866 Third Avenue, New York, N.Y. 10022
Collier-Macmillan Canada Ltd.

Library of Congress Catalog Card Number: 72-12452

First Printing

Printed in the United States of America

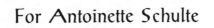

For Antoinette Schulte

CONTENTS

FOREWORD

This book presents a selection of unusual and classic recipes using fruit as a principal ingredient. In American cookery, fruits are generally relegated to salads or—more often—to desserts, but in Oriental, Middle Eastern, and much European cuisine, the complementary addition of fruit to meat, poultry, fish, and vegetable dishes is as old as cooking itself. The emphasis here, therefore, is on the relatively unexplored areas of main- and side-dish preparation possible with fruit; at the same time, I hope the book does not neglect the kind of fruit cookery more familiar to most of us.

The book is divided into five parts. Part I presents, in alphabetical order, fruits commonly found in grocery stores and supermarkets, either fresh, frozen, canned, or dried. Each fruit is introduced by a brief account of its botanical type and history. Then follow recipes using these individual fruits, arranged according to customary menu divisions: soups and appetizers, meats, poultry, fish, vegetables, farinaceous dishes, salads, breads, desserts, sauces and dressings, and beverages. Because there are more familiar than unusual fruit dishes in the salad, bread, dessert, and beverage categories, commensurately fewer recipes are given for them. Classic recipes, which time has tampered with or which fashion has changed, are given, insofar as possible, in their original form. The majority of recipes are intended to be suggestive (they are surely not designed to be restrictive or rigid); therefore, allow your imagination to soar—experiment! In creativity lies the delight of cooking. Better an interesting creation that does not quite work than a dull dish that succeeds in a trite and humdrum way. (I should add here that rhubarb, a vegetable commonly used as a fruit, is included, whereas tomatoes, cucumbers, and other fruits generally considered vegetables are omitted.)

Part II concerns *mixed* fresh, frozen, or canned fruits used in various combinations. Part III, dealing with *mixed* dried fruits, presents recipes for their use. Part IV offers conserves and relishes of special interest to the cook intrigued by the possibilities of unusual fruit cookery. Part V suggests recipes for "exotic" fruits, highly seasonal or only occasionally available. It must be admitted that, given the opportunity to enjoy fresh papaya or ripe mango, for example, only the adventurous cook would hazard to combine their delicacy with other flavors. The recipes, I feel, enhance rather than diminish the taste of the unusual fruits selected.

Most of the recipes are designed to serve six persons. They may be made from ingredients readily available, for the most part, from the supermarket, occasionally from a specialty or health food shop. When they may be doubled, refrigerated, or frozen, indication to this effect is made. For the convenience of the cook, the time required to prepare the recipe and the time needed to cook it are given. The recipes show when one may stop in the preparation or cooking of the dish in order to continue later; thus the recipe may be completed in two sessions, if desired, rather than in one longer period. Cross-referencing precludes the necessity of repeating basic recipes.

The recipes have been begged, borrowed, and stolen from friends, restaurants, and research sources. They have been invented "out of whole cloth." All have been altered and adapted to the purposes of this book, to the availability of ingredients, and to the limited number of cooking techniques incorporated here. The nationalities of many recipes are given and, when particular dishes have special significance for me, I add a personal note about them, feeling that cooks enjoy the human interest which lies behind recipes. When a prepared mix may be substituted for "making it from scratch," this suggestion is made; some few of the recipes stipulate prepared ingredients from the outset. A lexicon of terms used throughout the book is included for the user's convenience.

I happily express gratitude to my neighbor, Mrs. Mallory Danforth, who typed the (illegible) manuscript both cheerfully and accurately. Appreciation is also due the staff and crew, and especially Mr. Harvey Simmonds, of the steamer *Delta Queen*; here, a large section of the manuscript was written as she plied from Cincinnati to New Orleans and from Cincinnati to Peoria. The personnel searched out places where I could work quietly; I am sure there is no more complete removal from daily, and continually interrupted, living than being on board a boat! Warm thanks are due Marjorie Zaum for the privilege of working with her once more; this book is the third on which we have collaborated, she as illustrator, I as author. I hope more will follow. Finally, I want to thank family and friends, who subsisted for something over two years on fruit-recipe testing. That they survived, did not complain, and sometimes flattered, gave me enthusiasm to continue with the book which, now completed, will bring, I hope, pleasure to its user.

Robert Ackart

Katonah, New York
   1973

DEFINITIONS AND TERMS

The following terms and techniques, arranged alphabetically, recur throughout the book. Here they are defined and described (sometimes with prejudice) for the ready use of the cook.

Acidulated water: 1 quart of cold water with 1 or 2 tablespoons of lemon or lime juice, or ½ cup dry white wine added to it; used to prevent fruit and vegetables from discoloring and to soak certain meats, such as sweetbreads, before they are cooked.

"At this point you may stop and continue later": a signal useful to the cook unable to complete the dish at one time. Also helpful if the cook prefers not to reheat the completed casserole. It is assumed that not longer than 2 or 3 hours intervene in the preparation process; if so, the casserole should be refrigerated. (See also remarks under *Refrigeration* below.)

Bacon: (See *Salt pork.*)

Bouquet garni: the French term for a selection of herbs, tied together and sometimes put into a piece of cheesecloth to facilitate their removal from the completed dish. The classic *bouquet garni:* 3 stalks of parsley, 1 stalk of thyme, 1 bay leaf. A piece of orange zest (see definition below) is sometimes added, as is marjoram, lemon, thyme, or savory.

Browning meats and poultry: many of the recipes combining meats or poultry and fruit are cooked in a casserole; the meats are often cut into bite-sized pieces and the poultry is described as serving-pieces—a wing, thigh, or other portion. To brown the meat or poultry, follow the directions given in individual recipes. This process is not a pleasurable pastime; it is boring and can be messy (albeit a combination of butter and oil, as suggested, reduces the spattering). Because I am a lazy cook, I recommend browning a fairly large quantity of meat or chicken, using what an individual recipe requires, and freezing the remainder against the day when I want to make a dish calling for it. There is a less arduous way of browning meat and poultry: arrange the pieces (skin side down, if poultry) on a broiler rack, season the top side, and proceed as if you were going to broil the meat, lightly parboiling it until it is only *barely* golden; turn the pieces and repeat. The essences which drip through, once chilled and the fat removed, are excellent in stock and sauces (the essence) and for use in cooking other dishes (the fat). (See also *Seasoned flour* below.)

Bulgur: also spelled "bulghur," cracked buckwheat groats, used throughout the Middle East as often as rice, has both a more distinctive texture and a more distinctive flavor than white polished rice. Because it has more body, it tends to "hold" better for delayed serving and for freezing. Available at speciality and Middle Eastern food stores and, sometimes, at grocery stores.

Butter (and margarine): butter is called for in these recipes; but in cooking, margarine will serve equally well. You will find that 2 Tablespoons butter (or margarine) and 2 Tablespoons oil will suffice for browning undredged meats and poultry. In browning meats and poultry dredged in seasoned flour, you may want to add butter and oil as needed.

Casserole size: one of the aims of this book is to enable preparation of the main dish in one utensil, or sometimes two. For this reason, use a commodious casserole. Casserole sizes are sometimes difficult to judge. They come in several graduations: 5-, 5½-, and 6-quart sizes are available. I use a 5½-quart enamelized iron casserole; it is big enough to work in but sufficiently compact to keep the dish "together." For doubling these recipes, you will, of course, need a larger casserole.

Chicken broth: in these recipes, frequently a 10½-oz. can of chicken broth is called for. I use it undiluted. Chicken bouillon cubes or powder may be used to make chicken broth. The thrifty cook will make his own: save all bones from chicken dishes, as well as bits of skin and fat which may have been cut from the serving portions before cooking. In a soup kettle, put these, together with 1 or 2 bay leaves, a generous pinch of marjoram, sage, and thyme, and salt and pepper (I also use a bit of sugar); add water to cover and simmer for about 3 hours. Sieve the broth through a colander, then sieve it through a cloth into a tall, narrow container (I use a 2-quart plastic refrigerator jar); allow it to cool, chill it, and then remove the fat. This fat, incidentally works well in place of butter and oil for the next time you brown chicken.

Condiments for curries: serve in small side dishes to be sprinkled over the curry dish: mango chutney, chopped sweet pickles, raisins, chopped hard-boiled eggs, chopped scallions, pineapple tidbits, shredded coconut, peanuts, thin-sliced bananas.

Crème pâtissière: also known as confectioner's custard or baker's custard, this thick French cream is used to fill tarts and cakes. It is particularly good used with fruit. See page 130.

Curry: curry powders may consist of five spices or fifty, all dried and ground before being combined. Commercial curry may blend fifteen or twenty herbs; one of the better commercial curry powders is compounded of cumin, coriander, turmeric, fenugreek, cardamon, and red and black peppers. In certain of these recipes, the curry is made from individual species and herbs, giving quite a different flavor from commercial curry powder.

Deglazing: after browning and removing meat or poultry, add, over high heat, the liquid specified in the recipe; stir the mixture vigorously and scrape the bottom of the utensil to bring up the browned bits.

Dredging: in a waxed-paper bag, shake together a few pieces of meat or poultry and seasoned flour. This method assures an even coating of flour. You may also dredge by pressing the meat into flour which has been put in a dish. (See *Seasoned flour* below.)

Dried fruit: generally *tenderized* dried fruits are packaged in boxes; they are pliant to the touch and, unless a recipe specifies doing so, require no soaking before being combined and cooked with the other ingredients. Dried fruit requiring soaking is usually bought in bulk; it should be rinsed, put in a bowl and covered with boiling water, and allowed to stand for 30 minutes before being combined and cooked with the other ingredients. The fruit water may often be used as part or all of the liquid ingredient in the recipe.

Farinaceous foods: foods having a high starch content. Some foods commonly considered farinaceous are rice, *pastas* (spaghetti, noodles, etc.), and potatoes.

Fish: recipes calling for fish filets refer to white-fleshed lean fish: cod, flounder, scrod, and sole. Halibut and haddock also work in these recipes, although because they usually are thicker cuts of fish, they require additional cooking time. Filets of flounder and sole may be rolled and skewered with toothpicks, making an attractive presentation in serving. Filets of cod and scrod may be cut into serving portions before they are cooked.

Freezing: fruit does not freeze well; it loses its texture and often turns watery. When indication is made that a completed recipe may be frozen (which is not often), it should be remembered that some loss of quality is inevitable.

Frozen foods: in general, I prefer using fresh foodstuffs, rather than frozen products. Often, however, frozen foods are welcome time-savers. It is the consistency of frozen foods, not their taste, which I find disturbing. Frozen vegetables, for example, turn to mush if over-cooked. Frozen chopped onion is difficult to cook until golden, because of its high water content. Still, some of these recipes call specifically for frozen foods; when this occurs, use them in good heart!

Fresh ginger: fresh ginger root is available at Oriental and specialty food stores. Buy a pound, peel off the bark, cut the root into walnut-sized pieces, put them in jars, add dry sherry to cover, and store the ginger in the refrigerator. The root will keep indefinitely this way. I prefer the tanginess of fresh ginger to the milder taste of preserved ginger; the latter, however, is available at the supermarket.

"Heat the butter and oil . . .": not to the point that the combination smokes or discolors, but so that it is very hot and will seal in juices and sear the flesh of meat and poultry for added flavor. A drop of water in the casserole, wildly dancing, will show you that now is the time.

Herbs: whenever possible, use fresh herbs; their taste is much superior to the taste of dried herbs. If you have a spare window sill, try growing a few: basil, marjoram, parsley, sage, summer savory, and thyme are obliging plants, eager to thrive and to flavor a dish. If you use commercial dried herbs, select the best brand available; do not stint here, for quality makes the difference between real *bouquet* and no taste at all.

Julienne: a term derived from French cooking which means cut into very thin slices lengthwise. (We see the term on restaurant menus, offering julienne of ham and chicken in chef's salad.)

Ketchup: a name referring to any of several highly spiced sauces. Known also as *catsup*, of which the English essayist Steele wrote in the eighteenth century, the name derives from a now-archaic Chinese word meaning fish brine.

Lemon butter: a combination of melted butter and lemon juice, added to taste. A savory butter is made by stirring the juice of 1 lemon into ¼ lb. melted butter. Lemon butter is a fine sauce for fish and is sometimes used as an ingredient in these recipes.

Margarine (see also *Butter*): may be used in place of butter in these recipes. Or you may want to use half and half. For delicate dishes, try unsalted butter—truly a delight to the palate.

Marinating: do not hesitate to lengthen the suggested marinating times, but never shorten them. Marination tenderizes and adds its own particular flavor. I recommend marinating at room temperature; if the marination period is longer than 4 hours, allow 4 hours *outside* the refrigerator, and the remainder *inside*. Unless otherwise specified, save the marinade as an ingredient of the sauce.

Oil: in cooking, use either the finest grade of pure olive oil, a mixture or half olive oil and half corn oil, or a tasteless oil, such as peanut or sesame seed. In salad, the finest grade of pure olive oil is my recommendation; it will add flavor to the dressing, but, if top quality, will not taste "heavy."

Parsley: available in two varieties (the American curly leafed and the Italian flat leafed) and in three forms, fresh, dried, and frozen. Use fresh whenever possible. Rinse the parsley with cold water, shake it well, and put it in a container with tight-fitting lid; stored this way in the refrigerator, parsley will keep well. Frozen parsley tends to be watery. I think dried parsley tastes like hay, but that is only my opinion.

Pepper: there are three popular peppers: black, white, and red. Unless otherwise specified, black is the pepper called for in these recipes. I prefer to use peppercorns, grinding freshly as I need the spice. White pepper does not differ from black; it has merely had the dark hull removed. Red pepper differs markedly from both black and white, and from its red cousin, paprika; in these recipes it is *not* used unless specifically directed.

Pine nuts: also commonly called *pignoli*, these kernels from the cone of a variety of pine growing in the Southwestern United States, Southern Europe, and the Middle East, are very often used in Turkish, Balkan, and Italian cooking and as a garnish for meat dishes, vegetables, and salads. They are generally available in supermarkets and are easily procurable in specialty food stores.

Plumping (currants and raisins): in a mixing bowl, barely cover the currants or raisins with very hot or boiling water, allow them to stand for 5 minutes before draining them in a colander.

Refrigeration: the majority of dishes in this book may be refrigerated. This enables the cook to prepare the meal the morning before or even a day ahead, chill it, and reheat it before serving. Please note, however, that reheating is done after the chilled casserole has come fully to room temperature. Take it out of the refrigerator 2 or 3 hours before reheating and reheat it gently to avoid overcooking. If a dish cannot be refrigerated, notation to that effect is made, Chinese and Japanese food should be refrigerated only when you intend to use them as leftovers; refrigeration destroys their crisp-tender quality and the freshness of their color.

Rice: there are two readily available varieties in the supermarket. (Wild rice is not rice at all, but a member of the wheat family.) White or polished rice is most used. Brown rice, free of its hull but unpolished, is the second variety, and the one I prefer. It takes longer to cook than white rice, but it has more body, more taste, "holds" better for a delayed meal, and retains some degree of texture when frozen. I avoid precooked or processed rice; it is not as flavorful, has a somewhat nondescript texture, and will not freeze well.

Rose water: a flavoring for sweet dishes, creams, and cakes, and used widely in the Balkans, the Middle East, and India. It is made by infusing rose petals in or combining rose oils with water. It is available at Middle Eastern and specialty food shops. Orange-flower water, prepared from orange blossoms, may be used for the same purpose and is obtainable from the same sources.

Roux: equal amounts of melted fat (usually butter) and flour, well mixed, and used as the thickening agent for many sauces. A *roux* is improved by being cooked over gentle heat for 2 or 3 minutes before the liquid ingredient of the sauce is added.

Salt pork: in a flame-proof casserole, render (cook until crisp and golden) ¼ lb. salt pork, finely diced. With a slotted spoon, remove the cooked bits to absorbent paper and reserve them. In the remaining fat, brown the meat or poultry called for in the recipe. This technique makes for a richer dish. Some of these recipes direct doing so; many may be so treated if desired. Recipes which offer a very delicate or light flavor are better made as suggested. The pork bits make a tasty garnish cooked with the casserole or added at the time of serving. Six strips of bacon, diced, and prepared in the same way may be substituted for ¼ lb. salt pork.

Scalding (milk and cream): heat milk or cream, either over direct heat or over hot water in the top of a double boiler, to a point just short of boiling; at scalding temperature the liquid will shimmer and a thin surface film forms on it. Scalding prevents milk and cream from curdling when used in combination with other foods and liquids.

Seasoned flour: combine ⅔ cup flour, 1½ teaspoons salt, and ½ teaspoon pepper together in a waxed paper bag; in this, shake pieces of meat or poultry, a few at a time. Add a bit of the remaining flour when making the sauce. (I prefer using white pepper, which will not speckle the sauce.)

"Serving-pieces of chicken for 6 persons:" this phrase, referring to young chicken—fryers and broilers, not stewing fowl—appears in

each recipe for chicken cooked in casserole. Often chicken parts are available, thus enabling you to buy what you like best. I prefer the second joint, or thigh; it is more flavorful and moist than other parts of chicken and much less expensive than the breast, which can be dry and stringy unless cooked with great care. The chicken recipes can be prepared equally well with whole young chicken which you cut into serving-pieces yourself. Depending upon the parts used, allow two or perhaps three pieces per serving.

Shrimp, basic preparation of: for 6 persons, allow 1½ lbs. fresh shrimp. Wash them. (If they are frozen, thaw them in cold water.) With a shrimp cleaner or your fingers, peel off the shells and remove the black vein. To cook the shrimp, bring 2 cups water to the boil in a saucepan. Add 1 teaspoon salt and, if desired, a bay leaf, parsley sprig, onion slice, 1 whole clove, and 1 teaspoon of vinegar. Add the shrimp, bring them to the boil, and cook them for 5 minutes, or until they are just pink. (Overcooking shrinks and toughens them.)

Stir-frying: the Chinese technique for fast cooking in which sliced or chopped meats and vegetables are stirred rapidly and constantly in a small amount of oil over high heat. Stir-frying requires that all ingredients be prepared and ready at hand. It produces crisp-tender dishes and does not change the color of the ingredients.

Stuffing (dressing): allow 1 cup of stuffing per 1 pound of fowl. Do not pack stuffing; rather, allow room for it to expand while cooking. Extra stuffing may be cooked, covered, in a buttered baking dish. Handle dressing lightly to prevent its becoming heavy and sodden. Stuff the fowl (or other meat) just before cooking it to assure that the breadstuff does not sour.

Turmeric: this tropical herb has very little flavor of its own, but is invaluable in coloring curry powders. I recommend it for coloring dishes made with rice. Saffron, too, will color, but saffron is costly and highly flavorful; save saffron for an occasion demanding it, use turmeric for color.

Wine (cooking and table): recipes requiring wine should be cooked in enamelized or crockery ware; otherwise, the wine will take on the metallic utensil taste. Unless otherwise suggested, *dry* wines, both red and white are called for. "Cooking wine" does not exist, despite the popularity of that phrase. There is only good and not-so-good wine. It is unnecessary to cook with wine of rare vintage or costly price; your palate, however, will convince you that the quality of the dish reflects the quality of wine used in it. As for table wines, I do not hold that "with chicken and fish, white wine." The heartier dishes in this book taste well served with red wine. White wine is always acceptable with fruits, and *vin rose* is often welcome. I leave the selection to you; availability and prices of wine are so much a matter of geographical location. I do not recommend imported over domestic wines; there are admirable wines in both groups. Good wine, modestly priced or costly, must be ferreted out.

Wok: available at Chinese stores and indispensable to the cook who wants to prepare Chinese dishes in the Chinese way, a *wok* is a two-handled cooking pan, rounded at the bottom. It heats quickly and evenly and makes stir-frying easy. They do not work on electric ranges.

Zest: the zest of lemon, lime, or orange is the outer part of the peel which contains the flavorful oils. A vegetable peeler is the handiest tool to use in cutting the peel. Zest has none of the white pith attached, which is bitter and without taste of the parent fruit.

FRUITS IN COOKING

COOKING
WITH
INDIVIDUAL
FRUITS

PART

I

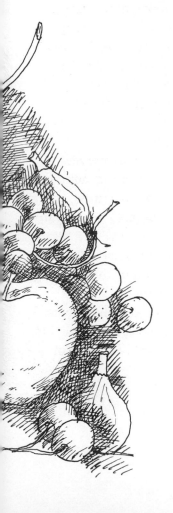

The world of fruit—how varied it is and how various the images it evokes. There is the comfortable familiarity of apples baked in pies or puddings, of oranges gracing the toes of Christmas stockings, of peaches eaten out of hand on summer evenings. There is the strange exciting world of mangoes perfuming tropical shores, of papayas proferred by sloe-eyed Circes, of legendary fruits far more mysterious and perhaps no less fateful than Eden's apple.

The botanist quickly dispells these fantasies by reminding us that fruits are simply the fleshy seed containers of certain trees, shrubs, bushes, and canes. This lack-lustre definition applies to all fruits—bananas, grapes, tomatoes, or apricots. The flesh of fruit protects the developing seeds and, once they are mature, aids in their distribution.

Botanically, there are four principal groups of fruits. Those having cores with small seeds (apples and pears, for example) are called *pomes*. Those having single stones or pits (cherries and plums) are *drupes*. Then there are *berries*, which have seeds scattered throughout their juicy flesh (grapes, blueberries—and oranges!). And, last, there are the *aggregate fruits*, in reality many small fruits growing together (raspberries and blackberries). There are some "fruits" which are not fruits at all (strawberries, which are neither berries nor fruits) and rhubarb (which is a vegetable but used as a fruit), as well as tomatoes and cucumbers (which are fruits but used as vegetables). Cooks attach a less rigid meaning to the term "fruit" than do botanists, so we may dismiss the fact that peas and beans are fruits and delight in the knowledge that over 160 species of "honest" fruits are eaten the world over.

Many, if not most, of the fruits known today originated in the Fertile Crescent, that area of the prehistoric and ancient world which had a Mediterranean climate of rainy winters and sunny summers and which was bounded on the south by the Arabian Desert and on the north by the Armenian mountains, extending from Babylonia and Persia to Assyria and the Mediterranean Ocean. The Fertile Crescent corresponds to the area of Hebrew tradition described in the Bible. Here systematic agriculture was first practiced, sometime around 8000 B.C. And here originated apricots, various berries, dates, figs, grapes, lemons, limes, melons, peaches, pomegranates, and perhaps apples, cherries, and pears. Rhubarb also originated here, as did cucumbers and peas and beans, those "non-fruits" already mentioned.

Common fruits from the New World are avocados, tomatoes, certain berries including cranberries, certain grapes, grapefruit, pineapples, and papayas. The origins of exotic or unusual fruits selected for this book are described under their specific entries.

All fruits provide the B-complex vitamins (which steady nerves and sharpen appetites) and vitamin C (which aids in healing wounds, maintaining muscle tone, and fighting head colds). Many fruits (apricots, peaches, plums, and blackberries among others) are rich in iron.

The cooking of the Orient, Middle East, and the Pacific islands relies heavily on fruits. Certain regional cooking, such as that of the Caribbean, is based largely on the use of fruit; one cannot imagine West Indian cuisine devoid of guavas, mangoes, papayas, pineapples, coconuts, breadfruits, plantains, and bananas. This book is designed to stimulate an interest in the world-wide, ancient, but ever-new use of fruit in cookery.

CABBAGE AND APPLE SOUP

(German)

Serves 6
Doubles
Refrigerates

Preparation: 30 minutes
Cooking: 2½ hours

1 medium head (1½ to 2 lbs.) young cabbage, shredded
1 8-oz. can tomato puree
½ cup cider vinegar
¾ cup dark brown sugar
Juice of 2 lemons
3 apples, peeled, cored, and chopped
2 10½-oz. cans condensed chicken broth

(1) In a soup kettle, combine these seven ingredients. Bring the mixture to the boil, reduce the heat, cover, and simmer for 2½ hours.

½ cup raisins
Salt
Pepper

(2) Add the raisins 15 minutes before serving. At the time of serving, adjust the seasoning to taste.

PUMPKIN AND APPLE SOUP

(American)

Serves 6
Doubles
Refrigerates
Freezes

Preparation: 25 minutes
Cooking: 20 minutes

(continued)

2 **cups pumpkin puree**
3 **tart green apples, peeled, and grated**
4 **Tablespoons butter**
2 **teaspoons sugar**
1½ **teaspoons salt**
½ **teaspoon white pepper**
¼ **teaspoon nutmeg**

(1) In a saucepan, combine the pumpkin, apple, butter, and seasonings. Over gentle heat, cook the mixture for 10 minutes, stirring constantly.

1 **10½-oz. can condensed chicken broth**
3 **cups milk, scalded**

(2) Gradually add the broth and then the milk, stirring constantly. Simmer the soup for 5 minutes. (If desired, pour soup into electric blender and set at high speed for 1 minute to eliminate any graininess from the apple. Reheat before serving.)

LAMB STEW AND APPLES

(French)

Navarin de Mouton is a classic French stew made with potatoes. This one, with apples, is my invention.

Serves 6
Doubles
Refrigerates

Preparation: 20 minutes
Cooking: 1½ hours
Preheat oven: 350°

3 **Tablespoons bacon fat**
3 **lbs. shoulder of lamb, cut in bite-sized pieces**
Salt
Pepper

(1) In a flame-proof casserole, heat the bacon fat and brown the lamb. Season the meat to taste and remove it to absorbent paper.

4 **onions, chopped**

(2) Discard all but 3 Tablespoons of the fat; in the remaining fat, cook the onions until translucent.

2 Tablespoons flour
½ teaspoon celery seed
½ teaspoon marjoram
½ teaspoon thyme

(3) Into the onions, stir the flour and seasonings. Replace the lamb.

At this point you may stop and continue later.

2 cups apple juice
6 firm, ripe tart apples, peeled, cored, and quartered

(4) Pour the apple juice over the contents of the casserole. Cover and bake at 350° for 1½ hours, or until the lamb is tender. Add the apples during the final 30 minutes of cooking.

PORK AND APPLE RAGOUT

(Flemish)

Serves 6
Doubles
Refrigerates
Freezes

Preparation: 30 minutes
Cooking: 2 hours
Preheat oven: 300°

3 lbs. fresh pork, cut into bite-sized pieces
Salt
Pepper

(1) Trim excess fat from pork and render in a flame-proof casserole. When fat is hot, brown the pork pieces well. Season to taste and remove.

12 to 18 small onions

(2) In the remaining fat, glaze the onions. Remove. Discard all but 3 Tablespoons fat.

3 Tablespoons flour
1 12-oz. can beer at room temperature

(3) Into the fat, stir the flour. Gradually add the beer, stirring constantly until the sauce is thickened and smooth.

(continued)

7

2 tart apples, peeled, cored, and coarsely grated
½ teaspoon oregano
½ teaspoon rosemary, crumbled
½ teaspoon sage

(4) To the sauce, add the apples and seasonings. Replace the pork and onions.

At this point you may stop and continue later.

4 tart apples, peeled, cored, and cut into eighths

(5) Bake the casserole, covered, at 300° for 1½ hours. Add the apple slices and continue to cook the ragout, covered, for an additional 30 minutes.

A variation of this recipe produces an English pork and apple pie: In a buttered casserole, alternate layers of pork, onions, and apple slices; sprinkle each layer with the herbs; add ½ cup condensed chicken broth; bake the casserole, well covered, at 325° for 1½ hours, or until the pork is tender (more broth may be added as necessary). Just before serving, top the pie with mashed potatoes and brown under the broiler.

CHICKEN AND APPLES

Serves 6
Doubles
Refrigerates

Preparation: 30 minutes
Cooking: 1 hour
Preheat oven: 350°

2 Tablespoons butter
2 Tablespoons oil
Serving-pieces of chicken for 6 persons
Salt
Pepper

(1) In a flame-proof casserole, heat the butter and oil and brown the chicken; season it. Remove chicken. Discard all but 3 Tablespoons of the fat.

3 Tablespoons flour
2 10½-oz. cans condensed chicken broth
Water

(2) To the remaining fat, add the flour, stirring; over gentle heat, cook the *roux* for a few minutes. To the broth, add water to equal 3 cups. Gradually add the liquid, stirring. Over moderate heat, cook the mixture, stirring constantly, until it is thickened and smooth.

6 carrots, scraped and thickly sliced **12 small onions**	(3) Add the vegetables to the sauce.
	At this point you may stop and continue later.
	(4) Replace the chicken in the casserole. Cover and bake at 350° for 35 minutes.
4 apples, peeled, cored, and sliced into eighths	(5) Gently stir the apples into the sauce, cover the casserole and continue cooking for 20 minutes.
1 9-oz. box frozen peas, fully thawed to room temperature	(6) Add the peas and continue cooking the dish, covered, for 10 minutes longer.

CHICKEN AND APPLES WITH CURRY

(Indian)

Serves 6
Doubles
Refrigerates

Preparation: 40 minutes
Cooking: 1 hour
Preheat oven: 350°

2 Tablespoons butter **2 Tablespoons oil** **Serving-pieces of chicken for 6 persons** **Salt** **Pepper**	(1) In a flame-proof casserole, heat the butter and oil and brown the chicken; season it. Remove chicken.
3 medium onions, chopped	(2) In the remaining fat, cook the onion until translucent.
3 or 4 green apples, peeled, cored, and diced **1 Tablespoon curry powder (or to taste)** **3 Tablespoons flour**	(3) Add the apples, stirring well to coat with fat. Then add the curry powder and flour; cook the mixture, stirring, for several minutes.

(continued)

1 10½-oz. can condensed chicken
broth
Apple juice

(4) Add apple juice to the chicken broth to equal 2½ cups. Gradually add the liquid to the apple mixture and cook, stirring, until thickened and smooth. Replace the chicken, spooning the sauce over it.

At this point you may stop and continue later.

(5) Bake the casserole, covered, at 350° for 1 hour, or until the chicken is tender.

CHICKEN LIVERS AND APPLES

(Finnish)

The dish is prepared so rapidly that there is no need to "stop and continue later."

Serves 6
Doubles
Refrigerates

Preparation: 20 minutes
Cooking: 10 minutes

4 Tablespoons butter
6 apples, peeled, cored, and cut into eighths
4 Tablespoons sugar

(1) In a skillet, melt the butter, add the apple slices, and sprinkle them with sugar. Cook the apples over gentle heat for 10 minutes, or until they are tender but still retain their shape.

4 Tablespoons butter
1½ lbs. chicken livers
Salt
Pepper
½ cup hot water

(2) In a second skillet, melt the butter and, over gentle heat, cook the livers 5 minutes, stirring often. Season them. Add the water and continue to cook them for 5 minutes.

1½ Tablespoons cornstarch, mixed with 2 Tablespoons cold water
1 cup apple juice
2 Tablespoons honey
2 Tablespoons lemon juice

(3) In a saucepan, combine the cornstarch mixture with the apple juice, honey, and lemon juice, stirring until they are well blended. Cook the sauce until it is thickened and smooth.

(4) On a serving dish, arrange the apple slices, top them with the chicken livers, and pour the sauce over all.

HELEN McCULLY'S APPLE SLICES BAKED IN BUTTER*

Serves 6
Doubles
Refrigerates

Preparation: 20 minutes
Cooking: 25 minutes
Preheat oven: 300°

4 or 5 all-purpose apples
  Salt
  Sugar
  Juice of 1 lemon
4 Tablespoons butter, melted

(1) Pare, core, and thinly slice the apples. In a flat, lightly buttered baking dish, arrange the apples in slightly overlapping rows. Sprinkle the apples with a little salt and, generously, with sugar. Add the lemon juice and pour the butter over the fruit.

(2) Bake the apples, basting them occasionally, at 300° for 25 minutes.

At this point you may stop and continue later.

  Sugar
  Butter

(3) Just before serving, sprinkle the apples with a little more sugar, dot with butter, and put them under the broiler until their edges turn golden.

* Helen McCully is a many-faceted person. She shines not only as Food Editor of *House Beautiful*, but also as the author of *Cooking with Helen McCully Beside You*, a book which, once mastered, virtually guarantees the ability to cook well. This recipe may be served with roast pork, goose, duck, or game; *or* as a dessert accompanied by heavy cream.

BEETS AND APPLES
(Ukrainian)

This side dish, or relish, is served with roast meats.

Serves 6
Doubles
Refrigerates

Preparation: 40 minutes
Cooking: 5 minutes

6 or 7 large beets

(1) Boil beets until tender (approximately 20 minutes), peel and grate them.

2 teaspoons cornstarch
1 cup sour cream
3 Tablespoons butter
½ teaspoon salt
¼ teaspoon pepper

(2) In a saucepan, blend the cornstarch and sour cream until smooth. Add the butter and seasonings. Cook the mixture, stirring constantly, until it comes to the boil.

4 tart apples, peeled, coarsely grated, and sprinkled with the juice of ½ lemon
Sugar (optional)

(3) To the sour cream mixture, add the grated beets and apples, stirring gently. Cook the mixture over moderate heat for about 5 minutes; do not allow it to boil. If desired, stir in a little sugar to taste.

BRUSSELS SPROUTS AND APPLES
(American)

Serves 6
Doubles
Refrigerates

Preparation: 25 minutes
Cooking: 35 minutes
Preheat oven: 350°

2 pints Brussels sprouts, trimmed
  and rinsed
3 apples, peeled, cored, and sliced
¾ cup grapefruit juice

(1) In a buttered baking dish, arrange the Brussels sprouts and apple slices. Pour the grapefruit juice over them. Cover and bake at 350° for 25 minutes, or until the sprouts are just tender.

½ cup sour cream
4 Tablespoons butter, melted
½ teaspoons ground cumin seed
  Salt
  Pepper

(2) Combine the sour cream and butter; season the mixture with the cumin and salt and pepper to taste.

At this point you may stop and continue later.

(3) Bring the sour cream mixture to the boil, pour it over the sprouts, cover, and continue cooking them for 10 minutes longer.

ONION AND APPLE PIE

(American)

This eighteenth-century recipe makes an excellent supper dish, as well as a pleasant accompaniment to roast meats.

Serving: one 9-inch pie

Preparation: 45 minutes*
Cooking: 1 hour
Preheat oven: 375°

Short pastry for a two-crust 9-inch pie

(1) Line a 9-inch pie pan with a bottom crust. Reserve pastry for top crust.

* Preparation time does not include readying the pastry, page 458.

(continued)

3 or 4 apples, peeled, cored, and sliced
3 potatoes, peeled and thinly sliced
6 medium onions, peeled and thinly sliced
6 hard-boiled eggs, sliced

(2) Over the crust, make a layer of each of these four ingredients. Repeat.

½ teaspoon mace
½ teaspoon pepper
2 teaspoons salt
Softened butter
¼ cup water

(3) Mix together the seasonings and sprinkle them over the top layer. Dot the layer generously with butter. Sprinkle over the water.

Top crust

(4) Arrange the top crust over the pie, crimping it at the edges with a fork. Make several cuts in it with a sharp knife.

At this point you may stop and continue later.

(5) Bake the pie at 375° for 1 hour, or until the crust is golden brown. Serve the pie hot.

RED CABBAGE AND APPLE

(*Swiss*)

Serves 6
Doubles
Refrigerates

Preparation: 15 minutes
Cooking: 2 hours
Preheat oven: 350°

1 medium-sized red cabbage, finely shredded
1 onion, chopped
3 or 4 apples, peeled and grated
6 slices of raw thick-sliced bacon, diced
½ cup wine vinegar

(1) In a large mixing bowl, toss together thoroughly all the ingredients.

1½ **cups dry red wine**
  3 **Tablespoons dark brown sugar**
1½ **teaspoons salt**
 ¼ **teaspoon pepper**

(2) In a casserole, bake the cabbage, covered, at 350° for 2 hours, stirring once or twice during the cooking. Serve the vegetable hot.

A Dutch variation omits the bacon, but directs that the cabbage be sauteed briefly in 4 or 5 Tablespoons butter before being combined with the other ingredients.

ZUCCHINI AND APPLES

Serves 6
Doubles

Preparation: 20 minutes
Cooking: 30 minutes
Preheat oven: 350°

4 **medium-sized zucchini, cut crosswise in ½-inch slices**
3 **tart apples, peeled, cored, and cut Into eighths**

(1) In a lightly buttered casserole, combine the zucchini and apples.

1 **teaspoon ground coriander**
3 **Tablespoons brown sugar**
1 **teaspoon salt**
  Grating of pepper
  Juice of 1 lemon

(2) Sprinkle the seasonings over the contents of the casserole.

4 **Tablespoons butter, melted**

(3) Add the butter and toss the mixture gently but thoroughly.

½ **cup cider, apple juice, or chicken broth**

(4) Pour the liquid over the apple mixture and bake the casserole, covered, at 350° for 15 minutes; remove the cover and continue to bake the dish for 15 minutes, or until the vegetable is tender.

15

APPLE SALAD WITH CELERY AND PEAS

Serves 6
Doubles
Refrigerates

Preparation: 30 minutes
Chilling time: 1½ hours (minimum)

4 large apples, peeled, cored, and diced
Juice of 1 lemon

(1) As you prepare the apples, put the diced pieces into a plastic container with a tight-fitting lid; add the lemon juice, cover and shake vigorously. The lemon juice will prevent the apples from turning brown. Drain.

2 9-oz. packages frozen small peas, fully thawed to room temperature
1½ cups celery, chopped
½ green pepper, chopped
3 scallions, chopped, with as much green as is crisp
½ cup Orange Mayonnaise (page 262)
Pinch of salt
Grating of pepper

(2) In a large mixing bowl, toss together the apples, and the other ingredients. Season to taste. If necessary to bind the salad, add a little more mayonnaise. Chill the mixture thoroughly.

Fresh salad greens

(3) To serve, arrange the salad mixture on a bed of greens.

HOT APPLE SLAW

(German)

Serves 6
Doubles

Preparation: 25 minutes
Cooking time: 5 minutes

¼ lb. salt pork, diced or ¼ lb. thick-sliced bacon, diced	(1) In a skillet, render the pork or bacon bits and remove them to absorbent paper; reserve them.

¼ cup cider vinegar 3 Tablespoons water 2 Tablespoons sugar ¾ teaspoon ground celery seed 1½ teaspoons salt	(2) To the remaining fat, add these five ingredients. Bring the mixture to a boil.

3 cups, packed, cabbage, finely shredded 2 apples, peeled, cored and coarsely grated	(3) To the boiling dressing, add the cabbage and apples, stirring gently. Simmer the slaw for a minute or two. Serve it at once, garnished with the reserved pork or bacon bits.

WALDORF SALAD

(American)

A conceit of the famous Oscar of the Waldorf, this salad is a classic of American cuisine. The original recipe, given here, has gone through various mutations; some of the variations are indicated below.

> Serves 6
> Doubles
> Refrigerates

Preparation: 30 minutes
Chilling time: 1½ hours (minimum)

4 firm eating apples, peeled, cored, and diced (note: peeling is optional) Juice of 1 lemon	(1) In a container with tight-fitting lid, toss the apple with the lemon juice; this step will prevent the apples from discoloring. Drain.

1 cup celery, chopped ½ cup walnut meats, broken	(2) Combine the apples, celery, and walnut meats.

¼ cup mayonnaise 1 Tablespoon sugar 1 teaspoon lemon juice	(3) In a mixing bowl, combine these three ingredients.

(continued)

½ cup heavy cream, whipped
Salad greens

(4) Into the mayonnaise mixture, fold the whipped cream. Fold the dressing into the apple mixture and serve the salad on crisp lettuce or other mild greens of your choice.

Variations: broken pecans may be used in place of walnuts; pineapple may be used in place of celery; raisins or chopped dates may be added to the listed ingredients; if desired, Orange Mayonnaise, page 262, may be used.

<hr>

APPLE BREAD

(American)

Serving: one 9-inch loaf

Preparation: 20 minutes
Cooking: 1 hour
Preheat oven: 350°

2 cups flour
1½ teaspoons baking powder
½ teaspoon soda
1 teaspoon salt

(1) In a mixing bowl, sift together these dry ingredients.

8 Tablespoons soft butter
⅔ cup sugar

(2) In a separate bowl, cream together the butter and sugar until the mixture is light.

2 eggs

(3) To the butter-sugar mixture, add the eggs, one at a time, beating after each addition.

1 cup apple, unpeeled, cored, and coarsely grated
½ cup American or sharp Cheddar cheese, grated

(4) Add the apple and cheese to the butter-egg mixture.

(5) Add half the dry ingredients, mixing until the flour is moistened. Repeat with the remaining flour.

(6) Into a buttered 9-inch loaf pan, spoon the batter. Bake the apple bread at 350° for 1 hour, or until a knife inserted at the center comes out clean. Allow the bread to cool for several minutes in the pan before removing it to a rack.

APPLE MUFFINS

12 to 18 muffins
Doubles
Refrigerates
Freezes

Preparation: 15 minutes
Cooking: 20 minutes
Preheat oven: 400°

2 cups flour
2 teaspoons baking powder
4 Tablespoons sugar
½ teaspoon cinnamon
½ teaspoon salt

(1) In a mixing bowl, sift together the dry ingredients.

1 cup milk
1 egg
4 Tablespoons butter, melted
1 cup apple, peeled, cored, and grated

(2) In a separate mixing bowl, beat together the milk and egg. Stir in the melted butter and apple.

(3) Add the apple mixture to the dry ingredients, stirring only enough to moisten the flour.

(4) Into buttered muffin tins, spoon the batter (the cups should be ⅔ full). Bake the muffins at 400° for 20 minutes, or until they are golden brown.

BAKED APPLES

Serves 6
Doubles
Refrigerates

Preparation: 20 minutes
Cooking: 30 minutes
Preheat oven: 400°

6 large apples, peeled half way down and cored
Sugar
Cinnamon
Nutmeg
Soft butter
Boiling water

In a baking dish, arrange the apples with the peeled ends up. In each cavity, put 1 Tablespoon sugar; dust each apple with cinnamon and nutmeg, and dot each with butter. Cover the bottom of the dish with boiling water and bake the apples, uncovered, at 400° for 30 minutes, or until they are tender. Baste them often with the pan juices. Serve them hot or cold with cream.

A Russian variation (*Iablochko*): Fill each apple with brown sugar and dust each one with cinnamon. In place of the water, use 1 cup dry red wine, added after the first 15 minutes of baking. Baste the apples with this. Serve the apples sprinkled with toasted filbert nuts and softly whipped cream.

Jellied Baked Apples: Follow the directions given in the main recipe above. However, before baking the apples, pour over them the following syrup: 2 cups sugar, 1 cup water, the zest and juice of 1 lemon; boil for 5 minutes. Bake the apples at 325°, basting them often, for 45 minutes or until the fruit is tender.

APPLE BROWN BETTY

(*American*)

As American as Johnny Appleseed himself and evocative of childhood memories, this classic dessert is a friendly dish at any age.

Serves 6
Doubles
Refrigerates

Preparation: 30 minutes
Cooking: 40 minutes
Preheat oven: 350°

2 cups breadcrumbs or graham cracker crumbs
4 Tablespoons butter, melted

(1) In a mixing bowl, use fork to toss together the crumbs and butter.

½ cup dark brown sugar, gently packed
1 teaspoon cinnamon
Grated rind and juice of 1 lemon

(2) Add the sugar, cinnamon, grated lemon rind, and lemon juice, tossing as before.

4 cups apple slices, peeled
½ cup hot water
Soft butter (optional)

(3) In a buttered baking dish, arrange a layer of the crumbs and then a layer of apples; repeat, saving a layer of crumbs as topping. Sprinkle water over the mixture. Dot with butter. Bake the Brown Betty at 350° for 40 minutes, or until the apples are tender. If the dessert browns too rapidly, cover it; remove the cover later to brown the top. Serve the dessert hot with cream.

APPLE CAKE

(Danish)

This delicate dessert is a specialty from the Isle of Mon, south of Copenhagen.

Serves 6

Preparation: 30 minutes
Cooking: 1 hour
Preheat oven: 350°

8 Tablespoons soft butter
¾ cup sugar

(1) In a mixing bowl, cream together the butter and sugar until light.

2 eggs

(2) Add the eggs one at a time, beating thoroughly after each addition.

(continued)

Grated rind and juice of 1 lemon

(3) Beat in the grated lemon rind and 1 Tablespoon juice. (Reserve rest of juice for later use.)

1 cup flour
Pinch of salt

(4) Add the flour and salt to the butter-egg mixture; beat the batter until smooth.

5 cooking apples, peeled, cored, and thinly sliced
Reserved lemon juice

(5) Gently toss the apple slices with the remaining lemon juice.

Soft butter
¼ cup sugar

(6) Arrange the batter in a buttered 9-inch pan (either spring form or one with removable bottom). Over the batter, arrange the apple slices. Dot generously with butter and sprinkle over the sugar. Bake the cake at 350° for 1 hour, or until the apples are golden and the cake pulls away from the side of the pan.

1 cup heavy cream, lightly whipped
Cinnamon

(7) Cool the cake on a rack. It may be served either while still warm or when completely cooled. Serve the whipped cream and cinnamon separately.

APPLE COBBLER AND APPLE PANDOWDY

(American)

There is little information on the difference between a cobbler and a pandowdy. Cobblers are made with fruit topped by a simple cake batter and baked. Pandowdies are made with fruit sweetened with molasses or brown sugar topped with shortcake dough (page 381) and baked—a somewhat heartier dish. The pandowdy, native to New England, is also enjoyed by the Pennsylvania Dutch; the origin of the name is unknown. If you refrigerate or freeze either dessert, it should be fully at room temperature before you warm it for serving. Cooking the fruit before adding the dough is necessary only for raw fruits; the time requisite to cook them and the amount of sweetening they will need will vary from fruit to fruit, as well as with the degree of ripeness. It is better to watch and taste rather than to follow any rule.

APPLE COBBLER

Serves 6
Refrigerates
Freezes

Preparation: 30 minutes
Cooking: 1 hour
Preheat oven: 350°

3 cups apples, peeled, cored, and sliced
½ cup sugar
¼ teaspoon cinnamon
¼ teaspoon nutmeg
¼ teaspoon salt
Juice of ½ lemon

(1) In a mixing bowl, toss together the apple slices and seasonings.

(2) Arrange the fruit mixture in a lightly buttered 1½- or 2-quart baking dish. Cook the apples, uncovered, in a 350° oven for 20 minutes, or until they are just tender.

1½ cups flour
2 teaspoons baking powder
½ cup sugar
½ teaspoon salt

(3) Meanwhile, in a mixing bowl, sift together these dry ingredients.

2 eggs
¾ cup milk
1 teaspoon vanilla
Grated rind of 1 lemon
4 Tablespoons butter, melted and cooled

(4) In a separate mixing bowl, combine the liquid ingredients; beat them with a rotary beater. Stir in the grated lemon rind and butter.

(5) Combine the dry and liquid ingredients, beating until the batter is smooth. Pour it over the apples and bake the cobbler, uncovered, at 350° for 1 hour, or until the cake begins to draw away from the sides of the dish.

APPLE PANDOWDY

Serves 6
Refrigerates
Freezes

Preparation: 30 minutes
Cooking: 1 hour
Preheat oven: 350°

3 cups apples, peeled, cored, and sliced
½ cup molasses or brown sugar, packed
¼ teaspoon cinnamon
¼ teaspoon nutmeg
¼ teaspoon salt
Juice of ½ lemon

(1) In a mixing bowl, toss together the apple slices and seasonings.

(2) Arrange the apple mixture in a lightly buttered 1½- or 2-quart baking dish. Cook the apples, uncovered, in a 350° oven for 20 minutes, or until they are just tender.

(3) Cover the apples with shortcake dough, page 381, and bake the pandowdy, uncovered, at 350° for 1 hour, or until the crust is delicately browned.

Cobblers and pandowdies may be made with various fresh, frozen, canned, or stewed dried fruits. Frozen, canned, and stewed dried fruit should be thoroughly drained. If the fruit is soft, you may omit step #2 in the pandowdy recipe. Serve the dessert with heavy or whipped cream, with vanilla ice cream, page 457, or with Custard or Lemon Sauce, page 460.

APPLE CREAM

(German)

Serves 6
Refrigerates

Preparation: 40 minutes
Chilling time: 4 hours

½ cup orange juice
1 packet unflavored gelatin
3 Tablespoons sugar
Juice of 1 lemon

(1) In a saucepan, combine the orange juice and gelatin; allow the gelatin to soften and then, over high heat, dissolve it, stirring constantly. Add the sugar, stirring to dissolve it. Pour the liquid into a large mixing bowl and allow it to cool. Stir in the lemon juice.

6 firm, ripe apples

(2) One at a time, peel and coarsely grate the apples into the juice mixture, stirring gently to cover the fruit. Do not grate the apple core. Chill the mixture for 15 minutes.

1 cup heavy cream
3 Tablespoons sugar
½ teaspoon vanilla or 2 Tablespoons dark rum

(3) In a mixing bowl, whip the cream, adding the sugar, one Tablespoonful at a time. Add the seasoning.

(4) Into the apple mixture, fold some of the cream. Then fold the apple mixture into the remaining cream. In a serving dish or mold, chill the dessert for 4 hours or until it is set.

APPLE CRISP

This recipe from my mother's collection of family dishes yields a tasty "pudding" with flavorful crisp bits varying the texture.

Serves 6

Preparation: 15 minutes
Cooking: 30 minutes
Preheat oven: 350°

(continued)

1 cup flour
1 cup dark brown sugar, packed
½ cup butter, melted

(1) With a fork, mix together the flour and brown sugar until there are no lumps; add the butter, stirring only enough to moisten the flour.

8 large apples, peeled, cored, and sliced
Cinnamon

(2) Butter a flat baking dish and in it arrange a layer of one-half of the apples, season with a sprinkling of cinnamon, and add one-half of the flour mixture; repeat.

Heavy cream, whipped cream, or vanilla ice cream (optional)

(3) Bake the dessert at 350° for 30 minutes. Serve it warm or at room temperature with the cream, if desired (whipped cream and vanilla ice cream are also good).

APPLE MOUSSE

(Russian)

In Russia, the dessert would perhaps not be prepared in this manner; but the blender makes for quick preparation, and the results are very good indeed.

Serves 6
Refrigerates

Preparation: 30 minutes
Chilling time: at least 3 hours

¼ cup apple juice (or cold water)
1 envelope unflavored gelatin
½ cup boiling apple juice (or water)

(1) Soften the gelatin in ¼ cup of the cold juice. Dissolve it fully by adding it to the boiling juice and stirring well.

1 egg
½ cup sugar
Pinch of salt
Grated rind and juice of 1 lemon
¼ cup rum
4 large apples, peeled, cored, and coarsely grated

(2) In the container of an electric blender, combine these seven ingredients. On medium speed, whirl them until the mixture is smooth. Add the gelatin mixture and blend for another few seconds. Pour the mixture into a large mixing bowl.

1 cup heavy cream, whipped until stiff

(3) Fold a little of the blended apple mixture into the cream; then fold all of the cream into the apple.

(4) Pour the dessert into a serving bowl or mold, rinsed with cold water. Chill it for at least 3 hours before unmolding and serving it.

APPLE PIE

(*American*)

A Pennsylvania Dutch version of the classic dessert.

Serving: one 9-inch pie

Preparation: 20 minutes*
Cooking: 40 minutes
Preheat oven: 400°

Short pastry for a two-crust 9-inch pie

(1) Line a 9-inch pie pan with bottom crust. Reserve pastry for top crust.

¾ cup brown sugar, packed
¼ teaspoon salt
½ teaspoon cinnamon
¼ teaspoon nutmeg
1 Tablespoon flour
Grated rind of 1 lemon

(2) In a mixing bowl, toss together these six ingredients.

6 to 8 tart, juicy apples, peeled, cored, and sliced
Soft butter

(3) Using 2 forks, toss the apples in the sugar mixture. Arrange the mixture in a mound over the pastry shell. Dot with butter. Cover with the top crust, crimping the edges together. Make several slashes on the top crust with a sharp knife.

(4) Bake the pie at 400° for 40 minutes, or until the crust is golden brown.

There are several variations of apple pie:

Apple Pie with Honey: follow the directions given above, using, in place of the brown sugar, ¾ cup honey mixed with ½ cup sour cream; stir in the seasonings and then the apples; spoon the mixture into the shell; omit the butter.

* Preparation time does not include readying the pastry, page 458.

Dutch Apple Pie: Follow the directions given above, using, in place of a top crust, the following crumb mixture: ¾ cup flour, ½ teaspoon cinnamon, and ½ cup brown sugar, packed; add ½ cup soft butter and stir the mixture with a fork until it is crumbly.

Pork and Apple Pie (a very rich American dish dating back to the eighteenth century): Follow the directions given above, using, in place of the soft butter for dotting the apple mixture, ¼ lb. lean salt pork, trimmed of the rind and diced. Bake the pie at 450° for 10 minutes; reduce the heat to 350° for 1 hour.

POACHED APPLES

(Turkish)

Serves 6
Doubles
Refrigerates

Preparation: 20 minutes
Cooking: 20 minutes

1 cup water
1 cup sugar
15 whole cloves
2 3-inch pieces cinnamon stick

(1) In a saucepan, combine these four ingredients; bring the mixture to the boil, stirring. Reduce heat and simmer the liquid, uncovered, until it becomes a thin syrup.

6 ripe, firm eating apples, peeled and cored

(2) Meanwhile, prepare the apples.

(3) In a large saucepan, arrange the apples in one layer. Pour the syrup over them. Simmer the apples covered, basting them frequently, for 15 minutes, or until they are tender. Uncover them and allow them to cool in the syrup.

Rose water (optional)
Heavy cream, whipped (optional)

(4) To serve the dessert, arrange the apples in a serving dish or in individual dishes. Put 2 or 3 drops of rose water in the cavity of each apple, pour over the syrup, strained, and, if desired, offer a side dish of whipped cream.

APPLE PUDDING

(*Russian*)

Follow the directions for Apricot Pudding, page 45, using: 4 cups tart apple slices, peeled; 2½ cups cold water; ⅓ cup sugar; ¼ teaspoon cinnamon; pinch of salt; pinch of nutmeg.

HORSERADISH AND APPLE SAUCE

For fish and boiled meats.

Serving: about 1½ cups

4 apples, peeled and grated
½ cup prepared horseradish
¼ cup vegetable oil
2 Tablespoons cider vinegar
   Honey

In a mixing bowl, combine the first four ingredients, stirring to blend them well. Add honey, stirring, to taste (the sauce should only suggest sweetness).

APPLE AND RAISIN STUFFING

(*German*)

For chicken and turkey.

Serving: about 8 cups

Preparation: 40 minutes

4 Tablespoons butter
4 onions, chopped

(1) In a large skillet, melt the butter and cook the onion until translucent. Remove it to a large mixing bowl.

¼ lb. butter
3 cups white bread, cubed
3 cups pumpernickel, cubed

(2) In the skillet, melt the butter, add the bread cubes, and cook them, stirring often, until they are well toasted. Add them to the onions in the mixing bowl.

(continued)

4 large apples, peeled, cored, and
  coarsely grated
¼ cup golden raisins
1 teaspoon salt
¼ teaspoon pepper

(3) To the breadstuff, add the apples, raisins, salt, and pepper. Using two forks, lightly toss the stuffing until it is well mixed.

APPLE SALAD DRESSING

For use on shredded cabbage (white or red or a combination), romaine, and such greens as have a sturdy taste of their own—watercress, arugola, etc.

      Serving: about 1½ cups

Preparation: 10 minutes
Chilling time: 1 hour (minimum)

3 apples, peeled and grated
1 clove garlic, chopped
½ cup sour cream or cream-style
  cottage cheese
1 teaspoon prepared Dijon mustard
3 Tablespoons mayonnaise
½ teaspoon salt
  Pinch white pepper
  Juice of 1 lemon

In the container of an electric blender, combine all the ingredients and whirl them on medium speed until the mixture is smooth. Chill the dressing.

APRICOTS

Apricots, the fruit of the *prunus armeniaca*, lie—
botanically speaking—somewhere between a
plum and a peach. This stone fruit, or drupe,
formerly thought to be native to the Caucasus
(hence the name *armeniaca*), is now believed to
have originated in China. Apricots traveled by
trade routes to central and southeastern Asia and
thence to southern Europe and northern Africa.
There is little doubt, however, that apricot
cultivation started in China; a character meaning
"apricot" in Chinese caligraphy is over 4,000
years old. A legend tells how a wise man of
China was born under an apricot tree; his name
was Lao-tse, which means "apricot."

Apricots arrived in England at the time of Henry
VIII; they were called "hastie peches" because
of their early ripening. Spanish mission fathers
introduced them to the New World when they

came to California in the early 1700s.

Although killed by late freezes, apricot trees are drought-resistant and will live from fifty to one hundred years. Tree-ripened apricots are one of our tastiest fruits; unfortunately, to assure safe transportation, they are picked underripe and are thus robbed of considerable flavor. Apricots from the Loire Valley in France are considered the world's best.

Apricots, both fresh and dried, are much used in Middle Eastern cooking. The finest quality of dried apricots, which have a stronger flavor and darker color than fresh ones, come from California and Australia. The dried fruit is rich in iron and contains less sugar than apples (they are often allowed in a diabetic diet). Apricots, when canned, are whole or halved, but their tender skin requires no peeling.

In the United States, commercial production is largely centered on the Pacific Coast and in the intermountain states. The annual crop may reach 200,000 tons, with California leading as the largest producer. A major portion of this crop is dried. Other producers of apricots include Iran, Syria, Spain, France, Italy, and Yugoslavia.

APRICOT SOUP

(*Norwegian*)

This soup may be served hot or cold, as an appetizer or as a dessert.

Serves 6
Doubles
Refrigerates

Preparation: 45 minutes
Cooking: 15 minutes

1 lb. dried apricots
5 cups water

(1) In a saucepan, soak the apricots in the water for 1 hour.

½ cup sugar

(2) Add the sugar and cook the fruit until it is very tender (about 45 minutes). Sieve the liquor and the apricots into a second saucepan.

At this point you may stop and continue later.

¼ cup quick-cooking tapioca
Juice of ½ lemon

(3) Heat the puree to the boiling point; add the tapioca and cook, stirring, until the mixture thickens. Stir in the lemon juice.

BEEF AND APRICOT SOUP-STEW

(*Russian*)

This soup-stew, hearty and flavorful, makes a satisfying one-dish meal. Serve it with pumpernickel and sweet butter.

Serves 6
Doubles
Refrigerates
Freezes

Preparation: 3½ hours

(continued)

3 lbs. chuck, cut in bite-sized pieces 1 onion, stuck with 4 cloves 1 carrot, sliced 2 stalks celery, chopped, with leaves 1 teaspoon salt 1 teaspoon sugar 1 bay leaf 6 cups water	(1) In a soup kettle, combine these ingredients and simmer them, covered, for 3 hours, or until the meat is tender. Remove the beef with a slotted spoon; strain and reserve the broth.
4 Tablespoons butter 2 onions, chopped 2 tomatoes, peeled, seeded, and chopped	(2) In the soup kettle, melt the butter and cook the onions until translucent. Add the tomatoes and simmer the mixture until nearly all the liquid is evaporated.
2 Tablespoons flour Reserved stock 1 10½-oz. can condensed beef broth (optional)	(3) Stir in the flour and when it is well blended, add the reserved broth (degreased if necessary), stirring. If desired, add the broth.
3 cups potatoes, peeled and diced 1 cup tenderized dried apricots, cut in halves 1½ teaspoons salt	(4) Add the potatoes, apricots, and salt. Bring the liquid to the boil, reduce the heat, and simmer the mixture, covered, for 15 minutes, or until the potatoes are tender.
Reserved beef ¼ cup parsley, chopped	(5) Add the beef pieces and simmer the soup for 5 minutes. When serving, garnish with parsley.

BEEF TIMBALE AND APRICOTS

(South African)

Serves 6
Doubles

Preparation: 25 minutes
Cooking: 50 minutes
Preheat oven: 350°

1½ lbs. ground round
½ cup bread crumbs
1 medium onion, grated
2 teaspoons curry powder
Juice of 1 lemon
18 tenderized dried apricots, cut in fine julienne
⅓ cup mango chutney
1¼ teaspoons salt
¼ teaspoon pepper

(1) In a mixing bowl, combine these nine ingredients.

1½ cups milk
3 eggs

(2) In a separate mixing bowl, blend the milk and eggs with a rotary beater.

(3) Measure 1 cup of the liquid, add it to the meat, and blend all the ingredients thoroughly. Reserve rest of liquid for later use.

2 bay leaves, broken

(4) In a lightly buttered baking dish, arrange the meat mixture; it should be level. Insert the bay leaf bits.

At this point you may stop and continue later.

(5) Bake the meat, uncovered, at 350° for 20 minutes.

(6) Remove the dish from the oven, discard the bay leaf, pour over the remaining liquid, and return the timbale to the oven, uncovered, for 30 minutes, or until the custard is set.

LAMB SHANKS AND APRICOTS

Follow the directions for Lamb Shanks and Grapes, page 157, using in place of the grapes, ¾ cup tenderized dried apricots, halved, added for the final 30 minutes of cooking.

PORK CHOPS AND APRICOTS

Serves 6
Doubles
Refrigerates
Freezes

Preparation: 45 minutes
Cooking: 45 minutes
Preheat oven: 350°

2 Tablespoons butter
6 double pork chops
Salt
Pepper

(1) In a skillet, heat the butter and brown the chops on each side for 6 minutes. Season them. Arrange them in one layer in a baking dish, or stand them on their sides in a casserole.

(2) While the chops are browning, prepare Apricot Sauce, page 47.

½ cup tenderized dried apricots

(3) Arrange the apricot halves on top of or in between the chops (depending upon whether a baking dish or casserole is used). Pour the apricot sauce over the meat.

At this point you may stop and continue later.

(4) Bake the chops, covered, at 350° for 30 minutes; uncover them and continue to bake them for 15 to 20 minutes, or until they are tender.

CHICKEN AND APRICOTS WITH CHINESE VEGETABLES

A heartier dish than the following one, this recipe is an adaptation from the Chinese, preserving the tender-crisp quality of the vegetables.

Serves 6
Doubles
Refrigerates

Preparation: 30 minutes
Cooking: 1 hour
Preheat oven: 350°

2 Tablespoons butter	(1) In a flame-proof casserole, heat
2 Tablespoons oil	the butter and oil and brown the
Serving-pieces of chicken for 6 persons	chicken; season it. Remove.
Salt	
Pepper	

2 Tablespoons butter
2 Tablespoons oil
  Serving-pieces of chicken for 6 persons
  Salt
  Pepper

(1) In a flame-proof casserole, heat the butter and oil and brown the chicken; season it. Remove.

8 scallions, chopped, with as much green as is crisp
3 stalks celery, thinly chopped
1 5-oz. can water chestnuts, thinly chopped
1 5-oz. can bamboo shoots

(2) Add these vegetables to the remaining fat, stirring to coat them well. Cook them gently for 5 minutes. Remove and reserve.

1 10½-oz. can condensed chicken broth
1 Tablespoon cornstarch
2 Tablespoons soy sauce

(3) With the broth, deglaze the casserole. Mix the cornstarch with the soy sauce and add to the broth. Cook the sauce, stirring, until it is thickened and smooth. Replace the chicken.

At this point you may stop and continue later.

(4) Bake the casserole, covered, at 350° for 40 minutes.

The reserved vegetables
¾ cup tenderized dried apricots, halved
½ cup toasted slivered almonds (optional)

(5) Add these remaining ingredients and continue to cook the casserole, covered, for 20 minutes, or until the chicken is tender.

CURRIED CHICKEN AND APRICOTS
(Indian)

Serve the dish with rice and the condiments for curry, page xv.

Serves 6
Doubles
Refrigerates

Marination: 3 hours (minimum)
Preparation: 30 minutes
Cooking: 1 hour
Preheat oven: 350°

(continued)

3 onions, coarsely chopped
3 cloves garlic, coarsely chopped
Pinch cayenne
¼ teaspoon cinnamon
1 teaspoon ground coriander
1 teaspoon ground cumin
1 teaspoon ground ginger
1 teaspoon turmeric
Grated rind and juice of 1 orange
1 6-oz. can tomato paste
1 10½-oz. can condensed chicken broth
1¼ teaspoons salt
¼ teaspoon pepper

(1) In the container of an electric blender, combine these ingredients and whirl them on high speed for 15 seconds.

Serving-pieces of chicken for 6 persons

(2) In a shallow dish, arrange the chicken pieces, pour the marinade over them, and allow them to stand for at least three hours; turn them occasionally.

2 Tablespoons butter
2 Tablespoons oil
3 bay leaves, broken

(3) In a flame-proof casserole, heat the butter and oil. Wipe the chicken pieces clean with a rubber spatula and brown them. Add the bay leaves. Pour the marinade over the chicken.

At this point you may stop and continue later.

(4) Bake the casserole, covered, at 350° for 45 minutes.

1 cup tenderized dried apricots, halved

(5) Arrange the apricots over the chicken and continue to bake the dish, covered, for 15 minutes longer, or until the chicken is tender.

DUCKLING AND APRICOTS*

If desired, the duck may be quartered into serving-pieces, baked as suggested and then basted with the sauce. In this case, the stuffing may either be omitted entirely or cooked in a separate baking dish.

Serves 4
Doubles
Refrigerates
Freezes

Preparation: 45 minutes
Cooking: 1 hour, 45 minutes
Preheat oven: 325°

1 5- to 6-lb. duck
1 teaspoon salt
½ teaspoon pepper
Apricot stuffing, page 48

(1) Rub the cavity of the duck with the salt and pepper; stuff and truss the fowl. Prick its breast, legs, and thighs several times with a fork. Arrange the duck on a rack in a roasting pan and bake it at 325° for 1 hour.

1 cup tenderized dried apricots
1 12-oz. can apricot nectar

(2) Meanwhile, in a saucepan, simmer the apricots in the nectar until they are tender, stirring often.

3 cloves garlic, chopped

(3) In the container of an electric blender, combine the apricots and garlic and whirl them on medium speed until the mixture is smooth. Drain off and discard the duck fat.

At this point you may stop and continue later.

(4) Arrange the duck in a casserole, pour the apricot sauce over it, and continue to cook it, uncovered, at 325° for about 45 minutes, or until it is tender.

* This recipe is contributed by Phyllis Curtin, the Metropolitan Opera soprano who has been called "the singer's singer," because of her remarkable musicality and ability to learn impossibly difficult music. In private life the wife of Eugene Cook, the photographer, Phyllis has been a close friend for many years; thoughts of her always evoke feelings of warmth, humor, honesty, and whole-hearted enthusiasm for the experience of living.

DUCK AND APRICOT PILAF

(Middle Eastern)

Serves 6
Doubles
Refrigerates
Freezes

Preparation: 25 minutes
Cooking: 2 hours
Preheat oven: 325°/350°

**Serving-pieces of duck for 6
persons
Salt
Pepper**

(1) On a rack in a broiling pan, arrange the pieces of duck, season them, and bake them at 325° for 1 hour. Remove the duck to absorbent paper and discard all but 3 Tablespoons of the fat.

**1 onion, chopped
½ teaspoon ground allspice
¼ teaspoon each: cinnamon, clove, and nutmeg
½ teaspoon turmeric
1½ teaspoons salt**

(2) In a flame-proof casserole, heat the fat and in it cook the onion until translucent. Stir in the spices.

**1 cup natural raw rice
1 cup tenderized dried apricots, chopped**

(3) Add the rice, stirring to coat each grain; add the apricots; replace the duck.

At this point you may stop and continue later.

2 10½-oz. cans condensed chicken broth

(4) Over the contents of the casserole, pour the chicken broth. Bake the dish, covered, at 350° for 1 hour, or until the duck and rice are tender and the liquid is absorbed.

SHRIMP AND APRICOTS

This dish has a Chinese aura, but to my best knowledge it originated in my country kitchen. All the ingredients may be prepared in advance and assembled at the time of cooking.

Serves 6
Doubles
Refrigerates

Preparation: 45 minutes
Cooking: 15 minutes

36 **tenderized dried apricots, quartered in strips**
4 **Tablespoons vegetable oil**

(1) In a casserole or Chinese *wok*, heat the oil and in it cook the apricots, stirring constantly, for 5 minutes.

1½ **lbs. shrimp, shelled and deveined**

(2) Add a little more oil, if necessary, and, when it is hot, add the shrimp and cook them over high heat, stirring constantly, until they are pink.

1 **12-oz. can apricot nectar**
4 **teaspoons cornstarch**
1 **Tablespoon soy sauce**
Juice of ½ lemon
3 **Tablespoons preserved ginger, chopped**
1 **clove garlic, put through a press**
Grating of pepper
6 **scallions, chopped, with as much green as possible**
½ **cup toasted slivered almonds (optional)**

(3) Add the apricot nectar. Mix the cornstarch with the soy sauce and lemon juice; add it and cook the mixture, stirring constantly, until the sauce is thickened and smooth. Add the remaining ingredients and heat them through, stirring. Serve the dish with rice.

SWEET POTATOES AND APRICOTS

Serves 6
Doubles
Refrigerates

Preparation: 30 minutes
Cooking: 25 minutes
Preheat oven: 375°

3 large or 6 small sweet potatoes

(1) Boil the sweet potatoes, in their jackets, for 25 minutes, or until they are tender. Remove the jackets and halve the potatoes lengthwise. Arrange them, cut side down, in a buttered baking dish.

1½ cups dark brown sugar, packed
4 teaspoons cornstarch
Grated rind of 1 orange
½ teaspoon salt
Pinch of pepper

(2) Combine these five ingredients in a saucepan; stir them well.

1 cup liquid from a 17-oz. can apricot halves
Juice of 1 orange
3 Tablespoons butter

(3) Add the liquids to the sugar-cornstarch mixture and cook the sauce over high heat, stirring constantly, until it is thickened and smooth. Stir in the butter.

Reserved apricot halves, drained

(4) Arrange the apricots, cut side down, over the potatoes. Pour the sauce over all.

At this point you may stop and continue later.

(5) Bake the dish, uncovered, at 375° for 25 minutes.

RICE AND APRICOTS
(Middle Eastern)

Serves 6
Doubles
Refrigerates

Preparation: 1 hour
Cooking: 30 minutes
Preheat oven: 375°

1 cup dried apricots
½ cup golden raisins
  Boiling water

(1) Soak the apricots and raisins in hot water to cover for 30 minutes. Drain thoroughly.

1½ cups natural raw rice
2 10½-oz. cans condensed chicken broth
  Water

(2) In a saucepan, simmer the rice, covered, in the broth plus enough water to equal 3 cups, for 15 minutes, or until the rice is tender and the liquid is absorbed.

4 Tablespoons butter
2 onions, chopped
½ green pepper, chopped
¾ teaspoon curry powder

(3) In a skillet, melt the butter and in it cook the onions and pepper until the onion is translucent. Stir in the curry powder.

½ cup pine nuts (optional)

(4) In a large mixing bowl, toss together the drained fruit, the onion mixture, the rice, and the pine nuts. Arrange the mixture in a buttered baking dish.

At this point you may stop and continue later.

(5) Bake the rice, uncovered, at 375° for 30 minutes.

SPAGHETTI AND APRICOT SAUCE

Follow the directions for Spaghetti and Raisin Sauce, page 357, using, in place of the raisins, ¾ cup tenderized dried apricots, chopped.

QUICK APRICOT BREAD

Fruit breads seldom taste strongly of the particular fruit for which they are named. This bread is more redolent of apricot than, I believe, are most.

Serving: one 9x5-inch loaf

Preparation: 30 minutes
Cooking: 1 hour
Preheat oven: 350°

3 **cups flour**
¾ **teaspoon salt**
1 **teaspoon soda**
1 **Tablespoon baking powder**
¾ **teaspoon cinnamon**

(1) Sift together these five ingredients.

4 **Tablespoons butter, melted and cooled**
2 **eggs, lightly beaten**
 Grated rind and juice of 1 lemon

(2) Combine the butter, eggs, lemon rind, and juice.

1 **cup apricot pulp, prepared by whirling in an electric blender 1 30-oz. can apricot halves, thoroughly drained**

(3) Add the fruit pulp to the egg mixture.

1 **cup reserved apricot liquid**
1 **cup tenderized dried apricots, quartered**
½ **cup nut meats, broken (optional)**

(4) Add the dry ingredients, together with the liquid, to the egg mixture. Stir only to blend the batter. Fold in the apricot quarters and, if desired, the nut meats.

(5) Spoon the batter into a buttered 9x5-inch loaf pan. Bake the bread at 350° for 1 hour, or until a knife inserted at the center comes out clean. Cool the bread in the pan for 10 minutes before removing it to a rack.

For other quick fruit breads, peaches, pears, or prunes, well drained, may be substituted for the apricots to make the puree. Similarly, dried peaches, pears, or prunes may be chopped and added, and peach, pear, or prune nectar or juice may be used as the liquid ingredient. If desired, 1½ cups whole-wheat flour may be substituted for 1½ cups of the white flour.

APRICOT BROWN BETTY

Follow the directions for Apple Brown Betty, page 20, using, in place of the apples: 2 cups of stewed apricots, well drained; use the apricot water in place of clear water.

APRICOT PUDDING

(Russian)

This type of fruit pudding made with potato flour or cornstarch is called a *kisel* and is popular in Russia. The recipe lends itself to several variations.

Serves 6
Doubles
Refrigerates

Preparation: 45 minutes
Chilling time: 3 hours (minimum)

1½ cups dried apricots
4 cups water

(1) In a saucepan, combine the fruit and water. Bring to the boil, reduce the heat, and simmer the fruit, covered, for 15 minutes, or until it is tender.

(2) In the container of an electric blender, puree the fruit; return it to the saucepan.

⅓ cup sugar
Pinch of salt
Pinch of powdered allspice

(3) Add the sugar and seasonings. Cook the puree, stirring, until it boils. Reduce the heat to moderate.

1 Tablespoon potato flour
1 Tablespoon cool water

(4) Mix the potato flour and water. When the liquid is smooth, add it to the apricot puree and cook the mixture, stirring, until it reaches the boil and thickens slightly. Cool the *kisel* partially, pour it into individual dishes, and chill it for at least 3 hours.

STEAMED APRICOT PUDDING
(English)

The recipe adapts itself to many canned fruits, thoroughly drained and, if necessary, seeded. The pudding should be served hot.

Serves 6
Refrigerates
Freezes

Preparation: 15 minutes
Cooking: 2 hours

1 cup canned apricot halves, drained
½ cup milk
½ teaspoon vanilla

(1) In the container of an electric blender, whirl these three ingredients on high speed until the mixture is smooth.

1 cup flour
½ cup sugar
1 teaspoon baking powder
½ teaspoon salt
¼ teaspoon ground ginger
¼ teaspoon nutmeg

(2) In a mixing bowl, sift together these six ingredients.

½ cup golden raisins
Custard Sauce, page 460

(3) Into the flour mixture, stir the raisins. Add the liquid mixture, stirring to blend the dough well.

(4) Pour the batter into a buttered 1-quart mold (or a 1-lb. coffee can with tight-fitting lid). Steam the pudding for 2 hours. Serve it with Custard Sauce.

APRICOT SOUFFLE

Serves 6

Preparation: 15 minutes
Cooking: 30 minutes
Preheat oven: 350°

1 28-oz. can apricot halves,
thoroughly drained
Dash of salt
1 Tablespoon lemon juice

(1) In the container of an electric blender, reduce the apricots to a puree. Pour into a saucepan. Stir in the salt and lemon juice and warm the puree over gentle heat.

4 egg whites, beaten stiff
Custard Sauce, page 460
(optional)

(2) Fold the puree into the egg whites. Pour the mixture into a lightly oiled souffle dish. Bake the dessert at 350° for 30 minutes, or until it is well risen and slightly golden. If desired, serve it with Custard Sauce.

This recipe adapts itself to peaches, pears, prunes, and strawberries—fresh, frozen, or canned. The fruit should be well drained (the drier the puree, the lighter the souffle) and the puree may be seasoned to taste with sugar, dissolved when heating the puree before being combined with the egg whites.

APRICOT WHIP

Follow the directions for Prune Whip, page 339, using, in place of the prunes, an equal amount of stewed dried apricots, thoroughly drained.

APRICOT SAUCE

(*Hawaiian*)

A pleasantly sharp sauce for roasted or grilled meats.

Serving: about 1¾ cups
Refrigerates

Preparation: 45 minutes

1 cup dried apricots
1¼ cups water

(1) In a saucepan with tight-fitting lid, combine the apricots and water. Simmer the fruit, covered, until it is tender and most of the liquid is absorbed.

(2) Puree the fruit in an electric blender.

(continued)

½ **cup cider vinegar**
6 **Tablespoons honey**
½ **teaspoon chili powder**
½ **teaspoon paprika**
¼ **teaspoon salt**

(3) Add these five ingredients and blend the sauce well.

APRICOT SAUCE

For cake, ice cream, or pudding.

> Serving: about 2½ cups
> Doubles
> Refrigerates
> Freezes

Preparation: 45 minutes

1 **cup tenderized dried apricots**
¼ **cup sugar**
2 **cups water**
¾ **teaspoon cinnamon**
½ **teaspoon mace**
 Pinch of salt

(1) In a saucepan, combine these six ingredients. Bring the mixture to the boil, reduce the heat, and simmer the fruit, covered, until it is very tender (about 35 minutes). Cool.

½ **cup Southern Comfort whiskey**

(2) In the container of an electric blender, combine the contents of the saucepan and the liquor. Whirl the mixture on high speed until it is a smooth puree. Store the sauce in a covered jar.

APRICOT STUFFING

For poultry, lamb, and pork.

Preparation: 15 minutes

For *each* 4 cups of seasoned bread crumbs, seasoned croutons, or packaged dressing:

1 cup tenderized dried apricots, coarsely chopped
½ cup celery, chopped
½ teaspoon cinnamon
½ teaspoon salt
Pinch of pepper

¼ cup butter, melted

(1) In a large mixing bowl, combine the breadstuff, apricots, celery, and seasonings.

(2) Add the butter and, with two forks, lightly toss the stuffing. If desired, a little water may be added for a moister dressing.

AVOCADOS

Avocados are the fruit of *Persea americana* of the family Lauraceae. In other words, they are members of the laurel family, whence also came the wreaths which once crowned Greek and Roman athletes and which includes cinnamon, camphor, and sassafras. The word "avocado" is a sound substitute for the Aztec *ahuacatl*, as is the Jamaican "alligator" pear, for the original name heard by the Spanish explorers.

Once believed to be aphrodisiac, avocados are native to the southern regions of the Western Hemisphere. Although probably domesticated in Peru several thousands of years ago, the tall spreading tree with its long elliptic leaves and small green petalless flowers was first known in Europe during the early sixteenth century through the written description of the *conquistadors*.

Today avocados are grown commercially wherever the climate is suitable to them. The three principal exporters of the fruit are California, Africa, and Israel. There are several varieties of avocado, differing in size, shape, and color. Some are the size of a hen's egg; others may weigh 4 pounds. Some are round; others are pear-shaped. Some are green; others are dark purple. And some have thin skins, while others are thick-skinned.

All avocados have rich, buttery flesh with a nutty flavor. Excepting the olive, no fruit contains such a high percentage of vegetable fat. Avocados, commonly an ingredient of salads, are also used in soups and desserts, as a sandwich filling, and in the manufacture of certain soaps and shampoos.

If the fruit yields to gentle pressure, it is ready to eat. Avocados may be kept at room temperature to ripen. Peeling them from the narrow end makes this operation easier. Lemon juice brushed on the exposed flesh prevents discoloring in the air.

AVOCADO COCKTAIL SPREAD

I have a strong prejudice against the word "dip"—it is evocative of glop made from packaged mixes. Nonetheless, a dip is what *this* is, and quite a good one, too.

> Serving: 2 cups
> Doubles
> Refrigerates

Preparation: 10 minutes
Chilling time: 2 hours

2 avocados, peeled, seeded, and coarsely chopped
3 Tablespoons lemon juice
4 Tablespoons olive oil
1 clove garlic, coarsely chopped
1 teaspoon salt
1 Tablespoon chopped chives
1½ teaspoons dill weed
2 or 3 drops Tabasco sauce

In the container of an electric blender, combine all the ingredients and, on medium speed, whirl them until the mixture is smooth. Chill the spread before serving it.

GUACAMOLE

> *(Mexican)*

A classic dish from Mexico, *guacamole* serves equally well as a cocktail appetizer or as a salad topping on greens of your choice.

> Serves 6
> Doubles
> Refrigerates

Preparation: 20 minutes
Chilling time: 2 hours

3 ripe avocados, peeled, seeded, and coarsely chopped

(1) In an earthenware or plastic bowl, using a silver fork, mash the avocado; it should be a paste, but with bits of avocado in it.

1 onion, grated
1 clove garlic, pressed
2 Tablespoons lemon juice
2 tomatoes, peeled, seeded, and
  chopped
1 teaspoon salt
¾ teaspoon chili powder
2 or 3 drops Tabasco sauce
1 teaspoon sugar

(2) Add the remaining ingredients and seasonings to the avocado. Stir thoroughly to blend the mixture well. Chill the *guacamole* before serving it as an appetizer or salad. (To prevent its discoloring, lay plastic wrap directly on it.)

AVOCADO SOUFFLE

Serves 6

Preparation: 25 minutes
Cooking: 35 minutes
Preheat oven: 375°

5 Tablespoons butter
6 Tablespoons flour
2 cups milk, scalded
1 teaspoon salt
¼ teaspoon white pepper
¼ teaspoon nutmeg

(1) In a saucepan, heat the butter and add the flour, stirring the mixture well. Gradually add the milk and stir the sauce until it is thickened and smooth. Stir in the seasonings.

2 ripe avocados, peeled, seeded,
  and coarsely chopped
5 egg yolks

(2) In the container of an electric blender, combine the avocado and egg yolks. On medium speed, whirl them until very smooth.

(3) Add the avocado mixture to the white sauce and, over gentle heat, cook the mixture, stirring; do not let it boil.

At this point you may stop and continue later.

6 egg whites, beaten until stiff

(4) Into the avocado mixture, fold the egg whites.

(5) Butter and flour a 2-quart souffle dish; pour in the batter. Bake the souffle at 375° for 35 minutes, or until it is browned on top and well puffed. Serve it at once.

AVOCADO SOUP I

A richer soup than the following one.

Serves 6
Doubles
Refrigerates
Freezes

Preparation: 20 minutes

1 large ripe avocado, peeled, seeded, and coarsely chopped
1 10½-oz. can condensed chicken broth, heated to the boiling point

(1) In the container of an electric blender, combine the avocado and broth; blend the mixture on low speed until it is smooth (about 15 seconds).

2 cups heavy cream
½ cup dry white wine
2 teaspoons lemon juice
Salt
Pepper
Pinch of cayenne

(2) To the contents of the container, add the cream, wine, and lemon juice. Season the soup to taste.

Dill weed, fresh or dried

(3) Before serving, garnish the soup with fresh or dried dill.

The soup may be served chilled or heated (in the top of a double boiler over hot water). If the soup has been frozen, thaw it fully and then homogenize it in an electric blender.

AVOCADO SOUP II

(American)

This rich and festive soup from New Orleans is a fine prelude to a light meal.

Serves 6
Doubles
Refrigerates
Freezes

Preparation: 20 minutes

6 Tablespoons butter 6 Tablespoons flour 6 cups warm milk 1 teaspoon salt ¾ teaspoon ground ginger ¼ teaspoon white pepper Grated rind of 1 orange	(1) In a saucepan, heat the butter. Add the flour, stirring until the mixture is smooth. Over gentle heat, cook the *roux* for a few minutes. Gradually add the milk, stirring constantly until the mixture is somewhat thickened and smooth. Stir in the seasonings.
2 ripe avocados, peeled, seeded, and coarsely chopped	(2) In the container of an electric blender, combine the avocado with a little of the milk mixture. On medium speed, whirl the ingredients until they are smooth. Stir the avocado into the remaining milk mixture.
Croutons lightly browned in butter Paprika	(3) Serve the soup hot, garnished with the croutons, and a sprinkling of paprika.

AVOCADO SOUP III*

Serves 6
Doubles
Refrigerates

Preparation: 20 minutes
Chilling time: 2 hours (minimum)

3 large ripe avocados, peeled, seeded, and coarsely chopped 2 10½-oz. cans condensed beef broth 1 cup sour cream	(1) In the container of an electric blender, whirl these three ingredients on medium speed for 15 seconds, or until the mixture is smooth.
4 large ripe tomatoes, peeled, seeded, and finely chopped ½ cup scallions, finely chopped 1½ teaspoons salt ¼ cup lemon juice Dash of Tabasco sauce	(2) Pour the avocado mixture into a plastic or earthenware bowl. Stir in the remaining ingredients. Chill the soup thoroughly before serving it.

* This subtle and delicious recipe is contributed by the actress Jacqueline Coslow, who, as Mrs. Theodore Eliopoulos, is my near neighbor in the country. Jackie and Ted bought a very old—and incommodious—house and have completely remodeled it themselves; they have also landscaped, terraced, and established gardens. They are no less delightful than they are energetic and some of my pleasantest times in the country are spent in their company.

AVOCADO AND GROUND BEEF TACOS*

Serves 6
Doubles
Refrigerates

Preparation: 30 minutes
Cooking: 15 minutes

3 **Tablespoons olive oil**
3 **onions, chopped**
1 **clove garlic, chopped**
2 **lbs. ground round**
4 **ripe tomatoes, peeled, seeded, and chopped**
½ **teaspoon chili powder**
½ **teaspoon ground cumin**
¼ **teaspoon oregano**
1 **teaspoon salt**

(1) In a skillet, heat the oil and in it cook the onions and garlic until they are translucent. Add the meat and brown well. Add the tomatoes and seasonings, stirring to blend the mixture well. Cook the mixture, stirring, for 5 minutes, or until it is fairly dry; drain off the excess fat.

12 **frozen flour tortillas (available in many supermarkets), fully thawed**
1 **cup cheddar cheese, grated**
2 **large ripe avocados, peeled, seeded, and sliced lengthwise**

(2) On each tortilla, arrange some of the meat, sprinkle it with cheese, and top it with slices of avocado. (Reserve 12 slices of avocado for later use.) Fold the tortillas over the meat "like an envelope—both sides, one over the other, and top and bottom."

At this point you may stop and continue later.

Cooking oil

(3) In a skillet, heat a generous amount of oil and fry the tortillas, taking care not to open the "envelopes." Drain them on absorbent paper.

Sour cream
Reserved avocado slices

(4) Serve the tortillas garnished with sour cream and an additional piece of avocado.

* This authentic Mexican delicacy is contributed by my country neighbor, Jacqueline Coslow Eliopoulos. Of this dish, Jackie says, "It is very rich and one tortilla per serving is adequate for lunch or supper—two, perhaps, for dinner."

The recipe was given Jackie's mother by friends who own the largest chili pepper ranch in the United States; they, in turn, were given the recipe by a Mexican woman working on the ranch, who brought the directions for *chimichangas* from her native state in Mexico.

CURRIED CHICKEN AND AVOCADO

Follow the directions for Curried Chicken and Papaya, page 446, using, in place of the papaya, 3 ripe avocados, peeled, halved lengthwise, and seeded.

CHICKEN AND AVOCADO WITH GRAPES

(American)

Serves 6
Doubles
Refrigerates

Preparation: 30 minutes
Cooking: 1 hour
Preheat oven: 350°

Seasoned flour
Serving-pieces of chicken for 6 persons
2 Tablespoons butter
2 Tablespoons oil

(1) In the seasoned flour, dredge the chicken. (Reserve remaining seasoned flour for later use.) In a flameproof casserole, heat the butter and oil and brown the chicken. Remove.

2 onions, chopped
1 clove garlic, chopped
1 small green pepper, seeded and chopped

(2) In the remaining fat, cook the onions, garlic, and pepper until the onion is translucent.

2 Tablespoons remaining seasoned flour
1 large ripe tomato, peeled, seeded, and chopped
½ cup golden raisins
2 teaspoons salt
1 cup dry white wine

(3) To the onion mixture, add the flour, stirring to blend the mixture well. Add the tomato, raisins, salt, and wine, and cook the sauce, stirring constantly, until it is thickened and smooth. Replace the chicken.

At this point you may stop and continue later.

(4) Bake the casserole, covered, at 350° for 1 hour, or until the chicken is tender.

(continued)

1 ripe avocado, peeled, seeded, sliced, and sprinkled with lemon juice

1½ cups seedless grapes, rinsed and dried on absorbent paper

Cinnamon

(5) Over the top of the chicken, arrange the avocado slices and grapes. Dust the fruit with a light sprinkling of cinnamon. Return the casserole, covered, to the oven for 5 minutes, or only long enough to heat the fruit.

CREAMED TURKEY AND AVOCADO

A festive way to use up the Thanksgiving bird.

Serves 6
Doubles

Preparation: 30 minutes

6 Tablespoons butter
6 Tablespoons flour

(1) In the top of a double boiler, melt the butter, add the flour, stirring, and, over gentle heat, cook the *roux* for a few minutes.

1 10½-oz. can condensed chicken broth
Water
2 eggs, beaten
2 Tablespoons lemon juice
¼ cup dry sherry
1½ teaspoons salt
¼ teaspoon nutmeg
¼ teaspoon white pepper

(2) To the broth, add water to equal 2 cups. In a mixing bowl, combine the liquid, eggs, lemon juice, and sherry. Gradually add the liquid mixture to the flour. Over simmering water, cook the sauce, stirring constantly, until it is thickened and smooth. Stir in the seasonings.

3 or 4 cups cooked turkey, diced
1 large avocado, peeled and diced

(3) Stir in the turkey and avocado. Allow them to heat through. Serve the dish with rice.

CRAB MEAT AND AVOCADO

This summer supper recipe works well also for lobster meat or shrimp.

Serves 6
Doubles
Refrigerates

Preparation: 20 minutes

1 lb. crab meat
3 stalks celery, chopped
½ teaspoon celery seed

(1) In a mixing bowl, toss together these three ingredients.

3 ripe avocados, halved lengthwise and seeded
Lemon juice

(2) Brush the inside of the avocados with lemon juice to prevent discoloration. Fill the cavities equally with the crab meat mixture.

Ripe olives, pitted and halved
Orange Dressing, page 262

(3) Serve the filled avocado halves on salad greens with a garnish of olives. Offer the sauce separately.

SHRIMP AND AVOCADO

Serves 6
Refrigerates

Preparation: 45 minutes
Chilling time: 1 hour (minimum)

4 Tablespoons olive oil
2 Tablespoons tomato paste
1 small onion, grated
Juice of 1 lime
½ teaspoon salt
¼ teaspoon white pepper

(1) In a mixing bowl, combine these six ingredients and blend them well.

1 lb. small or medium shrimp, shelled and deveined

(2) Prepare the shrimp, page xx. Sieve them and allow them to cool.

(3) Toss together the shrimp and sauce. Chill the mixture for at least 1 hour.

(continued)

3 ripe avocados, halved lengthwise
    and seeded
Lemon juice
Lemon slices

(4) Brush the inside of the avocados with lemon juice to prevent discoloration. Fill the cavities equally with the shrimp mixture. Serve with lemon slices.

BAKED OMELET AND AVOCADO

An adaptation of a dish from the West Indies.

Serves 6

Preparation: 15 minutes
Cooking: 20 minutes
Preheat oven: 350°

2 large avocados, peeled, seeded,
    and cut into cubes
Juice of 1 lime

(1) Sprinkle the avocado with the lime juice. Discard any excess juice. Reserve the fruit.

2 Tablespoons butter
2 Tablespoons flour

(2) In a saucepan, melt the butter and add the flour; over gentle heat, stir the *roux* for a few minutes.

1 cup milk
½ teaspoon salt
Pinch of white pepper

(3) To the *roux*, add the milk, stirring until the sauce is thickened and smooth. Stir in the seasonings. Fold in the avocados, and keep them warm in a serving bowl. This is the sauce that will be served separately later.

2 Tablespoons flour
¼ cup milk

(4) Mix the flour and milk, stirring until the mixture is smooth.

6 egg yolks, beaten
⅓ cup milk
¾ teaspoon salt
Pinch of white pepper

(5) In a mixing bowl, combine these four ingredients; to them add the flour mixture.

6 egg whites

(6) In a mixing bowl, beat the egg whites until they stand in stiff peaks. Fold the whites into the egg mixture. Pour the mixture into a well-buttered, heated skillet or baking dish and bake the omelet at 350° for 20 minutes. Serve it at once, cut in wedges, accompanied by the avocado sauce to be spooned over it.

GRILLED AVOCADO

Serves 6
Doubles

Preparation: 20 minutes
Cooking: 10 minutes

4 Tablespoons butter
2 onions, chopped
1 cup breadcrumbs
2 tomatoes, peeled, seeded, and chopped
½ teaspoon salt
Grating of pepper
¾ teaspoon basil or dill weed or marjoram
Juice of ½ lemon

(1) In a skillet, heat the butter and in it cook the onions until translucent. Add the bread crumbs, stirring to absorb the butter evenly. Add the tomatoes and seasonings, stirring to blend the ingredients. Over gentle heat, simmer the mixture, uncovered, for 3 minutes.

At this point you may stop and continue later.

3 ripe avocados (at room temperature), halved lengthwise seeded, and painted with lemon juice

(2) Fill the avocado cavities with the breadcrumb mixture, arrange the fruit in a flame-proof baking pan and put it under a hot broiler for 10 minutes, or until the crumb filling is browned.

AVOCADO IN SAVORY SAUCE

(Colombian)

Serves 6
Doubles

Preparation: 30 minutes

½ lb. thick-sliced bacon diced, rendered, and drained on absorbent paper

(1) Prepare the bacon and reserve it.

¼ cup olive oil
2 onions, chopped
1 clove garlic, chopped
2 green peppers, chopped

(2) In a skillet, heat the oil and in it cook the ingredients until the onion is translucent.

¼ cup tomato sauce
⅓ cup cider vinegar
1 teaspoon salt

(3) To the onion mixture, add these three ingredients and blend them well. Over very low heat, simmer the sauce for 20 minutes.

3 ripe avocados at room temperature, peeled, seeded, and coarsely chopped
Lemon juice

(4) Toss the avocado with lemon juice to prevent discoloring. Discard any excess lemon juice.

(5) In a serving dish, arrange the avocado pieces, pour the hot sauce over them, and sprinkle the top with the bacon bits. Serve at once.

AVOCADO ASPIC

(Mexican)

Serves 6
Refrigerates

Preparation: 30 minutes
Chilling time: at least 3 hours

1 10½-oz. can condensed chicken broth
Water
1 packet unflavored gelatin

(1) In a saucepan, combine the broth and water to equal 1½ cups. Stir in the gelatin. Heat the broth, stirring until the gelatin is dissolved. Allow the mixture to cool.

2 large ripe avocados, peeled, seeded, and coarsely chopped
1 cup cream-style cottage cheese
3 Tablespoons mayonnaise
2 Tablespoons fresh chives, chopped
½ teaspoon salt
¼ teaspoon white pepper
Juice and grated rind of 1 lemon or 1 lime

(2) In the container of an electric blender, combine these eight ingredients and, on medium speed, whirl them until the mixture is smooth.

(3) Add the avocado mixture to the broth, stirring to blend well. Pour it into a ring mold rinsed with cold water, and chill the aspic for at least 3 hours.

Salad greens of your choice
1 9-oz. package frozen artichoke hearts, cooked; or boiled shrimp (or crab meat); or fresh tomatoes, peeled and sliced; or cucumbers, peeled and sliced
Orange Dressing, page 262

(4) On a serving platter, unmold the aspic, surround it with salad greens, and fill the center with a food of your choice. Dress the filling with the orange dressing.

AVOCADO CREAM

Serves 6
Doubles
Refrigerates

Preparation: 15 minutes
Chilling time: at least 3 hours

(continued)

3 **large ripe avocados, peeled, seeded, and coarsely chopped**
6 **Tablespoons sugar**
1 **teaspoon vanilla**
 Grated rind and juice of 1 lemon
 Pinch of salt

(1) In the container of an electric blender, combine all the ingredients and, on medium speed, whirl them until the mixture is smooth. Chill the dessert in individual dishes.

 Toasted slivered almonds

(2) When serving, garnish with a sprinkling of almonds.

AVOCADO ICE CREAM*

Serving: 1½ quarts
Doubles
Freezes

Preparation: 30 minutes

1 **large, ripe avocado, peeled, seeded, and coarsely chopped**
1 **can frozen orange juice concentrate, thawed**

(1) In the container of an electric blender, combine the avocado and orange juice; reduce the mixture to a puree (about 15 seconds).

2 **cups milk, heated to the boiling point**
¾ **cup sugar**
 Pinch of salt

(2) Combine these three ingredients, stirring until the sugar is dissolved. Allow the mixture to cool.

2 **Tablespoons lemon juice**

(3) Combine the avocado and milk mixtures; add the lemon juice. Blend the mixture briefly. Chill the dessert until it is "slushy."

2 **cups heavy cream, whipped to the consistency of soft peaks**

(4) Fold in the whipped cream and freeze the dessert fully in ice trays or some other shallow container.

* This unusual and tasty dessert is contributed by Jack Brown, a country neighbor, whose profession is stage design, whose hobby is gardening, and whose by-no-means "minor" accomplishment is cooking.

AVOCADO TART*

Serving: one 8-inch tart
Refrigerates

Preparation: 15 minutes†
Chilling time: at least 3 hours

1½ teaspoons unflavored gelatin
¼ cup cold water

(1) Soften the gelatin in the cold water and dissolve it in a double boiler over simmering water.

⅔ cup lemon juice
2 large ripe avocados, peeled, seeded, and coarsely chopped

(2) In the container of an electric blender, combine the lemon juice and avocado. On medium speed, whirl them until the mixture is smooth.

Pinch of salt
1 14-oz. can sweetened condensed milk

(3) With the motor running, add to the contents of the blender the gelatin, salt, and, in a steady stream, the condensed milk.

Prepared pie shell, cooled

(4) Pour the avocado mixture into the pie shell. Chill the tart for at least 3 hours before removing it from the refrigerator 20 minutes before serving it.

Heavy cream, whipped (optional)

(5) The tart may be garnished with whipped or slightly sweetened sour cream, but the calorie count is then considerable.

* This recipe is contributed by the J. M. Klines, a delightful couple I met when traveling on the sternwheeler *Delta Queen*. Conversation about food led to this dessert which Kay makes with her own avocados and lemons growing in the garden of their La Mesa, California, home. Kay recommends a graham cracker crust.

† Preparation time does not include readying the pastry, page 458.

AVOCADO SAUCE FOR POACHED OR BAKED FISH

(Cuban)

Serving: 2 cups
Doubles
Refrigerates

2 **large avocados, peeled, seeded, and coarsely chopped**
  Juice of 1 lime
1 **small onion, grated**
4 **Tablespoons olive oil**
1 **teaspoon salt**
¼ **teaspoon white pepper**

In the container of an electric blender, combine all the ingredients and whirl them on medium speed until the mixture is smooth. (To prevent its discoloring, lay plastic wrap directly on it.)

BANANAS

Not all bananas are sweet, and some require as much cooking as potatoes. One legend says that the Serpent hid in a bunch of bananas when offering Eve the fatal apple; thus, one variety of banana is called *Musa paradisiaca*, or "heavenly fruit." Another tradition is that philosophers sought out the cooling shade of the banana tree to stimulate their contemplation; hence, another variety is called *Musa sapientum*, or "fruit of knowledge." The word *Musa* derives from an Arabic word for the fruit, *mouz*, in use during the thirteenth century. Perhaps as many as 300 varieties of the genus *Musa* are under cultivation. The term "banana" derives from an African tribal name for the varieties eaten raw. Those varieties requiring cooking are called "plantains."

The banana plant is really a giant herb which springs from underground stems, or rhizomes.

These grow into a false trunk, perhaps 12 feet tall. At the top of this trunk-like growth appears a large flower spike, bending downward, where a single bunch of as many as 150 of the fruit will grow in clusters. Botanically, the banana is a large berry, albeit its seeds never ripen to fertility. After the banana "tree" has fruited, it dies; it is replaced by suckers from its underground stems.

Sweet bananas are native to Asia, whence they spread to West Africa and the Pacific Islands. Pliny mentions them in connection with Alexander the Great's Indian expedition. Their dessemination seems to have accompanied that of the human race. Still, the banana is the only member of its family grown for food; two other members are the bird-of-paradise flower and the sisal plant producing hemp for rope manufacture.

Once considered a gastronomic luxury, the banana is a food staple wherever it is grown, capable of sustaining human life for a very long time. In the tropics, unripe bananas are dried and ground into a bread flour. Although eaten raw, they are more often cooked.

Commercially, the *Gros Michel*, a Caribbean variety, is the most important. Indigenous to Asia its cultivation spread first to Jamaica and then to Costa Rica and Panama. The West Indies and West Africa, respectively, are the world's largest exporters of the fruit, sending about 4 million tons a year to the United States, Great Britain, and continental Europe. Picked green, the bananas are transported in specially designed refrigerator ships. Africa produces about nineteen billion pounds of bananas a year, only 10 percent of which are exported; South and Central America produce about 14 billion pounds, of which most are exported.

CURRIED BANANA AND APPLE SOUP
(American)

Although traditionally served cold, this soup may also be served hot.

Serves 6
Doubles
Refrigerates
Freezes

Preparation: 30 minutes
Cooking: 12 minutes

1 10½-oz. can condensed chicken broth
3 or 4 apples, peeled, cored and coarsely grated
1 large, very ripe banana, peeled
1 onion, coarsely chopped
1 Tablespoon curry powder
Pinch of salt

(1) In the container of an electric blender, combine these ingredients and, on high speed, reduce them to a smooth puree.

1 10½-oz. can condensed chicken broth
1 large potato, peeled and finely diced

(2) In a large saucepan, combine the chicken broth, potato, and the contents of the blender. Bring the mixture to the boil, reduce the heat, and simmer the soup, covered, for 15 minutes, or until the potato is tender.

1 pint light cream (or half-and-half), scalded

(3) While the soup is cooking, scald the cream.

(4) Either sieve or whirl in the blender the hot mixture to make it as smooth as possible.

Chopped chives

(5) To the soup, add the scalded cream, pouring it through a sieve; stir to blend the mixture. When serving, garnish the soup with chives.

PEANUT AND BANANA SOUP*

(Mexican)

Serves 6
Doubles
Refrigerates

Preparation: 20 minutes

6 cups rich (preferably homemade) chicken stock or 5 10½-oz. cans condensed chicken broth
4 Tablespoons smooth peanut butter

(1) In the container of an electric blender, combine half of the chicken stock with the peanut butter. On medium speed, blend the ingredients for 15 seconds, or until the mixture is homogenous. Combine it with the remaining stock in a saucepan.

Salt
Pepper
3 ripe bananas, peeled, free of threads, and thinly sliced
Roasted peanuts

(2) Heat the soup to a gentle simmer and cook it, covered, for 10 minutes. Season it to taste with salt and pepper. Just before serving the soup, add the banana, stirring gently, and heat the fruit through. Serve the soup garnished with a few peanuts.

* This recipe is contributed by Charles Blum, the painter. Charles lived for some years in Mexico, where he knew the woman who said she created this soup. The woman, a cook in a private family, misunderstood the complaints of her mistress, who insisted on her breakfast being served *Todo junto! Todo junto!* ("All together"). Obligingly, the cook combined in a large pitcher: orange juice, scrambled eggs, toast, and coffee and presented the mixture to her horrified employer.

STEAK AND BANANAS*

Serves 6

Preparation: 5 minutes†
Cooking: 12 minutes
Preheat broiler

* Helen McCully, who contributed this recipe, says of it: "Just before the turn of the century, *broiled sirloin à la Stanley* was very fashionable, and such cookbooks as *The Epicurean* (a compilation of recipes from Delmonico's) and Lemcke's *European and American Cuisine* gave versions of it. Essentially, it is steak served with baked bananas and horseradish sauce."

† Preparation time does not include preparing the Baked Bananas, page 75.

1 6-lb. sirloin or porterhouse steak 1½-inches thick	(1) Allow the steak to come to room temperature. Slash the fat in several places to prevent the sides from curling. Place it on a well-buttered broiling pan and, in a preheated broiler, cook it for about 4 minutes; turn it and cook it for 5 minutes (the timing is for rare steak).
Salt Pepper Soft butter Watercress Baked Bananas Horseradish sauce	(2) Remove the steak to a serving platter, season it with a sprinkling of salt, a generous grating of pepper, and a spreading of butter. Garnish it with watercress and baked bananas. Serve the horseradish separately.

DUCKLING AND BANANA

(Japanese)

Serves 4
Doubles
Refrigerates

Preparation: 45 minutes
Cooking: 1 hour
Preheat oven: 400°/300°

1 4- to 6-lb. duck, quartered, trimmed of excess fat, and pricked with a fork in several places	(1) On a roasting rack, bake the duck at 400° for 30 minutes. Discard the fat and arrange the pieces in a baking dish. (Turn oven down to 300° if you are completing the recipe now.)
1 egg 2 teaspoons soy sauce	(2) In a small bowl, beat together the egg and soy sauce. Brush the duck with this mixture.
1 3-oz. can flaked coconut ¼ cup flour 1½ teaspoons salt ¼ teaspoon pepper	(3) In a mixing bowl, toss together these four ingredients.

(continued)

Liquid from 1 11-oz. can
mandarin oranges
½ cup honey
4 teaspoons cornstarch
Grated rind and juice of 1 lemon
Grated rind and juice of 1
orange
3 Tablespoons soft butter

(4) In the top of a double boiler combine all of these ingredients except the butter and, over high heat, cook the mixture, stirring constantly, until the sauce is thickened and smooth. Stir in the butter. Cover the sauce and reserve it.

At this point you may stop and continue later.

(5) Sprinkle the duck with the coconut mixture. Bake the duck, uncovered, at 300° for 45 minutes to 1 hour or until the duck is tender and the coconut well toasted.

3 ripe bananas, peeled and sliced

(6) Into the sauce, heated over boiling water, fold the banana slices. When they are heated through, pour the sauce over the duck and serve.

FISH FILETS AND BANANAS*

Serves 6
Doubles

Preparation: 20 minutes
Cooking: 8 minutes
Preheat oven: 450°

Fish filets for 6 persons, page xv

(1) In a flat, well-buttered baking pan, arrange the fish.

6 firm, ripe bananas, peeled and cut
in fairly large pieces
Salt
Lemon juice
Butter

(2) Arrange the bananas over and around the fish, season the dish with a sprinkling of salt and lemon juice; dot the bananas with butter.

* A fine recipe of Helen McCully's (page 11).

At this point you may stop and continue later.

(3) Broil the fish and bananas at 450° for about 8 minutes, or until the fish flakes easily. Do not turn the fish.

(4) Serve the fish with lemon butter.

FISH STEAK AND BANANAS

This dish, less elegant than Fish Filets and Bananas, page 72, is good made with steak of halibut or other white fish.

Serves 6

Preparation: 15 minutes
Cooking: 15 minutes
Preheat oven: 450°

Serving portions of fish steak for 6 persons
Soft butter
Salt
Pepper

(1) In a broiling pan, arrange the fish steaks, spread them with butter, and season them with salt and pepper. Broil them at 450° for about 15 minutes, or until they flake easily. Do not turn them.

(2) Arrange the fish on a serving dish.

3 bananas, peeled, halved and sliced lengthwise
6 Tablespoons butter
Toasted slivered almonds (optional)

(3) Top the fish steaks with the bananas. Heat the butter until it foams, and pour it over the bananas. Garnish the dish with almonds.

SHRIMP AND BANANA CURRY

This dish, quickly cooked, may be prepared in a Chinese *wok*. The "stop and continue later" point is when all the ingredients are readied. Serve the curry on rice.

> Serves 6
> Doubles
> Refrigerates

Preparation: 40 minutes
Cooking: 15 minutes

2 **Tablespoons butter** 2 **onions, chopped** 1 **clove garlic, minced**	(1) In a *wok* or large saucepan, heat the butter; in it cook the onions and garlic until translucent.
2 **teaspoons curry powder (or to taste)** 1 **Tablespoon preserved ginger, minced** 1 **Tablespoon cider vinegar** ½ **teaspoon ground allspice** ½ **teaspoon salt**	(2) Stir in the seasonings.
1½ **lbs. fresh shrimp, shelled and deveined**	(3) Add the shrimp and cook them, stirring constantly, until they are just barely pink.
1 **cup cider or apple juice** 1 **Tablespoon cornstarch, mixed with a little cold water**	(4) Add the cider and cornstarch and cook the mixture, stirring constantly, until it is thickened and smooth.
4 **ripe bananas, peeled, cut in ½-inch slices, and gently tossed in a little lemon juice**	(5) Add the bananas, stirring gently. Cook them only long enough to heat them through.

BANANA OMELET

(*Colombian*)

Follow the directions for Baked Omelet and Avocado, page 60. On the bottom of the buttered skillet or baking dish, arrange 6 firm, ripe bananas, peeled, halved lengthwise, and sauteed for 5 minutes in 6 Tablespoons hot butter. Pour the egg mixture over the bananas and cook as directed. Garnish the dish with chopped parsley.

SHERRY-BAKED BANANAS

(American)

A Creole side dish, excellent with roast meats.

> Serves 6
> Doubles

Preparation: 15 minutes
Cooking: 30 minutes
Preheat oven: 350°

⅓ **cup dry sherry**
⅓ **cup dark brown sugar**
4 **Tablespoons apricot preserves**
4 **Tablespoons cooled melted butter**
Juice of 1 lemon

(1) In a mixing bowl, combine these five ingredients and blend them well.

6 **firm, ripe bananas, peeled and halved lengthwise**

(2) In a very lightly buttered baking dish, arrange the bananas with their flat side down. Over them evenly spread the sherry mixture.

At this point you may stop and continue later.

(3) Bake the bananas at 350° for 30 minutes or until they are tender.

BAKED BANANAS HELEN MCCULLY

To accompany Steak and Bananas, page 70, or to be served as a vegetable.

> Serves 6
> Doubles
> Refrigerates

Preparation: 10 minutes
Cooking: 12 minutes
Preheat oven: 450°

(continued)

6 firm, ripe bananas, peeled **Butter** **Sugar** **Lemon juice**	In a well-buttered, flame-proof baking dish, arrange the bananas. Sprinkle them with a little sugar and lemon juice. Dot them with butter. Bake them at 450° for 10 minutes. Slide them under the broiler for about 2 minutes, or until the bananas are flecked with gold.

BAKED BANANAS WITH APPLE

Serves 6
Doubles

Preparation: 10 minutes
Cooking: 20 minutes
Preheat oven: 400°

Butter **3 tart apples, peeled, cored, and coarsely grated**	(1) In a well buttered baking dish, arrange a bed of the grated apple.
6 firm ripe bananas, peeled and, if desired, halved lengthwise **Juice of 1 lemon** **Salt** **Pepper** **Generous sprinkling of ground coriander or cumin**	(2) Over the apple, arrange the bananas (if halved, with the cut side up). Sprinkle them with the lemon juice and season them with salt, pepper, and either the coriander or cumin. (If desired, the bananas may be sprinkled with brown sugar and dark rum; in this case, retain the lemon juice but omit the coriander and cumin.)
	(3) Bake the bananas at 400° for 20 minutes and serve at once.

For an Italian flavor, omit the apple, and, in a shallow dish, mix together ¾ cup Italian-seasoned breadcrumbs, ⅓ cup grated Parmesan cheese, and 4 Tablespoons soft butter. After you have sprinkled the bananas with lemon juice, dredge them in the crumb mixture; sprinkle any remaining crumbs on top before baking the fruit.

BROILED BANANAS

Serves 6

Preparation: 10 minutes
Cooking: 10 minutes
Preheat broiler

6 firm, ripe bananas, peeled
   Lemon juice

   Melted butter
   Salt
   Nutmeg

(1) Brush the bananas with the lemon juice.

(2) On a lightly buttered broiler rack, arrange the bananas. Brush them with the melted butter and season them with a sprinkling of salt and nutmeg.

At this point you may stop and continue later.

(3) Broil the bananas for 5 minutes per side, or until they are browned. When turning them, brush the turned sides with melted butter and season them.

BAKED EGGPLANT AND BANANAS

(American)

Serves 6
Doubles
Refrigerates

Preparation: 1 hour
Cooking: 40 minutes
Preheat oven: 350°

(continued)

Vegetable oil
1 **large eggplant, cut in ¼-inch slices**
 Salt
 Thyme

(1) In a large skillet, heat about 3 Tablespoons of oil until it is very hot. In it, brown several eggplant slices, seasoning them with salt and thyme. Drain the eggplant on absorbent paper. Repeat the process until all the eggplant is browned.* (Pour off any excess fat.)

4 **Tablespoons butter**
3 **or 4 large, very ripe bananas, peeled and sliced in half lengthwise**
 Nutmeg

(2) Add the butter to the skillet and, when it is very hot, brown the banana slices, seasoning them with nutmeg.

1 **28-oz. can tomatoes, drained**

(3) Butter a 1½- or 2-quart baking dish. In it, arrange alternate layers of eggplant, banana, and tomatoes. Repeat as necessary. Over the casserole pour the butter remaining in the skillet. Add a sprinkling of salt and thyme.

At this point you may stop and continue later.

(4) Bake the dish, uncovered, at 350° for 40 minutes, or until it bubbles and the eggplant is tender.

* In step #1, if desired, the raw eggplant slices may be arranged on a buttered baking sheet, spread lightly with soft butter, and seasoned with salt and thyme; bake, uncovered, at 400° for 15 minutes. This method of precooking the eggplant is neater and less time-consuming. Proceed with the remainder of the recipe.

SWEET POTATO AND BANANA CASSEROLE

Serves 6
Doubles

Preparation: 25 minutes
Cooking: 10 minutes
Preheat oven: 475°

5 medium sweet potatoes (already boiled until tender and peeled)
Salt
Pepper
Nutmeg
¼ cup hot milk

(1) In a mixing bowl, mash the sweet potatoes and season them to taste with salt, pepper, and nutmeg. Beat in the hot milk.

2 firm ripe bananas, peeled and mashed until smooth

(2) Add the bananas to the potatoes.

2 egg yolks
2 egg whites, beaten until stiff

(3) Add the egg yolks and beat the mixture until it is light. Fold in the egg whites.

(4) Into a buttered casserole or souffle dish, spoon the potato mixture. Bake it at 475° for 10 minutes, or until it is lightly browned.

RICE AND BANANAS

(Mexican)

Serves 6
Doubles

Preparation: 20 minutes

1 cup natural raw rice
1 chicken bouillon cube
2 cups water

(1) In a saucepan, combine the rice, bouillon cube, and water. Bring the water to the boil, stirring to dissolve the bouillon cube. Reduce the heat to the lowest point and simmer the rice, covered, for 15 minutes, or until it is tender and the liquid is absorbed.

2 firm bananas, peeled, quartered lengthwise, and chopped

(2) With two forks, gently toss the banana bits with the hot rice and serve immediately.

BANANA MUFFINS

12 to 18 muffins
Doubles
Refrigerates
Freezes

Preparation: 10 minutes
Cooking: 15 minutes
Preheat oven: 400°

2 cups flour
1 Tablespoon baking powder
½ teaspoon salt
2 Tablespoons sugar
½ teaspoon ground coriander

(1) In a mixing bowl, sift together the dry ingredients.

2 eggs
1 cup milk
3 Tablespoons butter, melted
1 ripe banana, peeled and mashed until smooth

(2) In a mixing bowl, beat the eggs, add the milk, butter, and banana and blend the mixture well.

At this point you may stop and continue later.

(3) Butter 12 to 18 muffin cups (depending upon their size). Add the liquid to the dry ingredients, stirring only sufficiently to dampen the flour. Fill the cups ⅔ full and bake the muffins at 400° for 15 minutes, or until they are golden brown.

BAKED BANANAS AND RUM

Serves 6

Preparation: 15 minutes
Cooking: 30 minutes
Preheat oven: 350°

6 **firm bananas, peeled and halved lengthwise**
4 **Tablespoons butter, melted**

(1) In a lightly buttered baking dish, arrange the bananas, cut side down. Brush them well with the butter; pour over any remaining butter.

¼ **cup dark brown sugar**
¼ **teaspoon cinnamon**

(2) In a small mixing bowl, using a fork, toss together the sugar and cinnamon. Sprinkle the bananas with the mixture.

At this point you may stop and continue later.

(3) Bake the bananas at 350° for 30 minutes, or until they are tender.

½ **cup dark rum**

(4) At the time of serving, in a small saucepan, warm the rum and pour it over the bananas.

BANANA CAKE*

(American)

Serving: one 9- or 10-inch cake

Preparation: 35 minutes
Cooking: 50 minutes
Preheat oven: 350°

(1) Butter and flour a 9- or 10-inch tube pan. (If a 10-inch tube pan is used, double the recipe; a high cake will result.)

2 **cups flour**
¾ **teaspoon baking soda**
¼ **teaspoon baking powder**
½ **teaspoon salt**

(2) In a mixing bowl, sift together these dry ingredients.

* This delicacy should be entitled "Dorothea Wiggins's Banana Cake." Mrs. Wiggins is wife, mother, and nurse, active in church and civic affairs. Her activities would exhaust most people. Not Dorothea! She thrives on her busy schedule and takes pleasure in sharing it—including this dessert.

(continued)

1 cup butter
1 cup sugar

(3) In a separate bowl, cream the butter until soft; gradually add the sugar, beating constantly. Continue to beat the mixture until it is light and fluffy.

2 egg yolks, beaten

(4) One at a time, add the egg yolks to the butter mixture, beating well after each addition.

1 cup very ripe banana pulp, mashed
⅓ cup sour cream
1 teaspoon vanilla

(5) In a separate bowl, combine these three ingredients and mix them thoroughly.

(6) Gradually combine the wet and dry ingredients, beginning and ending with the dry; beat the batter well after each addition.

2 egg whites
½ cup sugar

(7) Beat the egg whites until soft mounds form; gradually add the sugar and continue beating until the egg whites are stiff. Fold them into the batter.

(8) Spoon the batter into the prepared pan and bake the banana cake at 350° for 50 minutes, or until a knife inserted at the center comes out clean. Remove the cake from the oven and allow it to cool 10 minutes before inverting the pan.

BANANA CREAM PIE

(American)

An American classic, very rich and very good—and a bane to calorie watchers!

Serving: one 9-inch pie
Refrigerates
Freezes (except for whipped-cream topping)

Preparation: 40 minutes*
Chilling time: at least 1 hour

* The preparation time does include readying the pastry shell, page 458.

½ cup sugar 5 Tablespoons flour ¼ teaspoon salt 3 egg yolks	(1) In a mixing bowl, sift together the first three ingredients. Beat in the egg yolks, one at a time.
2 cups milk 2 Tablespoons soft butter Grated rind of ½ lemon	(2) In a saucepan, combine these three ingredients. Heat them until the milk shimmers but does not boil.
½ teaspoon vanilla or 2 Tablespoons dark rum	(3) To the sugar mixture, slowly add the milk, stirring. Return the mixture to the pan and cook it over gentle heat, stirring constantly, until it is thickened and smooth. Stir in the vanilla or rum. Allow the custard to cool to room temperature.
½ cup heavy cream, whipped	(4) Into the custard, fold the whipped cream.
1 9-inch pie shell, baked 2 or 3 bananas, peeled and thinly sliced	(5) Over the bottom of the pie shell, spread a ¼-inch layer of custard. Over it, arrange a layer of banana slices. Repeat, ending with a layer of bananas.
½ cup heavy cream, whipped	(6) With a rubber spatula, spread an even layer of whipped cream over the pie. Chill the dessert for at least 1 hour before serving it.

BANANA ICE CREAM

Follow the directions for Helen McCully's Ice Cream, page 457, omitting the vanilla and using 3 very ripe bananas, peeled, sieved, and mixed with the juice of ½ lemon. Add the banana to the hot custard before cooling it.

BANANA PANDOWDY

Follow the directions for Apple Pandowdy, page 24, using, in place of the apple, 3 ripe bananas, peeled, sliced, and sprinkled with cinnamon, nutmeg, and ¼ cup dark brown sugar.

BANANA PUDDING

(Thai)

To say that the present recipe is Thai stretches a point; the original was
but it called for no leavening, egg, or shortening. For better or worse,
the changes are mine.

Serves 6
Refrigerates
Freezes

Preparation: 15 minutes
Cooking: 1 hour
Preheat oven: 350°

1 cup flour
⅔ cup sugar
1 teaspoon baking powder
Pinch of salt

(1) In a mixing bowl, sift together these dry ingredients.

1 3-oz. can shredded coconut

(2) Add the coconut to the dry ingredients and toss the mixture to blend it.

1 egg
1 cup milk
2 Tablespoons oil
1 teaspoon grated lemon rind

(3) In the container of an electric blender, combine these four ingredients and, on medium speed, whirl them for a few seconds.

(4) Add the liquid to the dry ingredients and stir the batter until it is smooth.

2 or 3 ripe bananas, sliced

(5) Fold in the banana.

Heavy cream or sauces specified

(6) Pour the batter into a buttered round baking dish. Bake the pudding at 350° for 1 hour, or until it tests done with a straw. Serve it at room temperature, cut in wedges, with cream or Sauce for Orange Crepes, heated, page 252, or Lemon Sauce, heated, page 460.

STEAMED BANANA PUDDING

Follow the directions for Steamed Apricot Pudding, page 46, using, in place of the apricots, 1 cup mashed banana.

BANANA WHIP

Serves 6
Doubles
Refrigerates

Preparation: 25 minutes
Chilling time: at least 3 hours

3 ripe bananas, peeled, mashed, and sieved
⅔ cup sugar
1 packet unflavored gelatin
¼ cup lemon juice
Pinch of salt

1 cup heavy cream, whipped
Toasted slivered almonds (optional)

(1) In a saucepan, soften the gelatin in the lemon juice; add the bananas, sugar, and salt. Cook the mixture over moderate heat, stirring constantly, until it comes just to the boil. Allow it to cool to room temperature.

(2) Into the cooked banana mixture fold the whipped cream. Spoon the dessert into a serving bowl and chill it for at least 3 hours. If desired, garnish it with the almonds.

BANANA SAUCE

For fresh fruit compotes.

Serving: about 1¼ cups
Refrigerates

Preparation: 15 minutes

(continued)

85

2 **ripe bananas, peeled and mashed until smooth**
  Juice of ½ lemon
2 **Tablespoons sugar**

(1) In a mixing bowl, blend these three ingredients.

½ **cup heavy cream**

(2) Stir in the cream. (If desired, the sauce may be made completely smooth by whirling it for a few seconds in the container of an electric blender.)

BERRIES

In America, wrote Captain John Smith, all berries are "four times bigger and better than ours in England." America boasts many different berries— black-, blue-, dew-, rasp-, whortle-, elder-, mul-, cran-, and straw- (which is actually neither a fruit nor a berry). Commercially, the most important berry is the blueberry, which has been cultivated in New Jersey since the early part of this century. Today, some 20,000 acres of high-bush blueberries are cultivated in the Garden State, in southwestern Michigan, and in eastern North Carolina. Blueberries are small-seeded members of the Heath Family, which thrives in an acid, well-drained soil. The huckleberry is the only variety of blueberry growing wild; it is smaller, drier, and tarter than its cultivated cousin, which is usually picked by machine.

Blackberries, dewberries, and raspberries are

also known as bramble fruits. The blackberry is a prickly plant native to the north temperate regions of the Old and New Worlds. It is used as a copse and hedge plant in Europe. The plant may stand erect or trail on the ground; the leaves are oval and coarsely toothed; the blossom is white, pink, or red; the fruit is black or red-purple. The blackberry plant, thousands of years old, propagates by suckers and root cuttings. It has been commercially cultivated since the second half of the nineteenth century; today, 20,000 acres in Oregon, Washington, and California are under blackberry cultivation. About 1,000 acres are cultivated in Great Britain. The fruit, a favorite for jams, jellies, pies, and puddings, deteriorates rapidly after picking. Blackberries are now available frozen in the supermarket.

The tender raspberry requires careful handling. The picked berry should be plump, but not soft or leaky, and of uniform color. Like the blackberry, it does not hold well after being picked. According to legend, Greek gods and goddesses, berrying on Mt. Ida, returned to Olympus with the raspberry. Apparently the gods shared their find, for raspberries grow in profusion in all temperate zones throughout the world. The American Indians had them, and the colonists dried the raspberry leaf for tea. Mentioned by Pliny as a wild fruit, raspberries have been cultivated since the early seventeenth century. Of the more than 200 species native to Asia, where the raspberry evolved, Britain and Europe now have but one, and the United States and Canada only three—the red, black, and western black. Twenty thousand acres in western Maryland, southern New Jersey, the Hudson Valley in New York, and areas of Michigan, Minnesota, Washington, and Oregon are under raspberry cultivation.

Currants and gooseberries, known as bush fruits, are hardy growers. Currants, of the genus *Ribes*, are commonly found in jams and jellies. (The dry "currant" used in cooking is actually a small raisin, unrelated to the true currant; originally obtained near Corinth, Greece, it was called *raisin de Corinthe*, from which the word "currant" has been anglicized. Recipes using the dried "currant" will be found in the section "Raisins and Currants," beginning on page 341.) Gooseberries, first cousins to currants, are cultivated in the United States as *Ribes hirtellum* and *missourienses*. Taken to England from the Continent in the sixteenth century, gooseberries were brought to America by the colonists, where, as in England, gooseberry pie was traditional Whitsuntide fare. Gooseberries are, however, more important today in Great Britain and Europe than in the United States. Abroad, they are cooked or eaten raw; in this country, they are relegated to jam, jelly, and pie. The Poorman is the best American gooseberry.

Most of the recipes in this chapter are adaptable to each of the four berries included—blackberries, blueberries, gooseberries, and raspberries. Fresh gooseberries require their stems *and* blossom ends to be removed.

BERRY SOUP
(Polish)

Serves 6
Doubles
Refrigerates

Preparation: 20 minutes
Chilling time: at least 2 hours

1 pint blackberries, blueberries, or raspberries, rinsed and picked over
1 lemon, very thinly sliced
2 cups water
1 3-inch piece cinnamon stick
2 whole allspice, crushed
⅓ cup sugar, or more, to taste

(1) In a saucepan, combine these six ingredients. Bring the mixture to the boil and simmer it for 10 minutes, or until the berries are very tender.

2 cups sour cream

(2) Sieve the berries, stir in the sour cream, and chill the soup before serving it.

MACKEREL FILETS AND GOOSEBERRIES
(English)

Serves 6
Doubles

Preparation: 30 minutes
Cooking: 30 minutes
Preheat oven: 450°

(continued)

½ **lb. gooseberries, picked, rinsed, and well drained***
¼ **cup water**
2 **Tablespoons brown sugar**
1 **hardboiled egg, sieved**
4 **Tablespoons soft butter**
¼ **cup minced parsley**
⅔ **cup dry white wine**
　Salt
　Pepper

(1) In a saucepan, cook the gooseberries in the water until they are soft. Add the next four ingredients, stirring until the butter is melted. Stir in the wine and season the sauce to taste.

6 **mackerel filets, rolled and skewered with toothpicks**

(2) In a lightly buttered baking dish, arrange the filets.

At this point you may stop and continue later.

(3) Pour the sauce over the fish and bake the dish, uncovered, at 450° for 30 minutes, or until the fish flakes easily.

* The recipe may be made with canned gooseberries, well drained. You will not need to cook the already tender berries.

BERRY MUFFINS

Follow the directions for Apple Muffins, page 19, using, in place of the apple, 1 cup berries, rinsed, drained on absorbent paper, and dusted with 1 Tablespoon flour.

BERRY CAKE

A dessert which may be made with all berries and many other fruits.

Serves 6 to 8
Refrigerates
Freezes

Preparation: 30 minutes
Cooking: 1 hour
Preheat oven: 350°

2 cups flour 1 cup sugar 4 teaspoons baking powder Pinch of salt	(1) In a mixing bowl, sift together these dry ingredients.
2 eggs, beaten ½ cup vegetable oil or melted butter, cooled ¼ cup milk 1 teaspoon vanilla	(2) In a mixing bowl, combine these liquid ingredients.
	(3) Add the liquid to the dry ingredients and beat them until they are smooth.

1 pint berries of your choice,
  rinsed, picked over, and drained
  on absorbent paper
	(4) Fold in the berries.

Crumb topping (optional)	(5) Spoon the batter into a 5 x 9 inch buttered pan. (If desired, a crumb topping may be added just before baking. Follow the directions for the topping of Berry Pie, page 92.) Bake the cake at 350° for 1 hour, or until a sharp knife, inserted at the center, comes out clean.

BERRY CREAM

(French)

Crème Bavaraise, a classic dessert in French cuisine.

Serves 6
Doubles
Refrigerates

Preparation: 40 minutes
Chilling time: at least 3 hours

(continued)

1 qt. black-, blue-, or raspberries, stewed until tender and sieved*
¾ cup sugar
1 packet unflavored gelatin, softened in ¼ cup cold water
Boiling water
2 Tablespoons lemon juice
Pinch of salt

2 cups heavy cream, whipped

(1) In a mixing bowl, combine the berry pulp and sugar, stirring to dissolve the sugar. Dissolve the gelatin by stirring it over the boiling water. Add it, together with the lemon juice and salt, to the berry pulp. Stir the mixture well and place it in the refrigerator.

(2) When the berry mixture is thickened and about to set, fold in the whipped cream. Spoon the dessert into a serving dish or mold rinsed with cold water; chill it for at least 3 hours.

* This dessert may be made with 2 1-lb. cans gooseberries, well drained and whirled in the container of an electric blender until smooth. The dessert may also be made with various fresh fruits, frozen fruits, canned fruits, or stewed dried fruits. Fruits with small seeds should be sieved. Frozen, canned, or stewed fruits should be well drained before being pureed in the container of an electric blender. The recipe requires 2 cups of fruit pulp.

BERRY ICE CREAM

Follow the directions for Helen McCully's Ice Cream, page 457, omitting the vanilla and using 1 quart berries of your choice, rinsed, picked over, drained on absorbent paper, and stewed with ½ cup sugar until they are soft; sieve the stewed berries and add them to the hot custard before cooling it.

BERRY PIE

(*American*)

Serving: one 9-inch pie

Preparation: 30 minutes*
Cooking: 40 minutes
Preheat oven: 425°

* The preparation time does not include readying the pastry, page 458.

2 pints berries of your choice, rinsed, picked over, and drained on absorbent paper	(1) Prepare the berries and reserve them.
½ cup sugar **3 Tablespoons flour** **¼ teaspoon salt**	(2) In a mixing bowl, sift together these dry ingredients and gently toss the berries with them.
¼ cup butter, melted **½ cup flour** **½ cup dark brown sugar, packed**	(3) In a mixing bowl, using a fork, stir together these three ingredients. The mixture should be crumbly.
1 unbaked pie shell	(4) In the unbaked pie shell, arrange the berry mixture and sprinkle it with the brown sugar topping. Bake the pie on the lower shelf of a 425° oven for 40 minutes, or until the crust is golden brown.

BERRY AND APPLE PIE

(English)

Serving: two 9-inch pies

Preparation: 30 minutes
Cooking: 25 minutes
Preheat oven: 425°

3 pints berries of your choice, rinsed, picked over, and drained on absorbent paper	(1) Prepare the berries and reserve them.
4 Tablespoons butter **3 tart apples, peeled, cored, and sliced**	(2) In a saucepan, melt the butter, add the apples, sugar and salt. Cook the apples, stirring them gently, until they are just tender. Cool the mixture.
¼ cup sugar **Pinch of salt** **Short pastry for 2 two-crust 9-inch pies** **¼ cup of sugar**	(3) Line two pie pans with short pastry. Add the berries and sprinkle them with the sugar. Add the cooked apples. Cover the fruit with a top crust, crimping the edges and puncturing the top crust with a fork.

* The preparation time does not include readying the pastry, page 458.

(continued)

Custard Sauce, page 460

(4) Bake the pies at 425° for 25 minutes, or until the crust is golden brown. Serve them with the Custard Sauce.

BERRY PUFF

Follow the directions for Strawberry Puff, page 379, using, in place of the strawberries, 1 quart ripe berries of your choice, picked over, rinsed, and drained on absorbent paper.

BERRY PUDDING I

This dessert is a combination of a French and an American recipe.

Serves 6
Doubles
Refrigerates

Preparation: 30 minutes
Cooking: 35 minutes
Preheat oven: 350°
Total chilling time: at least 2 hours

2 1-lb. cans berries of your choice (or any canned fruit)

(1) Drain the fruit and reserve the liquid. In a baking dish, arrange the berries.

4 Tablespoons quick-cooking tapioca

(2) To the reserved liquid, add water, if necessary, to equal 1½ cups. In a saucepan, combine the liquid and the tapioca; allow it to stand for 10 minutes, then cook the mixture, stirring constantly for 8 minutes, or until the tapioca is dissolved and the liquid thickened. Pour the sauce over the berries and chill the dish.

2 Tablespoons flour
3 Tablespoons sugar
Pinch of salt
2 cups sour cream
2 teaspoons vanilla
2 eggs

(3) In a mixing bowl, blend the dry ingredients. Add the sour cream, vanilla, and eggs. With a rotary beater, blend the mixture until it is smooth.

At this point you may stop and continue later.

(4) Over the chilled berries, pour the sour-cream mixture; do not stir. Bake the dessert, uncovered, at 350° for 30 minutes. Chill it.

Extra-fine granulated sugar

(5) Sprinkle the chilled dessert with the sugar and place it briefly under a very hot broiler for about 5 minutes to caramelize the sugar. Chill the dessert once more.

BERRY PUDDING II

(Russian)

Follow the directions for Apricot Pudding, page 45, using, in place of the apricots: 2½ pints blackberries, blueberries, or raspberries, rinsed, picked over, and drained on absorbent paper; 2 cups water; ⅔ cup sugar; pinch of salt; ¼ teaspoon ground allspice; juice of ½ lemon.

BERRY ROLYPOLY

(American)

This classic dessert lends itself to many juicy fruits. You will be rewarded by experimenting!

Serves 6

Preparation: 30 minutes
Cooking: 30 minutes
Preheat oven: 425°

Shortcake Dough, page 38
Melted butter

(1) Roll and shape the dough into an oblong ½-inch thick. Brush it with the melted butter.

(continued)

3 **pints berries of your choice, rinsed, picked over, and drained on absorbent paper**
1 **cup sugar**
½ **teaspoon salt**

(2) In a mixing bowl, toss the berries with the sugar and salt. Sprinkle half the berries over the shortcake dough and roll it (to resemble a jelly roll). Put the roll, with the fold on the bottom, in a buttered baking dish. Surround it with the remaining fruit.

Heavy cream, whipped cream, or ice cream

(3) Bake the Rolypoly at 425° for 30 minutes, or until it is golden brown. Serve it cut in slices accompanied by heavy or whipped cream, or ice cream.

GOOSEBERRY SAUCE

For poultry, meats, and fish.

Serving: about 1¼ cups
Doubles
Refrigerates

Preparation: 20 minutes

½ **lb. gooseberries**
½ **cup water**

(1) In a saucepan, combine the berries and water. Bring them to the boil, reduce the heat, and simmer them, covered, until they are very tender. Sieve them and return the mixture to the saucepan.

2 **Tablespoons sugar**
2 **Tablespoons soft butter**
1 **teaspoon cornstarch, mixed with 1 Tablespoon cold water**
  Pinch of salt

(2) Add these four ingredients and, over gentle heat, cook the sauce, stirring constantly, until it is slightly thickened.

BERRY SAUCE

Any berry sauce is delicious on ice cream or fruit puddings;
raspberry sauce, served over fresh strawberries, is a classic American
dessert.

> Serving: 1¼ cups
> Doubles
> Refrigerates

Preparation: 15 minutes

1 **package frozen blackberries,**
  blueberries, or raspberries, fully
  thawed
1 **teaspoon cornstarch**
  Pinch of salt
  Sugar

Into a saucepan, sieve the berries.
Mix the cornstarch with a little of the
juice. Add it to the contents of the
saucepan and cook the mixture,
stirring until it is slightly thickened.
Add the salt and stir in sugar to taste.
The sauce may be served warm or at
room temperature.

CHERRIES

Cherries are members of the Rose Family, as are apples, peaches, and pears. Some twelve species are known in America and a similar number grows in Europe. The greatest concentration of cherries, however, is in eastern Asia, where the trees may reach a height of 50 feet. Cherries spread from their native area near the Caspian Sea to the Balkans and hence to western Asia and eastern Europe, where they existed before recorded agricultural history. They were known in ancient Greece and Rome; the oldest known description of them was written by the Greek Theophrastus around the year 300 B.C. In America, where cherries were brought by the earliest settlers, they are the most popular fruit for the amateur grower; they are hardy, thriving far into Canada, and resistant to summer drouth.

The many varieties of cherries all belong to

either the sweet or sour strain. Even the real maraschino cherry is a small sour cherry, the *Marasca*, of southern Europe. Of the sour cherries, the Early Richmond is the first to ripen and the Montmorency is the most common for both commercial and home use; it is large, medium red, and pleasantly tart. Of the sweet cherries, the Black Tartarian is a medium-sized fruit with juicy flesh of excellent quality; the Yellow Spanish cherry, a good pollinator for other varieties, is light yellow with a flush of red; the Schmidt is one of the best firm-fleshed black cherries. Then there is the Napoleon Bigarreau, wrongly called "Royal Anne" in the United States, which is perhaps the best light-colored cherry, and the Bing, named for the Chinese horticulturalist who developed it in Oregon in 1875, which is the best midseason sweet cherry. The Windsor is the standard late-season black cherry. Finally, there are the Duke cherries, hybrids developed for their sweet-sour flavor, of which the best are the Olivet, the Reine Hortense, and the Royal Duke.

Eighty-five percent of the American commercial crop is raised under irrigation in the states of California, Washington, Utah, Oregon, and Idaho. The celebrated cherry trees in Washington, D.C., were given to the capitol by the city of Tokyo in 1912. There is, in all probability, no historical truth to the famous story of George Washington and the cherry tree; as a moral fable, however, it is an admirable eulogy of honesty.

CHERRY SOUP

Serves 6
Doubles
Refrigerates

Preparation: 25 minutes

2 1-lb. cans waterpack, pitted sour red cherries
⅓ cup sugar
4 teaspoons cornstarch
½ teaspoon salt
½ teaspoon cinnamon
Grated rind of 1 orange
1 cup orange juice

(1) In the container of an electric blender, combine these seven ingredients. On medium speed, whirl them for 15 seconds, or until the mixture is smooth.

1 cup dry red wine
Sour cream

(2) Pour the mixture into a saucepan; add the wine and cook the soup, stirring, until it is slightly thickened. Serve it hot or cold, garnished with a dollop of sour cream.

LAMB AND CHERRIES

(French)

This recipe is my fruited version of *daube à l'Avignonnaise*.

Serves 6
Doubles
Refrigerates

Marination: 8 hours (minimum)
Preparation: 40 minutes
Cooking: 2¾ hours
Preheat oven: 300°

1 onion, coarsely chopped
2 cloves garlic, coarsely chopped
Grated rind of 1 orange
2 Tablespoons olive oil
½ teaspoon ground allspice
1 bay leaf, broken
¼ cup parsley, chopped
½ teaspoon rosemary
1 teaspoon salt
½ teaspoon pepper
Juice of 1 orange
Liquid from 1 1-lb. can water-pack pitted sour cherries
Dry white wine

(1) In the container of an electric blender, combine all ingredients *except* the liquids. Combine the orange juice and cherry liquid; add the wine to equal 2 cups. To the contents of the blender, add the liquid and, on medium speed, blend the mixture for 15 seconds, or until the marinade is smooth.

3 lbs. shoulder of lamb, trimmed of excess fat and cut in bite-sized pieces

(2) In the marinade to cover, allow the lamb to stand for at least 8 hours. Drain and dry the lamb; reserve the marinade.

2 Tablespoons butter
2 Tablespoons oil

(3) In a flame-proof casserole, heat the butter and oil and brown the lamb. More butter and oil may be added, if necessary.

At this point you may stop and continue later.

1½ Tablespoons cornstarch mixed with 2 Tablespoons water

(4) In a saucepan, bring the marinade to the boil. Add the cornstarch and cook the mixture, stirring constantly until it is thickened and smooth.

Reserved sour cherries

(5) Pour the sauce over the lamb and bake the dish, covered, at 300° for 2½ hours, or until the meat is tender. Add the cherries and cook for an additional 15 minutes.

GROUND LAMB PILAF AND CHERRIES

(Iranian)

Serves 6
Doubles
Refrigerates*

Preparation: 45 minutes
Cooking: 15 minutes
Preheat oven: 350°

2 Tablespoons butter
1½ cups natural raw rice
2 10½-oz. cans condensed chicken broth
Water
1 teaspoon salt

(1) In a saucepan, heat the butter, add the rice, and, over medium heat, toast it for 3 minutes, stirring constantly to coat each grain. Combine the broth and water to equal 3 cups; pour the liquid over the rice and add the salt. Bring the liquid to the boil, reduce the heat, stir once with a fork, and simmer the rice, covered, for 12 minutes, or until it is just barely tender. Remove it from the heat.

1 lb. ground lamb
Salt
Pepper
2 Tablespoons butter
2 Tablespoons oil

(2) Season the lamb with the salt and pepper. Form it into ½-inch balls. In a skillet, heat the butter and oil and brown the meat balls. Remove them to absorbent paper. Discard all but 3 Tablespoons of the fat.

2 onions, minced
⅔ cup water

(3) In the remaining fat, cook the onions until translucent. Replace the lamb balls. Add the water and simmer the meat for 5 minutes.

1 1-lb. can pitted sour cherries and their liquid
2 Tablespoons sugar
2 Tablespoons butter

(4) In a saucepan, combine these four ingredients and, over gentle heat, simmer them to dissolve the sugar and melt the butter.

(5) In a lightly buttered casserole, gently toss together the rice with the meat mixture.

* *Note:* Refrigerating does not improve this dish; refrigerate only in order to use "leftovers."

At this point you may stop and continue later.

(6) Pour the cherries over the casserole. Bake the dish, uncovered, at 350° for 15 minutes, or until the liquid is absorbed.

VEAL AND CHERRIES

Serves 6
Refrigerates
Freezes

Preparation: 20 minutes
Cooking: 2 hours or more

1 3½- to 4-lb. veal roast
Salt
Pepper
Ground ginger
4 Tablespoons butter

(1) Rub the meat with the seasonings. In a large skillet, melt the butter and brown the veal in it.

At this point you may stop and continue later.

1 1-lb. can pitted sour cherries

(2) Drain ½ cup cherry liquid from the can of cherries. (Reserve remaining liquid and the cherries for later use.) Place the roast on a rack in a roasting pan. Pour over it the ½ cup of cherry liquid. Bake the veal, covered, at 300°, basting occasionally, for 2–2½ hours, or until it is tender, allowing 35 minutes to the pound.

(3) Remove the roast to a serving platter and keep it warm.

(continued)

2 Tablespoons cornstarch
2 Tablespoons sugar
  Remaining cherry liquid
  Reserved cherries

(4) Skim the fat from the pan drippings. Blend the cornstarch and sugar and add the mixture to the remaining cherry liquid. Stir the liquid into the pan juices and, over medium heat, cook the sauce, stirring constantly, until it is thickened and smooth. Add the reserved cherries. Serve the heated sauce with the veal.

CHICKEN BREASTS AND CHERRIES

Poulet Montmorency, so elegant, so easy, such good supper-party fare!

Serves 6

Preparation: 20 minutes
Cooking: 45 minutes
Preheat oven: 350°

For a special occasion, serve the dish with wild rice.

6 Tablespoons butter
3 large chicken breasts, halved
  and, if desired, boned
  Salt
  Pepper

(1) In a skillet, heat the butter and in it saute the chicken until it is golden brown. Season the pieces, turn them, and repeat the browning. Remove the chicken to a baking dish and bake it, covered, at 350° for 30 minutes.

2 1-lb. cans pitted dark sweet
  cherries
1 cup port wine

(2) Measure 1 cup of the cherry liquid, add to it the port, and simmer the liquid with the pan juices for about 10 minutes. (Reserve an additional ½ cup cherry liquid and all of the cherries for later use.)

½ teaspoon cinnamon
2 Tablespoons sugar
1 Tablespoon cornstarch
½ cup reserved cherry liquid
  Reserved cherries

(3) Mix together the cinnamon, sugar, and cornstarch, add them to the ½ cup reserved cherry liquid, stirring until the mixture is smooth. Add it to the simmering liquid in the skillet and cook the sauce, stirring constantly until it is thickened and smooth. Add the reserved cherries.

(4) Pour the cherry sauce over the chicken breasts and continue to bake the dish, covered, for 15 minutes.

CHICKEN PILAF AND CHERRIES

(Iranian)

Serves 6
Doubles
Refrigerates

Preparation: 30 minutes
Cooking: 1 hour
Preheat oven: 350°

2 1-lb. cans waterpack pitted sour cherries
⅓ cup sugar

(1) Drain the cherries and reserve the liquid for later use. In a saucepan, combine the cherries and sugar and cook them, stirring gently to dissolve the sugar. Remove the pan from the heat. (If a more tart dish is desired, step #1 may be omitted.)

2 Tablespoons butter
2 Tablespoons oil
Serving pieces of chicken for 6 persons
Salt
Pepper

(2) In a flame-proof casserole, heat the butter and oil and brown the chicken; season it. Remove.

2 onions, chopped
1 cup natural raw rice
½ teaspoon ground coriander
1 teaspoon ground cumin

(3) In the remaining fat, cook the onions until translucent. Add the rice and seasonings, stirring to coat each grain. Replace the chicken.

1 10½-oz. can condensed chicken broth
Reserved cherry liquid

(4) To the broth, add the reserved cherry liquid to equal 2 cups.

At this point you may stop and continue later.

(continued)

105

(5) Over the contents of the casserole, pour the broth mixture. Bake the casserole covered, at 350° for 1 hour, or until the chicken and rice are tender and the liquid is absorbed. Add the cherries during the final 15 minutes of cooking.

ROAST CHICKEN AND CHERRIES
(English)

Serves 6

Preparation: 30 minutes
Cooking: 1 hour
Preheat oven: 425°

1 cup natural raw rice

(1) Cook the rice until tender, using your own preferred method.

1 1-lb. can pitted sour cherries
1 Tablespoon curry powder
2 Tablespoons cornstarch
1½ teaspoons salt
1 Tablespoon vegetable oil

(2) Meanwhile drain the cherries and reserve some of the liquid. Mix the curry powder, cornstarch, salt and vegetable oil; add sufficient cherry liquid to yield a thin paste.

2 2½- or 3-lb. frying chickens

(3) With the paste, rub the outside of the chickens.

Reserved cherries
4 Tablespoons melted butter
½ teaspoon salt
3 Tablespoons brown sugar
Grating of pepper

(4) In a mixing bowl, using two forks, gently toss the cherries, cooked rice, and seasonings. With this mixture, stuff the chickens; truss them. Arrange them on a rack in a roasting pan.

At this point you may stop and continue later.

Soft butter

(5) Put the chickens in a preheated 425° oven. Immediately reduce the heat to 350° and roast the chickens, (allowing 20 minutes per pound) until they are tender. Baste them frequently with butter added to the pan juices.

CHICKEN AND CHERRY SAUCE
(for precooked chicken.)

Serves 6
Doubles
Refrigerates

Preparation: 30 minutes
Cooking: 20 minutes
Preheat oven: 300°

1 lb. fresh or frozen black cherries
¼ cup water
1 Tablespoon brown sugar
½ teaspoon salt
¼ teaspoon pepper
Pinch each: cinnamon, ginger, mace, nutmeg

(1) In a saucepan, combine the cherries and water; add the seasonings. Cook the cherries, covered, until they are very soft, about 20 minutes.

(2) Put the cherries through a sieve; discard the stones. Combine the cherry puree with the remaining pan liquor.

At this point you may stop and continue later.

Cooked pieces of chicken for 6 persons, at room temperature

(3) In a baking dish, arrange the chicken pieces, pour the sauce over them, and bake the dish, covered, at 300° for 20 minutes, or until it is well heated.

BRAISED DUCK AND CHERRIES

(French)

Canard Montmorency is a classic French poultry dish.

Serves 4
Doubles
Refrigerates

Preparation: 15 minutes
Cooking: 1¼ hours
Preheat oven: 350°

1 5- to 6-lb. duck, quartered and trimmed of excess fat
Salt
Pepper

(1) On a grill in a broiling pan, arrange the duck, skin side up. Prick the skin in several places with a fork. Season the pieces and bake them uncovered at 350° for 1 hour or until the thigh is fork-tender and the skin crisp and browned.

¼ cup cognac

(2) Arrange the duck pieces in a baking pan. Discard the fat. In a small saucepan, warm the cognac, ignite it, pour it over the duck, and allow it to burn out.

At this point you may stop and continue later.

1 1-lb. can pitted sweet dark cherries
1 Tablespoon cornstarch, mixed with 2 Tablespoons cold water
Grated rind of 1 orange
Zest of 1 lemon
3 Tablespoons cognac

(3) Drain the cherry liquid into a saucepan. (Reserve the cherries for later use.) To the liquid in the saucepan add the cornstarch mixture, the grated orange rind, lemon zest, and cognac. Bring the mixture to the boil, stirring constantly, until it is thickened and smooth.

Reserved cherries

(4) Over the pieces of duck, arrange the reserved cherries. Pour over the sauce and place uncovered in the 350° oven for 10 minutes.

FISH FILETS AND CHERRIES

Serves 6

Preparation: 10 minutes
Cooking: 20 minutes
Preheat oven: 400°

Butter
Fish filets for 6 persons, page xv
Salt
Pepper
Ground cumin
1 1-lb. can waterpack pitted sour
cherries

(1) In a lightly buttered baking dish, arrange the fish filets in a single layer. Season them with salt, pepper, and a generous sprinkling of cumin. Add the cherries and their liquid.

(2) Bake the fish, uncovered, at 400° for 20 minutes, or until it flakes easily.

SWEET AND PUNGENT SHRIMP AND CHERRIES

This dish, quickly cooked, may be prepared in a Chinese *wok*. The "stop and continue later" point is when all the ingredients are readied.

Serves 6

Preparation: 40 minutes
Cooking: 15 minutes

1 1-lb. can pitted dark sweet
cherries
6 Tablespoons cider vinegar
3 Tablespoons soy sauce
1 teaspoon salt
2 Tablespoons preserved ginger,
minced

(1) Drain the cherry liquid into a mixing bowl. (Reserve the cherries for later use.) Add the remaining four ingredients to the cherry liquid, mixing well.

(continued)

6 **scallions, cut into ½-inch lengths, with as much green as possible**	(2) Prepare the vegetables.
1 **6-oz. can water chestnuts, drained and sliced**	
1 **8-oz. can bamboo shoots, drained**	
4 **Tablespoons oil**	(3) In a *wok* or large saucepan, heat the oil, add the shrimp, and cook them, stirring, until they are just barely pink.
1½ **lbs. fresh shrimp, shelled and deveined**	
Reserved cherries	(4) Add the liquid mixture, bringing it rapidly to a boil. Then add the vegetables and the cherries, bringing them to a boil.
2 **Tablespoons cornstarch, mixed with a little cold water**	(5) Add the cornstarch and bring the dish quickly to the boil, stirring constantly until the sauce is thickened and smooth. Serve the dish at once.

CHERRY SALAD MOLD

Ordinarily, I eschew molded salads with more than a little vigor, but this one is very good and I recommend it.

Serves 6
Doubles
Refrigerates

Preparation: 30 minutes
Chilling time: at least 3 hours

2 **1-lb. cans pitted dark sweet cherries**	(1) Drain the cherries and reserve the liquid. In ¼ cup of the liquid, soften the gelatin.
1 **packet unflavored gelatin**	
1 **3-oz. package cream cheese at room temperature**	(2) Cream the cheese until fluffy. Add ⅓ cup cherry liquid and blend the mixture.
⅓ **cup cherry liquid**	

¼ **cup sweet sherry**
¾ **cup cherry liquid**
1 **Tablespoon lemon juice**

(3) In a saucepan, combine the sherry, ¾ cup cherry liquid, and lemon juice. Heat the mixture, add the gelatin, and stir until the gelatin is dissolved. Allow it to cool to room temperature.

Reserved cherries

(4) In a mold, rinsed with cold water, arrange the cherries. Combine the cream cheese and gelatin mixtures and pour over the cherries. Chill the salad for at least 3 hours.

CHERRY MUFFINS

Follow the directions for Apple Muffins, page 19, using, in place of the apple, 1 1-lb. can waterpack pitted sour red cherries, thoroughly drained on absorbent paper; mix together the grated rind of 1 lemon and 3 Tablespoons sugar. Just before baking the muffins, sprinkle each one with a little of this mixture.

CHERRIES JUBILEE
   (French)

A classic and festive sauce to be served with rich vanilla ice cream, page 457.

   Serves 6
   Doubles
   Refrigerates

Preparation: 15 minutes
Cooking: 10 minutes

3 **Tablespoons cornstarch**
2 **Tablespoons sugar**
2 **1-lb. cans pitted dark sweet cherries**
Port wine

(1) Combine the cornstarch and sugar. Combine the cherry liquid and wine to equal 2 cups. In a saucepan, combine the dry and liquid ingredients.

(continued)

Zest of 1 orange **Zest of 1 lemon**	(2) Add the fruit peel and cook the mixture, stirring constantly, until it is thickened and smooth. Discard the peel.
Reserved cherries **Juice of 1 lemon**	(3) Add the cherries and lemon juice.
	At this point you may stop and continue later.
½ cup cognac, warmed **Vanilla ice cream**	(4) Add the cognac, ignite it, pour it over the cherries (which have been reheated, if necessary). While they are still flaming, ladle the cherries jubilee over vanilla ice cream.

CHERRY PUDDING

(*French*)

"*Clafoutis aux cerises*," a traditional dish from the Limousin and Auvergne, was originally cooked in a skillet with unpitted cherries.

Serves 6

Preparation: 15 minutes
Cooking: 1½ hours
Preheat oven: 350°

4 eggs **½ cup sugar**	(1) In the container of an electric blender, combine the eggs and sugar and blend them until they are light.
½ cup soft butter **½ cup flour**	(2) Add the butter and blend it with the eggs and sugar; then add the flour, a little at a time, and blend it with the other ingredients.
1½ cups milk **Pinch of salt** **1½ teaspoons vanilla or 1 teaspoon almond extract**	(3) Add these three ingredients and blend the mixture once again.
3 cups cherries, pitted and, if canned, well drained **Cinnamon**	(4) In a well-buttered 8- or 9-inch baking dish, arrange the cherries and sprinkle them with cinnamon.

Heavy cream (optional)

(5) Pour the batter over the fruit and bake the pudding at 350° for 1½ hours. Serve it warm, with cream, if desired.

This recipe adapts itself to various fruits, fresh or canned—pears, plums, or peaches. Canned fruit must be thoroughly drained and, if desired, the liquid may be used in the batter, replacing the milk or supplementing it.

CHERRY TARTS

(English)

Serves 6
Doubles

Preparation: 25 minutes*
Cooking: 18 minutes
Preheat oven: 425°

1 1-lb. can dark sweet pitted cherries

(1) Drain the cherries, reserving the fruit and ¼ cup liquid.

¼ cup cherry liquid
¼ cup granulated sugar
¼ cup dark brown sugar
2 Tablespoons quick-cooking tapioca
Grated rind ½ lemon

(2) Combine these five ingredients. Allow them to stand for 15 minutes.

Pastry for 6 muffin cups

(3) Line 6 muffin cups with plain pastry.

Reserved cherries
Soft butter

(4) In each muffin cup, arrange an equal number of cherries. Over them, spoon an equal amount of the juice mixture. To each, add a dot or two of butter.

(5) Bake the tarts at 425° for 18 minutes, or until the pastry is golden. They may be served either hot or cold.

* The preparation time does not include readying the pastry, page 458.

CHERRY SAUCE
(Polish)

For baked, broiled, or poached fish. If desired, the fish may be poached in the sauce, rather than cooked first and then garnished with it.
Very good with boiled rice.

Serving: about 3 cups
Refrigerates

Preparation: 30 minutes

1 1-lb. can pitted sour cherries

(1) Drain the cherry liquid into a mixing bowl. (Reserve the cherries for later use.) To the liquid, add water to equal 1⅔ cups.

3 Tablespoons butter
¼ cup sugar
¼ teaspoon cinnamon
¼ teaspoon ground clove
1 cup dry red wine
2 Tablespoons cornstarch, mixed with ¼ cup cold water
Reserved cherries

(2) In a saucepan, combine the butter, sugar, cinnamon, clove, and wine. Bring the mixture to the boil. Add the cornstarch mixture, stirring constantly until the sauce is thickened and smooth. Add the reserved cherries.

As noted above, this recipe can be refrigerated. However, it should be warmed before serving.

CHERRY SAUCE

For ice cream, puddings, and cakes. This sauce may be served hot or cold.

Serving: about 2½ cups
Refrigerates

Preparation: 25 minutes

1 1-lb. can pitted dark sweet cherries
¼ cup sugar
¼ cup corn syrup
1 3-inch piece cinnamon stick
Zest and juice of 1 lemon

(1) Drain the cherry liquid into a saucepan. (Reserve the cherries for later use.) To the liquid, add the sugar, corn syrup, cinnamon, and lemon zest and juice. Simmer the mixture for 10 minutes. Remove the cinnamon stick.

2 **Tablespoons cornstarch mixed with 1 Tablespoon water**
Reserved cherries

(2) Add the cornstarch and cook the sauce, stirring constantly, until it is thickened and smooth. Gently stir in the cherries.

A Danish variation omits the cinnamon and lemon zest and juice, and flavors the sauce with ½ Tablespoon almond extract, or more, to taste.

CRANBERRIES

Like blueberries, cranberries are members of the Heath Family—together with rhododendron, mountain laurel, and trailing arbutus. They were known to the American Indians as *i-bimi,* "bitter berries," who taught the colonists uses for them. Cranberries were first cultivated by a farmer in Dennis, Massachussetts, in 1816. From this humble transplantation of some cranberry plants to a bog on the farmer's land has developed a crop which, today, yields 300 bushels of fruit per acre.

Growing in bogs where the soil is composed largely of decaying plants, cranberries are found virtually all over the world in some variety or other. The Scandinavian lingenberry is well known to us, and other kinds of cranberries are found throughout northern Asia and northern and central Europe.

The American cranberry, *Vaccinium macrocarpon*, grows wild from Newfoundland to the Carolinas, and west to Minnesota and Arkansas. Its round, oblong, or pear-shaped berry, varying from pink to dark red or mottled red and white, ripens from August to October. It is sold fresh, dried, or frozen and is used most often in sauces, pastries, and jellies. Fifty percent of the commercial crop is made into canned sauce. (The recipes in this book, it is hoped, may help rectify this rather monotonous use of the cranberry.)

Commercial cranberry cultivation centers in Massachusetts, New Jersey, Wisconsin, and the coastal areas of Oregon and Washington. The trailing plants are protected from winter's freezing by flooding the bogs. The United States produces over 3 million bushels of cranberries per year.

CABBAGE AND CRANBERRY SOUP
(Russian)

A substantial soup which, served with a hearty bread and dessert, makes a full meal.

Serves 6
Doubles
Refrigerates

Preparation: 40 minutes
Cooking: 20 minutes

2 cups cranberries, rinsed, drained, and put once through the coarse blade of a meat grinder
3 onions, chopped
3 cups cabbage, finely shredded
3 Tablespoons brown sugar
1 Tablespoon salt
¼ teaspoon pepper
3 10½-oz. cans condensed chicken broth

(1) In a large saucepan or soup kettle, toss together the first three ingredients. Add the seasonings. Pour over the broth and add water to equal 6 cups. Cook the mixture for 20 minutes, or until the vegetables are tender.

1 1-lb. can shoestring or diced beets
Sour cream

(2) Add the beets and their liquid and heat the soup through. When serving it, garnish with a spoonful of sour cream.

BEEF AND CRANBERRIES
(American)

Serves 6
Doubles
Refrigerates

Preparation: 40 minutes
Cooking: 2½ hours
Preheat oven: 300°

¼ lb. salt pork, diced

(1) In a flame-proof casserole, render the salt pork until crisp. Remove it to absorbent paper; reserve it.

2 onions, chopped
1 clove garlic, chopped

(2) In the remaining fat, cook the onions and garlic until translucent.

3 lbs. chuck, cut in bite-sized pieces
Seasoned flour

(3) Dredge the meat in the flour; brown it in the fat. Sprinkle over 2 Tablespoons of the remaining flour.

3 cups cranberries, rinsed and well drained
2 10½-oz. cans condensed beef broth
1 teaspoon marjoram
¾ teaspoon ground allspice
1 bay leaf, crumbled
3 Tablespoons brown sugar
1½ teaspoons salt
¼ teaspoon pepper

(4) Add the cranberries. Add the broth plus water to equal 3 cups. Add the seasonings.

At this point you may stop and continue later.

(5) Bake the casserole, covered, at 300° for 2½ hours, or until the meat is tender.

LAMB SHANKS AND CRANBERRIES
(American)

Follow the directions for Beef and Cranberries, page 118, using 6 lamb shanks and adding the grated rind and juice of 1 lemon and ½ teaspoon thyme. The cooking time will be about 2 hours. If desired, the dish may be made a day in advance of serving, cooled, refrigerated, and skimmed of excess fat before being reheated for serving.

PORK BUTT AND CRANBERRIES
(American)

Serves 6
Refrigerates

Preparation: 45 minutes
Cooking: 3 hours
Preheat oven: 300°

1 5-lb. pork butt
¾ cup water

(1) In a flame-proof casserole, arrange the pork butt, pour the water over it, and cook the meat slowly, uncovered, until the water is evaporated. Brown the meat in the remaining fat.

1 10½-oz. can condensed beef broth
½ cup dark brown sugar, packed
2 cups fresh cranberries, rinsed and well drained
½ teaspoon ground clove
½ teaspoon salt
Grated rind and juice of 1 lemon

(2) Add these seven ingredients.

At this point you may stop and continue later.

Beef broth or cranberry juice

(3) Bake the casserole, covered, at 300° for about 3 hours, or until the meat is tender. Broth or cranberry juice may be added as necessary.

PORK CHOPS AND CRANBERRIES
(American)

Serves 6
Refrigerates

Preparation: 30 minutes
Cooking: 1 hour
Preheat oven: 350°

2 Tablespoons butter
2 Tablespoons oil
6 double pork chops, trimmed of
   excess fat
   Salt
   Pepper
	(1) In a flame-proof casserole, heat the butter and oil and brown the chops; season them. Remove.

2 onions, chopped ½ teaspoon thyme ½ teaspoon rosemary, crumbled	(2) Discard all but 1 Tablespoon of fat; in it, cook the onions until translucent. Replace the chops and sprinkle them with the herbs.
2 cups fresh cranberries, rinsed and well drained ¾ cup honey ¼ cup water	(3) Add the cranberries. Combine the honey and water and pour the mixture over the contents of the casserole.

At this point you may stop and continue later.

(4) Bake the casserole, covered, at 350° for 1 hour, or until the meat is tender.

VEAL SHANKS AND CRANBERRIES

   (American)

Follow the directions for Beef and Cranberries, page 118, using 6 veal shanks and adding the grated rind and juice of 1 orange. The cooking time will be about 2 hours.

DUCKLING AND CRANBERRIES

   Serves 4
   Refrigerates

Preparation: 1½ hours
Cooking: 1 hour
Preheat oven: 350°/325°

(continued)

1 5- to 6-lb. duck, quartered, and excess fat removed	(1) Arrange the duck on the rack of a broiling pan and bake it at 350° for 1 hour. Discard all but 3 Tablespoons of the fat.
Reserved duck liver and giblets, chopped	(2) In a flame-proof casserole, cook the liver and giblets in the reserved fat for 5 minutes. Remove them to absorbent paper.
½ cup dry red wine **1 onion, chopped** **1 clove garlic, chopped** **1 bay leaf** **Few sprigs parsley** **½ teaspoon thyme** **½ cup brown sugar, packed** **2 cups fresh cranberries, rinsed and well drained** **Grated rind and juice of 1 lemon**	(3) To the casserole, add these ten ingredients and, over high heat, cook the mixture, stirring gently, until the cranberries pop.
1 Tablespoon cornstarch, dissolved in ¼ cup cool water	(4) Add the cornstarch mixture and continue to cook, stirring constantly, until the mixture is thickened and smooth. Stir in the reserved giblets and add the duck, spooning the sauce over it. *At this point you may stop and continue later.* (5) Bake the casserole, covered, at 325° for 1 hour, or until the duck is tender.

CRANBERRY AND HORSERADISH MOUSSE

(American)

Not really a vegetable, but serves as one to accompany boiled or roast meats. Not really a mousse, either!

Serves 6
Refrigerates

Preparation: 20 minutes
Chilling time: at least 4 hours

**2 cups Whole Cranberry Sauce,
page 132**
1 cup sour cream
**4 Tablespoons prepared
horseradish
Juice of ½ lemon**

(1) In a mixing bowl, combine these four ingredients.

1 packet unflavored gelatin
**½ cup cold water
Pinch of salt**

(2) In a small saucepan, soften the gelatin in the water. Add the salt. Then, over moderate heat, dissolve the gelatin, stirring constantly.

(3) Add the gelatin to the contents of the mixing bowl; fold together all the ingredients until they are well blended. Pour the mixture into a mold and chill it for at least 4 hours, or until it is set. Unmold the mousse before serving it.

SWEET POTATOES AND CRANBERRIES

Serves 6
Doubles
Refrigerates

Preparation: 30 minutes
Cooking: 20 minutes
Preheat oven: 350°

6 sweet potatoes, scrubbed

(1) In boiling salted water to cover, cook the potatoes for 20 minutes, or until they are tender. Drain and peel them.

**Soft butter
Cinnamon**
**2 cups (or more, to taste) Whole
Cranberry Sauce, page 132**

(2) In a lightly buttered baking dish, arrange the potatoes, halved lengthwise. Spread them with butter and sprinkle them with cinnamon. Spread the Cranberry Sauce over them.

At this point you may stop and continue later.

(3) Bake the potatoes, uncovered, at 350° for 20 minutes.

RED CABBAGE AND CRANBERRIES

(American)

Serves 6
Doubles
Refrigerates

Preparation: 20 minutes
Cooking: 30 minutes

1 medium-sized red cabbage, finely shredded
4 slices bacon, diced, rendered, and drained on absorbent paper (reserve the fat)
2 cups fresh cranberries, rinsed and drained
2 apples, peeled, cored, and cut into eighths

(1) In a soup kettle, toss together these four ingredients.

Reserved bacon fat
1 cup dry red wine
¼ cup cider vinegar
1¼ teaspoons salt
½ cup dark brown sugar, packed
Generous sprinkling nutmeg

(2) Mix together these six ingredients. Pour the mixture over the cabbage. Bring it to the boil, reduce the heat, and simmer, covered, for 30 minutes, or until it is tender. A little water may be added as necessary.

CRANBERRY BREAD

(American)

Serving: two 8-inch loaves

Preparation: 40 minutes
Rising: 1½ hours
Cooking: 50 minutes

¾ cup hot water
4 Tablespoons soft butter
3 Tablespoons light brown sugar
2 teaspoons salt

(1) In a mixing bowl, combine these four ingredients, stirring to melt the butter and to dissolve the sugar and salt.

2 cups cranberries, rinsed, drained, and put once through the coarse blade of a meat grinder
½ cup light brown sugar, packed
⅓ cup light molasses

(2) In a mixing bowl, combine these three ingredients; allow the mixture to sit for 30 minutes.

1½ cups flour
½ teaspoon mace
2 packets dry yeast

(3) In a large mixing bowl, sift together these three ingredients. (If desired, the bread may be made with half white and half whole-wheat flour.)

2 cups flour

(4) To the flour mixture, add first the cranberry mixture, stirring, and then the liquid. Stir the batter well. Add, by the half-cupful, the additional 2 cups flour, stirring in thoroughly each portion. The dough will be sticky.

(5) Put the bowl in a warm place and allow the dough to rise until doubled in bulk.

(6) Stir the dough down and spoon it into two buttered 8-inch loaf pans. Allow it to rise again.

(7) Put the pans into a cold oven; set heat for 400° and bake the bread at this temperature for 15 minutes. Reduce the heat to 325° and continue to bake the bread for 35 minutes, or until it sounds hollow when tapped.

CRANBERRY MUFFINS

(American)

12 to 18 muffins

Preparation: 15 minutes
Cooking: 25 minutes
Preheat oven: 400°

(continued)

2 cups flour
1 Tablespoon baking powder
⅔ cup sugar
½ teaspoon salt

(1) In a mixing bowl, sift together the dry ingredients.

1 cup fresh cranberries, rinsed and drained on absorbent paper
1 cup milk
3 Tablespoons butter, melted and cooled

(2) In the container of an electric blender, whirl these 3 ingredients on low speed only long enough to chop the cranberries roughly. (If desired, the grated rind of 1 orange may be added to the liquid ingredients.)

(3) Pour the liquid over the dry ingredients, stirring only enough to moisten the flour.

(4) Fill buttered muffin cups ⅔ full. Bake the muffins at 400° about 25 minutes, or until they are golden brown.

CRANBERRY CRISP

(American)

Serves 6

Preparation: 20 minutes
Cooking: 35 minutes
Preheat oven: 375°

2 cups Whole Cranberry Sauce, page 132
Grated rind of 1 orange
½ teaspoon cinnamon

(1) Into the Cranberry Sauce stir the grated orange rind and cinnamon.

3 cups unseasoned packaged croutons
8 Tablespoons butter, melted

(2) In a mixing bowl, toss together the croutons and melted butter.

(3) In a buttered baking dish, arrange alternate layers of the croutons and cranberries; the top layer should be croutons.

At this point you may stop and continue later.

Custard Sauce, page 460

(4) Bake the dessert, covered, at 375° for 20 minutes; uncover it and continue to bake 15 minutes longer, or until the top is golden. Serve it with Custard Sauce.

OPEN CRANBERRY TART

An American adaptation of the French Lemon Galette.

> Serves 6
> Refrigerates
> Freezes

Preparation: 45 minutes
Cooking: 30 minutes
Preheat oven: 400°

Follow the directions for Lemon Galette (page 204) using the following filling:

4 cups fresh cranberries, rinsed and well drained
¾ cup sugar
1 cup orange juice
Pinch of salt
Grated rind ½ lemon

(1) In a saucepan, combine and simmer these ingredients, covered, for 10 minutes; stir them occasionally. Allow the mixture to cool.

(2) In the container of an electric blender, whirl the mixture on high speed until it is a smooth puree. Return the mixture to the saucepan.

2 Tablespoons cornstarch
2 Tablespoons cold water

(3) Mix the cornstarch and water until smooth; add to the puree and over high heat cook the mixture, stirring constantly, until the filling is thickened and smooth. Allow it to cool before spreading it on the *galette* pastry. Bake as instructed in the *galette* recipe.

CRANBERRIES JUBILEE

(American)

Serves 6
Refrigerates

Preparation: 15 minutes

2 cups fresh cranberries, rinsed and well drained
1 cup sugar
½ cup water
½ teaspoon cinnamon
½ teaspoon nutmeg
¼ teaspoon ground clove

(1) In a saucepan or chafing dish, combine these six ingredients and, over high heat, bring the mixture to a boil; reduce the heat and simmer the berries until they are tender but still retain their shape, about 5 minutes.

1 teaspoon cornstarch, mixed with 1 teaspoon cold water
2 Tablespoons soft butter

(2) Add the cornstarch mixture, and cook the mixture over high heat, stirring gently but constantly, until the sauce is thickened and smooth. Remove it from the heat and stir in the butter.

⅓ cup cognac
Vanilla ice cream

(3) In a small saucepan, warm the cognac, ignite it, and pour it over the cranberries. Serve the sauce at once ladled over vanilla ice cream.

CRANBERRY AND RAISIN PIE

(American)

Serving: one 9-inch pie

Preparation: 30 minutes*
Cooking: 45 minutes
Preheat oven: 425°

2½ cups fresh cranberries, rinsed well drained, and coarsely chopped
1 cup golden raisins

(1) In a mixing bowl, combine the cranberries and raisins.

* The preparation time does not include readying the pastry for a two-crust pie, page 458.

4 teaspoons flour
1 cup sugar
½ teaspoon cinnamon
Pinch of salt

(2) In a mixing bowl sift together the dry ingredients. Add them to the fruit and, using two forks, toss the mixture lightly.

Unbaked 9-inch pie shell, chilled
Soft butter
Juice of ½ lemon
Unbaked top crust

(3) Fill the pie shell with the cranberry mixture; dot it with butter and sprinkle it with lemon juice. Add the top crust, crimping it sealed with a fork. With the tines of a fork, puncture the top crust to allow steam to escape.

(4) Bake the pie at 425° for 20 minutes; reduce the heat to 350° and continue baking for 25 minutes, or until the crust is golden brown.

CRANBERRY AND ORANGE TART I

Serving: two 8-inch tarts
Refrigerates
Freezes

Preparation: 40 minutes*
Cooking: 30 minutes
Chilling time: 3 hours

2 oranges, peeled, quartered, seeded, and the white pith removed. (If desired, substitute 3 tangerines for the oranges.)

(1) Put the oranges twice through the coarse blade of a meat grinder.

½ cup water
3 Tablespoons quick-cooking tapioca

(2) In a saucepan, combine the oranges, water, and tapioca. Bring the mixture to the boil, stirring constantly, and cook for five minutes.

1 lb. fresh cranberries, rinsed and drained
1 cup sugar

(3) Add the cranberries and sugar. Cook the berries, stirring, until they pop.

* Preparation time does not include readying the pastry, page 458.

(continued)

½ **teaspoon ground allspice**
½ **teaspoon cinnamon**
   Pinch of salt
2 **Tablespoons butter**

(4) To the cranberry mixture, add these four ingredients, stirring. Allow the mixture to cool slightly.

2 **8-inch pie shells, baked**
   Whipped cream, meringue, or vanilla ice cream (optional)

(5) Spoon the fruit into the pie shells and allow it to cool completely. The tarts may be topped with whipped cream or meringue, if desired; a scoop of vanilla ice cream also enhances the dessert.

CRANBERRY AND ORANGE TART II
(with Crème pâtissière)

A pleasant variation, applicable to many fruit pies, is the addition of *crème pâtissière*, a pastry custard filling.

   Serving: two 8-inch tarts
   Refrigerates
   Freezes

Preparation: 40 minutes*
Chilling time: 3 hours

3 **eggs**
1 **cup sugar**

(1) In a large mixing bowl, beat the eggs until light. Gradually add the sugar, beating constantly. Continue to beat the mixture until it is pale yellow and slightly thickened.

½ **cup flour**

(2) Add the flour gradually, beating constantly.

2 **cups scalded milk**
   Pinch of salt

(3) While beating the mixture, add the milk in a thin, steady stream. Add the salt.

(4) Pour the mixture into a saucepan. Over moderately high heat, bring it to the boil, stirring constantly with a wire whisk. Cook the creme at the boiling point, stirring for 2 minutes.

* Preparation time does not include readying the fruit filling (for this recipe, see Cranberry and Orange Tart I, page 129) or preparing baked pastry shells, page 458.

1 Tablespoon butter
3 Tablespoons kirsch or 1½
   Tablespoons vanilla

2 8-inch pie shells, baked
   Prepared fruit filling (Cranberry
   and Orange Tart I)
   Whipped cream, meringue, or
   vanilla ice cream (optional)

(5) Remove the mixture from the heat; beat in the butter, then the kirsch or vanilla; when it is smooth, allow it to cool.

(6) Spread a ½-inch layer of the custard over the bottom of the pie shell; add the fruit on top. Allow the tarts to cool completely. To serve, they may be topped with whipped cream or a meringue, or they may be served with a scoop of vanilla ice cream.

CRANBERRY PUDDING

(Russian)

Follow the directions for Apricot Pudding, page 45, using: 3 cups fresh cranberries, rinsed and well drained; 2 cups water; ¾ cup sugar; ¼ teaspoon mace.

STEAMED CRANBERRY PUDDING*

(American)

Serves 6
Refrigerates
Freezes

Preparation: 20 minutes
Cooking: 2 hours

1½ cups flour
 1 teaspoon baking powder
 2 teaspoons soda
 1 cup fresh cranberries, rinsed
   and drained on absorbent paper

(1) In a mixing bowl, sift together the first three ingredients. Add the cranberries and toss them lightly with the flour.

* *Note:* This pudding should be served hot; if you refrigerate or freeze it, allow it to return to room temperature before reheating it in a double boiler.

(continued)

131

½ cup cranberries, rinsed and
  well drained
½ cup light molasses
½ cup hot water
  Grated rind of 1 lemon

  Lemon sauce or custard sauce

(2) In a mixing bowl, combine these four ingredients. Add to the flour mixture and stir only enough to moisten the flour.

(3) Pour the batter into a lightly buttered double-boiler and cook it, tightly covered, over simmering water for 2 hours. Remove it to a warm plate, slice it, and serve it with either Lemon Sauce, page 460, or Custard Sauce, page 460.

CANDIED CRANBERRY SAUCE

To accompany roast meats and poultry.

> Serving: about 5 cups
> Refrigerates

Preparation: 10 minutes
Cooking: 1 hour
Preheat oven: 300°

8 cups (2 1-lb. boxes) cranberries,
  rinsed and lightly drained
3 cups sugar
1 teaspoon mace
½ teaspoon salt

(1) In a large bowl toss together the cranberries, sugar, and seasonings.

(2) Transfer the mixture to a deep casserole (the depth allows for easier stirring). Bake the cranberries, uncovered, at 300° for 1 hour, or until they are tender. Stir them often.

WHOLE CRANBERRY SAUCE
> *(American)*

To accompany roast meats and poultry.

> Serving: about 1 quart

Preparation: 20 minutes

2 **cups sugar**
Pinch of salt
1½ **cups water**

(1) In a large saucepan, bring these three ingredients to the boil, stirring until the sugar is dissolved. Boil the mixture, uncovered, for 5 minutes.

4 **cups fresh cranberries, rinsed**
and well drained
Zest of 1 orange

(2) Add the cranberries and orange zest. Cook the berries, uncovered, over gentle heat without stirring them for about 5 minutes, or until they are tender but still retain their shape. Skim the surface of the sauce and allow it to cool. Before serving, remove the orange zest.

CRANBERRY AND ORANGE STUFFING

For poultry and pork. Prepare the day before.

For *each* 4 cups of seasoned breadcrumbs, seasoned croutons, or packaged dressing:

1 **cup cranberries, rinsed and**
drained
½ **orange, quartered and seeded**

(1) Put the cranberries once through the coarse blade of a meat grinder; put the orange twice through the coarse blade of a meat grinder. In a mixing bowl, combine the two fruits.

¼ **cup sugar**
Grated rind of ½ lemon
¼ **teaspoon salt**
¼ **teaspoon cinnamon**

(2) Stir in the seasonings. Cover the bowl and allow the fruit to sit for 24 hours in the refrigerator.

½ **cup butter, melted**

(3) Allow the fruit to return to room temperature. Stir in the butter and toss the mixture lightly, using two forks, with the 4 cups of breadstuff.

DATES

Dates and coconuts are, oddly, the only fruits of the Palm Family cultivated for commercial use. Native to the shores of the Persian Gulf, dates are an important factor in the economy of the Arab countries. They are important, too, to California, which produces some 20,000 pounds annually from 5,000 acres under date cultivation.

All parts of the date palm yield products of economic value. The trunk is used for lumber. The hard ribs of the leaves are found in crates and furniture. The leaflets find their way into baskets. The leaf bases are burnt as fuel. From the fruit stalks, rope is made. Both alcohol and vinegar are derived from the fruit; and the sap of the tree is made into a beverage, either fresh or fermented.

Requiring hot summers and low humidity for ripening, dates are grown from Spain and the

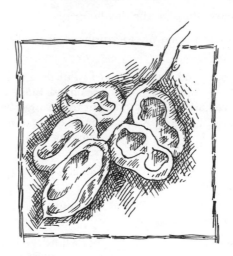

Canary Islands to North Africa, Southwest Asia, Pakistan, and India. Cultivated since remotest antiquity, dates were introduced to the New World by Spanish missionaries in the late eighteenth century. The fruit of the *Phoenix dactylifera* constitutes a rich and nourishing food upon which tribesmen in the deserts of Arabia have fed themselves for many thousands of years. In Iraq, which produces three-quarters of the world's supply, they continue to be a mainstay of the Bedouin diet.

The date palm, which can reach a height of 100 feet, is normally 60 to 80 feet high. It produces fruit after its eighth year and can continue to do so for over a century. The decorative leaves of the date palm, used in Palm Sunday observances and in the celebration of the Feast of the Tabernacle, can reach a length of 15 feet. The date flower is either male or female and is borne on separate palm trees; date palms under cultivation are pollinated artificially.

Actually, dates are berries with one seed. More or less oblong, they vary in size, color, shape, quality, and consistency of their flesh, according to their variety and environment. A single large bunch, weighing over 20 pounds, can contain as many as 1,000 individual fruits. A fresh ripe date, denied to most of the world, is superb; the dried fruit, as we commonly know it, is one-half sugar by weight.

BEEF AND DATES

Follow the directions for Beef and Oranges, page 229, using 1 cup sherry and ½ cup lemon juice; add 24 pitted dates for the final ½ hour of cooking.

CHICKEN AND DATES WITH CURRIED RICE

Although this dish appears to be of Middle Eastern or Indian origin, it actually had its genesis in my own experimental mood.

Serves 6
Doubles
Refrigerates

Preparation: 45 minutes
Cooking: 1 hour
Preheat oven: 350°

2 Tablespoons butter
2 Tablespoons oil
Serving-pieces of chicken for 6 persons
Salt
Pepper

(1) In a flame-proof 5½-quart casserole, heat the butter and oil and brown the chicken; season it. Remove.

3 onions, chopped
1½ cups natural raw rice
Grated rind of 1 lemon
1 Tablespoon curry powder (or to taste)

(2) In the remaining fat, cook the onions until translucent. Add the rice, stirring to coat each grain. Stir in the grated lemon rind and curry powder. Replace the chicken, spooning the rice over it.

At this point you may stop and continue later.

2 10½-oz. cans condensed chicken broth
Juice of 1 lemon or 1 Tablespoon cider vinegar (or, if more "snap" is desired, ½ lemon and ½ Tablespoon vinegar)
Water

(3) In a container, combine the broth, juice, and water to equal 3 cups. Pour the broth mixture over the contents of the casserole. Bake the casserole, covered, at 350° for 50 minutes.

1 **cup pitted dates, coarsely chopped**

(4) Add the dates and continue to cook the dish, covered, for 10 minutes, or until the chicken and rice are tender and the liquid is absorbed.

DATE BREAD

Follow the directions for Cranberry Bread, page 124, using, in place of the cranberries, 1½ cups chopped pitted dates.

DATE MUFFINS

Follow the directions for Apple Muffins, page 19, substituting ⅔ cup chopped pitted dates for the apples and dark brown sugar for white. Date Muffins are especially good when spread with cream cheese blended with milk to a soft consistency.

DATE CHIFFON PIE

Serving: one 8-inch pie
Doubles
Refrigerates

Preparation: 40 minutes*
Chilling time: at least 3 hours

1 **envelope unflavored gelatin**
¼ **cup sugar**

(1) In a saucepan, mix thoroughly the gelatin and sugar.

2 **egg yolks**
½ **cup orange juice**
⅓ **cup lemon juice**

(2) In a mixing bowl, beat together these three ingredients. Add them to the contents of the saucepan and, over gentle heat, cook the mixture, stirring constantly, until the gelatin is dissolved and the mixture slightly thickened. Allow it to cool.

½ **cup light cream**

(3) Add the cream, stirring.

* The preparation time does not include readying the pastry, page 458.

(continued)

2 **egg whites**
Pinch of salt
¼ **cup sugar**

(4) In a mixing bowl, beat the egg whites, with a pinch of salt added, until they stand in soft peaks. Add the sugar and continue beating until they stand in firm peaks. Fold a little of the custard into the egg whites; then fold all the whites into the custard.

⅔ **cup pitted dates, chopped**

(5) Fold in the dates, spoon the mixture into a prebaked 8-inch pastry shell, and chill the pie for at least 3 hours.

BAKED DATE PUDDING

Serves 6
Doubles
Refrigerates
Freezes

Preparation: 30 minutes
Cooking: 55 minutes
Preheat oven: 325°

1 **6½-oz. package pitted dates, chopped**
3 **Tablespoons butter**
1 **cup boiling water**

(1) In a mixing bowl, put the dates and the butter. Pour over them the boiling water and allow them to stand while the water cools slightly.

1 **egg beaten**
1 **cup dark brown sugar, packed**
Grated rind of 1 lemon

(2) Stir in the egg, sugar, and lemon rind.

1½ **cups flour**
1 **teaspoon baking soda**
1 **teaspoon salt**
½ **cup walnuts, chopped (optional)**

(3) In a mixing bowl, sift together these dry ingredients. (If desired, chopped walnuts may be added to the sifted dry ingredients.) To them, add the liquid mixture, stirring until the flour is moistened.

Custard Sauce, page 460

(4) Spoon the batter into a buttered 1½-quart baking dish and bake it in a 325° oven for 55 minutes, or until a knife inserted at the center comes out clean. Serve the pudding warm, with custard sauce.

RICE PUDDING WITH DATES

Follow the directions for Rice Pudding with Raisins, page 362, using, in place of the raisins, ¾ cup pitted dates, chopped.

STEAMED DATE PUDDING

Serves 6
Doubles
Refrigerates

Preparation: 30 minutes
Cooking: 2½–3 hours

3 Tablespoons butter
½ cup molasses
½ cup milk
2 eggs, well beaten

(1) In a saucepan, melt the butter. Add the molasses and milk, stirring to blend the mixture. Remove it from the heat. Stir in the eggs.

2 cups flour
1 teaspoon baking soda
½ teaspoon salt
½ teaspoon ground allspice
½ teaspoon ground clove
½ teaspoon nutmeg

(2) In a mixing bowl, sift together these dry ingredients.

½ lb. pitted dates, chopped fine

(3) Add the liquid to the dry ingredients, stirring until the flour is moistened. Stir in the dates.

(continued)

139

**Custard Sauce, page 460 or
Lemon Sauce, page 460**

(4) In a buttered 1-quart pudding mold or 1-lb. coffee can with tight-fitting lid, cover and steam the pudding in enough simmering water to cover one-half the container for 2½ or 3 hours, or until the pudding is firm but light. Serve it with the sauce of your choice.

DATE SOUFFLE

A sumptuous dessert, very rich and very good.

Serves 6

Preparation: 30 minutes
Cooking: 35–40 minutes
Preheat oven: 350°

1 cup pitted dates, chopped
½ cup milk

(1) In a saucepan, combine the dates with the milk and cook them, covered, for 20 minutes, or until they are very soft. Remove them from the heat and mash them until the paste is smooth.

2 Tablespoons dark rum
2 Tablespoons heavy cream
1 teaspoon vanilla
4 egg yolks, beaten

(2) Into the mashed dates, stir these four ingredients.

5 egg whites
½ cup sugar

(3) Beat the whites until they are stiff, gradually add the sugar until the mixture stands in firm peaks. Fold a little of the date mixture into the egg whites; then fold all the whites into the dates.

Heavy cream

(4) Spoon the batter into a souffle dish, buttered and sugared, and bake the dessert at 350° for 35 to 40 minutes, or until it is well risen and lightly browned. Serve the souffle immediately with heavy cream.

DATE SAUCE

For boiled meats, this sauce served hot is adapted from the ancient Roman gourmet, Apicius.

Serving: 2½ cups
Refrigerates

Preparation: 40 minutes
Cooking: 30 minutes

12 pitted dates, finely chopped
12 almonds, browned in butter and chopped
1 cup parsley, chopped
1 onion, minced
1½ Tablespoons olive oil
Dash of salt

(1) In a saucepan, combine these six ingredients and, over gentle heat, cook them, stirring often, for 6 minutes.

2 cups water
2½ Tablespoons cider vinegar
Salt
Pepper

(2) Add the water and vinegar and cook the sauce, uncovered, over medium high heat, for 30 minutes, or until the liquid is reduced by half. Season to taste with salt and pepper.

DATE SAUCE

Especially good on vanilla ice cream.

Serving: 2½ cups
Refrigerates

Preparation: 30 minutes
Chilling time: at least 3 hours

(continued)

¾ **cup light corn syrup**
½ **cup sweet sherry**
 3 **Tablespoons preserved ginger, minced**
   Grated rind of 1 orange
   Dash of salt

(1) In the top of a double boiler, cook these five ingredients over boiling water for 20 minutes.

 2 **cups pitted dates, chopped**

(2) Add the dates, cook the mixture for 10 minutes longer. Allow it to cool and chill it for at least 3 hours.

FIGS

When Cato advocated the conquest of Carthage,
he used as his crowning argument the
acquisition of the glorious North African figs—
and he forthwith drew from the folds of his
toga specimens for the Roman Senate to see!
And it was, indeed, the Romans who introduced
figs to all the temperate climates of Europe.
The French brought them to New Orleans and
the Spanish to California in the mid-eighteenth
century. Today, the principal cultivated varieties
are Mission, Calimyrna, Adriatic, Kadota, and
Smyrna.

The hundreds of different figs, which had their
genesis in the area between Smyrna and Syria
and then spread to Biblical Palestine, vary when
mature from greenish yellow to black. (The
fruit, incidentally, contains within it the fig tree
flower, which does not appear externally.) While

the tree is long-lived, the fruit is not, being very perishable when soft and ripe.

Figs, a multiple fruit, have a high sugar content and are therefore most often served as a dessert, albeit they are frequently used as an appetizer in Europe. The drying process—whose product we are more generally familiar with than the fresh fruit—causes the sugar to form a deposit on the surface of the fig, so that the fruit is really preserved in its own dried syrup. Dried figs are 60 percent sugar. Figs are grown commercially for drying and table use in Italy, Turkey, Algeria, Greece, Portugal, and Spain; and, in the United States, in California and Texas.

A member of the mulberry family, the genus *Ficus* (fig) varies in growth from a low trailing shrub to a giant tree. *Ficus carica*, the most common edible species, was cultivated by primitive man. The Egyptians made mummy cases from fig tree wood. In ancient Greece, Attic figs were so famous that laws governed their export. Pliny lists several varieties, preferring those which were imported and suggesting that domestically grown figs were fit food only for slaves. Sacred to Bacchus, figs were used in Roman religious festivals; and the fig tree, offering its protection to Romulus and Remus, was a symbol of prosperity and well-being.

BEEF AND FIGS I

Follow the directions for Beef and Oranges, page 229, using, in the final 30 minutes of cooking, either 18 dried figs, plumped in a vegetable steamer for 1 hour and chopped coarsely, or 18 tenderized dried figs, chopped coarsely.

BEEF AND FIGS II

(Indian)

Serves 6
Doubles
Refrigerates

Preparation: 30 minutes
Cooking: 2½ hours
Preheat oven: 300°

2 Tablespoons butter
2 Tablespoons oil
3 lbs. chuck, cut in bite-sized pieces
Salt
Pepper

(1) In a flame-proof casserole, heat the butter and oil and brown the meat; season it. Remove.

4 onions, chopped
4 carrots, scraped and sliced
3 Tablespoons flour

(2) In the remaining fat, cook the vegetables until the onion is translucent. Stir in the flour.

1½ teaspoons salt
½ teaspoon pepper
2 teaspoons cinnamon
¼ cup wine vinegar
½ cup honey

(3) Stir in these five ingredients. Replace the beef.

At this point you may stop and continue later.

2 10½-oz. cans condensed beef broth plus water to equal 3 cups
¾ cup cashews (optional)
¾ cup raisins
12 to 18 tenderized dried figs

(4) Add the broth and bake the casserole, covered, at 300° for 2 hours. Add the nuts, raisins, and figs. Continue to cook the dish, covered, for 30 minutes, or until the meat is tender.

CHICKEN AND FIGS

Follow the directions for Beef and Figs II, page 145, using, in place of the beef and beef broth, serving-pieces of chicken for 6 persons and 2 10½-oz. cans condensed chicken broth plus water to equal 3 cups. Bake the casserole, covered at 350° for 1 hour, or until the chicken is tender. Add the cashews, raisins, and figs for the second half-hour of cooking.

VEGETABLE CASSEROLE AND FIGS

Follow the directions for Vegetable Casserole and Grapes, page 166, using, in place of the grapes, 1 cup tenderized dried figs, quartered, and cooked with the vegetables for the full 20 minutes.

BAKED FIGS

Serves 6
Doubles
Refrigerates

Preparation: 40 minutes
Preheat oven: 300°

18 tenderized dried figs, stems removed
¼ cup sugar
¾ cup orange juice

(1) Prick the tenderized figs in several places with the tines of a fork. In a buttered baking dish, arrange the figs, sprinkle them with the sugar and add the orange juice. Bake them, uncovered, at 300° for 40 minutes, or until they are plumped and tender. Baste them frequently.

Ground clove
¼ cup orange-flavored liqueur
Whipped cream

(2) Remove them from the oven and sprinkle them lightly with the ground clove. In a small saucepan, warm the liqueur, ignite it, and pour it over the figs. Serve the dish, warm or cold, with the whipped cream.

STEAMED FIG PUDDING

Follow the directions for Steamed Date Pudding, page 139, using, in place of the dates, ½ lb. dried figs, chopped fine.

FIG SAUCE

For ice cream.

    Serving: 2 cups
    Doubles
    Refrigerates

Preparation: 30 minutes
Aging time: 2 weeks

¾ **cup sugar**
1½ **cups water**
  1 **3-inch piece cinnamon stick**
  3 **whole cloves**
    Zest and juice of 1 lemon

¾ **cup dried figs, chopped**
⅓ **cup pitted dates, chopped**
½ **cup nuts, chopped (walnuts, cashews, or almonds)**

(1) In a saucepan, combine these six ingredients. Bring them to a rolling boil and cook them, uncovered, for 30 minutes, or until the mixture is syrupy.

(2) In a container with tight-fitting lid, combine these three ingredients. Over them, strain the boiling syrup. Cover the container and let it age at room temperature for at least 2 weeks.

GRAPEFRUIT

So-called because the fruit may hang in clusters,
as do grapes, as well as singly, the *Citrus paradisi*
probably originated in Jamaica. It is not found in
southeastern Asia or on the East Indian Archipelago, where its cousin, the pommelo, is widely
grown. The grapefruit tree, as large as the orange,
has dense, dark, shiny green leaves and a large
white blossom.

The lemon-yellow fruit, twice the size of an
orange, is best used when well-shaped and heavy;
the weight is indicative of the juice content. Rich
in vitamin C, grapefruit were considered too sour
to be an important food in the United States
before 1900. Hybridization not only has made the
fruit sweeter, but also has given its flesh a clear,
pink, or dark red color.

The twenty-three varieties of grapefruit hy-
bridize easily with other members of the citrus

group. The tangelo, for example, is a cross of the mandarin orange and grapefruit. The aptly named ugli fruit is a cross of the tangerine with grapefruit; despite its descriptive name, ugli fruit, easily peeled and juicy, is nearly seedless and very sweet.

Grapefruit require a sandy but relatively fertile soil. In the United States, commercial orchards supplement fertilization. A mature tree may yield 1,500 pounds of fruit a year. Of the total world production, 90 percent is in the United States: Florida, Texas, Arizona, and California. Over one-half of this crop is canned or frozen. Israel, Jordan, South Africa, and Brazil are other large producers.

CROWN ROAST OF PORK AND GRAPEFRUIT

Serves 6
Refrigerates

Preparation: 30 minutes
Cooking: 40 minutes to the pound (size of roast will vary cooking time)
Preheat oven: 450°

1 12-rib crown roast of pork

(1) Wrap foil around the exposed ribs to prevent their charring. Arrange the pork on the rack of a roasting pan. Put it in a preheated 450° oven; immediately reduce the heat to 350° and cook the meat for 40 minutes per pound.

3 Tablespoons butter
1 onion, chopped
1 stalk celery, chopped

(2) In a saucepan, heat the butter and in it cook the onion and celery until translucent.

1½ cups cooked rice
2 cups croutons, toasted in butter
1 Tablespoon rubbed sage
1 teaspoon salt
¼ teaspoon pepper
Grated rind of 1 orange

(3) In a large mixing bowl, combine the cooked rice, croutons and seasonings. Add the onion mixture and, using two forks, toss the stuffing until it is well blended.

2 large grapefruit, peeled, sectioned, seeded, and the sections halved

(4) One hour before the meat is done, toss the stuffing with the grapefruit. Fill the center of the roast and baste it with the pan drippings. After 30 minutes of cooking, baste it again.

(5) When it is done, remove the roast from the oven and discard the foil on the ribs. If desired, a gravy may be made from the pan drippings.

VEAL AND GRAPEFRUIT

Serves 6
Doubles
Refrigerates

Preparation: 30 minutes
Cooking: 1½ hours

3 lbs. shoulder of veal, cut in
bite-sized pieces
Seasoned flour
2 Tablespoons butter
2 Tablespoons oil

(1) Dredge the veal in the seasoned flour. In a flame-proof casserole, heat the butter and oil and brown the veal, a few pieces at a time. Add butter and oil as necessary.

1 onion, chopped
1 clove garlic, chopped
2 bay leaves
1 teaspoon thyme
1 teaspoon salt
¼ teaspoon pepper
½ cup sugar
Grated rind of 1 orange

(2) Over the veal, sprinkle these ingredients.

1 6-oz. can frozen grapefruit juice
concentrate, thawed, plus water
to equal 2½ cups*

(3) Add the grapefruit juice.

At this point you may stop and continue later.

(4) Bring the casserole to the boil, reduce the heat, and simmer the veal, covered, for 1½ hours, or until it is tender.

1 large grapefruit, sectioned,
seeded, and with all white pith
removed*
Chopped fresh mint

(5) Add the grapefruit sections for the final 15 minutes of cooking. When serving, garnish the dish with a sprinkling of mint.

* If desired, the dish may be made with 2 1-lb. cans grapefruit sections, drained; in this case, use their liquid as part of the 2½ cups grapefruit juice.

BAKED FISH AND GRAPEFRUIT

Serves 6

Preparation: 30 minutes
Cooking: 50 minutes
Preheat oven: 400°

1 4- to 5-lb. baking fish (bass, blue fish, red snapper), cleaned
Salt

(1) Rub the cavity and exterior of the fish with a little salt.

4 Tablespoons butter
1 onion minced
1 cup croutons
½ cup cracker crumbs
¾ teaspoon dill weed
¼ cup parsley, chopped
Grinding of pepper

(2) In a saucepan, heat the butter and in it cook the onion until translucent. Add the remaining five ingredients, tossing them gently with a fork until the stuffing is well blended.

Sections of ½ grapefruit, seeded

(3) Toss the dressing with the grapefruit pieces and stuff the fish. Skewer it or tie it securely with string. Arrange the fish on greased foil in a baking pan.

At this point you may stop and continue later.

1 grapefruit, peeled, sectioned, and seeded
2 Tablespoons melted butter

(4) Bake the fish, uncovered, at 400° for 40 minutes. Toss the grapefruit sections with the butter and arrange them over the fish; continue to cook it for 10 minutes longer, or until it flakes easily.

GRAPEFRUIT PIE

Serving: one 9-inch pie

Preparation: 30 minutes*
Cooking: 30 minutes
Preheat oven: 400°

* The preparation time does not include readying the pastry, page 458.

1 **9-inch unbaked pie shell**
2 **1-lb. cans grapefruit sections, drained on absorbent paper**

1 **cup reserved grapefruit liquid**
⅔ **cup sugar**
½ **teaspoon ground allspice**
½ **teaspoon cinnamon**
2 **Tablespoons cornstarch**
   Pinch of salt

   Maraschino cherries, halved
   Pecan halves (optional)

(1) Line the pie shell with the grapefruit sections.

(2) In a saucepan, combine these six ingredients, stirring until they are blended. Over high heat, cook the mixture, stirring constantly, until it is thickened and smooth. Allow it to cool. Spoon it over the grapefruit sections in the pie shell.

(3) Garnish the pie with a few maraschino cherries and, if desired, pecan halves.

(4) Put the pie into a 400° oven for 10 minutes; reduce the heat to 350° and continue to bake the pie for 20 minutes, or until the crust is golden brown. Allow the pie to cool and to set before serving it.

GRAPES

Five hundred years before Columbus, Norwegian explorers called America "Vinland" because of the number of wild grapes found here. Today, 90 percent of the commercial United States grape crop is grown in California; European grapes are not successfully cultivated east of the Rocky Mountains. Both Lord Baltimore and Thomas Jefferson learned this fact, unhappily, when they planted and failed with European grapes. The leading grape native to America is the Concord, perfected by Ephraim Bull near Thoreau's Walden Pond; long before, however, "Concord" grapes had been eaten in their wild state by hungry New England Pilgrims.

Grape cultivation (viticulture, from *Vitis*, the grape genus) is annotated in Egyptian hieroglyphs of 2400 B.C. Noah planted a vineyard. In Homer's Greece, wine was a regular commodity. Pliny

lists over ninety different grapes and some fifty kinds of wine.

Vitis vinifera, the grape of the Bible and myth and which today continues
to produce wines, raisins, and the majority of table grapes, is a true berry
and had its origin around the Caspian Sea. From here it spread throughout
the whole of the ancient world. Wine cultivation and cellerage was brought to
a high degree of perfection by the Egyptians. The Phoenicians brought the
grape to France about 600 B.C.; the Carthaginians introduced it to Spain. The
Romans planted vineyards along the Rhine during the second century A.D.
and at about the same time brought grapes to England, where in 731 the
Venerable Bede wrote of native wines. The Bishop of Ely accepted English
wines as tithes. The English monasteries cultivated vineyards with considerable success and profit, but with their dissolution under Henry VIII,
English viticulture disappeared.

Table and wine grapes are two distinctive categories of *Vitis vinifera*,
from which comes 90 percent of the world's cultivated grapes. Any grape
can be made into wine—though with varying degrees of success—but few
wine grapes do well at the table. Color is the best guide to ripeness in table
grapes: darker varieties should be free of any green tinge and white or green
grapes should show an amber blush. Grapes require careful cultivation; they
must have long summers, temperate winters, light rainfall, and protection
from wind.

OXTAIL AND GRAPES

A contribution from Helen McCully, see page 11.

Serves 6
Doubles
Refrigerates

Preparation: 30 minutes
Cooking: 3½ hours
Preheat oven: 300°

¼ lb. salt pork trimmed of the rind and diced
2 large onions, chopped
4 large carrots, scraped and chopped
2 cloves garlic, chopped

(1) In a flame-proof casserole, render the salt pork, When it is brown, add the vegetables, reduce the heat, and cook them for 10 minutes.

4½ lbs. oxtail cut in 2-inch pieces
4 whole allspice
2 bay leaves
2 stalks parsley
½ teaspoon thyme
1½ teaspoons salt
¼ teaspoon pepper

(2) Add the oxtail and seasonings. Cook the meat, covered, over low heat for 20 minutes.

2 lbs. white seedless grapes, washed and slightly crushed

(3) Add the grapes. Bake the casserole, tightly covered, at 300° for 3 hours.

(4) Remove the oxtail and reserve it. Force the liquid and remaining ingredients through a sieve or food mill into a bowl; discard the allspice, bay leaves, and parsley. Allow the sauce to stand until the excess fat rises to the top; skim or siphen it off (if desired, the meat and sauce may be refrigerated and the fat is easily removed the following day).

At this point you may stop and continue later.

(5) In the casserole, combine the oxtail and the sauce. Bring the sauce to the boil; reduce the heat and simmer the dish for 30 minutes. The meat should fall from the bones; if it does not, cook it a little longer. Serve the stew with boiled new potatoes.

LAMB SHANKS AND GRAPES

(American)

The dish may also be made with veal shanks.

Serves 6
Doubles
Refrigerates

Preparation: 50 minutes
Cooking: 1½ hours
Preheat oven: 350°

2 Tablespoons butter **2 Tablespoons oil** **6 lamb shanks, trimmed of excess fat** **Salt** **Pepper**	(1) In a flame-proof casserole, heat the butter and oil and brown the lamb shanks; season them. Remove. Discard all but 3 Tablespoons of the fat.
1 onion, chopped **3 carrots, scraped and diced** **1 clove garlic, chopped**	(2) In the fat, cook the vegetables until the onion is translucent.
1 bay leaf **½ teaspoon ground ginger** **¼ teaspoon marjoram** **¼ teaspoon sage** **¼ teaspoon thyme**	(3) Into the vegetables, stir the seasonings. Replace the lamb shanks.
1½ cups dry white wine **1½ cups water**	(4) Add the liquid. Bake the casserole, covered, at 350° for 1½ hours, or until the meat is tender. Remove the casserole from the oven. *At this point you may stop and continue later.*

(continued)

(5) Remove the excess fat, reserving a little for the next step. (If desired, the casserole may be refrigerated overnight, which makes removing the excess fat much easier.) Remove the lamb shanks to a serving dish and keep them warm.

3 Tablespoons flour
A little of the removed fat
Juice of 1 lemon

(6) In a saucepan, make a *roux* of the flour and lamb fat. Add some of the broth to it, stirring. Then add the flour mixture to the broth, cooking it over high heat and stirring constantly until the sauce is thickened and smooth. Stir in the lemon juice.

3 cups seedless grapes, rinsed,
drained on absorbent paper, and
halved
⅓ cup parsley, minced
Grated rind of 1 lemon

(7) Into the sauce, stir the grapes and cook them for 3 minutes. Pour the sauce over the lamb shanks and garnish the dish with the parsley which has been mixed with the lemon rind.

SWEETBREADS AND GRAPES

(French)

Serves 6
Doubles
Refrigerates

Preparation: 1¼ hours*
Cooking: 40 minutes
Preheat oven: 325°

3 pairs sweetbreads
Acidulated water

(1) In a mixing bowl, soak the sweetbreads for 1 hour in acidulated water to cover. Drain them, remove and discard the membrane, and dry them on absorbent paper.

* Most of the preparation time of this delicate dish involves soaking the sweetbreads.

At this point you may stop and continue later.

Seasoned flour
2 Tablespoons butter
2 Tablespoons oil

(2) Dredge the sweetbreads in seasoned flour. In a flame-proof casserole, heat the butter and oil and saute the sweetbreads until they are faintly golden.

(3) Place the casserole, covered, in a 325° oven for 30 minutes. Baste them frequently with the pan juices (more butter may be added if necessary). Arrange the sweetbreads on a serving dish and keep them warm.

3 cups seedless grapes, rinsed, drained on absorbent paper, and halved
½ cup madeira wine
½ cup dry white wine
2 Tablespoons soft butter

(4) In the casserole, combine the grapes and wines and, over high heat, reduce the liquid by one-half. Stir in the butter and pour the sauce over the sweetbreads.

VEAL SCALLOPS AND GRAPES
(French)

Have all the ingredients and utensils readied. Then "stop and continue later." Like most Chinese dishes, this French one does not allow a respite once the cooking begins.

Serves 6
Doubles

Preparation: 25 minutes

Seasoned flour
Veal scallops for 6 persons, pounded flat
Butter

(1) In the seasoned flour, dredge the scallops. In a skillet, heat 3 Tablespoons of butter and in it brown both sides of the scallops, adding butter as necessary, until they are fork-tender. Remove them to a serving dish and keep them warm.

(continued)

1 onion, minced
1 Tablespoon flour
1 10½-oz. can condensed beef broth
3 Tablespoons marsala wine
¾ cup seedless grapes, rinsed, drained on absorbent paper, and halved.

(2) In the remaining fat, cook the onion until translucent. Add the flour, stirring until it turns brown. Gradually add the broth, stirring constantly until the mixture is thickened and smooth. Stir in the marsala wine. Add the grapes and heat them through. Pour the sauce over the veal scallops.

CHICKEN AND GRAPES

(Argentinean)

Serves 6
Doubles
Refrigerates

Preparation: 30 minutes
Cooking: 1 hour
Preheat oven: 350°

2 Tablespoons butter
2 Tablespoons oil
Serving-pieces of chicken for 6 persons
Salt
Pepper
Chili powder

(1) In a flame-proof casserole, heat the butter and oil and brown the chicken; season it with the salt, pepper, and a sprinkling of chili powder. Remove it.

2 10½-oz. cans condensed chicken broth
3 Tablespoons cornstarch, mixed with ¼ cup cold water

(2) With the broth, deglaze the casserole. Add the cornstarch, stirring constantly, until the mixture is thickened and smooth.

2½ lbs. seedless grapes, rinsed and drained on absorbent paper

(3) Stir in the grapes. Replace the chicken and pour the sauce over it.

At this point you may stop and continue later.

(4) Bake the chicken, covered, at 350° for 1 hour, or until it is tender.

CHICKEN AND GRAPES WITH RIPE OLIVES
(Greek)

Follow the directions for Chicken and Grapes, page 160, using, in place of the chili powder, 1 onion, chopped, and 1 clove garlic, chopped, both cooked until translucent in the butter and oil; substitute 1 cup dry white wine for 1 can of the condensed chicken broth. Season the sauce with 1 teaspoon each of chopped mint and chervil; use 2 cups prepared seedless grapes and 1 cup pitted ripe olives.

CHICKEN SALAD AND GRAPES "CHEZ VITO"*

Serves 6
Doubles
Refrigerates

Preparation: 30 minutes

3 cups cooked chicken, diced
1½ cups celery, diced
1 small onion, minced
1½ cups seedless grapes, stemmed, rinsed, and drained on absorbent paper
Salt
Pepper
Paprika, if desired

(1) In a mixing bowl, toss together the chicken, celery, onion, and grapes. (If desired, the recipe may be made with canned seedless grapes.) Season the mixture to taste.

¾ cup mayonnaise (Orange Mayonnaise, page 262, may be used, if desired)

(2) Add the mayonnaise and toss the ingredients again; there should be only sufficient mayonnaise to bind the mixture.

* Chez Vito was one of the rare dining experiences New York City offered. The food (for the better part, Northern Italian cuisine) was of the first rank and the musical entertainment of piano, strings, and a quartet of admirably schooled singers, will be long remembered. This recipe is contributed by Chez Vito's former chef.

(continued)

Salad greens
3 hard cooked eggs, shelled and halved
12 or 18 pitted ripe olives
2 tomatoes, peeled and cut into sixths
2 small oranges, cut in paper-thin slices and seeded

(3) On individual beds of salad greens, spoon equal portions of the chicken mixture. Garnish the salad with the eggs, olives, tomatoes, and oranges.

BRAISED DUCK AND GRAPES*

Serves 4
Doubles
Refrigerates

Preparation: 30 minutes
Cooking: 1 hour

2 Tablespoons butter
2 Tablespoons oil
1 5-lb. duck, quartered, trimmed of excess fat, and pricked several times with a fork
Salt
Pepper
Nutmeg

(1) In a flame-proof casserole, heat the butter and oil and brown the duck thoroughly on all sides. Season it with the salt, pepper, and a generous sprinkling of nutmeg. Discard the fat.

1¼ cups muscatel wine
4 Tablespoons currant jelly

(2) Mix together the wine and jelly and pour the mixture over the duck.

At this point you may stop and continue later.

(3) Bring the casserole to the boil, reduce the heat, and simmer it, covered, for 50 minutes or until the duck is tender.

* This welcome and delicious recipe is contributed by Patton Campbell, the talented costume designer whose work has embellished the stages of the New York City and Santa Fe Operas. Pat and I have been friends since Yale Drama School days—too long ago to be mentioned. I have since left the theater and he has gone on to enviable success. We continue to meet at the board, however, if not "on the boards," and share a delight in good food and drink.

2 **Tablespoons cornstarch, mixed**
 with ¼ cup cold water
1 **cup seedless grapes, rinsed,**
 drained on absorbent paper,
 and halved

(4) Remove the duck to a serving platter and keep it warm. To the pan juices, add the cornstarch, stirring constantly until the sauce is thickened and smooth. Stir in the grapes and simmer them for 5 minutes. Pour the sauce over the duck.

FILETS OF SOLE AND GRAPES
 (French)

Sole Véronique is a classic dish in French cuisine.

 Serves 6
 Doubles
 Refrigerates

Preparation: 45 minutes
Cooking: 20 minutes
Preheat oven: 400°

12 **filets of sole, rolled and**
 skewered with toothpicks
 2 **cups milk**

(1) In a flame-proof baking dish, arrange the fish in a single layer. Add the milk. Rapidly bring it to the boil, reduce the heat, and poach the fish for 5 minutes. Remove the skillet from the heat.

(2) Gently drain off the milk and reserve it.

12 **mushrooms, sliced**
 4 **Tablespoons butter**
 2 **cups seedless grapes, rinsed and**
 drained on absorbent paper

(3) In a saucepan, saute the mushrooms in the butter. Remove them with a slotted spoon and combine them with the grapes. Arrange the mixture over the fish.

3 **Tablespoons butter**
4 **Tablespoons flour**
 Reserved milk
 Salt
 Pepper

(4) In the saucepan, heat the additional butter, stir in the flour and, over gentle heat, cook the *roux* for a few minutes. Gradually add the milk, stirring constantly until the sauce is thickened and smooth. Season it to taste with salt and pepper. Pour it over the fish.

(continued)

At this point you may stop and continue later.

½ cup breadcrumbs, toasted in butter

¼ cup grated Gruyère cheese

(5) Over the sauce, sprinkle the breadcrumbs and then the cheese. Bake the dish, uncovered, at 400° for 20 minutes.

SHRIMP AND GRAPE CURRY

Follow the directions for Shrimp and Banana Curry, page 74, using, in place of the banana, 1½ cups seedless grapes, rinsed, drained, and cut in half lengthwise. Omit the onion and add 6 scallions, cut in ½-inch pieces, with as much green as possible.

CARROTS AND GRAPES

Serves 6
Doubles
Refrigerates

Preparation: 20 minutes

6 to 8 large carrots, scraped and cut in ⅛-inch slices

1 10½-oz. can condensed chicken broth

(1) In a saucepan, boil the carrots in the broth, covered, for 10 minutes, or until they are just tender.

2 teaspoons cornstarch

¼ cup dry white wine

(2) Combine the cornstarch and wine, add it to the carrots, and continue to cook them, stirring constantly, until the sauce is thickened and smooth.

At this point you may stop and continue later.

1 cup seedless grapes, rinsed and
   drained on absorbent paper
2 Tablespoons soft butter
1 teaspoon lemon juice
½ teaspoon salt
   Pinch of white pepper

(3) Stir in the grapes, butter, and seasonings. Continue stirring until the mixture comes to the boil. Remove it from the heat and serve.

CAULIFLOWER AND GRAPES*

Serves 6

Preparation: 20 minutes
Cooking: 22 minutes

1 large head cauliflower, washed
   and trimmed

(1) Leaving the cauliflower head whole if possible, steam it for 20 minutes, or until it is tender but still retains its crispness and shape.

⅓ cup each: red, black, and white
   grapes, halved and seeded (if
   different colors are not available,
   one variety of grape will do; to
   equal 1 cup)
8 Tablespoons butter
   Salt
   Pepper
½ teaspoon oregano
¼ teaspoon garlic powder
½ teaspoon paprika

(2) In a skillet, heat the butter until it foams and in it cook the grapes for 2 minutes. Flavor the cauliflower with the five seasonings and pour the grapes and butter over it.

* This treatment for cauliflower was suggested by a Boston friend, Joseph Shakra, whose ideas about food are creative, original, and tasty.

VEGETABLE CASSEROLE AND GRAPES*

Serves 6
Doubles
Refrigerates

Preparation: 20 minutes
Cooking: 20 minutes

4 **young zucchini**
4 **large celery stalks**
4 **tomatoes, peeled and seeded**
4 **onions**
1 **green pepper, seeded**
1 **teaspoon salt**
1/4 **teaspoon pepper**
1/2 **cup parsley, chopped**
Pinch of oregano
1/3 **cup water**

(1) Chop very coarsely all of the vegetables. Put them in a casserole, together with the seasonings. Add the water.

At this point you may stop and continue later.

1 **cup seedless grapes, rinsed and drained on absorbent paper**

(2) Bring the liquid to the boil, reduce the heat, and simmer the casserole, covered, for 15 minutes. Gently stir in the grapes and continue cooking the dish for 5 minutes.

* Louis Warth, a good friend who is a good decorator (responsible for the interior of my home in Katonah), is also a very good cook. He invents rather than going by the book. This dish is a fine invention, and the recipe was written down as he prepared the vegetables.

ASPARAGUS AND GRAPES IN ASPIC

Ordinarily, I do not like jellied salads. This one is an exception. Served with cold meat, it makes a pleasant summer supper.

Serves 6
Doubles
Refrigerates

Preparation: 30 minutes
Chilling time: at least 3 hours

2 9-oz. packages frozen asparagus spears	(1) In a saucepan, cook the asparagus, following the directions given on the package. Take care not to overcook it.
	(2) Drain the vegetable, reserving the cooking liquid. Plunge the asparagus into cold water for a minute or so. Allow it to drain before drying it on absorbent paper. Reserve it.
1 packet unflavored gelatin, softened in ½ cup cold water **Condensed chicken broth** **Salt**	(3) To the hot asparagus water, add the gelatin, stirring until it is dissolved. Add broth to equal 2 cups. Season the liquid and chill it until *slightly* thickened.
Reserved asparagus spears **2 cups seedless grapes, rinsed, drained on absorbent paper, and halved** **1 cup celery, diced**	(4) When the broth mixture is ready to set, rinse a mold with cold water; in it, arrange the asparagus, grapes, and celery. Pour the gelatin mixture over the vegetables and allow it to chill for at least 3 hours before unmolding it.

CONCORD GRAPE PIE

(American)

Serving: one 9-inch pie

Preparation: 45 minutes*
Cooking: 40 minutes
Preheat oven: 400°

1½ lbs. Concord grapes	(1) Slip the skins from the grapes and reserve them. In a saucepan, bring the pulps to a boil, reduce the heat, and simmer them, uncovered, for 5 minutes. Sieve them, discarding the seeds, and add them to the reserved skins.

* The preparation time does not include readying the pastry, page 458.

(continued)

1 cup sugar
⅓ cup flour
¼ teaspoon salt
1 Tablespoon lemon juice
3 Tablespoons butter, melted

(2) In a mixing bowl, combine the sugar, flour, and salt. Then stir in the lemon juice, butter, and the grape mixture.

Unbaked 9-inch pie shell

(3) Spoon the filling into an unbaked 9-inch pie shell, and bake the pie at 400° for 25 minutes.

Crumb topping (see Berry Pie, page 92)

(4) Add the crumb topping and continue baking the dessert for 15 minutes, or until the topping is browned.

GRAPE STUFFING

(Greek)

For chicken and turkey.

For *each* 4 cups of seasoned breadcrumbs, seasoned croutons, or packaged dressing:

2 cups seedless grapes, rinsed
  and drained on absorbent paper
½ teaspoon salt
½ teaspoon oregano

(1) In a mixing bowl, with the breadstuff of your choice, toss the grapes, salt and oregano.

¼ cup dry sherry
4 Tablespoons butter, melted
2 Tablespoons honey

(2) Blend the sherry, butter and honey. With this mixture dampen the dressing, tossing it gently with two forks.

KUMQUATS

In China, where they are used in cooking more frequently than in America, kumquats are called *Chin kan*, or "golden orange." Native to eastern Asia, the kumquat has long been cultivated in China and Japan, but it was not introduced to Europe until 1846, when Robert Fortune, a collector for the London Horticultural Society, brought home some specimens. From Europe kumquats came to America. There is limited cultivation of them in southern California and Florida.

Kumquats are evergreen shrub-trees of the genus *Fortunella*, closely related to but hardier than oranges and lemons. The plant, between 8 and 10 feet high, has dark green, glossy leaves; its white flowers are very similar to orange blossoms. The fruit, bright orange-yellow, may be round or ellipsoidal; it is mildly acid and has

a juicy pulp when thoroughly ripe and a sweet edible skin.

In the United States, kumquats are used largely as a candied fruit. Fresh ones are marketed, for some unexplicable reason, only at Thanksgiving and Christmas time. Granted that the season is short, it could be extended throughout the winter to allow kumquat enthusiasts opportunity to enjoy the fruit more fully.

Experimenting with kumquat cookery has been one of my chief pleasures in preparing this book. Most of the recipes which follow call for previously prepared kumquats; therefore, the preparation time given for each recipe does not include the time necessary to prepare the kumquats. Directions for preparing kumquats follow, page 171. My advice is to buy a large supply of kumquats when they appear in the market, prepare them as directed, refrigerate or freeze them, and then use them throughout the winter season. Your effort—and culinary experimentation—will be amply rewarded.

PREPARING KUMQUATS FOR COOKING

The following "puree" is used as the basic ingredient in the recipes made with kumquats.

> Serving: about 2 cups
> Doubles
> Refrigerates
> Freezes

Preparation: 40 minutes
Cooking: 30 minutes

2 quarts kumquats (as ripe as possible), stemmed and rinsed

(1) With a sharp knife, cut around the kumquat but not through it. Pull the fruit apart. One half of the pulp will come away from the rind. Peel the rind from the other half. (If the fruit is sufficiently ripe, you can make a single cut at the stem end of the fruit and squeeze out the pulp as you would with a grape.) Separate the pulp and rind and reserve both.

(2) Chop the rinds coarsely or put them once through the coarsest blade of a meat grinder.

Kumquat rind
Sugar
Water

(3) To each 2 cups of the kumquat rind, add ⅓ cup sugar, or a little more, to taste. In a saucepan, with only sufficient water to start to the boil (if, indeed, any is necessary), cook the rinds, covered, for 30 minutes, or until they are quite tender. Stir them often.

Kumquat pulp
Water
Sugar

(4) While the rinds are cooking, prepare the kumquat pulp. In a saucepan, with only sufficient water to start to the boil (ripe kumquats will not require water), cook the pulp, covered, for 30 minutes, or until it is very tender. Sieve it and measure the puree. For each 2 cups of puree, add ⅓ cup sugar, or a little more, to taste; stir to dissolve the sugar.

(continued)

(5) Combine the pulp puree and the rind, stirring to blend the mixture. Store it in jars or plastic containers in the refrigerator or freezer, for there is not adequate sugar in the mixture to preserve the fruit, as in the case with jams.

BEEF AND KUMQUATS

Follow the directions for Beef and Cranberries, page 118, using, in place of the cranberries, 2 cups prepared kumquats (page 171). In step #4 of the beef recipe, reduce the broth to 1 10½-oz. can, omit the water and the sugar.

LAMB SHANKS AND KUMQUATS

Follow the directions for Beef and Cranberries, page 118, using, in place of the cranberries, 2 cups prepared kumquats (page 171). In step #4 of the beef recipe, omit the water and sugar and add the grated rind and juice of 1 lemon and ½ teaspoon thyme. Use only 1 can of broth. The cooking time will be about 2 hours. If desired, the dish may be made a day in advance of serving, cooled, refrigerated, and skimmed of excess fat before being reheated for serving. When cooking, be sure that there is adequate liquid; more broth may be added as necessary.

PORK BUTT AND KUMQUATS

Follow the directions for Pork Butt and Cranberries, page 120, using, in place of the cranberries, 1½ cups prepared kumquats (page 171). In step #2 of the pork recipe, omit the sugar.

PORK CHOPS AND KUMQUATS

Follow the directions for Pork Chops and Cranberries, page 120, using, in place of the cranberries, 1½ cups prepared kumquats (page 171). In step #3 of the pork recipe, use 4 Tablespoons honey; add water as necessary (¼ cup will probably be too much).

CHICKEN AND KUMQUATS

Follow the directions for Chicken and Oranges, page 236, using, in place of the marmalade and orange rind, 1½ cups prepared kumquats (page 171); in step #4 of the chicken recipe, omit the orange slices.

CHICKEN AND KUMQUATS
(Indian)

Serves 6
Doubles
Refrigerates
Freezes

Marination: 6 hours
Preparation: 30 minutes
Cooking: 1¼ hours
Preheat oven: 350°

½ cup dry white wine
¼ cup lemon juice
¼ cup soy sauce
3 onions, coarsely chopped
4 cloves garlic, chopped
¾ teaspoon oregano
¾ teaspoon thyme
2 teaspoons curry powder
1½ teaspoons ground ginger
½ cup preserved kumquat liquid (page 436) or liquid from a 12½-oz. jar of preserved kumquats

(1) In the container of an electric blender, combine these ten ingredients; blend them on low speed for 15 seconds, or until the mixture is smooth.

(continued)

Serving-pieces of chicken for 6 persons

(2) In the sauce, marinate the chicken for 6 hours, turning it frequently. Drain the chicken and reserve the marinade.

2 Tablespoons butter
2 Tablespoons oil

(3) In a flame-proof 5½-quart casserole, heat the butter and oil and brown the chicken; remove it.

2 Tablespoons cornstarch, mixed with ¼ cup cold water

(4) In the casserole, combine the reserved marinade and the cornstarch mixture; cook them, stirring constantly, until the sauce is thickened and smooth. Replace the chicken and spoon the sauce over it.

At this point you may stop and continue later.

(5) Bake the casserole, covered, at 350° for 1 hour, or until the chicken is tender.

12 to 15 preserved kumquats (or the reserved fruit from the 12½-oz. jar of preserved kumquats)

(6) Arrange the kumquats over the chicken and continue to cook the dish, covered, for 10 minutes, or until the kumquats are heated.

DUCKLING AND KUMQUATS

Follow the directions for Duckling and Cranberries, page 121, using, in place of the cranberries, 2 cups prepared kumquats (page 171). In step #3 of the duckling recipe, use ½ cup dry white wine, omit the sugar, and stir the kumquats into the ingredients; in step #4, reduce the cornstarch to 1½ teaspoonsful.

FISH FILETS AND KUMQUATS

Serves 6
Doubles
Refrigerates*

Preparation: 15 minutes*
Cooking: 20 minutes
Preheat oven: 400°

Fish filets for 6 persons, page xv
Salt
Pepper

(1) In a lightly buttered baking dish, arrange the filets and season them.

1 cup prepared kumquats, page 171
½ cup water
1½ teaspoons cornstarch
1 Tablespoon soy sauce

(2) To the kumquats, add the water. Mix the cornstarch with the soy sauce and stir into the kumquats.

At this point you may stop and continue later.

(3) Bake the fish, covered, at 400° for 20 minutes, or until it flakes easily.

(4) Meanwhile, over high heat, cook the kumquat mixture, stirring constantly, until the sauce is thickened and smooth.

1 9-oz. package frozen small peas, fully thawed to room temperature (optional)

(5) Arrange the peas over the fish and pour over the sauce.

* The preparation time does not include preparing the kumquats. While refrigerating is possible, the dish loses freshness by it.

SHRIMP AND KUMQUATS

Follow the directions for Shrimp and Apricots, page 41, using, in place of the apricots, 2 cups prepared kumquats (page 171). In the shrimp recipe omit step #1; instead, in step #3, in place of the apricot nectar, use 1 10½-oz. can condensed chicken broth, combining the kumquats with the ingredients as suggested. The dish may be embellished with Chinese vegetables: 1 9-oz. package frozen pea pods, fully thawed to room temperature; 6 to 8 scallions, chopped; 1 6-oz. can water chestnuts, drained and sliced; and 1 8-oz. can bamboo shoots, drained.

KUMQUAT SALAD

Serves 6
Doubles
Refrigerates

Preparation: 25 minutes

18 fresh kumquats

(1) In a saucepan, boil the kumquats for 5 minutes. Drain and cool them.

1 8-oz. package cream cheese
½ teaspoon ground cumin
½ teaspoon salt

(2) Have the cream cheese at room temperature. In a mixing bowl, combine the cheese and seasonings and blend the mixture well.

Salad greens
Orange Mayonnaise, page 262

(3) Cut the kumquats in half, remove the seeds and pulp. Fill the cavity with the cream cheese. Serve the kumquats on the salad green of your choice and garnish the plates with orange mayonnaise.

KUMQUAT BREAD

Follow the directions for Cranberry Bread, page 124, using, in place of the cranberries, 2 cups prepared kumquats (page 171). In step #2 of the bread recipe, omit the molasses and brown sugar; use unbleached white flour throughout.

KUMQUAT MUFFINS

Follow the directions for Cranberry Muffins, page 125, using, in place of the cranberries, 1 cup prepared kumquats (page 171), drained of any excess liquid. In step #1 of the muffin recipe, use ¼ cup sugar; in step #2, use ¾ cup milk.

KUMQUAT CREPES

Follow the directions for Orange Crepes, page 252, using prepared kumquats (page 171) to spread over the crepes; add, if desired, a thin spreading of *crème pâtissière*, page 130. Roll the crepes, as directed. For the sauce, use ½ cup prepared kumquats, sieved, ¼ cup honey, and ¼ cup cognac, blended.

KUMQUAT GALETTE

Follow the directions for Open Cranberry Tart, page 127, using, in place of the cranberries, 2 cups prepared kumquats (page 171). In step #1 of the *galette* recipe, use ⅓ cup sugar.

KUMQUATS JUBILEE

Follow the directions for Cranberries Jubilee, page 128, using, in place of the cranberries, 1 cup prepared kumquats (page 171). In step #1 of the jubilee recipe, use ¼ cup sugar; in step #2, use 2 teaspoons cornstarch.

KUMQUAT PUDDING

Follow the directions for Persimmon Pudding, page 450, using, in place of the persimmon, 2 cups of prepared kumquats (page 171). In step #2 of the pudding recipe, reduce the sugar to 1 cup.

STEAMED KUMQUAT PUDDING

Follow the directions for Steamed Apricot Pudding, page 46, using, in place of the apricots, 1 cup prepared kumquats (page 171). Cook the pudding in a well buttered double-boiler over simmering water. Serve the pudding with the syrup suggested for Orange Crepes, page 252, somewhat thinned with additional water.

KUMQUAT SOUFFLE

Follow the directions for Apricot Souffle, page 46, using, in place of the apricots, 1 cup prepared kumquats (page 171).

KUMQUAT TART

Follow the directions for Cranberry and Orange Tart, page 129, adding a layer of *crème pâtissière*, page 130, to the baked pie shell and in place of the cranberry and orange, 2 cups of prepared kumquats, page 171, thickened with 1 Tablespoon cornstarch mixed with ½ cup water. To thicken the puree, combine it with the cornstarch mixture and, in a saucepan over moderate heat, cook it, stirring constantly, until it bubbles; allow it to cool, spread it over the *crème pâtissière*, and chill the tart.

BAKED KUMQUATS

A garnish for roast meats.

> Serves 6
> Doubles
> Refrigerates

Preparation: 25 minutes
Cooking: 15 minutes
Preheat oven: 350°

18 fresh kumquats, boiled for 5
minutes, drained and cooled
Cinnamon-sugar

(1) Cut the kumquats in half and remove the seeds and pulp. Fill the cavity with ½ teaspoon of cinnamon-sugar.

Orange juice

(2) In a shallow, lightly buttered baking dish, arrange the kumquats upright. Bake the fruit, uncovered, at 350°, for 15 minutes, basting it frequently with the orange juice.

KUMQUAT SAUCE

For meats.

Follow the directions for Hawaiian Apricot Sauce, page 47, using, in place of the apricots, 1 cup prepared kumquats (page 171). Omit step #1 of the sauce recipe; in step #3, use ¼ cup vinegar and 4 Tablespoons honey.

KUMQUAT STUFFING

For meats, duck, or goose.

Follow the directions for Cranberry and Orange Stuffing, page 133, using, in place of the cranberry and orange, an equal quantity of fresh kumquats, halved and seeded; put the fruit once through the coarse blade of a food chopper. If desired, when tossing the ingredients together, moisten the stuffing with a little chicken broth or water.

LEMONS

The origin of the lemon (*Citrus limon*) is uncertain. We take its name from the Persian *līmuñ*, but whether it is native to the Himalayan Mountains, whether it originated in Burma and India, or whether it had the citron and lime as its parent species, we cannot tell. It was unknown to the Greeks and Romans, but found its way from North Africa to Spain between 1000 and 1200 A.D., at the same time that the crusaders were bringing it back to Europe from Palestine. By the latter fifteenth century, it was cultivated in the Azores and since then its growth has spread to all tropical climates.

There are over twenty-five cultivated varieties of lemon, all of which grow on small, thorny trees with white, purple-tinged fragrant blossoms, similar to those of the orange. While, like the lime, the lemon cannot tolerate cold, it thrives in a cool

equitable climate, especially in coastal areas such as those found in California and Italy. The lemon tree, obligingly, blooms and bears continually upon maturing and can be harvested as many as ten times a year. The fruit reaches its full size while green, at which time it is picked (in the United States) and then ripens—unlike oranges which will not ripen off the tree. Commercial ripening is done at about 60° Fahrenheit and at a humidity of 85 percent. The fruit will keep for as long as three months.

The world crop yields something over 1,640,000 tons a year. The United States and Italy are the leading producers, supplying two-thirds of the total output. Spain, Greece, Turkey, Argentina, Chile, Brazil, Israel, and Australia are among other countries concerned with commercial lemon production. In the United States, 50 percent of the crop is sent to the market as fresh fruit; of this amount, the greater part is used in beverages. The oil of the peel is used in soaps, perfumes, and flavoring agents.

Citron (*Citrus medica*) is a variety of lemon, known in Europe from about 300 B.C. and today cultivated in the Mediterranean region and West Indies. Citrons, unlike their trim, pleasantly-colored cousins, are large, knobby, and unprepossessing. Their principal use is in candied peel, but the oil of the skin is also found in perfume and liqueur manufacture. One-half of the world's crop is consumed in the United States.

CHICK-PEA AND LEMON SPREAD

(Middle Eastern)

Hommos may be served as a cocktail spread, appetizer salad, or as a cheese-and-cracker course.

Serves 6
Doubles
Refrigerates

Preparation: 20 minutes

1 20-oz. can chick-peas
½ cup lemon juice
2 cloves garlic, coarsely chopped

(1) Drain the chick-peas and reserve the liquid. In the container of an electric blender, combine the peas, lemon juice and garlic; on medium speed, whirl them until the mixture is smooth. If necessary, add a little of the reserved liquid.

⅓ cup tahini (sesame seed puree, available at specialty food stores)
Salt
White pepper

(2) Add the *tahini* and continue blending the mixture until it is homogenous. Adjust the seasoning, to taste.

SPEZZATE (Bits of Veal in Lemon Sauce) *

(Italian)

Serves 6
Doubles
Refrigerates

Preparation: 30 minutes
Cooking: 15 minutes

* This recipe is contributed by Leyna Gabriele, the former owner of New York's Chez Vito. Leyna, a beautiful singer with a silvery lyric-coloratura soprano created the title role of *The Ballad of Baby Doe* by Douglas Moore when the now-classic opera was given its world premiere at the Central City Opera House in Colorado. I was production manager. Since that time we have been the closest friends.

Of the dish, Leyna writes "*Spezzate,* meaning 'broken bits,' refers to the veal, which is in very small pieces. The dish comes from my family's native village Bagnoli del Trigno in the Abruzzi-Molise mountains. The village dates from the Etruscan era and today is dominated by brooding remains of a feudal castle. I think the best Italian cooks are from Abruzzi—but I admit I'm prejudiced!"

3 Tablespoons olive oil 1½ lbs. lean veal, cut in ½-inch cubes 2 Tablespoons water Salt Pepper	(1) In a skillet, heat the oil and lightly brown the veal. Add the water and, over gentle heat, simmer the veal, covered, until it is very tender. Season it.
6 egg yolks Juice of 2 lemons, sieved	(2) In a mixing bowl, lightly beat together the yolks and lemon juice.
	(3) When the veal is cooked, remove it briefly to absorbent paper, meanwhile wiping the skillet clean. Replace the meat and pour over the egg-lemon mixture. Over *very low* heat, cook the dish, stirring constantly, until the sauce thickens; overcooking will curdle the sauce. Serve the dish, accompanied by a piece of Italian bread toasted and buttered.

CHICKEN AND LEMON SOUP
   (Greek)

Soupa Avgolemono seems as Greek to us as the Parthenon. The soup will not "hold," however; the prepared broth and egg mixtures should be combined only at the time of serving.

   Serves 6
   Doubles

Preparation: 30 minutes

4 10½-oz. cans condensed chicken broth ⅓ cup natural raw rice	(1) In a large saucepan, heat the broth; add the rice, stirring to prevent the grains from sticking. Cook the rice, covered, for 15 minutes, or until it is tender.
4 eggs Juice of 1 lemon	(2) Meanwhile, beat the eggs and lemon juice until the eggs are light.

(continued)

Salt
White pepper

(3) Just before serving, stir ½ cup of the hot broth into the egg mixture, 1 Tablespoonful at a time. Then stir the egg mixture into the broth, removed from the stove. Season the soup to taste and serve it at once.

LAMB AND LEMON SAUCE

(American)

This dish has truly a "lemon-fresh" flavor.

Serves 6
Doubles
Refrigerates

Preparation: 45 minutes
Cooking: 1½ hours

2 Tablespoons butter
2 Tablespoons oil
3 lbs. shoulder of lamb, boned and cut into bite-sized pieces
Salt
Pepper
1 teaspoon dill weed

(1) In a flame-proof casserole, heat the butter and oil and sear the meat until it is just barely colored; season it. Remove.

6 scallions, chopped, with as much green as possible
1 large head Boston lettuce, rinsed, dried on absorbent paper, and shredded

(2) In the remaining fat, cook the vegetables, stirring until they are limp. Replace the lamb.

Dry white wine
Grated rind and juice of 1 lemon

(3) Add the wine barely to cover the meat. Add the lemon rind and juice. Bring the liquid to the boil; reduce the heat, and simmer the meat, covered, for 1½ hours, or until it is tender.*

At this point you may stop and continue later.

* If desired, the casserole may be cooked in the oven rather than on top of the stove: Preheat oven to 350°, cover the casserole, and cook for 1½ hours, or until lamb is tender. Then continue with steps (4) and (5).

2 teaspoons cornstarch **Juice of 1 lemon**	(4) Mix the cornstarch with the lemon juice and add it to the hot broth, stirring until the mixture is slightly thickened. Remove the casserole from the heat.
3 egg yolks, lightly beaten	(5) To the egg yolks, add a little of the hot sauce, stirring. Then add the yolk mixture to the contents of the casserole, stirring constantly. Over *very low* heat, stir the sauce until it is thickened. *Do not allow it to boil.*

LAMB AND LEMON SAUCE WITH OLIVES
(Moroccan)

Follow the directions for Lamb and Lemon Sauce, page 184, using, in place of butter and oil, 4 Tablespoons olive oil; in place of the scallions and lettuce, 3 cups onions, chopped, and 1 clove garlic, chopped. To the wine, add ½ teaspoon ground ginger, ½ teaspoon saffron, crumbled, 1 teaspoon ground coriander, and 3 lemons, sliced paper-thin and seeded. Before adding the cornstarch, add 24 pitted green olives, halved lengthwise.

LAMB SHANKS AND LEMON

If desired, the dish may be made a day in advance of serving, cooled, and refrigerated overnight. This facilitates the removal of any excess fat and, I think, improves the flavor of the casserole.

> Serves 6
> Doubles
> Refrigerates
> Freezes

Preparation: 30 minutes
Cooking: 1 hour
Preheat oven: 350°

(continued)

2 Tablespoons butter
2 Tablespoons oil
2 cloves garlic, split
6 lamb shanks
　Seasoned flour
1 teaspoon paprika

(1) In a flame-proof casserole, heat the butter and oil and cook the garlic until the fat is flavored; remove the garlic. Dredge the lamb shanks in the seasoned flour to which the paprika has been added. Brown the lamb shanks. Discard any excess fat.

At this point you may stop and continue later.

1½ cups dry white wine
　Grated rind and juice of 2 lemons
1 bay leaf, broken

(2) To the contents of the casserole, add these four ingredients. Bake the lamb shanks, covered, at 350° for 1 hour, or until they are tender.

PORK STEW AND LEMON
　(Greek)

　Serves 6
　Doubles
　Refrigerates

Preparation: 30 minutes
Cooking: 1½ hours

2 Tablespoons butter
2 Tablespoons oil
3 lbs. lean pork, cut in bite-sized pieces
　Salt
　Pepper

(1) In a flame-proof casserole, heat the butter and oil and brown the pork; season it. Remove it to absorbent paper. Discard all but 3 Tablespoons of the fat.

2 onions, chopped
1 clove garlic chopped

(2) In the remaining fat, cook the onions and garlic until translucent.

¼ cup parsley, chopped
2 Tablespoons flour
½ cup dry white wine
　Grated rind and juice of 1 lemon
　Water

(3) Add the parsley and flour, stirring. Add the wine and lemon juice, and grated rind, stirring. Replace the pork. Add water just to cover. Bring the liquid to the boil, reduce the heat and simmer the pork, covered, for 1¼ hours.

At this point you may stop and continue later.

6 celery hearts, split (or 6 large stalks of celery, coarsely chopped)

(4) Add the celery hearts and continue to cook the dish, covered, for 15 minutes longer, or until the meat is tender. Remove the pork and celery to a serving plate and keep them warm.

3 egg whites
3 egg yolks
Juice of 2 lemons

(5) In a mixing bowl, beat the whites until stiff. Add the yolks and beat the mixture until it is light yellow. Beat in the lemon juice.

1 cup reserved stock
1 Tablespoon cornstarch mixed with a little cold water

(6) In a saucepan, bring the stock to the boil. Add the cornstarch. Cook the mixture, stirring constantly, until it is thickened and smooth.

(7) Slowly add the thickened stock to the egg mixture, beating the sauce constantly. When it is smooth and the consistency of heavy cream, pour it over the pork. Let it rest for a minute or two before serving.

VEAL SCALLOPS AND LEMON

(Italian)

Vitello piccato is a classic meat dish in Italian cuisine. Very quickly prepared and very fresh tasting.

    Serves 6
    Doubles
    Refrigerates

Preparation: 15 minutes

Seasoned flour
Veal scallops for 6 persons (about 1½ lbs.)

(1) Dust the veal scallops with the seasoned flour.

4 Tablespoons butter
4 Tablespoons oil

(2) In a skillet, heat the butter and oil and brown the scallops.

(continued)

¼ cup dry white wine
3 Tablespoons lemon juice
2 lemons sliced paper-thin and
 seeded
¼ cup parsley, minced

(3) Add the wine and lemon juice and simmer the meat for 5 minutes. Arrange the veal on a warmed serving plate and garnish it with the lemon slices and parsley.

MEAT LOAF AND LEMON

The dish may also be made with ground chuck alone.

Serves 6
Doubles
Refrigerates
Freezes

Preparation: 30 minutes
Cooking: 1½ hours
Preheat oven: 350°

½ lb. ground chuck
½ lb. ground veal
½ lb. ground pork
3 Tablespoons butter, melted
1½ teaspoons salt
½ teaspoon pepper
 Grated rind and juice of 2
 lemons
2 cups breadcrumbs
2 eggs, lightly beaten
1½ cups milk

(1) In a large mixing bowl, combine all the ingredients and mix them well. Pack the mixture into a 9x5-inch loaf pan.

At this point you may stop and continue later.

1 lemon, sliced paper-thin and
 seeded

(2) Bake the meat loaf, uncovered, at 350° for 1½ hours. For the final 10 minutes of cooking, garnish the meat loaf with the lemon slices.

CHICKEN AND LEMON I

Follow the directions for Lamb and Lemon Sauce, page 184, using, in place of the lamb, serving-pieces of chicken for 6 persons; in the casserole, bake the chicken, covered, at 350° for 1 hour, or until it is tender. Remove it to a serving dish and keep it warm while you prepare the sauce as directed. Pour the sauce over the chicken.

CHICKEN AND LEMON II*

(Algerian)

Serves 6
Doubles
Refrigerates
Freezes

Preparation: 30 minutes
Cooking: 1 hour
Preheat oven: 350°

* This recipe is contributed by Jack Kauflin, perhaps the best amateur cook I know—amateur in the sense that he has not declared himself a professional. Jack used to live in New York, where I knew him, cooked with him, and learned from him. Now he lives in Los Angeles, where he teaches dance. To say that I miss his cooking nearly as much as I do his good company sounds like insult, but is truly a compliment.

Jack found this dish at a small restaurant outside of Marrakech. The establishment was run by a demobilized French soldier and his wife, both of whom cooked, waited on table, recommended the wines, and, happily, shared the secret of their chicken and lemon.

(continued)

2 **Tablespoons butter**
2 **Tablespoons oil**
2 **onions, chopped**
2 **carrots, scraped and sliced**
  Serving-pieces of chicken for 6
  persons
1 **clove garlic, finely chopped**
8 **coriander seeds**
2 **Tablespoons parsley, finely**
  chopped
¼ **teaspoon saffron threads,**
  crumbled
1 **teaspoon salt**
¼ **teaspoon pepper**
2 **10½-oz. cans condensed chicken**
  broth plus water to equal 3 cups

(1) In a flame-proof casserole, heat the butter and oil and cook the onions and carrots until the onion is translucent. Over the vegetables, arrange the chicken; sprinkle over the garlic and seasonings. Add the broth.

At this point you may stop and continue later.

(2) Bake the casserole, covered, at 350° for 1 hour, or until the chicken is tender.

2 **egg yolks, lightly beaten**
½ **cup heavy cream**
8 **or 10 mushrooms, quartered**
  Zest and juice of 1 lemon (cut
  the zest into julienne)

(3) Meanwhile, in a mixing bowl, combine these five ingredients.

3 **Tablespoons butter**
3 **Tablespoons flour**

(4) In the top of a double boiler, over simmering water, melt the butter. Add the flour and cook the *roux*, stirring constantly, for 3 minutes.

(5) Remove the chicken to a serving dish and keep it warm. Sieve the stock.

(6) Add the stock to the *roux* and cook the mixture, stirring constantly, until it is thickened and smooth.

Parsley, finely chopped
1 lemon, sliced paper-thin and
seeded

(7) To the egg mixture, add a little of the hot sauce, stirring. Then add the egg to the sauce and, over simmering water, cook the sauce, stirring constantly, until it is smooth. *Do not let it boil.* Pour the sauce over the chicken and garnish the dish with the parsley and lemon.

CHICKEN AND LEMON III

(Rumanian)

Easy, fresh to the palate, and elegant to serve—good party fare!

Serves 6
Doubles
Refrigerates
Freezes

Preparation: 30 minutes
Cooking: 1 hour
Preheat oven: 350°

2 Tablespoons butter
2 Tablespoons oil
Serving-pieces of chicken for 6 persons
Salt
Pepper

(1) In a flame-proof casserole, heat the butter and oil and brown the chicken; season it. Remove.

3 Tablespoons flour
2 cups sour cream
1 10½-oz. can condensed chicken broth

(2) Into the remaining fat, stir the flour and, over gentle heat, cook it for a few minutes. Stir in the sour cream and then the broth.

½ lb. mushrooms, sliced
⅓ cup parsley, chopped
4 teaspoons poppy seeds
2 Tablespoons chives, chopped
Grated rind and juice of 1 lemon

(3) Stir in these six ingredients. Replace the chicken, spooning the sauce over it.

At this point you may stop and continue later.

(continued)

191

1 lemon, sliced paper-thin and seeded

(4) Bake the casserole, covered, at 350° for 1 hour, or until the chicken is tender. For the final 10 minutes of cooking, add the lemon slices.

FISH FILETS AND LEMON SAUCE

Serves 6
Doubles
Refrigerates

Preparation: 25 minutes

2 Tablespoons butter
3 scallions, minced, with as much green as possible
1 cup dry white wine

(1) In a skillet, heat the butter and cook the scallions until translucent. Add the wine and bring it to the boil.

Fish filets for 6 persons, page xv

(2) To the contents of the skillet, add the filets, reduce the heat and simmer them for 12 minutes, or until they flake easily. With a slotted spoon, carefully remove them to a serving platter and keep them warm.

1 teaspoon cornstarch
Juice of 1 lemon
2 egg yolks, lightly beaten

(3) Into a saucepan, strain the broth. Mix the cornstarch and lemon juice, add it to the broth, and over high heat, cook the mixture, stirring constantly, until it is thickened and smooth. Remove the saucepan from the heat. To the egg yolks, add a little of the broth. Then add the yolk mixture to the contents of the saucepan. Over *very* gentle heat, cook the sauce, stirring constantly, until it is thickened. *Do not allow it to boil.*

1 lemon, sliced paper-thin and seeded
¼ cup parsley, minced

(4) Pour the sauce over the fish. Garnish the dish with the lemon slices and sprinkle the parsley over all.

POTATOES AND LEMON
(American)

The vegetable may, of course, be prepared without stopping to continue later; in some ways preferable, for the potatoes are already hot from the lemon-butter sauce.

> Serves 6
> Doubles
> Refrigerates

Preparation: 25 minutes
Cooking: 5 minutes

6 medium potatoes, peeled and halved

(1) In a saucepan, in salted water to cover, boil the potatoes for 20 minutes, or until they are tender. Drain and reserve them.

6 Tablespoons butter
¼ cup parsley, chopped
Grated rind and juice of 1 lemon
½ teaspoon salt
Pinch of white pepper

(2) Meanwhile, in the saucepan, melt the butter. To it, add the remaining ingredients, stirring to blend them. Remove the pan from the heat.

At this point you may stop and continue later.

(3) Reheat the butter mixture and in it toss the potatoes, covered, until they are well covered and heated through.

VEGETABLE MOLD AND LEMON

A fine summer supper dish.

> Serves 6
> Doubles
> Refrigerates

Preparation: 1 hour
Chilling time: at least 3 hours

(continued)

2 packets unflavored gelatin **½ cup cold water**	(1) Soften the gelatin in the cold water.
2 cups water **Zest of 1 lemon**	(2) In a saucepan, combine the water and lemon juice. Bring it rapidly to the boil, add the softened gelatin and stir the mixture until the gelatin is dissolved.
⅓ cup sugar **1¼ teaspoons salt** **½ cup lemon juice**	(3) Add these three ingredients, stirring to dissolve the sugar. Discard the lemon zest and chill the mixture until it begins to set (about 1 hour).
⅔ cup pitted ripe olives, halved lengthwise **1½ cups cabbage, finely shredded** **¾ cup celery, diced** **¾ cup shredded carrot** **1 green pepper, seeded and chopped** **1 sweet red pepper, seeded and chopped**	(4) Meanwhile, in a mixing bowl, combine these six vegetables.
Orange Mayonnaise, page 262	(5) When the gelatin is almost ready to set, pour it over the vegetables, stirring to blend the mixture well. Pour it into a 2-quart mold rinsed with cold water. Chill the salad for at least 3 hours, or until it is firmly set, before unmolding it. Serve it with the orange mayonnaise.

LEMON MUFFINS

Follow the directions for Apple Muffins, page 19, using, in place of the apple, the grated rind of 1 lemon. When baking the muffins, press gently into the top of each one ½ lump of sugar soaked in lemon juice.

LEMON BREAD

Serving: two 8-inch loaves

Preparation: 20 minutes
Rising time: 1¾ hours
Cooking: 45–50 minutes
Preheat oven: 325°

¾ **cup milk**
8 **Tablespoons butter**
⅓ **cup sugar**
½ **teaspoon salt**

¼ **cup warm water**
2 **packets dry yeast**
2 **eggs, lightly beaten**
   Grated rind and juice of 1
   large lemon

4½ **cups flour**

(1) In a saucepan, scald the milk, add the butter, sugar, and salt, stirring to melt the butter. Allow the mixture to cool to lukewarm.

(2) In a large mixing bowl, over the warm water, sprinkle the yeast, stirring until it is dissolved. Stir in the milk mixture and the eggs. Stir in the lemon rind and juice.

(3) Add the flour, 1 cup at a time, mixing the batter after each addition until it is smooth.

(4) On a floured board, knead the dough for 5 minutes. Put it in a greased bowl and, in a warm place, allow it to rise until doubled in bulk.

(5) Punch the dough down. Form it into two loaves. Put them in 8-inch baking pans, buttered. Allow the dough to rise until it is half doubled in bulk (about 45 minutes).

(6) Bake the loaves at 325° for 10 minutes. Raise the heat to 350° and continue baking the bread for 35–40 minutes, or until the crust is golden and the loaves sound hollow when tapped.

LEMON BARS*

Serving: about 24 cookies

Preparation: 25 minutes
Cooking: 25 minutes
Preheat oven: 350°

2 cups flour
½ cup confectioner's sugar
½ lb. butter
  Grated rind of 1 lemon

(1) In a mixing bowl, sift together the flour and sugar. Cut in the butter and grated lemon rind. When the pastry clings together, press it into a 13 x 9 x 2-inch baking pan. Bake the crust at 350° for 20 minutes, or until it is lightly browned.

4 eggs
2 cups granulated sugar
⅓ cup lemon juice
¼ cup flour
2 teaspoons baking powder

  Confectioner's sugar

(2) In a mixing bowl, beat the eggs until light. Beat in the sugar, then the lemon juice and, finally, the flour and baking powder.

(3) Pour the lemon mixture over the baked crust. Bake the dessert at 350° for 25 minutes. Sprinkle it with confectioner's sugar, allow it to cool, and cut it into bars.

* These delicious cookies are contributed by Justine Macurdy, wife of the Metropolitan Opera basso, John Macurdy. John's musical performances, esteemed by every opera lover, are more celebrated than his wife's culinary ones, but the entire family admits that Justine's status at home is inviolate.

LEMON CAKE

Follow the directions for Orange Cake, page 250, using, in place of the grated orange rind and juice: the grated rind of 1 lemon and 1 teaspoon lemon-flavored extract, the juice of 1 lemon plus water to equal 1 cup, and 1 package of the best quality lemon cake mix. For the icing, if desired, use 3 Tablespoons lemon juice, the grated rind of 1 lemon, and the sugar.

LEMON ICE CREAM*

Serving: 1½ pints
Doubles
Freezes

Preparation: 15 minutes
Chilling time: at least 3 hours

Juice of 1½ lemons
1 cup sugar
1 pint light cream
2 teaspoons grated lemon rind

(1) In a mixing bowl, beat together the lemon juice and sugar. Gradually add the cream, beating until the sugar dissolves. Stir in the grated lemon rind.

(2) Pour the mixture into a refrigerator tray and freeze it, without stirring, for 3 hours, or until it is solid.

* This refreshing and easily prepared recipe is contributed by Richard Foster, one of the most accomplished vocal coaches and accompanists I have known. He started his career under the aegis of the great Povla Frijsh and has since worked with and helped many celebrated singers.

LEMON MOUSSE

Light in flavor and texture, this mousse is a pleasant dessert with which to end a substantial meal. If desired, the unchilled mousse mixture may be spooned over 1 pint strawberries, hulled, rinsed, and drained on absorbent paper, halved lengthwise, and arranged on the bottom of the serving dish. Then chill the dessert.

Serves 6
Doubles
Refrigerates
Freezes

Preparation: 25 minutes
Chilling time: at least 3 hours

2 Tablespoons cornstarch
¼ cup teaspoon salt
1 cup sugar

(1) In the top of a double boiler, mix these three ingredients.

(continued)

1 cup milk

(2) Add the milk and, over boiling water, cook the mixture, stirring often, for 15 minutes.

3 egg yolks

(3) In a mixing bowl, beat the egg yolks until light; slowly pour the hot mixture over the yolks, stirring constantly. Return the custard to the double boiler and cook it for 1 minute, stirring.

Grated rind of 1 lemon
⅓ cup lemon juice

(4) Stir in the grated lemon rind and juice. Allow the mixture to cool somewhat and then chill it in the refrigerator.

2 cups heavy cream, whipped

(5) Into the chilled lemon mixture, fold the whipped cream. Spoon the mousse into a serving dish and put it in the freezer for at least 3 hours to set.

LEMON PIE

(American)

A classic American dessert, best, I feel, in a plain short-pastry crust, but the custard may be varied (see below). A meringue topping, though optional, is desirable.

Serving: one 9-inch pie

Preparation: 45 minutes*

4 Tablespoons cornstarch
4 Tablespoons flour
½ teaspoon salt
1½ cups sugar

(1) In the top of a double boiler, mix these four ingredients.

1½ cups boiling water

(2) Add the boiling water and, over direct heat, bring the mixture to the boil. Over hot water, cook the mixture for 20 minutes.

* The preparation time does not include readying the pastry, page 458.

2 **Tablespoons butter**
Grated rind of 1 lemon
⅓ **cup lemon juice**
4 **egg yolks, lightly beaten**
1 **9-inch pie shell, baked**

4 **egg whites**
3 **Tablespoons sugar (optional)**

(3) To the hot mixture, add these four ingredients and continue to cook the custard, stirring constantly, until it is thick. Allow it to cool and spoon it into the pie shell.

(4) If a meringue is desired, beat the egg whites until frothy. Gradually add the sugar, beating constantly. When the egg whites stand in stiff peaks, spoon them onto the lemon filling and bake the pie at 425° for 5 minutes, or until the meringue is golden. Allow the pie to cool to room temperature.

Filling II—This recipe of my mother's yields a custard of softer consistency than that above. In a saucepan, mix together 3 Tablespoons flour and ¾ cup sugar; add 2 cups of boiling water and cook the mixture until it is thick. Remove it from the heat. Stir in thoroughly 3 eggs, well beaten, 3 Tablespoons butter, and the grated rind and juice of 2 lemons. Allow the custard to cool somewhat and pour it into the baked pie shell.

Filling III—This variation comes from my great-great grandmother. My grandfather, visiting his relatives on the farm, called the dessert "bug pie," because of the currants sprinkled over it: In a mixing bowl, blend 1½ cups sugar with 1 Tablespoon flour and a pinch of salt; cream the sugar with ¼ cup soft butter; add 4 eggs, well beaten, and the grated rind and juice of 2 lemons. Mix well. Stir in 1½ cups milk. Pour the mixture into an *unbaked* pastry shell, set in a buttered pie pan and brushed with slightly beaten egg whites. Bake the pie at 450° for 10 minutes, reduce the heat to 300°, and continue baking it for 45 minutes, or until the custard is firm. If desired, garnish the pie with 3 Tablespoons currants.

Filling IV—This filling, which can be used in pies or cakes, is very rich: In a mixing bowl, beat together 6 egg yolks and 2 cups of sugar; add the grated rind of 2 lemons and juice of 4. Stir in ½ cup butter, melted and partially cooled. Cook the mixture in a double boiler over simmering water, stirring constantly, until it is thickened and coats the spoon. *Do not allow it to boil.* Cool it somewhat and pour it into a baked pie shell. Chill the pie until it is set.

Filling V (a Virginia recipe from colonial days)—Cream together 4 Tablespoons soft butter, 2½ cups sugar, and 4 eggs, beaten; add the juice of 2 lemons plus water to equal 2 cups; stir in 7 teaspoons cornmeal and 4 teaspoons flour; beat the mixture well, pour it into an *unbaked* 9-inch pastry shell and bake the pie at 350° for 40 minutes, or until the crust is golden brown and a knife inserted at the center comes out clean.

LEMON PUDDING

Easy to make and a good "keeper."

Serves 6
Doubles
Refrigerates
Freezes

Preparation: 30 minutes
Cooking: 45 minutes
Preheat oven: 350°

½ **cup hot water**
  Grated rind of 2 lemons

(1) Combine the hot water and grated lemon rind. Set aside and reserve the mixture.

5 **Tablespoons soft butter**
⅔ **cup sugar**
2 **egg yolks**
  Juice of 2 lemons

(2) In a mixing bowl, cream together the butter and sugar. Add the egg yolks and lemon juice. Beat the mixture well.

2 **cups breadcrumbs**
  Reserved lemon water

(3) Add the breadcrumbs and lemon water. Stir the mixture well.

(4) Bake the pudding in a 1½-quart baking dish, buttered, at 350° for 30 minutes, or until it is set.

2 **egg whites**
4 **Tablespoons sugar**

(5) In a mixing bowl, beat the egg whites until they are frothy. Gradually add the sugar, beating constantly until the whites stand in stiff peaks. Cover the pudding with the meringue and bake it at 350° for 15 minutes, or until it is golden.

LEMON SNOW PUDDING

A classic lemon dessert, cool, light, and summery.

Serves 6
Doubles
Refrigerates

Preparation: 1½ hours
Chilling time: at least 3 hours

½ cup cold water
2 packets unflavored gelatin
2 cups boiling water
1½ cups sugar

(1) In a mixing bowl, combine the cold water and the gelatin. Add the boiling water and sugar and stir until the gelatin and sugar are dissolved.

½ cup lemon juice

(2) Add the lemon juice. Chill the mixture until it is partially set (about 1 hour). Beat it until it is frothy.

3 egg whites, beaten until stiff
Custard Sauce, page 460

(3) Fold in the egg whites. Pour the mixture into a mold rinsed with cold water. Chill the dessert for at least 3 hours before unmolding it. Serve it with the Custard Sauce.

LEMON SHERBET

Serves 6
Doubles
Freezes

Preparation: 1½ hours
Freezing time: at least 3 hours

1 package unflavored gelatin
1 cup boiling water
½ cup sugar
2 cups milk
Pinch of salt
¼ cup lemon juice
Grated rind of 1 lemon

(1) In a mixing bowl, pour the boiling water over the gelatin and stir until the gelatin is dissolved. Add the sugar and stir until it is dissolved. Add in order the remaining ingredients. Allow the mixture to cool to room temperature.

(continued)

(2) Pour the mixture into refrigerator trays and refrigerate it until it is partially set (about 1 hour).

1 cup heavy cream, whipped

(3) With a wire whisk, beat the gelatin-mixture lightly. Add the whipped cream, and continue beating gently until the mixture is homogenous. Return it to the freezer for 3 hours.

LEMON SOUFFLE

Serves 6

Preparation: 25 minutes
Cooking: 35 minutes
Preheat oven: 350°

2 Tablespoons butter
3 Tablespoons flour
Pinch of salt

(1) Over hot water, in a double boiler, melt the butter. Stir in the flour and salt. Allow the mixture to cook for 3 minutes.

1 cup milk
⅓ cup sugar

(2) Gradually add the milk, stirring constantly until the mixture is thickened and smooth. Stir in the sugar. Remove the double boiler from the heat.

3 egg yolks
2 teaspoons grated lemon rind
¼ cup lemon juice

(3) In a mixing bowl, beat the yolks until they are light. Beat in the grated lemon rind and juice.

(4) Stir a little of the hot mixture into the yolks. Then stir the yolks into the hot mixture.

3 egg whites

(5) In a mixing bowl, beat the egg whites until they are stiff; they should not be dry. Fold the lemon mixture into the egg whites.

(6) Pour the mixture into a buttered and sugared 1½-quart souffle dish. Bake the dessert at 350° for 35 minutes, or until it has a golden crust and is well puffed.

COLD LEMON SOUFFLE

Follow the directions for Cold Lime Souffle, page 216, using, in place of the lime, lemon rind and juice.

LEMON SOUFFLE PIE
(American)

Serving: one 9-inch pie
Refrigerates

Preparation: 30 minutes*
Cooking: 40 minutes
Preheat oven: 400°

2 egg whites
Pinch of salt

(1) In a mixing bowl, beat the egg whites until frothy. Add the salt and continue beating until they are stiff.

2 egg yolks
¾ cup sugar
¼ cup flour
1 cup milk
¼ cup lemon juice
1 Tablespoon butter, melted and cooled
Grated rind of 1 lemon

(2) In a second mixing bowl, beat the egg yolks lightly. Beat in, first the sugar and then the flour. When the mixture is smooth, add gradually, beating constantly, first the milk and then, in sequence, the lemon juice, butter, and grated lemon rind.

* The preparation time does not include readying the pastry, page 458.

(continued)

Reserved egg whites

(3) Into the lemon mixture, fold the egg whites. Spoon the filling into a pie shell which has been baked until just barely golden. Bake the pie at 400° for 12 minutes; reduce the heat to 350° and continue baking it for 25 minutes, or until a knife inserted at the center comes out clean. Allow the pie to cool and serve it at room temperature.

OPEN LEMON TART

(French)

Galette au citron is a classic dessert in France, traditionally served at Twelfth Night. If you refrigerate or freeze the tart, allow it to come fully to room temperature before warming it slightly in the oven.

Serves 6
Refrigerates
Freezes

Preparation: 45 minutes
Cooking: 30 minutes
Preheat oven: 400°

1 cup flour
½ teaspoon salt
2 Tablespoons sugar

(1) In a mixing bowl, sift together these three ingredients.

9 Tablespoons soft butter

(2) Make a hole in the center of the flour, add the butter, and blend the mixture quickly with the finger tips.

1 egg
1 Tablespoon water
1½ Tablespoons lemon juice

(3) In a mixing bowl, beat together these three ingredients, add this to the flour mixture, blend the dough well, and refrigerate it for at least 30 minutes.

4 egg yolks
1 cup sugar
Grated rind and sieved juice of 1 lemon

(4) In a mixing bowl, combine these four ingredients and, with an electric beater, blend them on high speed for 5 minutes.

(5) On a baking sheet, spread the dough in a circular shape, about 12 inches in diameter and ⅛ inch thick. Turn up the edges ½ inch. Add in a smooth layer the lemon mixture. Bake the *galette* at 400° for 25 to 30 minutes, or until the crust is golden brown. (The filling may be covered with foil if it browns too rapidly.)

EGG AND LEMON SAUCE

(*Greek*)

Avgolemono Saltsa is a basic of classic Greek cookery. For meat and fish.

Serving: 2 cups

Preparation: 20 minutes

3 egg whites
3 egg yolks
  Juice of 2 lemons

(1) In a mixing bowl, beat the egg whites until stiff. Add the yolks and beat the mixture until it is a light yellow. Gradually add the lemon juice, beating.

(2) In a saucepan, combine the stock and cornstarch. Over high heat, cook the mixture, stirring constantly, until it is thickened and smooth.

1 cup meat or fish stock, sieved
1 Tablespoon cornstarch, mixed
  with 3 Tablespoons water ·

(3) Slowly add the hot stock to the egg mixture, beating constantly to prevent the sauce from curdling. When the sauce is creamy and smooth, pour it over the meat or fish.

LEMON SAUCE

For boiled or poached fish.

Serving: 2 cups

Preparation: 20 minutes

(continued)

2 Tablespoons butter 3 Tablespoons flour	(1) In a saucepan, heat the butter, add the flour, stirring the mixture well; over gentle heat, cook the *roux* for 3 minutes.
1¾ cups milk (or ¾ cup light cream and 1 cup fish stock) Salt White pepper	(2) Add the liquid and cook the mixture, stirring constantly, until it is thickened and smooth. Season it to taste.
Juice of 1 lemon Pinch of cayenne	(3) Stir in the lemon juice and cayenne.
1 egg yolk 2 Tablespoons cream	(4) In a mixing bowl, beat the egg with the cream. Remove the sauce from the heat, and into it stir the egg mixture.

LEMON STUFFING FOR CHICKEN

For *each* 4 cups of seasoned breadcrumbs, seasoned croutons, or packaged dressing:

¼ cup parsley, chopped ¾ teaspoon thyme Grated rind and juice of 1 lemon 4 Tablespoons butter, melted	Toss the mixture, using two forks. If desired the dressing may be moistened with a little warm water.

LEMON AND SOUR CREAM DRESSING

(*Austrian*)

For delicate salad greens.

Serving: 1 cup

Preparation: 10 minutes

1 cup sour cream Juice of 1 lemon 2 teaspoons sugar ½ teaspoon salt Pinch of white pepper	In the container of an electric blender, combine all the ingredients. Whirl them at medium speed for 15 seconds, or until the mixture is smooth and homogenous.

LEMONADE SYRUP

(*English*)

For a cooling drink, add either water or soda water to 2 Tablespoonsful of syrup per serving. It keeps well in the refrigerator.

> Serving: about 1½ pints
> Refrigerates

Preparation: 15 minutes

Zest of 8 lemons
1 cup water

(1) In a saucepan, combine the lemon zest and water. Simmer the mixture, covered, for 10 minutes. Remove the zest and reserve the liquid.

Juice of 8 lemons

(2) To the reserved lemon water, add the lemon juice. Measure the liquid.

1 cup sugar (or more, to taste)

(3) For each 2 cups of liquid, add 1 cup of sugar. Boil this mixture until it is syrupy. Store the syrup in sterilized jars.

LIMES

Like many of our foods, limes were brought from the East Indian archipelago and the nearby Asian mainland, the regions of their origination, to the eastern Mediterranean area and Africa. Thence they were carried to Europe by returning crusaders. On his second voyage, Columbus brought lime seeds to the West Indies. Today, lime trees are partially naturalized in the West Indies, Florida, and Mexico, a leading producer of the fruit.

The small, many-thorned tree has pale green leaves and clusters of small white blossoms. The fruit, oval to nearly round, is thin-skinned and green-yellow; its tender pulp contains one-third more citric acid and more sugar than do lemons. Limes are used principally to flavor drinks, food, and confections. Its juice, rich in vitamin C, may be concentrated, dried, frozen, or canned.

British sailors, at the time of Elizabeth I, suffered acutely from scurvy until it was discovered that their Portuguese counterparts, who consumed limes regularly, did not suffer from the dread disease. (Indeed, the Portuguese cultivated limes in large quantity on the island of St. Helena—on the sailing routes to and from the Orient.) A regulated consumption of limes cured the English scurvy—a fact leading, in all probability, to the English sailor's sobriquet of "limey."

CHICKEN AND LIME
(American)

Similar to the Indian Chicken Breasts and Lime, page 211, this recipe does not require marinating the poultry. It is a blander dish.

Serves 6
Doubles
Refrigerates
Freezes

Preparation: 30 minutes
Cooking: 1 hour
Preheat oven: 350°

Seasoned flour
Serving-pieces of chicken for 6 persons
2 Tablespoons butter
2 Tablespoons oil

(1) In the seasoned flour, dredge the chicken. In a flame-proof casserole, heat the butter and oil and brown the chicken. Remove it.

1 onion, chopped
1 clove garlic chopped
1 Tablespoon ground coriander
½ teaspoon chili powder
½ teaspoon ground ginger
½ teaspoon turmeric

(2) In the remaining fat, cook the onion and garlic until translucent. Stir in the seasonings. Replace the chicken.

½ cup lime juice
1½ cups dry white wine
3 Tablespoons sugar

(3) Combine the lime juice, wine, and sugar. Pour the liquid over the contents of the casserole.

At this point you may stop and continue later.

(4) Bake the chicken, covered, at 350° for 45 minutes.

Grated rind of 3 limes
1 Tablespoon cornstarch

(5) Mix together the grated lime rind and cornstarch. Gently stir the mixture into the casserole. Continue to bake the chicken, covered, for 15 minutes or until it is tender and the sauce is slightly thickened.

CHICKEN BREASTS AND LIME

(Indian)

This dish may also be made with lemon.

Serves 6
Doubles
Refrigerates
Freezes

Marination: 3 hours
Preparation: 30 minutes
Cooking: 40 minutes
Preheat oven: 350°

3 large chicken breasts, halved
Juice of 3 limes
Grated rind of 1 lime
½ teaspoon salt
1 teaspoon ground cardamon
Pinch of cayenne
1 Tablespoon ground coriander
1 teaspoon ground cumin
1 piece fresh ginger root, the size of a walnut, grated
1 teaspoon sugar
3 scallions, chopped

(1) In a shallow dish, arrange the chicken breasts. In the container of an electric blender, combine the other ingredients and, on medium speed, whirl them for 15 seconds, or until the mixture is smooth. Pour the marinade over the chicken and allow the breasts to sit for 3 hours, turning them occasionally.

3 Tablespoons butter

(2) With a rubber spatula, wipe the chicken pieces clean. (Reserve the marinade for later use.) In a skillet, heat the butter and brown the chicken pieces. Remove them to a baking dish.

1 10½-oz. can condensed chicken broth
1 teaspoon cornstarch, mixed with 1 teaspoon sugar
⅓ cup golden raisins (optional)

(3) In a saucepan, combine the broth, cornstarch, and sugar. Over high heat, cook the mixture, stirring constantly, until it is thickened and smooth. Stir in the reserved marinade and the raisins. Pour the sauce over the chicken.

At this point you may stop and continue later.

(continued)

211

(4) Bake the chicken, covered, at 350° for 40 minutes, or until it is tender.

===

FISH IN LIME JUICE

Ceviche, or *seviche* is a popular dish throughout Latin America and Mexico. It is found also in Polynesian cuisine. Fish "cooked" by marination in lime juice, or a combination of lime and lemon juice, is usually served as an appetizer. I enjoy it also as a warm weather supper dish—a cold soup, *ceviche*, a good, robust bread, a salad, and cheese. *Ceviche* is capable of several variations, as you will see below. I find it a wonderful dish!

> Serves 6
> Doubles
> Refrigerates

Preparation: 20 minutes
Marinating time: at least 3 hours

2 cups lime juice, or 1 cup lime juice mixed with 1 cup lemon juice
1 teaspoon chili powder
2 large red onions, sliced and separated into rings
1 clove garlic put through a press
1 teaspoon salt
1 teaspoon sugar

(1) In a large mixing bowl, combine these six ingredients.

2 lbs. flounder filet, cut into bite-sized pieces

(2) In a flat glass or ceramic dish, arrange the fish pieces. Over it, pour the lime-juice mixture. Make sure the fish is covered by the marinade. Cover the dish and refrigerate it for at least 3 hours. When the fish is white and opaque, it is ready to eat.

Variations: Any white-fleshed, lean fish may be used—cod, haddock, halibut, or sole. Sea scallops (halved, if they are large) may be used. So, also, may fresh salmon, boned and skinned; marinate for 6 hours.

3 tomatoes, peeled, seeded and coarsely chopped, may be added to the marinade.

6 scallions, chopped, with as much green as possible, may be used in place of the red onion. Yellow onion, also, may be used.

¼ cup of green or sweet red pepper, diced, may be added to the marinade.

¼ cup parsley, chopped, may be added to the marinade.

For a richer dish, ¼ cup olive oil may be added to the marinade.

If desired, the fish may be removed from the marinade, together with the red onion rings (if used), and folded into 1 cup sour cream, mixed and with some of the marinade, seasoned to taste.

RICE AND LIME WITH SAFFRON

(Indian)

Serves 6
Doubles
Refrigerates

Preparation: 15 minutes
Cooking: 20 minutes

¼ teaspoon saffron
3 Tablespoons boiling water

(1) Into a small bowl or cup, crumble the saffron and pour the boiling water over it. Allow it to stand while you prepare the recipe.

4 Tablespoons butter
1½ cups natural raw rice
24 whole cashew nuts
1 Tablespoon ginger root, grated
½ teaspoon ground clove
1 teaspoon chili powder
4 Tablespoons chopped parsley
1 teaspoon salt

(2) In a large saucepan or casserole, melt the butter and add the rice, stirring to coat each grain. Stir in the next six ingredients.

Juice of 2 limes
Grated rind of 1 lime
Reserved saffron water
Chicken broth

(3) Combine the lime juice, grated rind, and saffron water. Add chicken broth to equal 3 cups.

At this point you may stop and continue later.

(continued)

⅓ **cup grated coconut, lightly toasted**

(4) Bring the liquid to the boil, pour it over the rice, stirring once with a fork. Simmer the rice, covered, for 15 minutes, or until it is tender and the liquid is absorbed. (If desired, a casserole may be baked at 350°, covered, for about 25 minutes, or until the rice is tender and the liquid is absorbed.) Garnish the dish with the coconut.

LIME CAKE

Follow the directions for Orange Cake, page 250, using, in place of the orange rind and juice, the grated rind of 3 limes and the juice of 2 limes plus water to equal 1 cup; for the icing, if desired, use 3 Tablespoons lime juice and the sugar (omit the grated rind).

LIME GRANITE

(Italian)

This dessert is a pleasant one, and easy—easier than the sherbet, page 201—but less reliable, as overfreezing produces, not *granite*, but merely a chunk of lime-flavored ice.

Serves 6
Doubles
Freezes

Preparation: 15 minutes
Freezing time: 3 hours

2 cups sugar
4 cups water
Grated rind of 2 limes
¾ **cup lime juice**

(1) In a saucepan, over high heat, boil the sugar and water, uncovered, for 5 minutes. Remove the syrup from the heat, add the lime rind and juice, and allow the mixture to stand, uncovered, until it cools to room temperature.

(2) Into refrigerator trays, sieve the mixture. Freeze the *granite* until it is granular.

LIME MERINGUE PIE

(American)

Serving: one 9-inch pie

Preparation: 45 minutes*
Cooking: 15 minutes
Preheat oven: 325°

1 **cup sugar**
¼ **cup flour**
   Pinch of salt
3 **Tablespoons cornstarch**

(1) In a saucepan, combine these four ingredients, stirring with a fork to mix them well.

2 **cups water**

(2) Gradually add the water, stirring. Cook the mixture, stirring constantly, until it is thickened and smooth.

3 **egg yolks, beaten**

(3) To the yolks, add a little of the cornstarch mixture, stirring. Then add the yolks to the contents of the saucepan. Over gentle heat, cook the mixture, stirring for 2 minutes.

1 **Tablespoon butter**
⅓ **cup lime juice**
   Grated rind of 2 limes
3 **or 4 drops green food coloring**

(4) Add these four ingredients, stirring to blend the mixture well. Allow the custard to cool slightly.

1 **9-inch pie shell, baked**

(5) Pour the custard into the baked pie shell and allow it to cool completely.

3 **egg whites**
   Pinch of salt
¼ **teaspoon cream of tartar**
3 **Tablespoons sugar**

(6) In a mixing bowl, beat the egg whites and salt until they are frothy; add the cream of tartar and beat them until they are stiff. Add the sugar by the Tablespoonful, beating constantly. When the meringue stands in stiff peaks, spread it over the pie and bake it at 325° for 15 minutes, or until it is golden. Allow the pie to cool at room temperature.

* The preparation time does not include readying the pastry, page 458.

LIME SHERBET

Follow the directions for Lemon Sherbet, page 201, using, in place of the lemon rind and juice, equal quantities of lime rind and juice.

COLD LIME SOUFFLE*

Serves 6
Refrigerates

Preparation: 30 minutes
Chilling time: at least 3 hours

A 1½- or 2-quart straight-sided souffle dish
Aluminum foil
Vegetable oil
Tape

(1) Prepare the souffle dish as follows: Fold in half lengthwise sufficient foil to go around the dish with a good margin for taping. With the folded edge as the "up" edge, lightly oil the side which will face the center of the dish. Wrap the foil around the dish and secure it with tape so that 4 inches stand above the rim.

¼ cup fresh lime juice
1 envelope unflavored gelatin

(2) In the lime juice, soften the gelatin.

½ cup fresh lime juice
Zest of 1 lime, coarsely chopped

(3) In the container of an electric blender, whirl the juice and zest until the zest is chopped into fine particles.

* This recipe was contributed by Jack Brown, a country neighbor, who is, at one and the same time, a stage designer, a landscape architect, and a cook *par excellence*. It is not easy to tell which of the three activities he does best, but this souffle sets a standard for anyone to emulate.

4 **egg yolks, lightly beaten**
½ **cup sugar**
  Pinch of salt
1 **or 2 drops green food coloring**
  (optional)

(4) In the top of a double boiler, combine the yolks, sugar, and salt. Add the juice and zest and, over simmering water, cook the mixture, stirring constantly, until it coats the spoon. Remove it from the heat and stir in the gelatin mixture and food coloring. Continue stirring until the gelatin is dissolved.

6 **egg whites**
½ **cup sugar**

(5) In a mixing bowl, beat the egg whites until they hold a soft shape; gradually add the sugar beating constantly, until the whites form stiff peaks.

1 **cup heavy cream, whipped**
  Mint leaves

(6) Gently fold and blend the cream and egg whites into the lime mixture. Pour it into the prepared dish and chill it for at least 3 hours, or until it is set. Before serving, remove the foil collar and garnish the souffle with a few fresh mint leaves.

MELONS

There are many types and varieties of the hard-skinned, juicy melon, but all of them belong to only one of two species—the muskmelon or the watermelon genera—and all are members of the gourd family (*Cucurbitaceae*), which includes pumpkins, cucumbers, and squashes.

Muskmelons (*Cucumis melo*), originating in Iran and Transcaucasia, were probably grown by the Egyptians (melons appear in Egyptian tomb paintings of 2400 B.C.) and were certainly on Greek and Roman menus (Pliny describes them in some detail). They were introduced to China at the beginning of the Christian era and have since spread throughout the warmer, less humid temperate zones of the world.

The muskmelon plant is a trailing vine with coarse heart-shaped leaves 3 to 5 inches across and yellow five-lobed wheel-shaped flowers. The

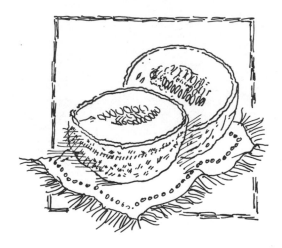

fruit itself varies in weight from 2 to 9 pounds, in shape from oblate to round, or globular to tapered, in texture from smooth- to wrinkled-skinned, and in flesh color from green to orange. Insect-pollinated, muskmelons intercross easily and are harvested between 85 and 125 days after planting. When a crack appears around the stem, most muskmelons (the casaba is the exception) have attained their highest sugar content and are best for picking.

Muskmelons include the honeydew, Persian, casaba, and cantaloupe. The latter is named for the castle of Cantalupo ("wolf song") near Rome, where it was developed in the seventeenth century. The honeydew, introduced to the United States from France at the beginning of this century, becomes sweeter after picking; other muskmelons do not.

The watermelon (*Citrullus vulgaris*) is related to the muskmelon only as a member of the gourd family. It originated in Africa and was cultivated there over 4,000 years ago. It spread to the Middle East (a word designating watermelon exists in Sanskrit) and to the warmer climates of Russia, at last reaching Europe by means of Arab and Moorish trading caravans. Colonists brought it to the Western Hemisphere and Pacific Islands. The watermelon was common fare in Massachusetts at the start of the seventeenth century.

This smooth-skinned green melon with its pink-to-red flesh is very juicy but has less flavor than the muskmelon. Today it is widely cultivated in all temperate zones and grows on trailing vines which are similar to its cousin's. The fruit, however, is much larger than the muskmelon; some varieties weigh as much as 50 pounds.

MELON SOUP I

(*Chinese*)

So easy, so delicately flavored. It has been said that there are only two great cuisines, the French and the Chinese. I do not agree; I feel there are more—such as traditional American cooking. Still, such a dish as this *does* influence one's opinions in favor of our Oriental neighbors.

> Serves 6
> Doubles
> Refrigerates

Preparation: 20 minutes

3 10½-oz. cans condensed chicken broth plus water to equal 6 cups, or 6 cups homemade chicken stock

(1) In a saucepan, bring the chicken broth to a boil.

Flesh of 1 large, ripe cantaloupe, diced
¼ lb. raw pork, cut into the fine julienne
½ teaspoon salt
1 teaspoon sugar
2 teaspoons soy sauce

(2) To the boiling liquid, add the cantaloupe, pork, salt, and sugar. When the soup returns to the boil, reduce the heat and simmer it, uncovered, for 5 minutes. Stir in the soy sauce and adjust the seasoning. Serve the soup at once.

Variations: If desired, 6 mushrooms, thinly sliced, may be added to the broth with the melon and pork. Also, ¼ lb. boiled ham, cut in fine *julienne* may be used in place of the fresh pork.

MELON SOUP II

A delectable cold soup for summer!

> Serves 6
> Doubles
> Refrigerates

Preparation: 20 minutes
Chilling time: at least 2 hours

1 large, ripe cantaloupe or honeydew, peeled, seeded, and
   chopped
½ teaspoon cinnamon
3 cups orange juice
2 Tablespoons lime juice, or more
   to taste

(1) In the container of an electric blender, combine all the ingredients and on medium speed, whirl them for 15 seconds, or until the mixture is smooth. Adjust the seasoning and chill the soup.

   Fresh mint leaves, chopped

(2) When serving the soup, garnish it with the chopped mint.

HAM STEAK AND MELON

An elegant way to serve ham steak.

   Serves 6

Preparation: 30 minutes

½ cup butter, melted
½ cup mango chutney, chopped fine
2 teaspoons curry powder

(1) In a mixing bowl, prepare the sauce by mixing together these three ingredients.

1 3-lb. ham steak, trimmed of
   excess fat

(2) On an oiled broiling rack, arrange the ham steak; brush it with the sauce. Broil it for 7 minutes.

(3) Turn the steak, brush it with the sauce, and broil it for 7 minutes. Remove the steak to a serving platter and keep it warm.

2 ripe cantaloupes, cut into sixths
   and seeded

(4) Arrange the cantaloupe slices on the broiling rack; brush them with the sauce. Broil them for 2 minutes.

(5) Turn the cantaloupe slices, brush them with the sauce and broil them for 2 minutes. Garnish the ham platter with cantaloupe.

221

LAMB CURRY AND MELON WITH MANGO

(Indian)

Made with the mango, this dish is truly "something else"; it is not necessary, however, and without it the dish is still very good.

Serves 6
Doubles
Refrigerates

Preparation: 30 minutes
Cooking: 1¼ hours

5 Tablespoons butter
3 onions, chopped
3 lbs. lean lamb, cut in bite-sized pieces

(1) In a flame-proof casserole, heat the butter and cook the onions until translucent. Add the lamb and cook it until it changes color, but not until it is brown.

2 teaspoons salt
¼ teaspoon pepper
1 teaspoon sugar
2 Tablespoons curry powder, or more to taste
½ teaspoon dried mint leaves
1 10½-oz. can condensed beef broth

(2) Add the seasonings and then the broth. Bring the liquid to the boil, reduce the heat, and simmer the lamb covered, for 1 hour, or until it is tender.

At this point you may stop and continue later.

1 medium ripe melon (cantaloupe or honeydew), peeled, seeded, and cut into bite-sized pieces
1 large ripe mango, peeled, seeded, and cut into bite-sized pieces (optional)

(3) Add the melon and mango and cook them for 5 minutes.

½ cup lime juice
½ cup heavy cream

(4) In order, stir in first the lime juice and then the cream. *Do not allow the sauce to boil.* Serve the curry with rice and condiments for curry, page xv.

SAUTEED MELON WITH CURRY

An accompaniment to roast or broiled meats.

> Serves 6
> Doubles

Preparation: 20 minutes

4 Tablespoons butter
2 large or 3 small ripe melons (cantaloupe, honeydew, or Persian) peeled, seeded, and cut into bite-sized pieces
Salt

(1) In a skillet, heat the butter and in it saute the melon, turning it to cover it well with the butter. Add more butter as necessary. Season the melon with a sprinkling of salt. Remove it to a serving dish and keep it warm.

1 onion, minced
Curry powder

(2) In the remaining butter, cook the onion until translucent. Spread the onion over the melon and sprinkle the dish with curry powder to taste.

SAUTEED WATERMELON RIND

To accompany roast meats.

> Serves 6
> Doubles
> Refrigerates

Preparation: 20 minutes
Cooking: 10 minutes

Watermelon rind

(1) Trim the green from the rind. Using a coarse shredder, prepare 6 cups of shredded rind.

6 pieces thick-sliced bacon, diced
1 onion, chopped

(2) In a skillet, render the bacon until crisp; remove it to absorbent paper and reserve it. In the remaining fat, cook the onion until translucent.

(continued)

223

Salt
Pepper

(3) Add the prepared watermelon rind, stirring; cook the rind, covered, for 10 minutes, or until it is just tender. Season it to taste with salt and pepper and garnish it with the reserved bacon bits.

MELON WITH PORT WINE
(Spanish)

This recipe provides an elegant and unusual way to serve melon.

Serves 6
Doubles
Refrigerates

Marination: 5 hours
Preparation: 15 minutes

1 large ripe Spanish melon or 2 large ripe cantaloupes or Persian melons
1 cup port wine

(1) At the stem end of the melon, cut out a plug; reserve it. Into the melon, pour the wine; replace the plug and refrigerate the melon for several hours.

(2) Remove the plug and drain the melon, reserving the wine.

(3) Halve the melon, seed it, and cut it into serving portions. Over each piece pour some of the wine.

ORANGES
AND
TANGERINES

England's Henry IV is said to have served oranges
at a royal banquet in 1399. Henry VIII's Cardinal
Wolsey carried a pomander of orange studded
with cloves to protect his delicate nose from evil
smells. During the reign of Elizabeth I, oranges
began to be sold in London streets and, some
years later, the most famous of all orange girls,
Nell Gwyn, became the mistress of Charles II.
And some say the golden apple given Paris in
classical myth was really an orange.

Probably originating in southern China and the
Indo-Chinese region (hence the name *Citrus
sinensis*), the orange spread throughout the
Mediterranean area, and thence to Europe, by
means of Arab traders, Roman conquests, Islamic
expansion, and the Crusades. Oranges were
brought to the West Indies by Columbus on his
second voyage.

Our word "orange" derives not from the color of the fruit, for color is no guide to its ripeness, but from its Sanskrit name, *nāranga*. The orange color, at least in the United States, is largely a product of ethylene gas in which the ripe fruit is fumed (unripe fruit will remain green, despite the gas). Ethylene, given off naturally by bananas and some apples, is used by the Florida, California, and Arizona fruit-growers. In South America, where often oranges have a fuller flavor than their Florida-grown cousins, the fruit sometimes turn a faint yellow and sometimes remain green.

Oranges are not strictly a tropical fruit. They thrive best where the semi-dormant trees are chilled somewhat by occasional night frost; if the tree has achieved its annual growth, it can tolerate temperatures as low as 30 degrees. Perhaps for this reason, orange trees, protected in *orangeries*, were popular in seventeenth- and eighteenth-century England and France, where nobles and royalty enjoyed their own home-grown fruit. Louis XIV at Versailles built a splendid *orangerie*, filled with fruit trees and tropical plants, which was the envy of Europe.

The orange tree, standing almost 30 feet high, has glossy evergreen leaves and fragrant white blossoms. The blossom produces what is, botanically, a berry. The peel is composed of two layers, the outer which is rich in oil, and the inner which is little more than cellulose. The pulp or flesh of this berry is arranged in edible segments (a fact true only of citrus fruits—other fruits are less orderly and organized!). These segments, or carpels, are made up of juice sacks, which contain some nourishment; but most of the good of an orange is within the juice itself: carbohydrates, organic acids, citric-, C-, and B-complex vitamins, and mineral salts.

Oranges are picked when ripe; they do not ripen after picking. For this reason, in the United States, it is unlawful to sell them before a certain maturity has been reached. Picked for the most part by machinery, the orange is then bathed in warm soapy water, scrubbed by revolving brushes, rinsed, brushed again, rinsed with a borax solution, rinsed again with clear water, dried in a forced-air tunnel, picked over by hand, graded for size, and finally— and, one imagines, in a state of exhausation—the poor orange is crated.

There are over one hundred varieties of sweet and mandarin (*Citrus reticulata*) oranges. World production equals about 2½ billion pounds per annum! Orange exportation is one of Israel's economic mainstays; the Jaffa, which is free of rag (the white inner skin), virtually seedless, sweet, and juicy, is the preferred variety. In the United States, 40 percent of the national crop is made into frozen orange juice. (Orange juice was nearly unknown to the American breakfast table before 1920.) Oils, pectin, candied peel, and preserves are the by-products of frozen orange juice concentrate. From the waste material, stock feed for cattle is made.

Mandarin oranges, which include tangerines and satsumas, are loose-skinned varieties. Easily peeled and sectioned, this variety in its many forms has a less acid flavor than that of the sweet orange and, unlike other oranges, its skin has a distinctive smell. We generally call mandarin oranges "tangerines," because Tangiers was the source of the first European importation of them in the early nineteenth century. The *Citrus reticulata*— the Mandarin orange—grows on a smaller tree than *Citrus sinesis*, its fruit is flatter and turns bright orange when ripe. Some varieties, such as the satsuma, are seedless. Mandarin oranges were cultivated in Japan over 2,000 years ago. *Mikan*, the only fresh fruit available throughout the Japanese winter, has been used as a remedy for headcolds for over 600 years; it is especially rich in vitamin C.

Tangerines and fresh Mandarin oranges are interchangeable in these recipes.

CHICKEN AND ORANGE CONSOMME

A delicately flavored, clear, rather elegant soup. Serve it hot or cold.

Serves 6
Doubles
Refrigerates

Preparation: 35 minutes

3 10½-oz. cans condensed chicken broth

(1) In a saucepan, allow the excess fat to rise to the surface; remove it by floating paper towels on it and discarding them quickly. Over high heat, reduce the broth to 3 cups.

3 cups orange juice, sieved
Salt
White pepper

(2) To the broth, add the orange juice. Season the liquid to taste with salt and pepper.

4 teaspoons cornstarch, mixed with ¼ cup orange juice

(3) Add the cornstarch mixture and, over high heat, cook the soup, stirring constantly, until it is slightly thickened and smooth.

6 orange slices, cut paper-thin and seeded

(4) Garnish each serving with an orange slice.

JELLIED CHICKEN CONSOMME AND ORANGE
(Caribbean)

Follow the directions for Chicken and Orange Consomme, above, using 2 envelopes unflavored gelatin sprinkled over the grease-free chicken broth; to this mixture, add the grated rind of 1 orange and simmer the liquid, stirring to dissolve the gelatin, for 3 minutes; add the orange juice but omit the cornstarch; chill the soup until it is slightly jellied.

TOMATO AND ORANGE CONSOMME*

Follow the directions for Chicken and Orange Consomme, page 228, using, in place of the chicken broth, 3 cups tomato juice, lemon juice and celery salt as the seasonings to taste; garnish the soup with chopped fresh chives or fresh dill or fresh mint, or a dollop of sour cream.

* This cool and refreshing soup is contributed by Odette Doguereau, a close friend who is as French as her name. When I was a graduate student at Harvard, one of the highlights of my week was to get out of the Widener Library and into the underground, bound for Odette's apartment, where, every Wednesday evening, we would cook supper together. I will never forget the first time, one spring evening, that Odette produced potato salad à la française (with oil-and-vinegar dressing in which several garlic cloves had been crushed). It was a revelation and for that salad (if not for a thousand other reasons) I have loved her for a quarter century!

BEEF AND ORANGES
(Spanish)

Sometimes called Beef Matador, this stew is delightfully aromatic.

Serves 6
Doubles
Refrigerates
Freezes

Preparation: 40 minutes
Cooking: 2½ hours
Preheat oven: 350°

2 Tablespoons butter **2 Tablespoons oil** **3 lbs. chuck, cut into bite-sized pieces** **Salt** **Pepper**	(1) In a flame-proof casserole, heat the butter and oil and brown the beef; season it. Remove.
4 onions, chopped	(2) In the remaining fat, cook the onions until translucent. Replace the beef.
1 3-inch piece cinnamon stick **2 Tablespoons quick-cooking tapioca**	(3) Add the cinnamon and sprinkle over the tapioca.

(continued)

1 **6-oz. can frozen orange juice concentrate, fully thawed**
1½ **cups sweet sherry**
2 **Tablespoons soy sauce**
1½ **teaspoons salt**
¼ **teaspoon pepper**
1 **teaspoon ground celery seed**
1 **teaspoon ground cumin**

(4) Mix together the liquids and seasonings and pour over the meat.

2 **oranges, sliced paper-thin and seeded**

(5) Over the contents of the casserole, arrange the orange slices.

At this point you may stop and continue later.

(6) Bake the casserole, covered, at 300° for 2½ hours, or until the meat is tender. (If the casserole is frozen, replace the orange slices with fresh ones when reheating for serving.)

POT ROAST AND ORANGE

Serves 6
Refrigerates
Freezes (except for the fruit garnish)

Marination: 6 hours
Preparation: ½ hour
Cooking: 3 hours

1½ **teaspoons salt**
½ **teaspoon pepper**
½ **teaspoon ground clove**
1 **teaspoon ground coriander**
1 **teaspoon ground cumin**
1 **teaspoon sugar**
Grated rind and juice of 1 orange
1 **6-oz. can frozen orange juice concentrate, thawed**
2 **onions, coarsely chopped**

(1) In the container of an electric blender, combine these ten ingredients and, on high speed, whirl them for 15 seconds.

3½- **to 4-lb. pot roast**

(2) In a mixing bowl, arrange the pot roast, pour the marinade over it, and let it stand for several hours in the refrigerator.

1 Tablespoon butter
1 Tablespoon oil
¼ cup orange-flavored liqueur
  Reserved marinade

(3) Wipe the meat clean with a rubber spatula, reserving the marinade. In a flame-proof casserole, heat the butter and oil and brown the meat. In a small pan, warm the liqueur, ignite it, and pour it over the meat. When it burns out, pour the marinade over the meat.

At this point you may stop and continue later.

2 oranges, cut into ⅛-inch slices
  and seeded

(4) Bring the marinade to the boil, reduce the heat, and simmer the pot roast, covered, for 2½ hours, or until it is tender. Garnish the dish with the oranges and continue cooking it, covered, for 15 minutes longer.

1 Tablespoon cornstarch
  Water

(5) Arrange the meat and orange slices on a warm serving dish. Skim the fat from the sauce. Blend the cornstarch with a little water, add it to the sauce, and cook the mixture, stirring constantly, until it is thickened and smooth. Serve the sauce separately.

LAMB BRAISED IN ORANGE SAUCE

(Puerto Rican)

What an unusually fresh-tasting dish this is. If desired, it may be made a day in advance and refrigerated, thus facilitating the removal of any excess fat.

> Serves 6
> Doubles
> Refrigerates
> Freezes

Preparation: 30 minutes
Cooking: 1½ hours
Preheat oven: 350°

(continued)

2 **Tablespoons butter**	(1) In a flame-proof casserole, heat
2 **Tablespoons oil**	the butter and oil and brown the
3 **lbs. lean lamb, cut in bite-sized**	lamb; season it. Remove it to
pieces	absorbent paper. Discard all but 2
Salt	Tablespoons of the fat.
Pepper	

2 **Tablespoons butter**
2 **Tablespoons oil**
3 **lbs. lean lamb, cut in bite-sized**
   pieces
   Salt
   Pepper

(1) In a flame-proof casserole, heat the butter and oil and brown the lamb; season it. Remove it to absorbent paper. Discard all but 2 Tablespoons of the fat.

1 **cup dry white wine**
¾ **cup orange juice**
2 **Tablespoons cornstarch**
¼ **cup lime juice**
   Grated rind of 1 orange
¼ **cup golden raisins**
2 **Tablespoons capers (optional)**
2 **cloves garlic, minced**
1 **teaspoon chili powder**
¼ **teaspoon ground clove**
1 **bay leaf, broken**

(2) With the wine, deglaze the casserole. Add the orange juice. Mix the cornstarch with the lime juice and add it to the casserole. Over high heat, cook the mixture, stirring constantly, until it is thickened and smooth. Stir in the remaining seven ingredients. Replace the lamb, spooning the sauce over it.

At this point you may stop and continue later.

2 **oranges, peeled, segmented, free**
   of all white pith, and seeded

(3) Bake the lamb, covered, at 350° for 1½ hours, or until it is tender. Add the orange sections during the final 15 minutes of cooking.

PORK CHOPS AND ORANGES
   (New Zealand)

The orange cuts the richness of the pork and, at the same time, enhances its delicate flavor.

   Serves 6
   Doubles
   Refrigerates
   Freezes

Preparation: 30 minutes
Cooking: 40 minutes
Preheat oven: 350°

2 Tablespoons butter
2 Tablespoons oil
6 shoulder chops of pork, about
   ½ lb. each, trimmed of excess
   fat
   Salt
   Pepper

(1) In a skillet, heat the butter and oil and brown the chops well; season them. Remove them to a flat baking dish; they should lie in one layer only. Discard the remaining fat.

1½ cups orange juice
½ cup dark brown sugar
   Juice of 1 lemon
1 teaspoon ground ginger
   Grated rind of 1 orange

(2) Combine these five ingredients and pour over the chops.

6 orange slices, cut paper-thin
   and seeded, or 1 orange, peeled,
   segmented free of all white
   pith, and seeded

(3) Over the chops, arrange the orange slices or segments.

At this point you may stop and continue later.

(4) Bake the chops, uncovered, at 350° for 40 minutes, or until they are tender. Baste them frequently with the pan juices.

4 teaspoons cornstarch mixed
   with 2 Tablespoons cold water

(5) Arrange the chops on a serving platter and keep them warm. Pour the pan juices into a saucepan (if the baking dish is not flame-proof). To the pan juices, add the cornstarch and, over high heat, cook the sauce stirring constantly, until it is thickened and smooth. Serve the sauce separately.

PORK ROAST AND TANGERINES

Serves 6
Refrigerates

Preparation: 15 minutes
Cooking: 3½ hours
Preheat oven: 325°

(continued)

1 teaspoon marjoram, crushed in a mortar
1 teaspoon dry mustard
1 teaspoon salt
5- to 6-lb. loin roast of pork

(1) Combine the marjoram, mustard, and salt and, with this mixture, rub the pork roast. Arrange the roast, fat side up, on the rack of a roasting pan.

(2) Roast the meat, uncovered, at 325° for 2 hours.

Grated rind of 3 tangerines
¾ cup tangerine juice
1 Tablespoon dark brown sugar
1 teaspoon Lea & Perrins Worcestershire Sauce

(3) While the meat is roasting, in a small mixing bowl, combine these ingredients.

(4) At the end of the 2-hour period, skim the fat from the pan juices. With the tangerine juice mixture baste the roast frequently as it cooks for 1 hour longer, uncovered.

(5) Arrange the roast on a serving platter and keep it warm.

3 Tablespoons flour
Pinch dry mustard
Pinch marjoram
Tangerine juice
3 tangerines, peeled, sectioned, all white pith removed, and each section halved and seeded

(6) From the pan juices, remove the excess fat; discard it. Stir in the flour and seasonings. Cook the mixture, stirring constantly, until it is thickened and smooth; add tangerine juice as necessary to produce the desired consistency. Stir in the tangerine sections and pour the sauce over the roast, or, if desired, serve the sauce separately.

VEAL AND ORANGES*

Serves 6
Doubles
Refrigerates

* This delectable recipe is contributed by Robert C. Kennedy, my closest friend when we were undergraduates together at Wesleyan University. Since that time—now in the rather dim past!—Bob has lived in the Middle East and New York City. In these places, as well as during his annual summer trip to Some Place Or Other, one of his principal interests is food and its preparation. "As a cook, I'm a rank amateur," he says, but a meal at his home gives such protestations the lie.

Preparation: 30 minutes
Cooking: 1½ hours

2 Tablespoons butter
2 Tablespoons oil
3 lbs. lean stewing veal, cut in
    bite-sized pieces
    Salt
    Pepper
	(1) In a flame-proof casserole, heat the butter and oil and brown the veal; season it.

12 to 18 small onions **3 oranges, sliced paper-thin and** **seeded**	(2) Over the meat, arrange the onions and then the orange slices.
3 Tablespoons cornstarch **2⅔ cups orange juice***	(3) In a saucepan, combine the cornstarch with a little of the orange juice; add the remaining juice and, over high heat, cook the mixture, stirring constantly, until it is thickened and smooth. Pour the sauce over the contents of the casserole. *At this point you may stop and continue later.* (4) Bake the casserole, covered, at 350° for 1½ hours, or until the veal is tender.

* If desired, sweet sherry may be used in addition to the orange juice. If so, use only 2 cups orange juice in step (3). Then, 15 minutes before serving, add ⅔ cup sherry and continue cooking at 350°.

VEAL CUTLETS AND ORANGE SAUCE

A last-minute meat dish, easily prepared if you have all the ingredients readied ahead of time.

> Serves 6
> Doubles
> Refrigerates
> Freezes

Preparation: 25 minutes

(continued)

6 **veal cutlets about 1-inch thick**
Salt
Pepper
4 **Tablespoons butter**

(1) Season the cutlets. In a skillet, heat the butter and brown the meat on both sides.

3 **scallions, chopped**

(2) Add the scallions and continue cooking the meat, turning it once, for 2 minutes on each side.

1 **cup orange juice**
½ **teaspoon meat glaze**
1 **teaspoon Lea & Perrins Worcestershire Sauce**
6 **orange slices, cut paper-thin and seeded**

(3) Combine the orange juice, meat glaze, and Worcestershire sauce; pour them over the meat; simmer the cutlets, covered, for 12 minutes, or until they are tender. More orange juice may be added, if necessary. Transfer the cutlets to a serving platter, garnish them with the orange slices, and keep them warm.

1 **teaspoon cornstarch, mixed with a little cold water**

(4) To the pan juices, add the cornstarch and, over high heat, cook the sauce, stirring constantly, until it is thickened and smooth. Pour the sauce over the veal cutlets.

CHICKEN AND ORANGE I

(Mexican)

Serves 6
Doubles
Refrigerates

Preparation: 30 minutes
Cooking: 1 hour
Preheat oven: 350°

2 **Tablespoons butter**
2 **Tablespoons oil**
Serving-pieces of chicken for 6 persons
Salt
Pepper

(1) In a flame-proof casserole, heat the butter and oil and brown the chicken; season it. Remove. Discard the remaining fat. (If desired, the chicken may be dredged in seasoned flour and then browned; in this case, the sauce evolves without the use of cornstarch.)

1 10½-oz. can condensed chicken
   broth
1 cup orange juice
¼ cup lemon juice
2 Tablespoons cornstarch, mixed
   with ¼ cup orange juice
¾ teaspoon ground ginger
1 teaspoon paprika

1 orange, thinly sliced and seeded
1 green pepper, chopped
¼ cup pimentos, chopped
12 mushrooms, quartered

(2) Using the broth and the two juices, deglaze the casserole. Add the cornstarch mixture and, over high heat, cook the sauce, stirring constantly, until it is thickened and smooth. Stir in the seasonings. Replace the chicken, spooning the sauce over it.

(3) Over the chicken, arrange these four ingredients.

At this point you may stop and continue later.

(4) Bake the chicken, covered, at 350° for 1 hour, or until it is tender.

CHICKEN AND ORANGE II

Follow the directions for Chicken and Orange I, page 236, using, in place of the chicken broth and lemon juice, a total of 2½ cups orange juice seasoned with ¼ cup honey, 1½ teaspoons Lea & Perrins Worcestershire Sauce, and the grated rind of 1 orange. Thicken the sauce as directed. Omit the green pepper, pimentos, and mushrooms.

CHICKEN BREASTS IN BITTER ORANGE SAUCE

Serves 6
Doubles
Refrigerates

Preparation: 20 minutes
Cooking: 30 minutes

6 Tablespoons butter
3 large chicken breasts, halved
  Salt
  Pepper

(1) In a flame-proof casserole, heat the butter and in it brown the chicken; season it. Remove.

(continued)

½ **teaspoon cinnamon**
¾ **teaspoon dry mustard**
2 **cups orange juice**
½ **cup bitter orange marmalade**
5 **teaspoons cornstarch, mixed with ¼ cup orange juice**
   Sugar

(2) Into the remaining butter, stir the cinnamon and mustard. Mix together and then add the orange juice and marmalade, stirring. Add the cornstarch mixture and, over moderate heat, cook the mixture stirring constantly, until it is thickened and smooth. Add a bit of sugar, to taste, if desired. Replace the chicken.

At this point you may stop and continue later.

6 **orange slices, cut paper-thin and seeded**

(3) Simmer the chicken, covered, for 30 minutes, or until it is tender. Add the orange slices for the second 15 minutes of cooking. Serve the chicken with wild rice.

CHICKEN AND TANGERINES

Serves 6
Doubles
Refrigerates

Preparation: 30 minutes
Cooking: 1 hour
Preheat oven: 350°

2 **Tablespoons butter**
2 **Tablespoons oil**
   Serving-pieces of chicken for 6 persons
   Salt
   Pepper

(1) In a flame-proof casserole, heat the butter and oil and brown the chicken; season it.

2 **Tablespoons cornstarch**
2½ **cups fresh tangerine juice**
   Grated rind of 3 tangerines

(2) In a saucepan, mix the cornstarch with a little of the tangerine juice. Add the remaining juice and the rind. Over high heat, cook the mixture, stirring constantly, until it is thickened and smooth. Pour the sauce over the chicken.

At this point you may stop and continue later.

4 **tangerines, peeled, sectioned, all white pith removed, and each section seeded**
⅓ **cup golden raisins (optional)**

(3) Bake the casserole covered, at 350° for 1 hour, or until the chicken is tender. Add the tangerine sections and raisins for the final 15 minutes of cooking.

DUCK AND ORANGE

(*French*)

Canard à l'orange is a well-known dish in classic French cooking.

Serves 4
Doubles
Refrigerates
Freezes

Preparation: 30 minutes
Cooking: 2 hours

2 **Tablespoons butter**
2 **Tablespoons oil**
1 **5- or 6-lb. duck, quartered and trimmed of excess fat**
Salt
Pepper

(1) In a flame-proof casserole, heat the butter and oil and brown the duck; season it. Remove it to absorbent paper. Discard the remaining fat. Replace the duck

Zest of 2 oranges, cut in fine julienne
3 **oranges, peeled, quartered, and free of all white pith**
1 **10½-oz. can condensed chicken broth**

(2) To the contents of the casserole, add these three ingredients. Simmer the duck, tightly covered, for 1½ hours, or until it is tender.

At this point you may stop and continue later.

(3) Remove the hot duck pieces, drain them, arrange them on a serving platter and keep them warm.

(continued)

239

⅔ cup orange juice
1 Tablespoon cornstarch, mixed
   with ¼ cup orange juice
¼ cup orange-flavored liqueur
   (optional)
1 small orange, sliced paper-thin,
   quartered, and seeded

(4) Pour off all but ⅔ cup of the pan juices. To them, add the orange juice. Bring the liquid to the boil, add the cornstarch mixture, and, over high heat, cook the sauce, stirring constantly, until it is thickened and smooth. (If desired, ¼ cup orange-flavored liqueur may be warmed, ignited, poured over the browned duck and allowed to burn out, before adding the sauce.) Strain the sauce over the duck and garnish the dish with the orange pieces.

FISH FILETS AND MANDARIN ORANGES

Serves 6
Doubles
Refrigerates

Preparation: 15 minutes
Cooking: 20 minutes
Preheat oven: 400°

Fish filets for 6 persons, page xv
Salt
Pepper

(1) In a lightly oiled baking dish, arrange the filets and season them with salt and pepper.

Liquid from one 11-oz. can
mandarin oranges (reserve the
fruit)
Water
1 6-oz. can frozen orange juice
   concentrate, fully thawed
1 Tablespoon cornstarch
1 Tablespoon soy sauce

(2) To the mandarin orange liquid, add water to equal 1 cup. Add the orange juice concentrate. Stir in the cornstarch. Add the soy sauce.

At this point you may stop and continue later.

(3) Bake the fish, covered, at 400° for 20 minutes, or until it flakes easily.

(4) Meanwhile, over high heat, cook the orange juice-cornstarch mixture, stirring constantly, until the sauce is thickened and smooth.

1 9-oz. packet frozen small peas, fully thawed to room temperature
Reserved orange sections

(5) Arrange the peas over the fish, pour over the sauce, and garnish the dish with the reserved mandarin orange sections.

FISH FILETS AND ORANGE

(Mexican)

Serves 6
Doubles
Refrigerates

Preparation: 20 minutes
Cooking: 20 minutes
Preheat oven: 400°

Fish filets for 6 persons, page xv
4 Tablespoons butter, melted
3 cloves garlic, put through a press
Grated rind of 1 orange
White pepper

(1) In a shallow baking dish, lightly buttered, arrange the fish filets. Combine the melted butter, garlic, and grated orange rind; pour the mixture evenly over the fish. Season the fish with a sprinkling of pepper.

4 Tablespoons butter
3 cloves garlic, sliced lengthwise
3 Tablespoons parsley, minced
Juice of 1 orange
Salt
Pepper

(2) In a saucepan, heat the butter and in it cook the garlic until the butter is flavored. Discard the garlic pieces. Add the parsley, orange juice, and salt and pepper to taste.

At this point you may stop and continue later.

(3) Bake the fish, covered, at 400° for 20 minutes, or until it flakes easily. Heat the sauce and pour it over the fish.

BAKED ORANGES

A pleasant accompaniment to roast chicken, duck, and turkey.

Serves 6
Doubles
Refrigerates

Preparation: 35 minutes
Cooking: 1½ hours

6 oranges
6 to 12 sugar lumps
   Lea & Perrins Worcestershire
   Sauce

In a saucepan, cover the oranges with cold water. Bring the water to the boil, reduce the heat, and simmer the oranges, covered, for 30 minutes. Drain the oranges, slice off their tops, and insert 1 or 2 sugar lumps, to taste, to each of which has been added ¼ teaspoon of Worcestershire sauce. Cook the oranges in the roasting pan with the fowl for the final 1½ hours of roasting time.

BEETS AND ORANGE

Serves 6
Doubles
Refrigerates
Freezes

Preparation: 40 minutes

12 to 18 beets, scrubbed

(1) In boiling salted water, cook the beets covered for 30 minutes, or until they are tender. Slip off their skins; slice. Reserve the beets.

At this point you may stop and continue later.

6 Tablespoons butter
Juice and grated rind of 1 orange
1 teaspoon Lea & Perrins Worcestershire Sauce
Fresh tarragon leaves, if available

(2) In a skillet, heat the butter and in it reheat the beets. Combine the orange rind, juice, and Worcestershire sauce; pour the liquid over the beets. Garnish the beets with a few tarragon leaves, chopped.

CARROTS AND ORANGE

(American)

Serves 6
Doubles
Refrigerates
Freezes

Preparation: 10 minutes
Cooking: 30 minutes

½ teaspoon salt
½ teaspoon ground ginger
1 teaspoon sugar
2 Tablespoons butter
1 cup orange juice
Grated rind of 1 orange

(1) In a saucepan with a tight-fitting lid and large enough to cook the carrots, combine these six ingredients and bring the mixture to the boil.

Carrots for 6 persons, scraped and cut in ½-inch slices
1 teaspoon cornstarch, mixed with 2 Tablespoons cold water (optional)

(2) Add the carrots, shaking the pan to cover them well with the orange sauce. Simmer the carrots, covered, for 30 minutes, or until they are tender. If desired, the carrots may be drained and served; or, if desired, the cornstarch may be added to the cooked carrots and gently stirred to thicken the sauce.

CUCUMBER AND ORANGES

(Puerto Rican)

Serves 6
Doubles
Refrigerates

Preparation: 20 minutes
Cooking: 5 minutes

6 large cucumbers, peeled, quartered lengthwise, and seeded

1½ cups orange juice
2 Tablespoons cornstarch
3 Tablespoons soft butter
Grated rind of 1 orange
Salt
White pepper

(1) In boiling, lightly salted water to cover, cook the cucumbers for 10 minutes; drain them well.

(2) In a saucepan, combine the orange juice and cornstarch. Over high heat, cook the mixture, stirring constantly, until it is thickened and smooth. Stir in the butter, grated orange rind, and seasonings to taste. Add the cucumbers to the sauce.

At this point you may stop and continue later.

(3) Over gentle heat, cook the cucumbers for 5 minutes, or until they are heated through.

ONIONS AND ORANGES

(American)

Serves 6
Doubles
Refrigerates

Preparation: 15 minutes
Cooking: 1 hour
Preheat oven: 350°

6 **large onions, peeled**
Grated rind of 1 orange
4 **Tablespoons brown sugar**
Salt

(1) In a lightly buttered baking dish, arrange the onions; sprinkle them with the rind and brown sugar and season them with salt.

6 **paper-thin orange slices, seeded**
Nutmeg

(2) Put an orange slice, sprinkled with nutmeg, on each onion.

½ **cup orange juice**

(3) Add the juice to the baking dish.

At this point you may stop and continue later.

(4) Bake the onions, covered, at 350° for 1 hour, or until they are tender but still hold their shape. More orange juice may be added as necessary.

BAKED BEANS AND ORANGE*

Serves 10
Doubles
Refrigerates
Freezes

Soaking: overnight
Preparation: 45 minutes
Cooking: 2½ hours
Preheat oven: 350°

* Robert Elick, Galley Steward of the steamer *Delta Queen*, is the originator of this recipe. For many years a *maître d'hotel*, he is presently in charge of the bills of fare on this sternwheeler which is happily evocative of Mark Twain and of life in a less complex era. Like the *Delta Queen* herself, the food aboard her is of honest American persuasion.

(continued)

2 lbs. Great Northern or navy beans, soaked overnight in enough water to cover **2 lbs. onions, finely chopped** **½ lb. bacon, finely diced** **2 6-oz. cans frozen orange juice concentrate, thawed** **Grated rind and juice of 2 oranges** **2 teaspoons salt** **½ teaspoon pepper**	(1) Drain the beans and reserve the liquid. In a large saucepan or soup kettle, combine the drained beans, onion, and bacon. Add the orange juice concentrate and the grated rind and orange juice. Add the reserved water just to cover the beans. Stir in the salt and pepper. Bring the liquid to the boil, reduce the heat, and simmer the beans, covered, for 30 minutes, or until they are just barely tender. More reserved bean water may be added, if necessary.
1 cup dark brown sugar **3 Tablespoons cider vinegar**	(2) Stir in the sugar and vinegar.
1 6-oz. can tomato paste **¼ teaspoon ground allspice** **½ teaspoon ground celery seed** **½ teaspoon chili powder** **½ teaspoon cinnamon** **¼ teaspoon ground clove** **2 teaspoons Lea & Perrins Worcestershire Sauce**	(3) In a small mixing bowl, combine the tomato paste and spices; stir the mixture until it is smooth and well blended. Stir the mixture into the beans.
1 orange, sliced paper-thin and seeded	(4) Transfer the beans and liquid to a bean pot or casserole. Over the beans, arrange a layer of the orange slices. Bake the beans, covered, at 350° for 2½ hours, or until they are tender and the excess liquid is absorbed.

MASHED POTATOES AND ORANGE

(American)

Particularly tasty with ham or veal.

>Serves 6
>Doubles
>Refrigerates

Preparation: 40 minutes

6 medium potatoes, peeled and
  boiled until tender
3 or 4 Tablespoons soft butter
  Salt
  Pepper

(1) Drain and mash the potatoes.
Add the butter and whip the potatoes.
Season them to taste with salt and
pepper.

Grated rind and sieved juice of 1
orange

(2) Add the orange rind and juice
and continue to whip the potatoes
until they are light.

RICE AND ORANGES

Serves 6
Doubles

Preparation: 10 minutes
Cooking: 15 minutes

1 Tablespoon butter
1½ cups natural raw rice
1 small onion, minced (optional)
1 teaspoon salt
  Pinch of white pepper

(1) In a saucepan, heat the butter
and in it cook the rice for 2 minutes,
stirring to cover each grain. (If
desired, 1 small onion, minced, may
be cooked until translucent in the
butter before the rice is added.) Stir
in the seasonings.

3 cups orange juice, sieved

(2) Prepare the orange juice.

*At this point you may stop and
continue later.*

Fresh mint (optional)

(3) Add the orange juice to the
contents of the saucepan. Over high
heat, bring the liquid to the boil; stir
the rice once. Over low heat, simmer
the rice, covered, for 15 minutes, or
until it is tender and the liquid is
absorbed. A few leaves of fresh mint,
chopped, make a nice garnish for rice
cooked in orange juice.

CUCUMBER AND ORANGE SALAD

Serves 6
Doubles
Refrigerates

Preparation: 25 minutes
Chilling time: at least 1 hour

2 large cucumbers, peeled, quartered lengthwise, seeded, and cut in 1-inch lengths
4 oranges, peeled, all white pith removed, sectioned, and seeded
1 cup sour cream
1 Tablespoon honey
2 Tablespoons fresh mint, chopped
½ teaspoon salt

(1) In a mixing bowl, combine all the ingredients. Toss the mixture gently. Chill it.

Salad greens

(2) Onto individual servings of salad greens of your choice, spoon the cucumber-orange mixture.

ORANGE AND OLIVE SALAD

(Italian)

Serves 6
Doubles
Refrigerates

Preparation: 20 minutes
Chilling time: 1 hour

3 or 4 oranges, sliced paper-thin and seeded
1 cup pitted black olives, sliced lengthwise
¼ cup olive oil
Salt
Freshly ground pepper
½ clove garlic, crushed (optional)

(1) In a large serving bowl, combine the orange slices and olives. Dress them with the oil and season the salad to taste with salt and pepper. (Freshly ground pepper is important to the flavor of this salad. If the garlic is used, crush it through a press into the oil about 1 hour before making the salad.)

Prepared salad greens

(2) Serve the salad on greens of your choice.

ORANGE BREAD

Serving: two 8-inch loaves

Preparation: 40 minutes
Rising: 1½ hours
Cooking: 50 minutes

Zest of 1 orange, cut into the finest julienne
¼ cup sugar
1 cup water

(1) In a saucepan, combine these three ingredients; bring them to the boil, reduce the heat, and simmer them, covered, for 10 minutes.

1 6-oz. can frozen orange juice concentrate, thawed to room temperature
4 Tablespoons soft butter
2 teaspoons salt

(2) To the rind mixture, add these three ingredients, stirring until the butter and salt are melted.

2 packets dry yeast

(3) When the juice mixture is lukewarm, sprinkle over the yeast and stir until it is melted.

1½ cups flour
½ teaspoon nutmeg

(4) In a large mixing bowl, sift together these two ingredients. Add the orange juice mixture, stirring well.

2 cups flour

(5) Add the flour by the half-cupful, stirring in thoroughly each addition. The dough will be sticky.

(6) Put the bowl in a warm place and allow the dough to rise until doubled in bulk (about 1 hour).

(7) Stir the dough down and spoon it into two buttered 8-inch loaf pans. Allow it to rise again (about 30 minutes).

(continued)

(8) Put the pans into a cold oven. Turn the oven on 400° and bake the bread at this temperature for 15 minutes. Reduce the heat to 325° and continue baking for 35 minutes, or until the bread sounds hollow when tapped.

ORANGE MUFFINS

Follow the directions for Apple Muffins, page 19, using, in place of the apple, the grated rind of 1 orange. Into the top of each unbaked muffin, press a sugar lump soaked in orange juice. Bake the muffins as directed.

ORANGE CAKE*

Serving: one 10-inch cake
Doubles
Refrigerates
Freezes

Preparation: 20 minutes
Cooking: 1 hour
Preheat oven: 350°

4 eggs
1 cup orange juice
½ cup vegetable oil
Grated rind of 1 orange
1 teaspoon orange-flavored extract

(1) In a mixing bowl, beat the eggs very thoroughly until they are frothy. Add the next four ingredients and stir to blend the mixture.

1 package instant lemon pudding
1 package best quality yellow cake mix

(2) To the liquid ingredients, add the pudding and cake mixes. Beat for 2 minutes with an electric beater or 300 strokes by hand.

* This recipe is contributed by my friend Mary Carver, an accomplished self-taught cook. She rarely reads a recipe all the way through, never writes anything down, and inevitably succeeds by look, feel, or taste. This recipe was written down as she prepared it.

(3) In a buttered, floured tube, loaf, or layer tin, arrange the batter. Bake the cake at 350° for 1 hour, or until a knife inserted at the center comes out clean. Cool in the pan for 10 minutes; remove the cake from the pan and cool the cake completely on a rack.

3 Tablespoons orange juice
Grated rind of 1 orange
1 cup confectioner's sugar

(4) If desired, the cake may be iced: beat together these three ingredients until the mixture is smooth. Ice the cake while it is still slightly warm.

ORANGE GINGERBREAD

A delicious, spicy, fresh flavor!

Serving: one 8 x 12-inch loaf

Preparation: 15 minutes
Cooking time: 35 minutes
Preheat oven: 350°

½ cup dark brown sugar
½ cup butter
1 egg, lightly beaten
1 cup light molasses or maple or pancake syrup

(1) In a mixing bowl, cream together the sugar and butter. Stir in the beaten egg and then the molasses.

2½ cups flour
1½ teaspoons baking soda
1½ teaspoons ground ginger
½ teaspoon cinnamon
¼ teaspoon ground clove
½ teaspoon salt
Grated rind of 2 oranges

(2) In a mixing bowl, sift together the dry ingredients. Add the grated orange rind and stir well to blend.

1 cup orange juice, boiling

(3) Combine the molasses and flour mixtures. Gradually add the orange juice, beating constantly to keep the batter smooth. Beat the batter for 3 minutes.

(continued)

251

(4) Spoon the batter into a lightly buttered 2-quart baking dish. Bake the gingerbread at 350° for 35 minutes, or until a knife inserted at the center comes out clean. Cool the loaf slightly before turning it out onto a rack.

ORANGE CREPES*

Serves 9 (about 18 crepes)
Refrigerates

Preparation: 1¼ hours
Cooking: 10 minutes
Preheat oven: 400°

1½ **cups flour**
¼ **cup powdered sugar**
½ **teaspoon salt**

(1) Sift together these three ingredients.

2 **eggs**
¾ **cup milk**
¾ **cup water**
1 **teaspoon vanilla or 3 Tablespoons cognac or orange-flavored liqueur**
5 **Tablespoons butter, melted**

Soft butter

(2) In the container of an electric blender, whirl these five ingredients. Gradually add the flour mixture until the batter is smooth (it will be thin). Allow the batter to stand for at least two hours before making the crepes.

(3) Heat a 5- or 6-inch frying pan and butter it lightly. Pour in sufficient batter just to cover the bottom of the pan. Tilt the pan to spread the batter evenly. Cook the crepes as you would pancakes, first one side and then the other, turning them with a spatula. Crepes may be refrigerated or frozen; put a piece of wax paper between each to prevent their sticking together.

* Sue Kelly, who contributed this recipe, is a neighbor in the country, a beautiful young wife and mother who takes an active part in the life of Katonah village. The current phrase for such a lady is, I believe, "young matron." What an inadequate phrase it is! In Sue's case, it gives no hint of the charm of her home, the energy she devotes to ecological programs, *or* the excellence of her cooking.

2 **cups sour cream or cream-style cottage cheese**
1 **3½-oz. can flaked coconut**

6 **oranges, peeled, segmented, and cleaned of white membrane**

½ **cup honey**
3 **Tablespoons frozen orange juice concentrate, thawed**

(4) Mix the sour cream and coconut and spread each crepe with 2 Tablespoons of the mixture.

(5) Arrange 3 orange segments on one half of each crepe. Roll the crepes into tubes and place them in a lightly buttered baking dish.

(6) Blend the honey and orange juice concentrate.

At this point you may stop and continue later.

(7) Pour the honey mixture over the crepes. Garnish the dish with any remaining orange segments. Bake the dessert, uncovered, at 400° for 10 minutes, or until the crepes are well heated.

Two crepes per serving will suffice for a dessert. The recipe may be varied by omitting the sour cream, coconut, and orange segments, using instead tart orange marmalade spread over the crepes, and *crème pâtissière*, page 130, spread over the marmalade before the crepes are rolled.

CREPES SUZETTE

(French)

Perhaps the most "classic" of all classic French desserts. Easier than one would expect, and very festive.

Serves 6
Doubles
Refrigerates

Preparation: 20 minutes*

* The preparation time does not include readying the crepes, page 252. Prepare the crepes before you begin the sauce.

(continued)

½ lb. soft sweet butter
½ cup confectioner's sugar
   Grated rind and juice of 1 orange
¼ cup orange-flavored liqueur or
   cognac

(1) Cream together the butter and sugar. Beat in the orange rind and juice, and then the liqueur.

Prepared crepes
Fine granulated sugar
Orange-flavored liqueur

(2) In a chafing dish, heat 3 Tablespoons of the sauce. Add 6 crepes and heat them through, spooning the sauce over them; add more sauce as necessary. When the sauce is syrupy and the crepes hot, sprinkle them with the sugar and pour over them orange-flavored liqueur, warmed in a small saucepan and ignite.

Two crepes per serving is adequate for a dessert portion.

BAKED ORANGE CUSTARD
(American)

Perhaps not as well known as vanilla-flavored baked custard, but, I feel, a much more interesting dish.

      Serves 6
      Doubles
      Refrigerates

Preparation: 15 minutes
Cooking: 45 minutes
Preheat oven: 325°

1 cup heavy cream
3 eggs, lightly beaten
   Grated rind of 1 orange
1 cup orange juice, sieved
¼ cup sugar
   Pinch of salt

(1) In a mixing bowl, combine all the ingredients; stir to blend the custard.

(2) Pour the custard into six ½-cup custard cups. Put the cups in a shallow pan of hot water.

(3) Bake the custard at 325° for 45 minutes, or until a knife inserted at the center comes out clean.

ORANGE FOOL
(English)

This recipe was made famous by Boodle's, one of London's renowned men's clubs. A "fool," a dessert made of fruit and cream or soft custard, dates back to Tudor England.

Serves 6
Doubles
Refrigerates

Preparation: 25 minutes
Chilling time: at least 1 hour

Juice of 4 oranges, sieved
Juice of 2 lemons, sieved
Grated rind of 2 oranges
Grated rind of 1 lemon
3 Tablespoons honey
2 cups heavy cream
Pinch of salt

(1) In a mixing bowl, combine all the ingredients. With a rotary beater, beat the mixture until it is thickened and frothy.

12 to 18 large lady fingers

(2) With the lady fingers, line a glass or silver serving bowl. Over the lady fingers, spoon the cream mixture. Chill the dessert for 1 hour before serving it.

TANGERINE MOUSSE

Quick and easy—an unusual dessert.

Serves 6
Refrigerates

Preparation: 25 minutes
Chilling time: at least 3 hours

(continued)

1 cup tangerine juice, heated but not boiling
2 packets unflavored gelatin

(1) In the container of an electric blender, whirl the hot juice on medium speed, adding the gelatin to dissolve it.

4 eggs
Grated rind of 2 tangerines
3 Tablespoons sugar
Pinch of salt

(2) To the contents of the blender, add these four ingredients; whirl them on medium speed for 15 seconds to dissolve the sugar.

1 cup cracked ice, packed
Orange Sauce I, page 263

(3) Add the ice and continue whirling the mixture for 10 seconds. Pour it into a quart mold or individual dishes. Chill the mousse for at least 3 hours before unmolding it. Serve the sauce separately.

ORANGE MERINGUE PIE

(American)

A delicacy from the South.

Serving: one 9-inch pie
Refrigerates

Preparation: 40 minutes*
Chilling time: at least 2 hours
Preheat oven: 450°

4 egg yolks
½ cup sugar
1 envelope unflavored gelatin

(1) In a mixing bowl, beat the yolks until they are light. Add the sugar and gelatin and continue beating for about 5 minutes.

1 13-oz. can condensed milk

(2) Add the milk to the egg mixture and, in a saucepan, over gentle heat, cook the custard, stirring constantly, until it coats the spoon. Remove the saucepan from the heat.

⅓ cup orange-flavored liqueur
Grated rind of 2 oranges

(3) Stir in the liqueur and grated rind and allow the mixture to cool.

* Preparation time does not include readying the pastry, page 458.

1 9-inch pie shell, baked and
  cooled
4 egg whites
3 Tablespoons sugar

(4) Pour the custard into the pie shell. Beat the whites until they are stiff, adding the sugar gradually. Arrange the meringue over the custard and bake the pie in a 450° oven for about 5 minutes, or until the meringue is golden. Allow the pie to set in the refrigerator for at least 2 hours.

TANGERINE CHIFFON PIE

Serving: one 9-inch pie
Refrigerates

Preparation: 45 minutes*
Chilling time: at least 3 hours

1 envelope unflavored gelatin
½ cup sugar
  Dash of salt

(1) In the top of a double boiler, combine these three ingredients.

4 egg yolks
¼ cup lemon juice
1 cup tangerine juice

(2) In a mixing bowl, beat together these three ingredients. Add them to the contents of the double boiler and, over gently boiling water, cook the mixture, stirring constantly, until the gelatin and sugar are dissolved and the mixture coats the spoon. Remove the pan from the heat.

Grated rind of 2 tangerines

(3) Into the custard, stir the tangerine rind. Chill the custard, stirring it occasionally, until it is partially set.

4 egg whites
⅓ cup sugar

(4) In a mixing bowl, beat the egg whites until they are frothy. Gradually add the sugar, beating constantly until the whites stand in stiff peaks.

* The preparation time does not include readying the pastry, page 458.

(continued)

1 9-inch pastry shell, baked

(5) Into the chilled gelatin mixture, fold the egg whites. Spoon the mixture into the pie shell. Chill the pie for at least 3 hours, or until it is set.

1 cup heavy cream, whipped, flavored with 3 Tablespoons orange-flavored liqueur
2 tangerines, peeled, sectioned, all white pith removed, and each section seeded

(6) Garnish the pie with the whipped cream and tangerine sections.

This recipe may be made with canned mandarin oranges; use their liquid in place of the tangerine juice; omit the grated tangerine rind, but add the reserved fruit of one can, halved, to the custard before adding the egg whites. Use the reserved fruit from the second can to garnish the completed pie.

ORANGE CUSTARD PIE

Serving: one 9-inch pie
Refrigerates

Preparation: 25 minutes*
Cooking: 35 minutes
Preheat oven: 425°
Chilling time: at least 2 hours

4 eggs, lightly beaten
1 9-inch pastry shell, unbaked

(1) With a little of the beaten eggs, brush the pastry shell. Chill the pastry while you prepare the remaining ingredients.

¾ cup sugar
1½ cups light cream, scalded
Grated rind of 1 orange
1⅓ cups orange juice, sieved

(2) In a mixing bowl, combine the eggs, sugar, and cream. Stir in the orange rind and juice. Pour the mixture into the pie shell.

(3) Bake the pie at 425° in the lower half of the oven for 35 minutes, or until a knife inserted at the center comes out clean. Cool the pie on a rack.

* The preparation time does not include readying the pastry, page 458.

2 oranges, peeled, all pith
   removed, sectioned, and seeded

(4) In a pattern of your choice, arrange the orange sections on top of the custard.

⅓ cup orange juice
1½ teaspoons cornstarch
¼ cup orange-flavored liqueur

(5) In a saucepan, combine the orange juice and cornstarch. Over high heat, cook the mixture, stirring constantly, until it is thickened and smooth. Stir in the liqueur and pour the mixture over the orange sections. Chill the pie.

ORANGE SHERBET

Follow the directions for Lemon Sherbet, page 201, using, in place of the lemon rind and juice, the grated rind of 1 orange and 1½ cups orange juice, sieved. Dissolve the gelatin by heating the orange juice and stirring the gelatin in it. Allow it to cool before continuing with the recipe.

ORANGE SOUFFLE

So easy. So elegant.

Serves 6

Preparation: 30 minutes
Cooking: 30 minutes
Preheat oven: 375°

3 Tablespoons butter
3 Tablespoons flour

(1) In a saucepan, melt the butter, add the flour, and, over gentle heat, cook the *roux* for a few minutes.

1 6-oz. can frozen orange juice
   concentrate, fully thawed
¼ cup water

(2) Combine the orange juice and water and gradually add the liquid to the *roux*, stirring constantly. Cook the mixture, stirring, until it is thickened and smooth.

4 egg yolks, lightly beaten

(3) Stir the egg yolks into the orange mixture.

(continued)

½ cup ginger or orange marmalade
¼ cup orange-flavored liqueur

(4) Combine the marmalade and liqueur, stirring to blend the mixture. This sauce may be used as a garnish over the top of the completed souffle, or it may be served separately.

At this point you may stop and continue later.

4 egg whites
Pinch of salt

(5) In a mixing bowl, beat the egg whites until they are frothy. Add the salt and continue beating until the whites are stiff but not dry.

(6) Fold half of the egg whites into the orange mixture. Then lightly fold the orange mixture into the remaining egg whites.

Soft butter
Sugar

(7) Butter and then sugar a 2-quart souffle dish. Into the dish, spoon the souffle mixture and bake it at 375° for 30 minutes, or until it is well puffed and golden.

COLD ORANGE SOUFFLE

Serves 6
Refrigerates

Preparation: 25 minutes
Chilling time: at least 3 hours

Follow the directions for Cold Lime Souffle, page 216, using as the liquid ingredient 1 6-oz. can frozen orange juice concentrate, fully thawed to room temperature. Use ¼ cup of the concentrate to soften the gelatin, and the remaining ½ cup to combine with the zest of 1 orange, whirled in a blender to chop the rind finely.

TANGERINE TART

(American)

Serving: one 9-inch tart
Refrigerates

Preparation: 30 minutes*
Chilling time: at least 3 hours

¼ **cup sugar**
4 **teaspoons cornstarch**
Dash of salt
1⅓ **cups tangerine juice**

(1) In a saucepan, mix the sugar, cornstarch, and salt. Gradually add the tangerine juice and over high heat, cook the mixture, stirring constantly, until it is thickened and smooth. Allow it to cool.

3 **tangerines, peeled, sectioned, all white pith removed, and seeded**

(2) Add the tangerine sections to the cornstarch mixture.

1 **8-oz. package cream cheese**
⅓ **cup orange-flavored liqueur**
1 **9-inch pie shell, baked**

(3) In a mixing bowl, cream together the cheese and liqueur. Spread the mixture evenly over the bottom of the baked pie shell.

(4) Over the cheese, spoon evenly the tangerine mixture. Chill the tart for 3 hours.

* The preparation time does not include readying the pastry, page 438.

ORANGE BUTTER

Serving: about 1 cup

For fruit muffins.
Follow the directions for Crepes Suzette Sauce, page 253, omitting the orange-flavored liqueur and chilling the prepared butter until it is firm.

ORANGE DRESSING

Serving: 1¼ cups

For fruit salads, for mild-tasting green salads, and for salad herbs with decided flavors, such as watercress and arugola.

⅓ cup frozen orange juice
   concentrate, thawed
⅔ cup olive or salad oil
2 Tablespoons lemon juice
½ teaspoon salt
¼ teaspoon dry mustard
½ teaspoon white pepper
   Grated rind of 1 orange

In a jar with a tight-fitting lid, combine all the ingredients and shake them vigorously until the sugar and salt are dissolved. If desired, the dressing may be prepared by combining the ingredients in the container of an electric blender and whirling them on medium speed for 15 seconds.

ORANGE MAYONNAISE

Serving: 1½ cups

1 egg
½ teaspoon dry mustard
½ teaspoon salt
4 Tablespoons frozen orange juice
   concentrate, thawed
1 Tablespoon lemon juice or cider
   vinegar
¼ cup olive or salad oil
   Grated rind of 1 orange

(1) In the container of an electric blender, combine these seven ingredients and, on medium speed, whirl them for 15 seconds.

¾ cup olive or salad oil

(2) Without turning off the motor, add the oil in a slow, steady stream. As soon as the oil has been absorbed, turn off the motor.

ORANGE SAUCE I

For desserts. Serve either warm or chilled.

Serving: 1 cup
Doubles
Refrigerates

Preparation: 20 minutes

1 cup orange juice, sieved Grated rind of 1 orange ¼ cup sugar 2 Tablespoons cornstarch Pinch of salt	(1) In the container of an electric blender, whirl these five ingredients at medium speed for 15 seconds, or until the mixture is homogenous.
2 Tablespoons soft butter ¼ cup orange-flavored liqueur (optional)	(2) In a saucepan, over high heat, cook the orange juice mixture, stirring constantly, until it is thickened and smooth. Stir in first the butter and then the liqueur.

ORANGE SAUCE II

A more elegant dessert sauce than the preceding one.

Serving: 2½ cups
Refrigerates (for a few hours)

Preparation: 20 minutes
Chilling time: 1 hour

1 cup sugar 5 Tablespoons flour Pinch of salt	(1) In the top of a double boiler, mix the sugar, flour, and salt.
Grated rind of 1 orange ½ cup orange juice Juice of ½ lemon 3 egg yolks, lightly beaten	(2) To the contents of the double boiler, add the orange rind and juice, the lemon juice, and egg yolks. Over simmering water, cook the mixture, stirring constantly, until it is thickened and coats the spoon.

1 **Tablespoon soft butter**

(4) Stir in the butter and cool the sauce.

1 **cup heavy cream, whipped**

(5) Into the sauce, fold the whipped cream. Chill the sauce.

ORANGE SAUCE III

For basting grilled meats and poultry.

>Serving: 3 cups
>Refrigerates

Preparation: 40 minutes

1 **cup olive oil**
3 **onions, chopped**
4 **cloves garlic chopped**

(1) In a saucepan, heat the oil and cook the onions and garlic until translucent.

3 **ripe tomatoes, chopped**
1 **cup dry red wine**
  Grated rind of 2 oranges
½ **cup orange juice**
½ **cup dark brown sugar**
¼ **cup parsley, chopped**
¼ **cup green pepper, chopped**
  Juice of 1 lemon
1 **teaspoon rosemary**
2 **Tablespoons Lea & Perrins Worcestershire Sauce**

(2) To the contents of the saucepan, add the remaining ingredients, and, over low heat, simmer the sauce, covered, for 25 minutes. Sieve it.

  Salt

(3) Correct the seasoning, if necessary, by adding a little salt.

ORANGE STUFFING

For roast lamb, pork, and poultry.

For *each* 4 cups of seasoned breadcrumbs, seasoned croutons, or packaged dressing:

Grated rind of 1 orange ½ **cup orange juice** 1 **orange, peeled, all white pith removed, segmented; the segments seeded and halved** 2 **stalks celery, finely chopped** 4 **Tablespoons butter, melted**	In a large mixing bowl, combine these five ingredients. To them, add 4 cups of breadstuff of your choice. Using two forks, quickly toss the mixture until it is well blended and uniformly moist.

ORANGEADE

For 1 person

When I was a child, I recall, one of the happier accompaniments to being ill was Mother's orangeade, made with the white of egg. The drink was cool, foamy, and nourishing. Now, a distressing number of years later, I still find the ade cool, foamy, and a pleasant midsummer's-day pick-up.

Juice of 3 oranges **Sugar** **White of 1 egg**	In a mixing bowl, combine the orange juice and sugar, to taste; add the egg white and beat the mixture vigorously until it is frothy. Pour it over cracked ice in a chilled glass.

FARMER'S BISHOP

A "bishop" was originally a red-wine based drink, and its name derives from its color. Bishops were common drinks in Tudor England. Farmer's bishop is so-called because of using plebian cider for the more aristocratic wine.

25 servings
Refrigerates

Preparation: 1 hour
Preheat oven: 400°

6 **oranges, each stuck with 12** **whole cloves**	(1) In a roasting pan, bake the oranges at 400° for 35 minutes, or until the juice begins to run from them.

(continued)

265

1 cup sugar
1 quart rum

(2) In a large saucepan, arrange the oranges; to them add the sugar and then the rum. Over gentle heat, cook the oranges until the sugar is dissolved. Remove the saucepan from the heat.

If the farmer's bishop is not to be served at once, *at this point you may stop and continue later*. The contents of the saucepan may be cooled and stored, tightly covered, at room temperature. (I have kept the mixture for up to four years.)

2 quarts cider, warmed
Cinnamon
Nutmeg

(3) In a large heat-proof bowl, put the warm oranges and rum. Ignite the rum. After a few seconds, add the cider. Season the individual servings with a dusting of cinnamon and nutmeg.

If the oranges are used again, add more rum to them.

PEACHES

Traveling westward from China, where written accounts of the fruit, *tao*, had appeared since 500 B.C., traders carried the peach (*Prunus persica*) from its original home to northern India, southeast Russia, and Persia. (The botanical name for the peach derives from a former belief, now discredited, that it originated in Persia.) From here, the fruit found its way to Greece; in 328 B.C., Alexander the Great ate it when camping at Samarkand, now part of Russia. Virgil sang the praises of peaches, and his compatriots spread the delicacy throughout Europe. Predictably, Spanish explorers brought peaches to Mexico and the New World in the late sixteenth century. The Indians, as well as colonists, were responsible for their spread on this continent.

Today, America produces nearly one-half of the world's peach crop, and most of the leading

thirteen commercial varieties, such as the free-stone Elberta, have been developed in this country. Italy, the leading European grower, is followed by France, Spain, and Greece. The nearly 2,000 varieties and the many uses of the fruit make the peach tree the third most important of the deciduous fruits, following closely the apple and pear.

The yellow-fleshed peach is four times richer in vitamin A than the orange. It is very low in caloric count; T. S. Eliot's J. Alfred Prufrock, worrying about his fading looks, asks "Do I dare to eat a peach?" Peaches are, however, highly subject to climatic conditions, a fact determining where they may be successfully produced; they are benefitted by cover crops in winter as protection of their roots.

Members of the Rose Family (*Rosaceae*), peaches are botanical cousins of cherries, plums, and apricots, the other principal drupes, or stone fruits. The bearded peach's sister, the smooth-skinned nectarine (*Prunus persica*, var. *nectarina*), is not, as some believe, a plum graft, but merely another form of peach. Sometimes both nectarines and peaches are found on the same tree as a result of bud variation or sporting. There are twelve common varieties of nectarine.

For centuries the cultivation and selection of peaches took place in the gardens of nobility, who alone enjoyed their delicate goodness. Commercial production is a nineteenth-century development in the United States. The medium-sized tree, with its glossy lance-shaped leaves and pink or white blossoms, rarely attains a height of 25 feet. It requires, however, constant pruning, for the tree overproduces its heavy fruit (which is 87 percent water), thus breaking its branches, which in turn necessitates unripe picking or mechanical bolstering of the limbs. Perhaps for these reasons, the life of the peach tree is short; eight to ten years is normal and a tree of twenty years is considered venerable indeed.

Gastronomically, the peach is best known through a dinner given by the singer Nellie Melba at London's elegant Savoy Hotel in 1892. Escoffier, the chef of the hotel, created Peach Melba for the occasion: around a swan carved in ice—recalling "Lohengrin"—were poached peaches on a bed of vanilla ice cream. It was later, at London's Carlton Hotel in 1899, that Escoffier embellished his dessert with additions of fresh raspberry puree and shredded green almonds.

In these recipes, ripe fresh peaches and nectarines may be used interchangeably.

BEEF AND PEACHES

Serves 6
Doubles
Refrigerates

Preparation: 30 minutes
Cooking: 2½ hours
Preheat oven: 300°

4-lb. boneless chuck steak
Salt
Pepper

(1) Season the meat to taste with salt and pepper. Arrange it in a casserole.

2 onions, coarsely chopped
1 12-oz. can peach nectar, plus
water to equal 2 cups
Grated rind and juice of 1 lemon
1 teaspoon salt
¼ teaspoon pepper
½ teaspoon cinnamon
1 teaspoon ground cumin
1 Tablespoon cornstarch
2 large ripe peaches, seeded
and coarsely chopped

(2) In the container of an electric blender, combine these ten ingredients and, on medium speed, whirl them until the mixture is smooth.

(3) Pour the sauce over the meat and bake the casserole, covered, at 300° for 2½ hours.

At this point you may stop and continue later.

3 large ripe peaches, halved and
seeded

(4) Arrange the fruit, skin side up, on the meat and continue to bake the dish, covered, for 15 minutes, or until the beef is tender.

CHICKEN AND PEACHES

(Polynesian)

Serves 6
Doubles
Refrigerates

Preparation: 30 minutes
Cooking: 1 hour
Preheat oven: 350°

2 Tablespoons butter
2 Tablespoons oil
Serving-pieces of chicken for 6 persons
Salt
Pepper

(1) In a flame-proof casserole, heat the butter and oil and brown the chicken; season it. Remove.

1 onion, chopped
1 green pepper, cut in julienne
2 tomatoes, peeled, seeded, and chopped

(2) In the remaining fat, cook the onion and pepper until translucent, stir in the tomatoes.

2 Tablespoons cornstarch
2 cups peach nectar (unsweetened, if available)
2 Tablespoons soy sauce
3 Tablespoons cider vinegar

(3) Mix the cornstarch with a little of the peach nectar. Add the remaining liquids and cornstarch mixture to the contents of the casserole. Cook the mixture, stirring constantly, until it is thickened and smooth. Replace the chicken.

At this point you may stop and continue later.

4 to 6 firm ripe peaches*, peeled, seeded and cut into eighths

(4) Bake the casserole, covered, at 350° for 40 minutes. Add the peach segments and continue cooking the chicken, covered, for 20 minutes longer, or until it is tender.

* This dish may also be prepared with canned peaches; use a 1 lb.-13 oz. can of sliced peaches, reserving the liquid to make the sauce; augment the liquid with water, if necessary, to equal 2 cups.

A variation (not Polynesian): following the browning of the chicken, warm, ignite, and pour over ¼ cup peach brandy, allowing it to burn itself out; as liquid for the sauce, use 1 10½-oz. can condensed chicken broth, ½ cup peach brandy, and water to equal 2 cups; flavor the sauce with ¼ teaspoon ground clove; for the final 20 minutes of cooking, add, with the peaches, ⅓ cup toasted slivered almonds.

CHICKEN AND PEACHES WITH BULGUR

Serves 6
Doubles
Refrigerates
Freezes

Preparation: 45 minutes
Cooking: 1 hour
Preheat oven: 350°

2 Tablespoons butter **2 Tablespoons oil** **Serving-pieces of chicken for 6 persons** **Salt** **Pepper**	(1) In a flame-proof casserole, heat the butter and oil and brown the chicken; season it. Remove.
2 onions, chopped	(2) In the remaining fat, cook the onions until translucent.
1½ cups bulgur **1 teaspoon cinnamon** **1 teaspoon ground ginger** **1 teaspoon salt**	(3) Add the bulgur, stirring to coat each grain. Stir in the seasonings. Remove the bulgur to a side dish.
12 to 18 dried peach halves	(4) In the casserole, arrange in layers the chicken, bulgur, and peaches; repeat, ending with a layer of the fruit. *At this point you may stop and continue later.*

(continued)

1 12-oz. can peach nectar
1 10½-oz. can condensed chicken broth
Water

(5) Combine the nectar and broth; add water to equal 3 cups. Bring the liquid to the boil, pour it over the contents of the casserole, and bake the dish, covered, at 350° for 1 hour, or until the chicken is tender and the liquid is absorbed.

DUCK AND PEACHES

Serves 4
Doubles
Refrigerates

Preparation: 1 hour
Cooking: 30 minutes
Preheat oven: 400°/325°

Salt
Pepper
Paprika
1 5- to 6-lb. duck, quartered

(1) With the salt, pepper, and paprika, rub the portions of duck. Arrange them on a broiling rack, fat side up, puncture them in several places with a fork, and roast them at 400° for 10 minutes. Reduce the heat to 325° and continue roasting for 50 minutes. Arrange the pieces of duck in a baking dish and discard all but 4 Tablespoons of the fat.

2 onions, chopped
1 carrot, scraped and thinly sliced
Reserved duck liver, chopped

(2) In a skillet, heat the duck fat and in it cook the onions, carrot, and liver until the onion is translucent.

1 cup dry red wine
1 cup peach nectar
4 teaspoons cornstarch
1 teaspoon Lea & Perrins Worcestershire Sauce

(3) Combine the wine and broth. Into a little of the liquid, stir the cornstarch. Add the liquids and the cornstarch to the contents of the skillet and, over high heat, cook the mixture, stirring constantly, until it is thickened and smooth. Stir in the Worcestershire sauce.

3 to 4 firm, ripe peaches*, peeled, halved, and seeded

(4) Arrange the peach halves over the duck pieces, round side up. Pour the sauce over the peaches.

At this point you may stop and continue later.

(5) Bake the dish, covered, at 325° for 30 minutes.

* If desired, the dish may be made with one 1 lb.-13 oz. can of sliced peaches; use the liquid to make the sauce.

ROAST DUCK AND PEACHES

Serves 4
Doubles

Preparation: 30 minutes
Cooking: 2½–3 hours
Preheat oven: 350°

1 1 lb.-13 oz. can sliced peaches
1 onion, chopped
1 cup breadcrumbs
½ teaspoon salt
½ teaspoon paprika

(1) Drain the peaches, reserving the liquid. Chop the peach slices. In a mixing bowl, combine the chopped peaches and the remaining four ingredients. Toss them together with two forks until they are blended.

1 5- or 6-lb. duck

(2) Stuff the duck with the peach-breadcrumb mixture; truss it.

Reserved peach liquid
½ cup port wine

(3) Arrange the duck on a rack in a roasting pan, breast side up. Puncture it in several places with a fork. Roast the duck at 350°, allowing 30 minutes to the pound. Baste it every 10 minutes with a mixture of the peach liquid and wine.

(continued)

273

2 **Tablespoons flour**
Water
Salt

(4) Remove the duck to a serving platter and keep it warm. Skim the excess fat from the pan juices, and discard it. Stir the flour into the pan juices and, adding water as necessary for the desired consistency, cook the mixture, stirring constantly, until it is thickened and smooth. Correct the seasoning. Sieve the sauce and serve it separately.

FISH FILETS AND PEACHES

I first enjoyed this dish at a restaurant in Amsterdam, where the menu listed it as "Filets Picasso." I have never seen the name since, but have prepared the recipe often.

Serves 6
Doubles

Preparation: 30 minutes
Cooking: 20 minutes
Preheat oven: 400°

¼ **lb. butter, cooked until slightly browned**
Fish filets for 6 persons, page xv
Salt
Pepper

(1) With a little of the browned butter, lightly grease a baking dish. In the dish, arrange the fish filets; season them with a sprinkling of salt and pepper. Pour the remaining butter over the fish.

3 **or 4 firm, ripe peaches, peeled, seeded and sliced (sliced canned peaches may be used, if desired)**
¼ **cup preserved ginger, finely chopped**

(2) Over the fish, arrange the peach slices and chopped ginger.

1 **cup peach nectar**
1 **Tablespoon cornstarch, mixed with 2 Tablespoons water**
2 **Tablespoons lemon juice**

(3) In a saucepan, combine these three ingredients and, over high heat, cook the mixture, stirring constantly, until it is thickened and smooth. Pour the sauce over the fish.

At this point you may stop and continue later.

(4) Bake the filets, uncovered, at 400° for 20 minutes, or until they flake easily.

PEACH MUFFINS

Follow the directions for Apple Muffins, page 19, using, in place of the apple, 1 cup of chopped ripe peaches.

BAKED PEACHES

A very old dessert, known throughout Europe for centuries. It appears in English cooking books of the Tudor era.

Serves 6
Doubles
Refrigerates

Preparation: 30 minutes
Cooking: 20 minutes
Preheat oven: 350°
Chilling time: at least 2 hours

6 ripe, whole peaches, peeled

(1) In a baking dish, arrange the peaches.

1 cup sugar
Zest and juice of 1 lemon
½ teaspoon mace
1 cup port wine (or dry red or white wine)

(2) In a saucepan, combine these five ingredients. Over high heat, bring them to the boil, stirring to dissolve the sugar.

(3) Pour the wine mixture over the peaches and bake them, covered, at 350° for 20 minutes, basting them occasionally with the pan juices.

(4) Cool the peaches in the baking dish. Chill them for 2 hours. Serve them topped with a spoonful of the syrup.

PEACH COBBLER

(American)

Follow the directions for Apple Cobbler, page 23, using, in place of the apples, 3 cups of sliced ripe peaches, peeled and sprinkled with lemon juice.

PEACH CUSTARD

(American)

The delicate flavor of fresh peaches in a rich custard.

Serves 6
Doubles
Refrigerates

Preparation: 30 minutes
Cooking: 35 minutes
Preheat oven: 325°

3 ripe peaches	(1) In a saucepan, cook the peaches in boiling water to cover for 3 minutes. Drain them and cover them with cold water. Peel, halve, and seed them. Arrange each half, cut side down, in individual baking dishes, or, if preferred, in a single layer in one large baking dish.
1 cup milk **1 cup heavy cream**	(2) In a saucepan, combine the milk and cream and scald them. Remove the saucepan from the heat.
3 eggs **2 egg yolks** **¼ cup sugar** **1 teaspoon vanilla** **Pinch of salt**	(3) In a mixing bowl, beat the eggs and yolks until they begin to thicken. Beat in the sugar. Add the hot milk, beating constantly, in a slow stream. Add the vanilla and salt.
Nutmeg	(4) Pour the custard over the peaches. Garnish with a grating of nutmeg.

(5) Place the dishes (or dish) in a shallow pan of boiling water on the middle rack of the oven. Bake the custard at 325° for 35 minutes, or until a knife inserted at the center comes out clean. Cool the custard; serve the dessert either chilled or at room temperature.

PEACH ICE CREAM WITH GINGER

(American)

This recipe is from the southern United States. The ginger provides a pleasant accent.

Follow the directions for Helen McCully's Ice Cream, page 457, adding 4 ripe peaches, peeled, seeded, and chopped, and ¼ cup preserved ginger, finely chopped, to the hot custard before cooking it.

PEACH KUCHEN

(German)

A classic German dessert, peach *Kuchen* is closely related to the American cobbler. There is sufficient difference, however, to warrant its inclusion here.

Serves 6
Doubles
Refrigerates

Preparation: 30 minutes
Cooking: 45 minutes
Preheat oven: 400°

2 cups flour
½ teaspoon baking powder
Pinch of salt
3 Tablespoons sugar

(1) In a mixing bowl, sift together these four ingredients.

(continued)

8 **Tablespoons soft butter**

(2) Add the butter and, working rapidly with the fingertips or a pastry blender, mix the ingredients until their consistency is a crumbly meal.

(3) Into a 8-inch baking pan, pat the dough evenly over the bottom and halfway up the sides.

6 **ripe peaches, peeled, seeded, and sliced**
1 **teaspoon cinnamon**
¼ **cup sugar**

(4) In an overlapping pattern, arrange the peach slices over the dough. Combine the cinnamon and sugar and sprinkle the mixture evenly over the peaches.

2 **egg yolks**
1 **cup sour cream**

(5) Bake the *Kuchen* at 400° for 15 minutes.

(6) Meanwhile, in a mixing bowl, beat together the egg yolks and sour cream. Pour the mixture over the dessert and continue to bake it for 30 minutes longer.

PEACH MELBA

For a note on this celebrated dessert, see page 268.

Serves 6
Doubles

Preparation: 1 hour*
Chilling time: 2 hours

1½ **cups water**
1 **cup sugar**

(1) In a saucepan, combine the water and sugar; bring the mixture to the boil, stirring constantly. Allow it to boil, uncovered, for 5 minutes.

* The preparation time does not include making the ice cream.

6 ripe peaches, peeled, halved, and seeded

(2) Add the peaches to the syrup and cook, uncovered, for 10 minutes. With a slotted spoon, remove them to a bowl, allow them to cool, and chill for 1 hour. (Allow the syrup to continue boiling while you complete step #3.)

1 9-oz. package frozen raspberries, fully thawed

(3) Sieve the raspberries and add the pulp to the syrup. Remove the mixture from the heat, allow it to cool, and chill it for 1 hour.

At this point you may stop and continue later.

Hellen McCully's Ice Cream (see page 457)

(4) Around the ice cream, arrange the peach halves. When serving the dessert, offer the raspberry sauce separately. This dessert may also be made with ripe, firm pears.

PEACH MOUSSE

(Brazilian)

Serves 6
Refrigerates

Preparation: 35 minutes
Chilling time: at least 3 hours

Ripe peaches, peeled, chopped, and sieved to equal 1¼ cups
¾ cup sugar
Pinch of salt

(1) In a mixing bowl, stir together these three ingredients and set them aside.

1½ packets unflavored gelatin
¼ cup orange-flavored liqueur
½ cup heavy cream

(2) Soak the gelatin in the liqueur for 5 minutes. Add the cream and, in the top of a double boiler, bring the mixture to the boil, stirring to dissolve the gelatin.

(continued)

2 **egg yolks, lightly beaten**
½ **teaspoon vanilla**

(3) Add the egg yolks and, over simmering water, cook the mixture, stirring constantly, until the custard coats the spoon. Stir in the vanilla and the peach mixture. Allow the custard to cool.

1½ **cups heavy cream, whipped**

(4) In a mixing bowl, fold together the custard and whipped cream.

(5) Pour the mousse into a 1-quart ring mold, rinsed with cold water. Chill the dessert for at least 3 hours.

3 **or 4 ripe peaches, peeled and
   sliced
   Juice ½ lemon
   Sugar
   Preserved kumquats (optional),
   page 436**

(6) Meanwhile, toss the peaches with the lemon juice; add the sugar and allow them to stand for 1 hour. Onto a serving dish, unmold the mousse and arrange the sliced peaches in the center of the ring. (If desired, a few preserved kumquats may be added to the sliced peaches.)

PEACH PIE

(American)

Peach pie, while not as celebrated, perhaps, as apple or blueberry pie, is a classic dessert of American cuisine.

Follow the directions for Apple Pie, page 27, using, in place of the apples, 5 cups peeled, sliced ripe peaches.

PEACH PUFF

Follow the directions for Strawberry Puff, page 379, using, in place of the strawberries, 3 cups peeled, sliced ripe peaches.

PEACHES IN SOUR CREAM

Serves 6
Doubles
Refrigerates

Preparation: 30 minutes
Chilling time: at least 2 hours

6 to 9 ripe peaches, peeled, seeded, and sliced
Juice of 1 lemon

(1) In a china or silver bowl, arrange the peaches. Sprinkle them with the lemon juice and toss them gently to cover the slices.

1 cup sour cream
⅓ cup maple syrup or orange-flavored liqueur

(2) Combine the sour cream and syrup (or liqueur) and fold the mixture into the peaches. Chill the dessert for 2 hours before serving.

This dessert may be made with various other fruits: fresh pineapple, bananas, strawberries, blueberries, pears—or a combination of your choice.

PEARS

Homer mentions pears as a fruit in the garden of Alcinous. In 100 B.C., the Romans cultivated six varieties of pears; by 100 A.D., forty-one varieties were grown throughout the empire and spread, with the Roman conquests, throughout Europe. The Romans considered pears a luxury, however, and Pliny said that "All pears whatsoever are but a heavy meat, unless they are well boiled or baked." At the time of Christ, grafting to improve the fruit was a common practice. Today there are thousands of varieties of pears, some brought to America by the northern colonists and the Spanish Mission Fathers. In America, pears were nearly as important to the pioneer as were apples; the fruit was eaten, the wood was valued for furniture and tools, the leaves produced a yellow dye, and from the juice pear cider—perry—was made.

Pyrus communis, a member of the Rose Family,

originated in southeast Europe and western Asia. The pear tree, requiring more care than many other fruits, is taller and more upright than the apple. Its foliage is rather oval-shaped and leathery, its blossom is white. The fruit, usually elongated, is sometimes round, especially in the Oriental varieties, and contains more protein, minerals, and sugar, but less vitamin A, than apples. The water content and caloric value are the same as those of apples. Less resistant to cold than the apple tree, the pear blooms earlier in the spring and thus is more susceptible to late frosts, despite its requiring winter cold during the dormant period. It is a long-lived tree (fifty to seventy-five years) and bears when between five and seven years of age.

Total pear production equals about 5 million tons a year, surpassing that of peaches, plums, and cherries. One-half of this output is from Europe, where Italy is the world's leading grower. In the United States, the second largest producer, California, Oregon, and Washington yield 90 percent of the domestic crop. China, Japan, Turkey, Argentina, Austria, and South Africa are among other important pear-growers. In the United States, one-half of the crop is canned; in Europe, canning is only of minor importance. Thirty percent of the French crop is made into perry.

The principal varieties grown in the United States are Giffard, Bartlett, Gorham, Seckel, Cayuga, Comice, Bosc, and Anjou. The European name for the Bartlett pear is Williams Bon Chrétien, known simply as Williams, so-called for the nurseryman who introduced it to the market. Upon its importation to the New World, however, the name changed, at least in the United States, to Bartlett, for the nurseryman, Enoch Bartlett of Dorchester, Massachussetts, who perhaps shrewdly foresaw that "Bartletts" would one day be the most famous of all "American" pears, making up 75 percent of our domestic crop.

PEAR SOUP

A delicate soup, best made with firm ripe fresh fruit, but also good made with canned pears, well drained—or, if desired, with 3 large ripe apples, peeled, cored, and chopped.

> Serves 6
> Doubles
> Refrigerates
> Freezes

Preparation: 35 minutes
Chilling time: 2 hours

4 scallions, chopped
1 onion, chopped
2 medium potatoes, peeled and chopped
2 10½-oz. cans condensed chicken broth
Pinch of white pepper

(1) In a saucepan, combine these five ingredients, bring them to the boil, reduce the heat, and simmer them, covered, for 20 minutes, or until they are very tender. In the container of an electric blender, whirl them on high speed for 15 seconds, or until the mixture is smooth.

3 large, ripe pears, peeled, cored, and chopped

(2) To the contents of the blender, add the pears, and whirl them until the mixture is smooth.

3 cups cold milk
Salt
Chopped chives or paprika

(3) Combine the pear mixture and the milk, adjust the seasoning, and chill the soup. When serving the soup, garnish it with chopped chives or paprika.

LAMB AND PEARS*

This light and refreshing dish goes well with rice.

Serves 6
Doubles
Refrigerates

Preparation: 30 minutes
Cooking: 1½ hours
Preheat oven: 350°

2 Tablespoons butter
2 Tablespoons oil
3 lbs. boneless lean lamb cut in
   bite-sized pieces
Salt
Pepper

(1) In a flame-proof casserole, heat the butter and oil and brown the lamb; season it. Remove it to absorbent paper and discard the remaining fat.

2 1-lb. cans pear halves
3 Tablespoons cider vinegar
1 Tablespoon Lea & Perrins
   Worcestershire Sauce
2 Tablespoons brown sugar
3 Tablespoons cornstarch, mixed
   with a little cold water
½ teaspoon nutmeg

(2) Drain the pears, reserving the liquid. In the casserole, combine the pear liquid and the remaining five ingredients and, over high heat, cook the mixture, stirring constantly, until it is thickened and smooth. Replace the lamb, spooning the sauce over it.

At this point you may stop and continue later.

6 scallions, chopped, with as much
   green as possible
3 or 4 stalks celery
1 green pepper, seeded and cut in
   julienne
Reserved pear halves

(3) Bake the lamb, covered, at 350° for 1½ hours. Add, in order, the vegetables and pears during the final 15 minutes of cooking.

* This recipe is a most welcome contribution from Metropolitan Opera *diva* Martina Arroyo, whom I first met when she was brought as a charming guest to a picnic at my home. By the afternoon's end, she was captain of a touch-football game, had helped lay out the supper, and concluded, after it was eaten, by doing much of the washing up. To compare this warm-hearted exuberance with the touching simplicity of her Madama Butterfly or the statuesque nobility of her Leonore (in *Il Trovatore*) is to have some intimation of her personality.

LAMB SHANKS AND PEARS

Follow the directions for Lamb Shanks and Grapes, page 157, using, in place of the grapes, 12 *dried* pear halves, added for the final 50 minutes of cooking.

CHICKEN AND PEARS

(Middle Eastern)

Serves 6
Doubles
Refrigerates

Preparation: 30 minutes
Cooking: 1 hour
Preheat oven: 350°

2 Tablespoons butter
2 Tablespoons oil
Serving-pieces of chicken for 6 persons
Salt
Pepper

(1) In a flame-proof casserole, heat the butter and oil and brown the chicken; season it. Remove.

2 onions, chopped

(2) In the remaining fat, cook the onions until translucent.

1 Tablespoon flour
½ teaspoon salt
¼ teaspoon pepper
1 teaspoon curry powder
Sprig of fresh mint, chopped
Zest and juice of 1 lemon
2 Tablespoons brown sugar

(3) Add the flour, stirring until it is well blended with the onions; stir in the remaining seven ingredients.

1 10½-oz. can condensed chicken broth
2 firm-fleshed ripe pears, peeled, cored, and coarsely chopped

(4) Gradually add the broth, stirring constantly until the sauce is thickened and smooth. Replace the chicken and top with the pears.

At this point you may stop and continue later.

4 firm-fleshed ripe pears, peeled, cored, and cut into eighths lengthwise

(5) Bake the casserole, covered, at 350° for 40 minutes. Add the pear slices and continue to cook the dish, covered, for 20 minutes, or until the chicken and pears are tender.

For a stronger taste of the fruit, increase the flour to 2 Tablespoons and for the chicken broth substitute one 1-lb. can Bartlett pear slices, pureed in an electric blender.

This recipe is adapted from one for veal and pears. If desired, the dish may be made with veal by using 2½ lbs. boneless meat, cut in bite-sized pieces, and by increasing the cooking time to 1½ hours, or until the meat is tender.

CHICKEN AND PEARS WITH RICE

Serves 6
Doubles
Refrigerates

Preparation: 30 minutes
Cooking: 1 hour
Preheat oven: 350°

2 Tablespoons butter
2 Tablespoons oil
Serving-pieces of chicken for 6 persons
Salt
Pepper

(1) In a flame-proof casserole, heat the butter and oil and brown the chicken; season it. Remove.

2 onions, chopped

(2) In the remaining fat, cook the onion until translucent.

1½ cups natural raw rice
2 teaspoons ground cumin
1 teaspoon nutmeg
1 teaspoon salt

(3) Add the rice, stirring to coat each grain. Stir in the seasonings. Remove the rice.

12 to 18 dried pear halves

(4) In the casserole, arrange in layers the chicken, rice, and dried pears; repeat, ending with a layer of the fruit.

(continued)

At this point you may stop and continue later.

1 **1-lb. can sliced Bartlett pears, sieved or whirled in a blender**
1 **10½-oz. can condensed chicken broth**
   Water

(5) Combine the pear puree and broth; add water to equal 3 cups. Bring the liquid to the boil, pour it over the contents of the casserole, and bake the dish, covered, at 350° for 1 hour, or until the chicken is tender and the liquid is absorbed.

CHICKEN AND PEARS WITH VEGETABLES

(Chinese)

Serves 6
Doubles
Refrigerates

Preparation: 45 minutes
Cooking: 15 minutes

2 **Tablespoons oil**
2 **whole chicken breasts, boned and cut into 2-inch julienne**

(1) In a *wok* or casserole, heat the oil and in it stir-fry the chicken for 2 minutes.

1 **10½-oz. can condensed chicken broth**
1 **6-oz. can water chestnuts, drained and sliced**
1 **9-oz. package frozen small peas, fully thawed to room temperature**
6 **scallions, chopped diagonally, with as much green as possible**

(2) To the chicken, add these four ingredients, bring the liquid to the boil, and cook them for 2 minutes.

4 **firm, ripe pears, peeled, cored, and cut into ½-inch dice (or Prepared dried pears and liquid***
4 **teaspoons cornstarch, mixed with 4 teaspoons soy sauce**

(3) Add the pears and cornstarch mixture. Over high heat, cook the dish, stirring constantly, until the sauce is thickened and smooth.

* If desired, the dish may be made with 8 *dried* pear halves, chopped, soaked in 1 10½-oz. can condensed chicken broth, brought to the boil and removed from the heat. Use this mixture in place of the fresh pears, but, because the dried pears will have "drunk" the liquid, use a second can of broth.

FISH FILETS AND PEARS*

Serves 6
Doubles
Refrigerates

Preparation: 20 minutes
Cooking: 20 minutes
Preheat oven: 400°

Butter
Fish filets for 6 persons, page xv
Salt
Pepper

(1) In a lightly buttered baking dish, arrange the fish filets in a single layer. Season them with salt and pepper.

3 firm, ripe pears, peeled, quartered, and cored
Juice of 1 lemon

(2) Allowing two pear quarters per serving, cut the quarters into thin slices, arrange them over the filets, and sprinkle them with lemon juice.

¼ cup parsley, finely chopped

(3) Bake the fish at 400° for 20 minutes; sprinkle them with parsley before serving.

Variations: This dish may also be made with bluefish filet, which will require 30 minutes to cook.

If desired, add Ribier grapes, halved and seeded; arrange them over the filets skin side up before adding the pears.

* This recipe is contributed by Oliver Smith, the well-known stage-set designer of *My Fair Lady, Hello, Dolly!,* and a host of other distinguished productions. For over a quarter of a century a luminary of our stage, he is also co-producer, with Lucia Chase, of the American Ballet Theater. As my neighbor in the country, however, he is thought of less in connection with stage fame and more in terms of companionable evenings in front of a winter's fire, where we are warmed, inside and out, by good food, good drink, and good talk.

POTATO AND PEAR SALAD
(Swiss)

A novel idea for a salad which, to many, means just mayonnaise and hardboiled eggs mixed with potato.

Serves 6
Doubles
Refrigerates

Preparation: 30 minutes

½ **cup condensed beef broth, hot**
¾ **teaspoon salt**
¼ **teaspoon pepper**
2 **teaspoons prepared Dijon mustard**
1 **Tablespoon red wine vinegar**
3 **Tablespoons oil**

(1) In the container of an electric blender, whirl these six ingredients for 8 to 10 seconds.

4 **medium potatoes, cooked in boiling water to cover and peeled and cubed while warm**
6 **firm, ripe pears, peeled, cored, and coarsely chopped**

(2) In a large mixing bowl, combine the potatoes and pears, add the blended dressing, and, using two forks, gently toss the salad until it is well mixed.

Freshly chopped chives
6 **slices bacon, diced, rendered, and drained on absorbent paper**
Salad greens

(3) Garnish the salad with the chives and bacon bits; serve it on greens of your choice.

PEARS AND CHOCOLATE
(American)

Either fresh or well-drained canned Bartlett pears may be used to make this classic, if unusual, dessert. The secret of the dish is in preparing it long in advance of serving, so that the chocolate flavor permeates the fruit and the sugar in the pears sweetens the cocoa.

Serves 6
Doubles
Refrigerates

Preparation: 10 minutes*
Chilling time: 3 hours

6 fresh firm, ripe Bartlett pears,
peeled, cored (leaving a hollow),
(or 12 canned Barlett pear halves,
well drained)
Unsweetened cocoa

(1) In a serving dish, arrange the pears, cut side up. Put ¾ teaspoon of the cocoa in each of the pear cavities. Cover the pears with wrap to keep them moist; chill them.

Custard Sauce, page 460

(2) Serve the pears, two halves per person, and offer the custard sauce separately.

* The preparation time does not include readying the Custard Sauce.

PEAR COBBLER

(American)

Follow the directions for Apple Cobbler, page 23, using, in place of the apple, firm ripe pears, peeled, cored, and sliced.

PEAR PIE

Serving: one 9-inch pie

Preparation: 30 minutes*
Cooking: 45 minutes
Preheat oven: 425°

½ **cup sugar**
¼ **cup dark brown sugar, packed**
 3 **Tablespoons flour**
½ **teaspoon cinnamon**
¼ **teaspoon ground clove**
½ **teaspoon ground coriander**
½ **teaspoon nutmeg**
  Pinch of salt

(1) In a mixing bowl, sift together these eight ingredients.

* The preparation time does not include readying the pastry, page 458.

(continued)

6 **firm ripe pears, peeled, cored, and sliced**
Grated rind and juice of 1 lemon

(2) Toss the pears with the dry ingredients, adding the lemon rind and juice. Add the pear brandy and toss.

3 **Tablespoons pear brandy (optional)**

(3) Line a pie pan with a bottom crust. Add the pear mixture and dot it with butter. Add a top crust, crimping the edges closed with a fork; cut a few slashes in the top to allow for escaping steam.

Pastry for a two-crust 9-inch pie
Soft butter (optional)

(4) Bake the pie at 425° for 45 minutes, or until the crust is golden brown.

POACHED PEARS

Serves 6
Doubles
Refrigerates

Preparation: 30 minutes
Chilling time: at least 2 hours

6 **firm, ripe pears, peeled, each studded with 4 cloves, and stems attached**

(1) Prepare the pears.

1 **cup sugar**
1 **cup orange juice**
½ **cup lemon juice**
2 **3-inch pieces cinnamon stick**
Pinch of salt

(2) In a saucepan, combine these five ingredients. Bring the mixture to the boil, stirring to dissolve the sugar. Boil the syrup vigorously for 5 minutes.

(3) To the syrup, add the pears. Poach them for 20 minutes, or until they are tender but still hold their shape. Remove the pears to a serving dish.

1 **cup seedless grapes**
  Whipped cream (optional)

(4) Continue boiling the syrup until it is reduced by half. Add the grapes and pour the syrup over pears. Chill the dessert well before serving it. The dessert may be garnished with whipped cream, if desired.

For Pears in Raspberry Sauce: reduce the syrup by half, as done in step 4 above; then, instead of the grapes suggested in the main recipe, add one 9-oz. package frozen raspberries, thawed to room temperature; cook the raspberries, uncovered, for 10 minutes, and sieve the sauce to remove the seeds.

PEARS AND GINGER

Serves 6
Doubles
Refrigerates

Preparation: 40 minutes
Chilling time: 2 hours

2 **cups water**
2 **cups sugar**
3 **3-inch pieces cinnamon stick**
  Piece of fresh ginger, the size of a walnut, chopped
  Zest and juice of 1 lemon

(1) In a saucepan, combine these six ingredients, bring them to the boil and, over high heat, cook them, uncovered, at a rolling boil for 10 minutes.

6 **firm ripe pears, peeled, cored, and quartered**

(2) To the syrup, add the pears and simmer them, uncovered, for 20 minutes, or until they are just tender but still hold their shape. Allow them to cool in the syrup.

3 **or 4 Tablespoons preserved ginger, finely chopped**
  Whipped cream (optional)

(3) With a slotted spoon, remove the pear quarters to a serving dish. Sieve the syrup over them and chill them. Garnish the pears with the preserved ginger. Serve them with whipped cream, if desired.

PEARS AND MADEIRA

Follow the directions for Pears and Ginger, page 293, making the syrup of 2 cups madeira wine, 1⅓ cups sugar, and the zest and juice of 1 lemon. Proceed with poaching the pears as indicated.

PEARS AND ORANGE SAUCE

Follow the directions for Pears and Ginger, page 293, making the syrup of 1½ cups orange juice, ½ cup orange-flavored liqueur, and the zest of 1 orange. Proceed with poaching the pears as indicated.

PEAR PUFF

Follow the directions for Strawberry Puff, page 379, using, in place of the strawberries, 3 cups peeled sliced ripe pears.

PEAR SAUCE

For ice cream and puddings.

Serving: 2½ cups

Preparation: 15 minutes

1 cup water
½ teaspoon ground ginger
3 Tablespoons sugar
Grated rind and juice of ½ lemon
1 ripe pear, peeled, cored, and coarsely chopped

(1) In the container of an electric blender, combine these six ingredients. On medium speed, whirl them for 15 seconds, or until the mixture is smooth.

3 ripe pears, peeled, cored, and coarsely chopped
¼ cup preserved ginger, finely chopped (optional)

(2) To the contents of the blender, add, one at a time, the three pears, whirling them to produce a smooth sauce. Turn off the motor and add the preserved ginger. The sauce is tastiest served at room temperature.

PINEAPPLES

Pineapples, originally growing wild in Brazil, were called *anana* ("excellent fruit") by the Guarani Indians, who cultivated and carried them north and west to the Isthmus of Panama. The Indians had used the pineapple or its plumed top as a symbol of welcome; the pineapple as an architectural motive derives from this tradition.

The first account of pineapples is given by Columbus who, returning from his second voyage, took them to Spain; here they were called *piña de los Indies* ("pine cone of the Indies") because of their resemblance to the pine cone. They were brought to England by Raleigh. In 1670, one of Charles II's gardeners harvested the first English pineapple and, tactfully, presented it to his monarch. Our name for the fruit is an English invention.

The Portuguese are responsible for the early

dissemination of pineapples; in 1502, they introduced them to the island of St. Helena, and from there took them to Madagascar and India. By the close of the sixteenth century, pineapples were cultivated in most tropical regions, including some of the Pacific islands—albeit we do not know with certainty how they got there. Today, however, Hawaii produces about 60 percent of the world's crop, most of which is canned, made into juice, or frozen. The first pineapple canning plant was built in Hawaii in 1892. Other important growers are Brazil, Cuba, Mexico, Formosa, Ceylon, Malaysia, the Philippines, and South Africa. Fifteen- to twenty-thousand plants can be grown to the acre; each plant bears for about ten years, although it is usually replaced after four years or so.

There are many varieties of the cultivated pineapple, *Ananas comosus*. They differ in size, shape, taste, and color of flesh. Pineapples are aggregate fruits, developing from tiny purple flowers clustered on the cone of the stalk. Each of these individual fruits, of which there may be one hundred or more spirally arranged on a thick central axis or core, is, in reality, a berry. Six to seven months are needed for the fruit to mature after the plant has flowered; for maximum flavor, the fruit must ripen on the plant.

In these recipes, fresh pineapple, always preferred unless otherwise indicated, is interchangeable with canned pineapple.

BEEF AND PINEAPPLE

Serves 6
Doubles
Refrigerates

Preparation: 30 minutes
Cooking: 2½ hours
Preheat oven: 300°

2 Tablespoons butter
2 Tablespoons oil
**2½ lbs. boneless chuck, cut in
bite-sized pieces**
Salt
Pepper

(1) In a flame-proof casserole, heat the butter and oil and brown the beef; season it.

**6 Tablespoons quick-cooking
tapioca**
1 bay leaf, broken
**2 teaspoons Lea & Perrins
Worcestershire Sauce**
**1 10½-oz. can condensed
chicken broth**
1 12-oz. can pineapple juice

(2) Sprinkle the tapioca over the meat; add the bay leaf; add the liquids.

At this point you may stop and continue later.

**1 medium pineapple, peeled, and
coarsely chopped**

(3) Bake the casserole, covered, at 300° for 2 hours. Add the pineapple and continue cooking the meat, covered, for 30 minutes longer, or until it is tender.

This dish may be made with chicken, lamb, pork, or veal. *Cooking times:* Chicken: 350° for 1 hour; lamb, pork, and veal: 350° for 1½ hours.

The dish may also be made with one 20-oz. can pineapple chunks: use the liquid in place of the canned pineapple juice; the total liquid ingredient should equal about 3 cups.

GROUND BEEF AND PINEAPPLE

This plain dish is tastiest if prepared and served at one time. At any rate, it is too simple a recipe to warrant stopping now and continuing later. It is pleasant on rice.

Serves 6
Doubles
Refrigerates

Preparation: 15 minutes
Cooking: 35 minutes

2 lbs. ground chuck
Oil, if necessary for browning
4 scallions, chopped, with as much green as possible
1 clove garlic, put through a press
½ cup golden raisins
½ teaspoon ground ginger
1¼ teaspoons salt
1 cup dry red wine

(1) In a large skillet, brown the beef. Add the remaining ingredients and stir to blend them well with the meat. Simmer the meat for 10 minutes.

1 8¾-oz. can pineapple tidbits

(2) Drain the pineapple and reserve the liquid. To the meat, add the pineapple tidbits.

Reserved pineapple liquid
1 Tablespoon cornstarch

(3) Combine the pineapple liquid and cornstarch and add it to the skillet. Cook the meat, stirring, until the sauce is thickened and smooth.

SWEET-AND-PUNGENT MEAT BALLS

(Chinese)

Serves 6
Doubles
Refrigerates
Freezes

Preparation: 25 minutes*
Cooking: 15 minutes

* The preparation time does not include readying the sauce.

1½ **lbs. ground round** 1 **egg** 1 **Tablespoon cornstarch** 1 **small onion, finely chopped** **Pinch of pepper**	(1) In a mixing bowl, combine these five ingredients and blend them thoroughly. Form the meat into balls about 1 inch in diameter.
2 **Tablespoons oil**	(2) In a skillet or saucepan, heat the oil and brown the meat balls well. *At this point you may stop and continue later.*
Sweet-and-Pungent Sauce, page 317 3 **green peppers (optional)**	(3) Add the sauce and, over medium heat, simmer the meat balls, uncovered, for 15 minutes, or until they are heated through. (If desired, 3 green peppers, seeded and cut in julienne may be added with the sauce.)

LAMB SHOULDER AND PINEAPPLE

In this recipe, there is no preparation. Just start the dish 2¼ hours before you wish to serve it, you do not even need to watch it, except to turn it once.

Serves 6
Refrigerates

Cooking: 2¼ hours
Preheat oven: 325°

⅓ **cup oil** 4 **onions, finely chopped** 2 **cloves garlic, finely chopped** ½ **teaspoon ground allspice** 1 **teaspoon cinnamon** 1 **Tablespoon ground coriander** ½ **teaspoon ground cumin** ½ **teaspoon turmeric** 1 **teaspoon salt** ½ **teaspoon pepper**	(1) In a large flame-proof casserole, heat the oil and cook the onions and garlic until translucent. Stir in the seasonings.

(continued)

1 4-lb. boned shoulder of lamb, trimmed of excess fat, rolled, and tied

(2) Add the lamb to the casserole and, over high heat, sear it on all sides, coating well with the onion mixture.

2 12-oz. cans unsweetened pineapple juice

(3) Add the pineapple juice and bake the lamb, covered, at 325° for 1 hour. Turn the lamb and continue baking it, covered, for 1 hour longer.

(4) Remove the lamb to a serving platter and keep it warm. Remove and discard the excess fat from the pan juices.

2 teaspoons cornstarch mixed with 2 Tablespoons cold water
1 ripe pineapple, peeled, cored, and cut into cubes

(5) Over high heat, reduce the pan juices to 1½ cups, add the cornstarch, and, over high heat, cook the mixture, stirring constantly, until it is thickened and smooth. Add the pineapple and simmer the sauce for 15 minutes. Serve the sauce separately.

PORK AND PINEAPPLE

(Polynesian)

Serves 6
Doubles
Refrigerates

Preparation: 45 minutes
Cooking: 1¾ hours
Preheat oven: 325°

1 3- or 4-lb. boneless pork loin (or pork cut in bite-sized pieces)
Salt
4 Tablespoons oil

(1) Rub the meat with salt. In a flame-proof casserole, heat the oil and in it brown the pork, turning it frequently. Remove the meat to absorbent paper and discard all but 2 Tablespoons of the fat.

3 onions, chopped
Ground cumin

(2) In the remaining fat, cook the onions until translucent. Replace the pork and sprinkle it with cumin.

⅓ cup soy sauce
1 12-oz. can unsweetened
  pineapple juice

(3) Combine the liquids, pour them over the pork, and bake the casserole, covered, at 325° for 1½ hours, or until the pork is tender.

At this point you may stop and continue later.

2 cups fresh pineapple, cut in
  chunks (or one 20-oz. can pineapple chunks or 2 packages
  frozen pineapple chunks, fully
  thawed to room temperature)
1 9-oz. package frozen pea pods,
  fully thawed to room
  temperature
1 8-oz. can bamboo shoots
1 green pepper, chopped

(4) Remove the meat to a serving dish and keep it warm. Add the fruit and vegetables to the casserole and allow them to heat through.

2 Tablespoons cornstarch
¼ cup water

(5) Blend the cornstarch and water. Add the liquid to the contents of the casserole, stirring constantly until the sauce is thickened and smooth. Pour the sauce over the pork and serve the dish with rice.

SWEET-AND-PUNGENT PORK

(Chinese)

Serves 6
Doubles
Refrigerates
Freezes

Preparation: 15 minutes*
Cooking: 1 hour

3 Tablespoons oil
1 clove garlic, finely chopped
  Salt
  Pepper
2½ lbs. lean pork, cut in bite-sized
  pieces

(1) In a flame-proof casserole, heat the oil, add the garlic, and, when the oil is flavored, brown the pork; season it. Remove it to absorbent paper; discard the remaining fat. Replace the pork.

* The preparation time does not include readying the sauce.

(continued)

Sweet-and-Pungent Sauce,
page 317
3 Tablespoons sweet sherry

(2) Combine the sauce and sherry and pour the mixture over the pork.

At this point you may stop and continue later.

(3) Simmer the casserole, covered, for 1 hour, or until the pork is tender.

SWEET-AND-PUNGENT SPARERIBS

(Chinese)

Serves 6
Doubles
Refrigerates

Preparation: 1¼ hours
Cooking: 25 minutes
Preheat oven: 325°

6 lbs. spareribs, separated into
serving pieces

(1) On a rack in a roasting pan, arrange the spareribs and bake them at 325° for 1¼ hours. (While the spareribs are baking, make the Sweet-and-Pungent Sauce, page 317.) Discard the excess fat and replace the spareribs without the rack.

Sweet-and-Pungent Sauce
2 green peppers, seeded and
coarsely chopped
1 clove garlic

(2) Combine the sauce and peppers. Add the garlic, putting it through a press. Stir the sauce well and pour it over the spareribs.

At this point you may stop and continue later.

(3) Bake the spareribs, uncovered, at 325° for 25 minutes.

VEAL AND PINEAPPLE WITH CHINESE VEGETABLES

Serves 6
Doubles
Refrigerates

Preparation: 45 minutes
Cooking: 1½ hours

2 Tablespoons butter
2 Tablespoons oil
2½ lbs. boneless veal cut in bite-sized pieces
Salt
Pepper

(1) In a flame-proof casserole, heat the butter and oil and brown the veal; season it. Remove.

2 onions, chopped
1 clove garlic, chopped
1 bay leaf

(2) In the remaining fat, cook the onions and garlic until translucent. Replace the veal. Add the bay leaf.

1 small ripe pineapple, peeled, cored, and coarsely chopped (reserve the juice)
Orange juice
½ cup dry white wine
1 teaspoon salt
¼ teaspoon white pepper
½ teaspoon ground ginger

(3) Strain the pineapple juice to eliminate any of the brownish skin. To it, add orange juice to equal 1¼ cups. Add the wine and seasonings, stirring.

(4) Pour the liquid over the veal, bring it to the boil, reduce the heat, and simmer the casserole, covered, for 1¼ hours, or until the veal is just tender.

At this point you may stop and continue later.

4 teaspoons cornstarch
¼ cup orange juice

(5) Mix the cornstarch and juice. Add the mixture to the simmering casserole, stirring gently until the sauce is thickened and smooth.

(continued)

Reserved pineapple
¼ cup whole almonds (optional)
1 6-oz. can water chestnuts, drained and sliced
1 8-oz. can bamboo shoots, drained
1 9-oz. package frozen pea pods, fully thawed to room temperature
¼ cup preserved ginger, chopped

(6) Stir in the reserved pineapple and remaining ingredients. Heat them and serve the dish with boiled rice.

CURRIED CHICKEN AND PINEAPPLE

Follow the directions for Curried Chicken and Papaya, page 446, using, in place of the papaya, 2 cups fresh pineapple, peeled, cored, and coarsely grated: add the pineapple to the curried chicken and cook it for 2 minutes, or until it is heated through. This dish is very good served with rice.

CHICKEN AND PINEAPPLE WITH CHINESE VEGETABLES*

Serves 6
Doubles
Refrigerates

Preparation: 30 minutes
Cooking: 1½ hours

2 Tablespoons butter
2 Tablespoons oil
Serving-pieces of chicken for 6 persons
Salt
Pepper

(1) In a flame-proof casserole, heat the butter and oil and brown the chicken; season it. Remove it to absorbent paper. Discard all of the remaining fat.

* This recipe is contributed by Robert Schmorr, the talented *comprimario* tenor of the Metropolitan Opera who, despite his un-Chinese name, takes pleasure in offering such fare as this to his friends, musical and non-musical.

1 **12-oz. can unsweetened pine-**
apple juice (or the reserved
liquid from one 20-oz. can
pineapple chunks)
1 **10½-oz. can condensed chicken**
broth
3 **Tablespoons soy sauce**

(2) In the casserole, combine these three ingredients. Over high heat, bring the liquid quickly to the boil and deglaze the casserole. Replace the chicken, reduce the heat, and simmer it, covered, for 1 hour, or until it is tender. Remove it to a serving plate and cover it to prevent its drying.

At this point you may stop and continue later.

2 **cups fresh pineapple, peeled**
and cut into chunks (or one 20-
oz. can pineapple chunks,
drained)
1 **9-oz. package frozen pea pods,**
fully thawed to room
temperature
1 **8-oz. can bamboo shoots, drained**
1 **6-oz. can water chestnuts, sliced**
6 **or 8 scallions, sliced, with as**
much green as possible
½ **cup chopped celery (optional)**

(3) While the chicken is being brought to serving temperature in a warm oven, bring the liquid in the casserole to a boil. Add these six ingredients and rapidly bring the mixture once again to the boil.

3 **Tablespoons cornstarch (plus 1**
teaspoon, if a thicker sauce is
desired), mixed with ¼ cup
cold water

(4) Immediately add the cornstarch and cook the mixture, stirring constantly, until the sauce is thickened and smooth. Pour the vegetables and sauce over the warmed chicken and serve at once.

CHICKEN (OR TURKEY) SALAD AND PINEAPPLE

Serves 6
Doubles
Refrigerates

Preparation: 30 minutes

2½ **cups cooked chicken or turkey,**
diced
2 **cups fresh ripe pineapple, diced**
½ **cup celery, diced (optional)**

(1) Prepare the meat and pineapple. (If desired, add the diced celery.)

(continued)

1 cup mayonnaise (or Orange
  Mayonnaise, page 262)
2 Tablespoons water
2 Tablespoons heavy cream
2 Tablespoons honey
  Juice of ½ lemon

(2) In a mixing bowl, combine these five ingredients. Stir them to blend the mixture well.

Salad greens
Toasted slivered almonds or
  berries (optional)

(3) To the dressing, add the poultry-pineapple mixture. Using two forks, gently toss the salad. Serve it on greens of your choice. If desired, top the salad with toasted slivered almonds, or with berries of your choice.

CHICKEN LIVERS IN SWEET-AND-PUNGENT SAUCE
(Chinese)

Serves 6
Doubles
Refrigerates

Preparation: 45 minutes
Cooking time: 5 minutes

1 lb. chicken livers

(1) Soak the chicken livers for 30 minutes in cold salted water, drain on absorbent paper and halve. Meanwhile, prepare the Sweet-and-Pungent Sauce, page 317.

2 Tablespoons oil
3 green peppers, seeded and cut in
  julienne

(2) In a saucepan, heat the oil and in it cook the chicken livers, stirring until they are just barely browned. Remove and reserve them.

(3) In the pan juices, cook the peppers for 3 minutes, or until they are barely wilted. Replace the chicken livers.

Sweet-and-Pungent Sauce

(4) Add the sweet-and-pungent sauce and simmer the livers and pepper, uncovered, for 5 minutes, or until they are heated through.

DUCK AND PINEAPPLE

(Chinese)

Serves 4
Doubles
Refrigerates

Preparation: 1 hour
Cooking: 40 minutes
Preheat oven: 400°/325°

¼ **cup soy sauce**
1 **Tablespoon sugar**
½ **teaspoon ground ginger**
1 **clove garlic, put through a press**
1 **5- to 6-lb. duck, quartered and trimmed of excess fat**

(1) In a small mixing bowl, combine the first four ingredients. With this mixture, generously brush the duck quarters. Arrange the duck, skin side up, on a rack in a broiling pan. With the tines of a fork puncture the skin in several places. Put the broiling pan into a 400° oven; reduce the heat to 325° and bake the duck for 1 hour.

(2) Remove the duck to a casserole or baking dish. Discard the fat.

2½ **cups pineapple juice**
2 **Tablespoons cornstarch**

(3) In a saucepan, combine the pineapple juice and cornstarch and, over high heat, cook the mixture, stirring constantly, until it is thickened and smooth. Pour the sauce over the duck.

At this point you may stop and continue later.

1 **medium-sized, ripe pineapple, peeled, cored, and cut into cubes**

(4) Bake the duck, uncovered, at 325° for ½ hour. Add the pineapple and continue baking the dish uncovered, for 10 minutes longer, or until the duck is tender and the pineapple is heated through.

SWEET-AND-PUNGENT DUCK

(Chinese)

Serves 4
Doubles
Refrigerates

Preparation: 1 hour
Cooking: 30 minutes
Preheat oven: 400°/325°

1 5- to 6-lb. duck, quartered and trimmed of excess fat

(1) On the rack of a broiling pan, arrange the duck quarters, skin side up; with the tines of a fork, puncture the skin in several places. Put the broiling pan into a 400° oven; reduce the heat to 325°, and bake the duck for 1 hour. Remove it to a casserole or baking dish. Discard the fat.

Sweet-and-Pungent Sauce, page 317

(2) While the duck is baking, prepare the sauce. Pour the sauce over the duck.

At this point you may stop and continue later.

(3) Bake the duck, uncovered, at 325° for 30 minutes, or until it is tender.

CURRIED SEAFOOD AND PINEAPPLE

Follow the directions for Curried Chicken and Papaya, page 446, using, in place of the chicken meat, ¾ lb. each raw shrimp, shelled and deveined, and sea scallops, halved, simmered in the curry sauce for 10 minutes, or until the shrimp are pink. In place of the papaya, use 3 pineapple "boats," made of 3 ripe fruits, halved lengthwise, the core cut out, and the flesh cut away from the outer skin so it may be easily removed and eaten.

FISH FILETS AND PINEAPPLE

Serves 6
Doubles
Refrigerates (fairly well)

Preparation: 20 minutes
Cooking: 20–25 minutes
Preheat oven: 400°

1 20-oz. can pineapple chunks (or 2 cups fresh pineapple, cut in large dice)

(1) Drain the canned pineapple and reserve the liquid. If fresh pineapple is used, a tastier dish will result; allow the fresh fruit to drain and reserve the liquid.

Orange juice

(2) To the reserved liquid, add orange juice to equal 2 cups.

2 Tablespoons cornstarch
½ teaspoon salt
1 teaspoon ground cumin

(3) To a little of the pineapple liquid, add the cornstarch, stirring until the mixture is smooth. In a saucepan, bring the reserved liquid to the boil, add the cornstarch, and cook the mixture, stirring constantly, until it is thickened and smooth. Stir in the salt and cumin.

Butter
Fish filets for 6 persons, page xv
Reserved pineapple
Salt
Pepper

(4) In a lightly buttered baking dish, arrange the filets. Season them with salt and pepper. Pour over the sauce and add the reserved fruit.

At this point you may stop and continue later.

(5) Bake the dish at 400° for 20 to 25 minutes, or until the fish flakes easily with a fork.

SWEET-AND-PUNGENT FISH

(Chinese)

Serves 6
Doubles
Refrigerates

Preparation: 10 minutes*
Cooking: 20 minutes
Preheat oven: 400°

Fish filets for 6 persons, page xv
1 **green pepper, seeded and cut in julienne**
3 **scallions, chopped**

(1) In a baking dish, arrange the fish filets. Over them arrange the green pepper and scallions.

Sweet-and-pungent Sauce, page 317

(2) Over the contents of the baking dish, pour the sauce.

At this point you may stop and continue later.

(3) Bake the filets, uncovered, at 400° for 20 minutes, or until they flake easily.

* The preparation time does not include readying the sauce.

SHRIMP AND PINEAPPLE

(Thai)

This dish is remarkably easy to prepare, good for summer days, when one wants to dine lightly and without great preparation.

Serves 6
Doubles
Refrigerates

Marination: 15 minutes
Preparation: 30 minutes

1 20-oz. can pineapple chunks
⅓ cup soy sauce
½ teaspoon cinnamon
¾ teaspoon ground ginger
1 teaspoon salt
Grating of pepper
1½ lbs. raw shrimp, shelled and deveined

(1) Drain the pineapple and reserve the liquid. In a mixing bowl, combine the pineapple liquid, soy sauce, and seasonings. In this mixture, marinate the shrimp for 15 minutes. Drain the shrimp and reserve the marinade.

6 Tablespoons butter
Reserved pineapple chunks

(2) In a skillet or saucepan, heat the butter and cook the shrimp, stirring, for 10 minutes, or until they are just pink. Add the pineapple.

Reserved marinade
1 Tablespoon cornstarch

(3) Mix the cornstarch with a little of the marinade. Add it and the remaining liquid to the skillet. Over high heat, cook the sauce, stirring constantly, until it is thickened and smooth. Serve the shrimp on rice.

SHRIMP AND PINEAPPLE SALAD

An attractive dish for luncheons or summer suppers.

Serves 6
Doubles
Refrigerates

Preparation: 30 minutes*

1 lb. fresh shrimp, shelled and deveined

(1) Prepare the shrimp and chill them (see page xx).

1 onion, minced
1 cup celery, chopped
1 20-oz. can pineapple chunks, well drained
Salt
White pepper

(2) In a large mixing bowl, combine the shrimp with these ingredients and lightly toss them together with salt and pepper to taste.

* Preparation time does not include preparing the shrimp or the mayonnaise.

(continued)

Orange Mayonnaise, page 262

(3) Fold the salad mixture with sufficient mayonnaise to bind it.

Salad greens, rinsed and shaken dry

6 strips of bacon, diced, rendered, and drained on absorbent paper (optional)

3 to 6 hard-cooked eggs, halved

(4) Line a large serving bowl with the greens of your choice. In the center, arrange the shrimp-pineapple mixture. Garnish the salad with the bacon bits and arrange the eggs around the edge.

SWEET-AND-PUNGENT SHRIMP

(*Chinese*)

Serves 6
Doubles
Refrigerates

Preparation: 30 minutes*
Cooking: 5 minutes

4 Tablespoons oil
1 clove garlic, split
1½ lbs. raw shrimp, shelled and deveined
2 onions, sliced and separated into rings
2 green peppers, seeded and cut in ¼-inch strips

(1) In a flame-proof casserole or *wok*, heat the oil and in it cook the garlic until the oil is flavored; discard the garlic. To the hot oil, add the shrimp and cook them, stirring constantly, until they are barely pink; remove and reserve them. In the remaining oil, cook the onions and green pepper until they are barely wilted. Remove the casserole from the heat. Replace the shrimp.

Sweet-and-Pungent Sauce, page 317

(2) Over the contents of the casserole, pour the sauce.

At this point you may stop and continue later.

* The preparation time does not include readying the sauce.

(3) Over medium-high heat, bring the contents of the casserole just to the boil. As soon as the shrimps are heated through, remove them from the heat and serve.

VEGETABLE CASSEROLE AND PINEAPPLE

Follow the directions for Vegetable Casserole and Grapes, page 166, using, in place of the grapes, one 20-oz. can pineapple chunks, drained.

SWEET-AND-PUNGENT VEGETABLES
(Chinese)

Serves 6
Doubles
Refrigerates

Preparation: 30 minutes*
Cooking: 5 minutes

¼ cup oil
1 head celery cabbage, cut in ¾-inch slices, rinsed and well drained
1 green pepper, seeded and coarsely chopped
½ lb. mushrooms, rinsed and sliced
1 9-oz. package frozen pea pods, fully thawed to room temperature
1 6-oz. can water chestnuts, sliced
1 8-oz. can bamboo shoots, drained
6 scallions, sliced diagonally, with as much green as possible.

(1) In flame-proof casserole or *wok*, heat the oil, add the cabbage and stir-fry it for 2 minutes. Add the pepper and mushrooms and cook them for 2 minutes. Add the pea pods and cook them for 2 minutes. Add the remaining vegetables and cook them for 2 minutes.

Sweet-and-Pungent Sauce, page 317

(2) Over the contents of the casserole, pour the sauce.

* The preparation time does not include readying the sauce.

(continued)

At this point you may stop and continue later.

(3) Over medium-high heat, bring the contents of the casserole just to the boil. As soon as the vegetables are heated through, remove them from the heat and serve.

PINEAPPLE MUFFINS

Follow the directions for Apple Muffins, page 19, using, in place of the apple, ¾ cup ripe fresh pineapple, grated; in a sieve, press against the pineapple with the back of a spoon to eliminate any excess juice.

PINEAPPLE AMBROSIA
(American)

This nineteenth-century dessert is a classic in American cooking.

Serves 6
Doubles
Refrigerates

Preparation: 45 minutes*
Cooking: 5 minutes
Preheat oven: 425°
Final chilling time: 3 hours

1 large ripe pineapple, peeled and coarsely grated
½ cup sugar

(1) In an oven-proof serving bowl, combine the pineapple and sugar and chill the mixture for 2 hours.

* The preparation time does not include the advance chilling time (step #1).

2 eggs
2 egg yolks
¼ cup sugar
Pinch of salt
2 cups milk, scalded and partially cooled
1 teaspoon vanilla

(2) In the top of a double boiler, beat together the eggs, yolks, sugar and salt. Gradually stir in the milk and, over simmering water, cook the custard, stirring, until it thickens and coats the spoon. Allow it to cool and stir in the vanilla.

2 egg whites
¼ cup sugar

(3) Pour the cooked custard over the chilled pineapple. Beat the whites until they are frothy; gradually add the sugar and beat them until they are stiff. Spread this meringue over the dessert and bake it at 425° for 5 minutes, or until it is golden. Chill the dessert well.

BAKED PINEAPPLE AND RUM

Follow the directions for Baked Bananas and Rum, page 80, using, in place of the bananas, 1 large ripe fresh pineapple, peeled, cored, and cut into cubes. Serve the pineapple with whipped or ice cream.

PINEAPPLE ICE CREAM

Follow the directions for Helen McCully's Ice Cream, page 457, reducing the vanilla to 1 teaspoonful, increasing the sugar to ¾ cup, and adding 1 cup very ripe pineapple, grated, to the hot custard before cooling it.

PINEAPPLE PIE

Follow the directions for Apple Pie, page 27, using, in place of the apple, 1 large ripe pineapple, peeled, cored, diced, and well drained. Mix the flour and sugar, adding if desired a grating of nutmeg or the grated rind of ½ lemon. Toss the diced pineapple in the dry mixture, fill the unbaked pie shell and proceed as directed. The secret of this recipe is in using a very ripe pineapple finely diced.

PINEAPPLE SPONGE

(American)

Serves 6
Refrigerates

Preparation: 30 minutes
Chilling time: at least 3 hours

½ cup sugar
1 cup unsweetened pineapple
juice

1 cup grated fresh ripe pineapple
1 packet unflavored gelatin,
softened in ½ cup water

2 egg whites, stiffly beaten

(1) In a saucepan, combine the sugar and pineapple juice; bring the liquid to the boil, stirring to dissolve the sugar.

(2) Stir in the pineapple and gelatin. When the gelatin is dissolved, chill the mixture until it begins to set.

(3) Into the pineapple gelatin, fold the egg whites. Pour the sponge into a 1½-quart mold or serving dish. Chill the dessert for at least 3 hours before unmolding it. A little green *crème de menthe*, served separately as a sauce, is a pleasant accompaniment.

PINEAPPLE SAUCE

For basting grilled fish, seafood, and roast pork.

Serving: 3 cups
Refrigerates

Preparation: 15 minutes

1 cup wine vinegar
1 cup dark brown sugar
1 cup water
1 8-oz. can pineapple chunks, with
juice
1 green pepper, seeded and
chopped
2 tomatoes, peeled, seeded, and
chopped

(1) In a saucepan, combine these eight ingredients and, over gentle heat, simmer them, covered, for 15 minutes.

1 Tablespoon Lea & Perrins
   Worcestershire Sauce
½ teaspoon dry mustard

4 teaspoons cornstarch, mixed with 2 Tablespoons cold water	(2) Add the cornstarch and cook the sauce, uncovered, stirring constantly until it is thickened and smooth.

SWEET-AND-PUNGENT SAUCE
   (*Chinese*)

For meat, poultry, fish and seafood, and vegetables. There are a variety of ways to make sweet-and-pungent (or sweet-and-sour) sauce. All derive their common characteristic from the flavor of sweet pineapple combined with the aromatic taste of vinegar.

> Serving: about 2 cups
> Doubles
> Refrigerates

Preparation: 15 minutes

3 Tablespoons sugar ¾ teaspoon salt ½ teaspoon ground ginger, or more to taste 2 Tablespoons cornstarch	(1) In a saucepan, mix together these four dry ingredients.
1 20-oz. can pineapple chunks ¼ cup cider vinegar 3 Tablespoons soy sauce	(2) Stir in the pineapple and its liquid, the vinegar, and the soy sauce. Over high heat, cook the mixture, stirring constantly until it is thickened and smooth.

PINEAPPLE STUFFING

For pork and duck.

> Serving: 4 cups

Preparation: 20 minutes*

* Preparation time does not include cooking the rice.

(continued)

2 Tablespoons butter
1 onion, finely chopped
⅓ cup carrot, grated
1 cup celery, diced
¼ cup parsley, chopped

(1) In a saucepan, heat the butter and in it cook the onion until translucent. Add, in order, the carrot, celery, and parsley, cooking each for 1 minute before the next addition.

¼ teaspoon ground clove
¾ teaspoon paprika
1 teaspoon salt
½ teaspoon pepper
1 cup cooked rice

(2) In a mixing bowl, using two forks, toss together the vegetable mixture, the rice, and seasonings.

1 cup ripe pineapple, grated
⅓ cup seedless raisins
2 cups dry breadcrumbs

(3) Add the pineapple, raisins, and breadcrumbs. Toss the stuffing until it is well blended.

PLUMS
AND PRUNES

The good taste of plums prompted the adoption of the word "plum" to mean a prize or something especially desirable. A cousin of the cherry and peach, plums come in four varieties. The common European plum, *Prunus domestica*, is native to southeastern Europe and western Asia, where it has been cultivated for over 2,000 years. Its cousin, *Prunus institia*, also of European and Asian origin, is usually used in jellies and jams. Another cousin, *Prunus salicina*, came first from China, but was domesticated in Japan, whence it traveled to America in 1870. Last, of the seven plums native to America, *Prunus americana*, the only one of any commercial importance is the *maritima*, beach plum, from which excellent preserves are made.

In the United States, the *domestica*, growing in the intermountain areas of the Pacific Coast

states, include the Reine Claude (or greengage, so-called after the Gage family who first imported it to England from France), the yellow egg plum, the red Lombard, and the dark purple Italian prune-plum. The *institia*, embracing the Damson or Damascus plums, also include the English Shropshire and the French Mirabelle. The *salicina,* perfected in this country by Luther Burbank, are red-skinned and red- or yellow-fleshed; not as adaptable to canning as the *domestica*, it is especially delicious eaten out of hand. The *americana* fed the Indians long before the colonists arrived with *Prunus domestica*; it has been improved by crossing with other plum strains.

Plums, most widely distributed of the drupe or stone fruits, rank second only to the peach in importance. Its tree, which may reach a height of 30 feet, is beautiful in shape and blossom, which is sometimes yellow overlaid in red. Yugoslavia leads world production with a potential 1 million tons a year; Germany is the second largest European producer, nearly equaling the output of the United States. Turkey and Japan are the leading Asian growers.

"Prune" is the name given to certain plums which can be dried into a firm long-lasting product with a high sugar content. In California, prunes are sun-dried; in Oregon and Washington, they are dehydrated artificially.

In these recipes purple plums (often called "blue" Italian plums), pitted, are interchangeable with prunes; the fresh fruit requires about one-half the cooking time of dried tenderized pitted prunes.

PLUM SOUP I

(German)

Serve this soup cold.

> Serves 6
> Doubles
> Refrigerates

Preparation: 30 minutes
Chilling time: at least 2 hours

1½ lbs. prune plums, seeded
½ cup sugar
1 2-inch piece cinnamon stick
8 cups water
Zest of 1 lemon

(1) In a saucepan, combine these five ingredients, bring them to the boil, reduce the heat, and simmer them, covered, for 30 minutes, or until the plums are soft.

(2) In the container of an electric blender, puree the mixture, a little at a time, by whirling it on medium speed for 15 seconds, or until it is smooth. Pour the puree into a second saucepan.

5 Tablespoons cornstarch, mixed
with ¼ cup cold water
½ cup dry white wine
Whipped or sour cream

(3) Add the cornstarch and, over moderate heat, cook the mixture, stirring constantly, until it is thickened and smooth. Stir in the wine. Cool the soup, chill it, and serve it garnished with whipped or sour cream.

PLUM SOUP II

Serve this soup hot.

> Serves 6
> Doubles
> Refrigerates

Preparation: 20 minutes

(continued)

1 30-oz. can purple plums

(1) Drain the plums, reserving the liquid. Seed them. In the container of an electric blender, whirl the plums, a few at a time, on medium speed for 15 seconds, or until they are pureed. Pour the puree into a saucepan.

1 cup reserved plum liquid
¼ cup brown sugar
1 Tablespoon cornstarch
¼ teaspoon salt
  Juice of 1 lemon
2 Tablespoons soft butter
2 Tablespoons dark rum

(2) Add 1 cup of the reserved plum liquid. Mix together the sugar and cornstarch and add them to the plums. Stir in the salt and lemon juice. Over moderate heat, cook the soup, stirring constantly, until it is thickened and smooth. Stir in the butter and rum.

Whipped or sour cream

(3) Serve the hot soup garnished with whipped or sour cream.

BEEF AND PLUMS WITH RIPE OLIVES*

Serves 6
Doubles
Refrigerates

Preparation: 30 minutes
Cooking: 2½ hours
Preheat oven: 300°

2 Tablespoons butter
2 Tablespoons oil
3 lbs. chuck, cut in bite-sized
  pieces
  Salt
  Pepper

(1) In a flame-proof casserole, heat the butter and oil and brown the beef; season it. Remove.

4 onions, chopped

(2) In the remaining fat, cook the onions until translucent. Replace the meat.

* This recipe is contributed by Lewis Core, an expert picnic maker and an intrepid sailor, who spent the better part of one summer at our house, where he prepared sumptuous picnic luncheons to be enjoyed on the beach following hair-raising sailing excursions along the coast of Great South Bay.

¼ **cup brandy**

(3) In a small saucepan, warm the brandy, ignite it, and pour it over the meat. Allow it to burn out.

2 **cups sour cream**
1 **10½-oz. can condensed beef broth**
   Grated rind and juice of 1 lemon
3 **Tablespoons flour**

(4) In the container of an electric blender, combine these five ingredients and, on medium speed, blend the mixture for 15 seconds, or until it is smooth.

At this point you may stop and continue later.

12 **firm, ripe Italian purple plums, stemmed, halved lengthwise, and seeded***
½ **cup ripe olives, halved**

(5) Over the contents of the casserole, pour the liquid. Bake the casserole, covered, at 300° for 2¼ hours. Add the plums and olives and continue to cook the dish, covered, for 15 minutes longer, or until the meat is tender.

* This dish may be prepared instead with dried tenderized pitted prunes. Halve lengthwise 12 prunes and add them to the contents of the casserole for the final 30 minutes of cooking.

BEEF AND PRUNES
(French)

Serves 6
Doubles
Refrigerates
Freezes

Preparation: 30 minutes
Cooking: 2½ hours
Preheat oven: 300°

2 **cups dry red wine**
1 **12-oz. package dried pitted prunes**

(1) In the wine, cook the prunes for 30 minutes. Drain them and reserve the wine.

(continued)

2 Tablespoons butter
2 Tablespoons oil
3 lbs. lean chuck, cut in
 bite-sized pieces
 Salt
 Pepper

(2) In a flame-proof casserole, heat the butter and oil and brown the beef; season it. Remove.

3 onions, chopped
1½ Tablespoons flour
2 bay leaves, broken
1 teaspoon cinnamon
2 Tablespoons sugar
 Reserved wine
2 Tablespoons wine vinegar

(3) In the remaining fat, cook the onions until translucent. Stir in the flour and remaining ingredients except the wine and vinegar. To the reserved wine, add the vinegar. To the contents of the casserole, gradually add the wine, stirring constantly; cook the mixture until it is thickened and smooth. Replace the beef, spooning the sauce over it.

At this point you may stop and continue later.

Reserved prunes

(4) Bake the casserole, covered, at 300° for 2 hours. Add the prunes and continue cooking the beef, covered, for 30 minutes, or until it is tender.

Try any or all of these variations: Madeira may be used in place of dry red wine; 3 medium potatoes, peeled and halved, may be added with the prunes for the final 30 minutes of cooking; 3 carrots, sliced, and 1 stalk of celery, chopped, may be added with the onions. The dish may also be made with veal, cut into bite-sized pieces.

LAMB AND PRUNES

(Czechoslovakian)

Serves 6
Doubles
Refrigerates

Preparation: 30 minutes
Cooking: 2¼ hours
Preheat oven: 300°

1½ cups fine egg noodles Boiling water	(1) In a mixing bowl, pour the boiling water over the noodles, cover the bowl, and allow the noodles to cook by simply setting.
3 lbs. boneless, fat-free lamb, cut in bite-sized pieces Seasoned flour	(2) Dredge the lamb in the seasoned flour.
2 Tablespoons butter 2 Tablespoons oil	(3) In a flame-proof 5½-quart casserole, heat the butter and oil and brown the lamb; remove it.
3 onions, chopped 1 clove garlic, chopped ½ teaspoon ground allspice ½ teaspoon cinnamon ¼ teaspoon ground clove ½ teaspoon nutmeg	(4) In the remaining fat, cook the onions and garlic until translucent. Replace the lamb and sprinkle it with the seasonings. *At this point you may stop and continue later.*
2 10½-oz. cans condensed beef broth	(5) To the contents of the casserole, add the broth and bake the dish, covered, at 300° for 2 hours.
1 12-oz. box dried pitted tenderized prunes Drained noodles 1 cup reserved noodle water	(6) To the contents of the casserole, add the prunes, cover them with the drained noodles, and pour over 1 cup of the noodle water. Continue cooking the dish, covered, for 15 minutes or until the lamb is tender.

LAMB SHANKS AND PRUNES

Ripe fresh purple plums, stemmed, halved, and pitted may also be used; add them for the final 15 minutes of cooking.

Follow the directions for Beef and Cranberries, page 118, using, in place of the beef and cranberries, 6 lamb shanks and 18 to 24 tenderized pitted prunes, added for the final 30 minutes of cooking. Cooking time: 2 hours at 300°.

PRUNE-STUFFED PORK LOIN

(Swedish)

Serves 6
Refrigerates

Preparation: 30 minutes
Cooking: 2½ hours
Preheat oven: 350°

1 onion, chopped
1½ teaspoons ground ginger
1 teaspoon rosemary
½ teaspoon pepper
1 3- to 4-lb. pork shoulder, boned
**12 to 14 dried tenderized pitted
    prunes**
1 Tablespoon salt

(1) Mix together the onion and seasonings and spread the mixture evenly over the pork, laid out flat. Over the onion, arrange the prunes. Roll and tie the meat. Rub it with the salt.

(2) Place the meat on the rack of a roasting pan and bake it at 350° for 1½ hours.

2 Tablespoons pork drippings
2 Tablespoons flour
2 cups dry red wine

(3) In a flame-proof casserole, combine the pork drippings and flour; stir to blend them well. Gradually add the wine and, over medium high heat, cook the mixture, stirring constantly, until it is thickened and smooth. Remove the pork to the casserole, spooning the sauce over it. Discard the excess fat.

At this point you may stop and continue later.

(4) Bake the casserole, covered, at 350° for 1 hour, or until the pork is tender.

PORK AND PRUNE PIE

(Alsatian)

This dish, in its native Alsace, is always made with pork; it may also be made with ground lean beef, lamb, veal, or a combination of meats.

Serving: one 9-inch pie
Refrigerates

Preparation: 30 minutes*
Cooking: 1¼ hours
Preheat oven: 450°

1 lb. fresh ham, ground
1 lb. smoked ham, ground
1 cup dried tenderized pitted prunes, chopped
1 onion grated

(1) In a mixing bowl, combine these four ingredients.

1 cup breadcrumbs
½ cup light cream
1 egg, beaten
1½ teaspoons salt
½ teaspoon pepper
¾ teaspoon marjoram
1 teaspoon sage

(2) In a separate mixing bowl, soak the breadcrumbs in the cream. Add the egg and stir in the seasonings.

(3) Add the breadcrumb mixture to the ground meat. Stir to blend the ingredients well.

At this point you may stop and continue later.

* The preparation time does not include readying the pastry, page 458.

(continued)

Short-pastry for a two-crust 9-inch pie

(4) Line a 9-inch pie tin with a bottom crust. Fill the pastry shell with the meat mixture, mounding it in the center. Add the top crust, crimping the edges together with a fork. Puncture the top crust in a few places. Bake the pie at 450° for 10 minutes; reduce the heat to 300° and continue to bake it for 1 hour longer. The pie may be served hot or cold, accompanied by Dijon mustard mixed with horseradish sauce, in equal parts.

CHICKEN AND PRUNES

(Russian)

Serves 6
Doubles
Refrigerates

Preparation: 30 minutes
Cooking: 1 hour
Preheat oven: 350°

2 Tablespoons butter
2 Tablespoons oil
Serving-pieces of chicken for 6 persons
Salt
Pepper

(1) In a flame-proof casserole, heat the butter and oil and brown the chicken; season it. Remove.

3 onions, chopped
1 carrot, scraped and sliced
1 stalk celery, chopped
4 sprigs parsley
1 bay leaf, broken
1 10½-oz. can condensed chicken broth

(2) In the remaining fat, cook the vegetables until translucent. Add the parsley and bay leaf. Replace the chicken. Add the broth.

At this point you may stop and continue later.

18 dried tenderized pitted prunes

(3) Bake the casserole, covered, at 350° for 30 minutes. Add the prunes and continue to cook the chicken covered, for 30 minutes longer, or until it and the prunes are tender.

Prune juice
1½ Tablespoons cornstarch

(4) Remove the chicken and prunes to a serving dish and keep them warm. Sieve the pan broth and to it add prune juice to equal 2 cups. Combine the cornstarch with a little of the liquid. Return the cornstarch mixture and the remaining prune liquid to the pan. Over high heat, cook the sauce, stirring constantly, until it is thickened and smooth. Adjust the seasoning and pour the sauce over the chicken.

PORK AND PLUM PILAF

(Spanish)

Serves 6
Doubles
Refrigerates
Freezes

Preparation: 30 minutes
Cooking: 1½ hours
Preheat oven: 350°

2 Tablespoons oil
2 lbs. pork, cut in bite-sized pieces
Salt
Pepper

(1) In a flame-proof casserole, heat the oil and brown the pork; season it. Remove it to absorbent paper.

2 onions, chopped
1 clove garlic, chopped
½ teaspoon basil
½ teaspoon marjoram
½ teaspoon savory
½ teaspoon thyme

(2) In the remaining fat, cook the onions and garlic until translucent. Stir in the seasonings.

(continued)

2 **tomatoes, peeled, seeded, and chopped**

¼ **cup sweet sherry**

(3) Stir in the tomatoes and sherry; simmer the mixture for 5 minutes.

1¼ **cups natural raw rice**

(4) Stir in the rice and replace the pork, spooning the rice mixture over it.

At this point you may stop and continue later.

2 **10½-oz. cans condensed chicken broth**

12 **firm, ripe Italian purple plums, stemmed, halved lengthwise, and seeded**

(5) Over the contents of the casserole, pour the broth. Bake the dish, covered, at 350° for 1½ hours, or until the pork is tender. Add the plums during the final 15 minutes of cooking.

POACHED FISH AND PRUNE SAUCE

(Czechoslovakian)

Serves 6
Doubles
Refrigerates

Preparation: 30 minutes

2 **cups wine vinegar**
4 **cups water**
2 **onions, chopped**
1 **clove garlic, chopped**
2 **stalks celery, chopped**
1 **carrot, thinly sliced**
2 **bay leaves, broken**
4 **whole cloves**
4 **whole allspice**
1 **teaspoon cumin seed**

(1) In a fish poacher or large skillet combine these ten ingredients. Bring the liquid to the boil, reduce the heat, and simmer the broth, covered, for 15 minutes.

2 **to 2½ pounds lean fish or fish filets of your choice, page xv**

(2) With the liquid just simmering, add the fish and poach it until it flakes when tried with a fork (the time will vary depending upon the size and variety of fish used). Carefully remove the fish to a serving plate and keep it warm.

1 cup reserved fish broth, sieved
2 cups cooked prunes, seeded
  Juice of 1 lemon
¼ cup sugar
  Pinch of salt
2 Tablespoons butter, melted
1½ Tablespoons cornstarch

⅓ cup golden raisins
¼ cup walnuts, chopped

(3) In the container of an electric blender, combine the broth and prunes. Add the lemon juice, sugar, salt, butter, and cornstarch. On medium speed, whirl the ingredients until the mixture is smooth.

(4) Transfer the mixture to a saucepan and, over high heat, cook the sauce, stirring constantly, until it is thickened and smooth. Stir in the raisins and nuts, heat them through, and pour the sauce over the fish.

VEGETABLE CASSEROLE AND PRUNES

Follow the directions for Vegetable Casserole and Grapes, page 166, using, in place of the grapes, 1 cup dried tenderized pitted prunes, quartered, cooked with the vegetables for the full 20 minutes.

LENTILS AND PRUNES

A substantial side dish, tasty as an accompaniment to roast meats.

    Serves 6
    Doubles
    Refrigerates

Preparation: 40 minutes

1 cup lentils, rinsed

(1) In a saucepan, cook the lentils, covered, in boiling salted water to cover for 30 minutes, or until they are tender but still hold their shape. Drain and replace them in the saucepan.

(continued)

1 **cup dried tenderized pitted
 prunes, chopped**
¼ **cup sherry**
1 **teaspoon salt**
 Juice of ½ lemon
3 **Tablespoons soft butter**

(2) To the lentils, add these five ingredients and, using two forks, toss the mixture to blend it. Heat the vegetable, covered, before serving it.

PRUNE BREAD

Follow the directions for Cranberry Bread, page 124, using, in place of the water and cranberries, prune juice, heated, and 1 cup dried tenderized pitted prunes, put through the coarse blade of a food chopper; omit the second (½ cup) addition of light brown sugar and the molasses; reduce the second (2 cups) measure of flour to 1 cup.

PRUNE CAKE

A hearty dessert, very pleasant as a wintertime dish.

> Serves 6
> Refrigerates
> Freezes

Preparation: 30 minutes
Cooking: 30 minutes
Preheat oven: 400°

5½ **Tablespoons soft butter**
 ⅓ **cup sugar**
 1 **egg**
 1 **cup milk**

(1) In a mixing bowl, cream together the butter and sugar. Beat in the egg and then the milk.

2½ **cups flour**
 1 **teaspoon salt**
 1 **teaspoon baking soda**
 2 **teaspoons cinnamon**

(2) In a separate mixing bowl, sift together the dry ingredients.

 1 **cup dried tenderized pitted
 prunes, chopped**

(3) Add the liquid to the dry ingredients, beating the batter until it is smooth. Stir in the prunes.

Lemon Sauce, page 460

(4) Spoon the batter into a flat 2-quart baking dish, buttered. Bake the cake at 400° for 30 minutes, or until a knife inserted at the center comes out clean. Serve the cake warm or cold with hot lemon sauce.

PLUM CAKE

Follow the directions for Berry Cake, page 90, using, in place of the berries, an equal amount of fresh, ripe plums, halved, seeded, and chopped. Serve the dessert with Lemon Sauce, page 460.

PLUM COBBLER

Follow the directions for Apple Cobbler, page 23, using, in place of the apples, an equal amount of fresh ripe plums, halved, seeded, and arranged with their cut sides down in the baking dish.

FRESH PLUM COMPOTE

Serves 6
Doubles
Refrigerates

Preparation: 15 minutes
Chilling time: at least 2 hours

⅔ **cup sugar**
1 **cup dry white wine**
1 **cup water**
4 **whole cloves**
1 **3-inch piece cinnamon stick**
Zest of 1 lemon

(1) In a saucepan, combine these six ingredients. Bring them to a rolling boil and cook them, uncovered, for 5 minutes.

(continued)

12 to 18 firm, ripe greengage or red plums, rinsed

(2) Add the plums, return the syrup to the boil, lower the heat, and simmer the plums for 5 minutes, or until they are tender but still hold their shape. Cool and then chill the plums in the syrup.

PRUNE CUSTARD
(Swedish)

The dessert may be served warm or cold.

Serves 6
Refrigerates

Preparation: 20 minutes
Cooking: 1 hour
Preheat oven: 350°

3 egg yolks
½ cup sugar

(1) In a mixing bowl, beat the yolks until they are a light yellow; add the sugar and beat the mixture until it is creamy.

1¾ cups chilled light cream
1 teaspoon vanilla

(2) Gradually add the cream, beating. Add the vanilla.

3 egg whites, beaten until stiff but not dry

(3) Fold in the egg whites.

18 to 24 cooked prunes, pitted and drained on absorbent paper
Whipped cream (optional)

(4) In a 1½-quart baking dish, arrange the prunes in a single layer. Pour the custard over the prunes. Put the baking dish in a pan of boiling water and bake the dessert at 350° for 1 hour, or until the custard is golden and a knife inserted at the center comes out clean. Serve the dessert with whipped cream, if desired.

BAKED PLUM COMPOTE

(Polish)

Serves 6
Doubles
Refrigerates (except the meringue)

Preparation: 15 minutes
Cooking: 55 minutes
Preheat oven: 350°/400°

1½ **cups dry red wine**
1½ **cups sugar**
  Zest of 1 lemon

(1) In a saucepan, combine these three ingredients, bring them to a rolling boil, stirring to dissolve the sugar; boil the syrup for 5 minutes.

 3 **lbs. purple plums, rinsed,**
   drained on absorbent paper,
   and pricked in several places
   with a pin

(2) In a 2-quart baking dish, lightly buttered, arrange the plums. Over them, pour the syrup; remove the lemon zest. Bake the plums, uncovered, at 350° for 50 minutes.

At this point you may stop and continue later.

 2 **egg whites**
½ **cup sugar**
½ **teaspoon almond extract**

(3) In a mixing bowl, beat the egg whites until frothy; gradually add the sugar and then the flavoring, beating until the whites are stiff. Over the plums spread the meringue. Bake the dish in a 400° oven for 5 minutes, or until the meringue is golden brown. Serve the compote hot or at room temperature.

A Scandinavian variation: omit the syrup; in the baking dish, layer the plums alternately with sugar, using 3 cups of sugar; over the plums, pour 1 cup dark rum. Bake the plums as directed. Serve the plums chilled in their syrup.

GREENGAGE ICE CREAM

Follow the directions for Helen McCully's Ice Cream, page 457, using, in place of the vanilla, 1½ cups pulp, made by thoroughly draining, seeding, and sieving canned greengage plums. Add the fruit to the hot custard before cooling it.

PLUM KUCHEN
(German)

Follow the directions for Peach *Kuchen*, page 277, using, in place of the peaches, 1½ lbs. ripe plums, halved and seeded, arranged skin sides down in the baking dish.

PRUNE CREAM PIE
(American)

Serving: one 9-inch pie
Refrigerates

Preparation: 5 minutes*
Cooking: 35 minutes
Preheat oven: 400°

3 eggs
½ cup prune juice
1 cup milk
4 Tablespoons flour
½ teaspoon salt
¼ teaspoon cinnamon
1 cup sugar
1 cup cooked prunes, drained and pitted

(1) In the container of an electric blender, whirl these eight ingredients on medium speed for 15 seconds, or until the mixture is smooth.

* The preparation time does not include readying the pastry, page 458.

1 9-inch pastry shell, unbaked
Whipped cream (optional)

(2) Pour the mixture into the unbaked pastry shell and bake the pie at 400° for 35 minutes, or until the custard is set and the crust golden brown. Cool the pie. If desired, garnish it with whipped cream at the time of serving.

PRUNE PUDDING

Follow the directions for Apricot Pudding, page 45, using dried tenderized pitted prunes in place of the apricots.

PRUNE SOUFFLE

The secret of this recipe is to have *everything* (even the simmering water) ready before you start.

Serves 6

Preparation: 20 minutes
Cooking: 1 hour

1 cup prune puree*
½ cup sugar
Pinch of salt
Juice of ½ lemon

(1) In a mixing bowl, stir together these four ingredients.

5 egg whites, beaten until stiff but not dry

(2) Fold the egg whites into the prune mixture.

(3) Immediately pour it into the top of a double boiler, lightly buttered, and, over simmering water, cook the souffle, covered, for 1 hour. *Do not uncover it.*

Whipped cream

(4) Onto a warm serving plate, turn out the souffle. Serve it at once with whipped cream.

* Baby food can be used for prune puree, or canned prunes, drained, seeded, and whirled in an electric blender.

PLUM TART

(American)

The recipe adapts itself to any canned fruit, thoroughly drained and, if necessary, sweetened with additional sugar. Suggested fruit: pitted cherries, peaches, pears, prunes.

Serving: one 9-inch tart
Refrigerates

Preparation: 30 minutes*
Cooking: 20 minutes
Preheat oven: 450°

2 1-lb. cans purple plums, thoroughly drained and seeded

1 9-inch pastry shell, unbaked

(1) Over the bottom of the pastry, arrange the plums.

Grated rind of 1 orange

1 cup sour cream (if desired, sweetened with 3 Tablespoons sugar or flavored with 1 teaspoon vanilla)

(2) Sprinkle the plums with the orange rind. Spread over the sour cream.

(3) Bake the tart at 450° for 20 minutes, or until the crust is golden brown.

* The preparation time does not include readying the pastry, page 458.

PRUNES BAKED IN WINE*

Serves 6
Doubles
Refrigerates

Soaking: overnight
Preparation: 15 minutes
Cooking: 1 hour
Preheat oven: 325°
Chilling time: 2 hours

* This recipe is contributed by Elizabeth Jane Wills, familiarly known as E. Jane. The wife of my oldest friend and mother of five, she is also an artist of unusual talent and a cook of pleasing originality, as evidenced by this compote, so much more interesting than common, garden variety stewed prunes.

2 pounds dried prunes
2 cups madeira wine or port

(1) In a mixing bowl, soak the prunes in the wine overnight.

(2) With a slotted spoon, remove the prunes to a baking dish. Transfer the wine to a saucepan.

Reserved wine
½ cup sugar
Pinch of salt
1 3-inch piece cinnamon stick
Zest and juice of 1 lemon
Additional madeira wine or port

(3) To the reserved wine, add the sugar, salt, cinnamon stick, and lemon zest and juice; heat the mixture, stirring, until the sugar is dissolved. Pour the syrup over the prunes. Add sufficient additional wine to cover the prunes.

Sour or whipped cream

(4) Bake the prunes, uncovered, at 325° for 1 hour, or until they are tender. Allow them to cool in the syrup; chill them. Serve them with sour or whipped cream.

PRUNE WHIP

(American)

Prune whip is a classic dessert in American cooking. The recipe may also be made with apricot pulp in place of the prune.

Serves 6
Refrigerates

Preparation: 30 minutes
Cooking: 45 minutes
Preheat oven: 300°

¾ cup pulp made by sieving cooked
prunes, drained
Sugar, to taste
Juice of ½ lemon
Pinch of salt

(1) In a saucepan, stir together the prune pulp and sugar. Over moderate heat, cook the mixture, stirring, until it is thickened. Stir in the lemon juice and salt. Cool the mixture.

(continued)

3 egg whites, beaten until stiff
Custard Sauce, page 460

(2) Fold the prune pulp into the egg whites, spoon the mixture into a souffle dish. Put the dish in a pan of hot water and bake the dessert at 300° for 45 minutes, or until it is firm. Serve it warm with the custard sauce.

PLUM SAUCE

(Caucasian)

To accompany roast or broiled fowl.

Serving: 2 cups
Refrigerates

Preparation: 30 minutes

½ lb. purple plums, seeded
Water

(1) In a saucepan, cook the plums, covered, in water just to cover for 20 minutes, or until they are soft. Drain them, reserving the liquid.

(2) In the container of an electric blender, whirl the plums on medium speed for 15 seconds, or until they are reduced to a smooth puree.

Reserved plum liquid

(3) With the blender running, add the plum liquid, a little at a time, stopping when the mixture reaches the consistency of heavy cream.

3 cloves garlic, coarsely chopped
Salt
Pepper
⅓ cup parsley, chopped

(4) Add the garlic and then the salt and pepper to taste. Return the sauce to the pan, add the parsley, and simmer it, uncovered, for 10 minutes.

RAISINS AND CURRANTS

Raisins, the dried fruit of certain varieties of grapes, were known in 2000 B.C. to the Persians and Egyptians. They are mentioned in the Bible in the story of Moses, and David was given "a hundred clusters of raisins" (I Samuel, XXV, 18). Greek and Roman athletic heroes were awarded raisins as well as laurel wreaths.

Until the present century, Turkey, Iran, and Greece were the principal producers of raisins. Today, however, the United States is first, with the industry based entirely in California. Australia ranks second in world production.

The word *raisin* is a contraction of *raisin sec*, French for "dried grape." The most important raisin grapes are the pale yellow Thompson seedless (also known as "sultana"); the white Turkish and Iranian kishmish; the large-seeded muscat or Alexandria; and the small seedless

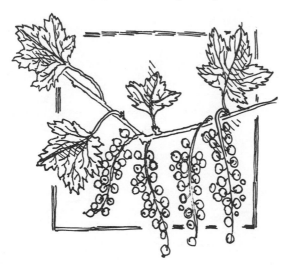

black corinth, also called the zante currant.

The zante currant, from the Ionian island of Zakinthos is not a currant at all, but rather a raisin, deriving its popular name from the French "raisin de Corinthe," the city to which the little island exported its raisins for marketing. (See page 88.)

Natural raisins are sun-dried and are grayish black with a rather tough skin. Golden raisins are dipped in 0.5 percent lye, exposed to fumes of burning sulfur for several hours, and then dried by artificial dehydration. These two methods of drying are the most important, but several others are also practiced.

High in carbohydrates and low in protein, raisins vary from 1,300 to 1,600 calories per pound.

In general, currants or black or golden raisins may be used inter-changeably in these recipes. Your choice of raisins over currants will somewhat affect the quantity of the completed recipe, (because raisins are much larger) and selecting golden rather than black raisins will affect the appearance of the dish.

The recipes in this section call for seedless raisins and currants, available boxed at your supermarket.

RAISIN AND ALMOND SOUP
(Mexican)

Serves 6
Doubles
Refrigerates

Preparation: 15 minutes
Cooking: 10 minutes

3 **Tablespoons lard** 1 **cup blanched almonds** 1 **cup raisins**	(1) In a skillet, heat the lard and in it cook the almonds and raisins until the raisins are a bit tender. Remove them.
2 **large onions, chopped**	(2) In the remaining lard, cook the onions until translucent. More lard may be added if necessary.
3 **large tomatoes, peeled and seeded**	(3) Through the finest blade of a meat grinder, put the tomatoes, the cooked almonds and raisins.
2 **10½-oz. cans condensed beef broth**	(4) In a saucepan, combine the onions and the raisin mixture. Add the broth, bring the soup to a boil, reduce the heat, and simmer it, covered, for 10 minutes.

BEEF AND RAISINS I

Follow the directions for Beef and Oranges, page 229, adding 1 teaspoon curry powder to the cooked onion; after replacing the beef, add ½ cup grated coconut and ¾ cup golden raisins, plumped for 5 minutes in hot water and drained.

BEEF AND RAISINS II

(Cuban)

Serves 6
Doubles
Refrigerates

Preparation: 1¼ hours
Cooking: 15 minutes

3 lbs. chuck, trimmed of excess fat and cut in bite-sized pieces
1½ teaspoons salt
¼ teaspoon pepper
Water

(1) In a saucepan, combine the beef, salt, pepper, and enough water to cover. Bring the liquid to the boil and skim any fat from the surface. Reduce the heat and simmer the meat, covered, for 1 hour, or until it is tender. Drain it and reserve the broth for another dish.

4 Tablespoons olive oil
3 onions, chopped
2 cloves garlic, chopped
4 green peppers, seeded and chopped
1¼ teaspoons chili powder

(2) In a flame-proof casserole, heat the oil and in it cook the onions, garlic, and pepper, seasoned with chili powder, until the vegetables are translucent.

6 tomatoes, peeled, seeded, and coarsely chopped
¼ teaspoon ground clove
1½ teaspoons salt
¼ teaspoon pepper
2 teaspoons sugar

(3) Add the tomatoes and seasonings. Cook the mixture, stirring until most of the liquid is evaporated and the sauce thickens slightly.

At this point you may stop and continue later.

¾ cup raisins
3 Tablespoons cider vinegar
⅓ cup pitted green olives, sliced lengthwise (optional)

(4) Into the sauce, stir the raisins, vinegar and olives. Add the reserved meat, spooning the sauce over it. Simmer the dish, covered for 15 minutes, or until the meat is well heated.

GROUND BEEF AND RAISINS

(Polynesian)

Serves 6
Doubles
Refrigerates

Preparation: 30 minutes
Cooking: 30 minutes
Preheat oven: 350°

2 Tablespoons oil **2 lbs. ground round** **Salt** **Pepper**	(1) In a skillet, heat the oil and brown the beef; season it.
2 6-oz. cans water chestnuts, drained and sliced **¼ lb. mushrooms, sliced** **¾ cup raisins** **1 package frozen small peas** **1 beef bouillon cube, dissolved in ½ cup hot water** **1 teaspoon curry powder** **1 Tablespoon soy sauce**	(2) In a mixing bowl, combine the meat and these seven ingredients. Using two forks, gently toss the mixture to blend it thoroughly.
1 orange, sliced paper-thin and seeded	(3) In a lightly oiled baking dish, arrange the meat mixture. Top it with the orange slices and bake it, uncovered at 350° for 30 minutes.

CABBAGE ROLLS AND RAISINS

(German)

This recipe is also known as German-style stuffed cabbage.

Serves 6
Doubles
Refrigerates

Preparation: 30 minutes
Cooking: 45 minutes
Preheat oven: 350°

(continued)

12 large cabbage leaves
   Boiling water

(1) In a large saucepan, arrange the cabbage leaves. Pour boiling water over them to cover. Let them stand about 5 minutes; drain them. With a sharp knife, remove the leaf base.

½ cup raisins
¾ lb. ground round
1½ cups cooked rice
1 onion, grated
1½ teaspoons salt
¾ teaspoon dill weed
3 Tablespoons water

(2) In a mixing bowl, combine and blend well these seven ingredients.

(3) Make six piles of two cabbage leaves each. Spoon the meat filling into the center in equal proportions. Fold in the edges of the leaves and then roll them, skewering them with toothpicks. Arrange the rolls in a skillet.

At this point you may stop and continue later.

1 10½-oz. can condensed beef broth

(4) Pour the broth over the cabbage rolls and simmer them, covered, for 30 minutes. Remove the rolls to a serving dish and keep them warm.

2 Tablespoons tomato paste
3 Tablespoons cider vinegar
1 Tablespoon cornstarch
⅓ cup raisins

(5) Pour the remaining broth into a saucepan, adding water to equal 1 cup. Add the tomato paste. Combine the vinegar and cornstarch and add it. Cook the sauce, stirring constantly, until it is thickened and smooth. Stir in the additional raisins. Pour the sauce over the cabbage rolls and bake them, covered, at 350° for 15 minutes. (If desired, the recipe may be fully prepared and then baked at the time of serving.)

LAMB AND RAISINS WITH ALMONDS

(Middle Eastern)

Serves 6
Doubles
Refrigerates
Freezes

Preparation: 30 minutes
Cooking: 1½ hours
Preheat oven: 350°

2½ **lbs. lean shoulder of lamb, cut in bite-sized pieces**
1 **Tablespoon turmeric**
1 **teaspoon ginger root, grated**
1 **onion, chopped**
1 **cup yoghurt**

(1) In a mixing bowl, combine these five ingredients, stirring to blend them well.

4 **Tablespoons butter**
1 **onion, chopped**
1 **teaspoon ginger root, grated**

(2) In a flame-proof casserole, heat the butter and in it cook the onion and ginger root until the onion is translucent.

1 **cup yoghurt**

(3) Add the lamb mixture and cook it, stirring, for 5 minutes. Stir in the yoghurt and bake the dish, covered, at 350° for 1 hour, or until it is just barely tender.

At this point you may stop and continue later.

1 **cup yoghurt**
½ **cup pine nuts**
¾ **cup raisins**

(4) Into the yoghurt, stir the pine nuts and raisins. Add the mixture to the contents of the casserole, and continue to bake it, covered, for 30 more minutes.

PORK ROLLS AND RAISINS

Serves 6
Doubles
Refrigerates

Preparation: 25 minutes
Cooking: 1 hour

1 2½-lb. pork steak, trimmed of excess fat, and cut into 6 thinly sliced serving pieces

(1) Prepare the meat and reserve it.

1½ cups breadcrumbs
¾ cup chopped apple
1 onion, chopped
¾ cup raisins
½ teaspoon salt
½ teaspoon thyme
2 Tablespoons water

(2) In a mixing bowl, combine these seven ingredients and, using two forks, toss them together. Divide the stuffing equally on each serving of pork. Roll and skewer each piece.

At this point you may stop and continue later.

3 Tablespoons butter
1 10½-oz. can condensed chicken broth

(3) In a flame-proof casserole, heat the butter and in it brown the pork rolls. Add the broth and simmer the dish, covered, for 45 minutes, or until the meat is tender.

1½ teaspoons cornstarch mixed with 1 Tablespoon water

(4) Remove the pork rolls to a serving dish and keep them warm. Skim the excess fat from the remaining broth, add the cornstarch mixture, and cook it, stirring constantly, until it is thickened and smooth. Pour it over the pork rolls.

FRESH TONGUE WITH RAISINS

(Dutch)

Do not be discouraged by the long preparation time; most of it is devoted to boiling the tongue, during which time you are free from kitchen duty!

Serves 6
Refrigerates
Freezes

Preparation: 3 hours
Cooking: 10 minutes

12 **fresh lamb tongues or 6 veal tongues or 1 beef tongue**
2 **onions, peeled and quartered**
2 **garlic cloves, peeled and split**
1 **bay leaf**
1½ **teaspoons salt**
6 **peppercorns**

(1) In a soup kettle, combine these six ingredients, and add water to cover them by one inch. Bring the liquid to the boil, reduce the heat, and simmer the tongue, covered, for 2 hours, or until it is fork-tender. Allow it to cool in the broth. Strain and reserve the stock. Skin the tongue and discard the waste. Arrange the tongue on a serving dish and keep it warm.

At this point you may stop and continue later.

2 **cups reserved stock**
¾ **cup raisins**
½ **cup brown sugar**
½ **teaspoon ground cumin**
½ **teaspoon marjoram**
3 **Tablespoons cider vinegar**
Salt

(2) Into a saucepan, measure the stock. Add the raisins and seasonings and bring the mixture to the boil, stirring, to dissolve the sugar. Add salt, if necessary.

2 **Tablespoons cornstarch mixed with ½ cup dry white wine**

(3) Add the cornstarch mixture and cook the sauce, stirring constantly, until it is thickened and smooth.

(continued)

(4) Pour the sauce over the tongue. (If beef tongue is used, it is more easily served if sliced away from the table; lamb or veal tongue may be served whole.) If desired, the tongue may be arranged in a casserole, the sauce poured over it, and the dish simmered for 10 minutes before serving. This method is easier when the dish is not prepared in one complete operation.

A pleasant variation in the sauce: omit the sugar and, in place of it, use ⅔ cup blackberry jelly, stirred until it is dissolved.

====

CHICKEN AND RAISINS IN ORANGE SAUCE*

Serves 6
Doubles
Refrigerates

Preparation: 30 minutes
Cooking: 1 hour
Preheat oven: 350°

2 Tablespoons butter
2 Tablespoons oil
Serving-pieces of chicken for 6 persons
Salt
Pepper
Paprika

(1) In a flame-proof casserole, heat the butter and oil and brown the chicken; season it. Remove it, and discard all but 3 Tablespoons of the fat.

2 onions, chopped
Cinnamon
Ginger
¾ cup golden raisins
½ cup slivered almonds (optional)

(2) In the remaining fat, cook the onion until translucent. Replace the chicken and sprinkle it with cinnamon and ginger. Add the raisins and, if desired, the almonds.

* A contribution of Joseph Florestano, page 389.

1 6-oz. can frozen orange juice concentrate, fully thawed
Water
2 Tablespoons cornstarch

(3) In a saucepan, combine the orange juice concentrate and water to equal 2½ cups (2½ cups fresh orange juice may also be used). Mix the cornstarch with a little of the orange juice and add it to the contents of the saucepan. Over high heat, cook the sauce, stirring constantly, until it is thickened and smooth. Pour it over the contents of the casserole.

At this point you may stop and continue later.

3 oranges, peeled, sectioned, and seeded

(4) Bake the chicken, covered, at 350° for 1 hour, or until it is tender. Garnish the dish with the orange segments.

CHICKEN AND RAISIN PILAF I

(Guinean)

Serves 6
Doubles
Refrigerates
Freezes

Preparation: 30 minutes
Cooking: 1 hour
Preheat oven: 350°

2 Tablespoons butter
2 Tablespoons oil
Serving-pieces of chicken for 6 persons
Salt
Pepper

(1) In a flame-proof casserole, heat the butter and oil and brown the chicken; season it. Remove.

1½ cups natural raw rice
1½ cups golden raisins
1 teaspoon salt
1 teaspoon nutmeg
Grated rind and juice of 1 lemon

(2) To the remaining fat, add the rice, stirring to coat each grain. Stir in the raisins and seasonings. Replace the chicken, spooning the rice over it.

(continued)

1 **cup light cream**
2 **10½-oz. cans condensed chicken broth**

(3) Combine the cream and broth and add the mixture to the casserole.

At this point you may stop and continue later.

(4) Pour over casserole and bake, covered, at 350° for 1 hour, or until the chicken and rice are tender and the liquid is absorbed.

CHICKEN AND RAISIN PILAF II

Follow the directions for Chicken and Raisins in Orange Sauce, page 350, adding 1 cup natural raw rice to the cooked onion, stirring the mixture well, and using 2½ cups orange juice (without cornstarch added to it).

CHICKEN LIVERS AND RAISINS
(French)

During most of the preparation time, the raisins are on their own— and so are you. A very easy dish.

Serves 6
Doubles
Refrigerates

Preparation: 1 hour
Cooking: 20 minutes

1 **cup raisins**
  Madeira wine

(1) In a mixing bowl, plump the raisins in enough madeira to cover for 1 hour.

2 **Tablespoons butter**
1 **onion, minced**

(2) Meanwhile, in a saucepan, heat the butter and in it cook the onion until translucent.

1 Tablespoon flour
A bouquet garni, see page xiii
1 cup dry white wine

(3) Stir in the flour and, over gentle heat, cook the mixture for 3 minutes. Add the *bouquet garni* and the white wine. Simmer the sauce, covered, for 30 minutes, stirring often.

1½ lbs. chicken livers

(4) Add the raisins, drained, and the chicken livers. Simmer the dish, covered, for 20 minutes or until the livers are cooked through but still tender.

COD FILETS AND CURRANTS
(Greek)

Serves 6
Doubles
Refrigerates*

Preparation: 20 minutes
Cooking: 25 minutes
Preheat oven: 400°

1 cup dry white wine
⅔ cup currants

(1) In a saucepan, heat the wine, remove it from the stove, add the currants, and let them stand.

½ cup olive oil
2 onions, minced
2 cloves garlic, minced
⅓ cup parsley, chopped
1 1-lb. can whole tomatoes, drained

(2) In a separate saucepan, heat the oil and cook the onions and garlic until translucent. Add the parsley and tomatoes, and simmer the mixture, uncovered, for 10 minutes.

Reserved wine and currants
½ teaspoon salt
Pinch of pepper
¼ teaspoon ground clove
Juice of 1 lemon

(3) Stir in the wine and currants. Then stir in the seasonings. Simmer the sauce for 5 minutes.

At this point you may stop and continue later.

* Only the sauce can be refrigerated.

(continued)

Cod filet servings for 6 persons (about 2½ lbs.)

(4) In a lightly oiled baking dish, arrange the filets in a single layer. Pour the sauce over them and bake the fish, uncovered, at 400° for 25 minutes, or until it flakes easily.

SPINACH AND RAISINS

Serves 6
Doubles

Preparation: 30 minutes
Cooking: 10 minutes

3 Tablespoons butter
3 Tablespoons oil
1 clove garlic, put through a press
⅓ cup golden raisins, plumped in hot water and drained on absorbent paper
⅓ cup pine nuts
Salt

(1) In a saucepan, heat the butter and oil and in it cook the garlic. Stir in the plumped raisins and pine nuts; season the mixture to taste.

At this point you may stop and continue later.

2 lbs. spinach, washed, picked over, cooked, and drained

(2) While the spinach is cooking, reheat the sauce.* Toss the prepared spinach with the sauce and serve it at once.

* The sauce can be prepared, refrigerated, heated, and added to the spinach when serving.

BULGUR AND CURRANTS WITH PINE NUTS

Serves 6
Doubles
Refrigerates
Freezes

Preparation: 10 minutes
Cooking: 15 minutes

2 **Tablespoons butter**	(1) In a saucepan, heat the butter
1¼ **cups bulgur**	and in it "toast" the bulgur, stirring
¼ **cup currants**	the grain constantly with a fork,
¼ **cup pine nuts**	until a few of the grains are golden
1 **teaspoon salt**	brown. Stir in the currants, pine nuts,
	and salt.

At this point you may stop and continue later.

2 **10½-oz. cans condensed**	(2) Add the chicken broth, bring the
chicken broth	liquid to the boil, stir the grain once
	with a fork, reduce the heat to low,
	and simmer it, covered, for 15
	minutes, or until the bulgur is tender
	and the liquid is absorbed.

NOODLES AND RAISINS

A substantial side dish to accompany roast meats and poultry.

Serves 6
Doubles
Refrigerates

Preparation: 30 minutes
Cooking: 40 minutes
Preheat oven: 375°

1 **lb. noodles**	(1) Cook the noodles in salted water
⅔ **cup golden raisins**	until tender; drain them. Meanwhile,
	plump the raisins by barely covering
	them with hot water. Let them stand.
5 **Tablespoons butter**	(2) In a saucepan, melt the butter
2 **onions, chopped**	and in it cook the onions until
	translucent. Add the raisins and
	raisin water.
	(3) In a mixing bowl, using two
	forks, toss the noodles with the raisin
	mixture. Arrange the noodles in a
	well-buttered baking dish.

(continued)

355

At this point you may stop and continue later.

(3) Bake the noodles at 375° for 40 minutes, or until they are brown and crusty on top. Cut them into squares when serving.

RICE AND CURRANTS

(Indian)

Serves 6
Doubles
Refrigerates

Preparation: 15 minutes
Cooking: 15 minutes

3 Tablespoons butter
1 onion chopped
¾ cup currants

(1) In a saucepan, melt the butter and in it cook the onion and currants until the onion is translucent.

1½ cups natural raw rice*
1 teaspoon salt
½ teaspoon curry powder
½ teaspoon saffron, crumbled

(2) Add the rice and salt, stirring to coat each grain. Stir in the seasonings.

2 10½-oz. cans condensed
chicken broth
Water

(3) To the broth, add water to equal 3½ cups. Pour the liquid over the rice, bring it to a boil, stirring it once with a fork; reduce the heat, and simmer the rice, covered, for 15 minutes, or until it is tender and the liquid is absorbed.

* This dish is particularly good made with brown rice, which takes about 50 minutes to cook. Prepare the onion-currant mixture, then separately prepare the rice and its seasonings, using an additional 2 Tablespoons butter. Add the currants for the final 15 minutes of cooking.

SPAGHETTI AND RAISIN SAUCE*
(Italian)

The recipe may be made with any spaghetti-like *pasta*. It is very good, though probably quite un-Italian, if tenderized pitted dried apricots, chopped, are substituted for the raisins.

Serves 6
Doubles

Preparation: 15 minutes
Cooking: 35 minutes

½ cup olive oil
2 cloves garlic, minced
6 Tablespoons chopped walnuts
6 Tablespoons pine nuts
6 anchovy filets, chopped
½ cup raisins, plumped for 5 minutes in hot water and thoroughly drained on absorbent paper
2 teaspoons oregano
¼ cup minced parsley

(1) In a deep skillet or casserole, heat the oil and cook the garlic until it is just barely golden. Add the remaining ingredients and simmer the sauce, covered, over low heat.

1 lb. spaghetti

(2) In a soup kettle, cook the spaghetti in salted water until it is barely tender. Drain it, reserving some of the water.

Grated Italian cheese

(3) Add the spaghetti to the sauce, together with some of the water, as needed. Over gentle heat, finish cooking the spaghetti in the sauce, tossing it frequently to meld the flavors (about 15 minutes). Serve the dish with grated cheese.

* This recipe is donated by Edward Giobbi, a friend and neighbor. Ed is a painter by profession and a cook by avocation. His first cookbook, *Italian Family Cooking*, is a collection of recipes from his native Abruzzi, illustrated by his three children. The tips on baking are his wife's, a bread-maker *par excellence*.

RAISIN BREAD

Follow the directions for Cranberry Bread, page 124, using, in place of the cranberries, 1½ cups raisins or currants, added after the third cup of flour.

BOSTON BROWN BREAD

Traditionally, brown bread is steamed, but baking is easier, perhaps.

Serving: two round loaves

Preparation: 45 minutes
Baking: 50 minutes
Preheat oven: 350°

2 cups buttermilk
½ cup dark molasses
1 egg

(1) In a mixing bowl, mix well the buttermilk, molasses, and egg.

2 cups whole wheat flour
½ cup white flour
2 teaspoons baking soda
1 teaspoon salt
1 cup raisins

(2) In a separate mixing bowl, blend well the dry ingredients and then add the raisins.

(3) Add the buttermilk mixture, stirring until the batter is smooth.

(4) Into two well buttered 1-lb. cans, spoon the batter equally. Allow it to stand 30 minutes.

(5) Bake the bread at 350° for 50 minutes, or until a sharp knife inserted at the center comes out clean. Remove the loaves from the cans to cool on a rack.

RAISIN MUFFINS

Follow the directions for Apple Muffins, page 19, using, in place of the apple, ½ cup raisins or currants added to the liquid ingredients.

RAISIN COMPOTE

(Rumanian)

Serves 6
Doubles
Refrigerates

Preparation: 1 hour*
Cooking: 10 minutes
Chilling time: at least 2 hours

2 cups golden raisins	(1) In a mixing bowl, soak the raisins in water to cover for 1 hour. Drain them, reserving 1 cup of the liquid.
Reserved liquid **½ cup honey**	(2) In a saucepan, boil the water and honey for 5 minutes.
	At this point you may stop and continue later.
Reserved raisins **Grated rind and juice of 1 lemon**	(3) To the honey syrup, add the raisins and lemon rind and juice. Simmer the raisins covered, for 10 minutes, skimming them as necessary.
3 Tablespoons pine nuts **Sour cream**	(4) Chill the compote. When serving it, stir in the pine nuts and garnish each portion with a dollop of sour cream.

* The "preparation" consists of little more than soaking the raisins.

RUM RAISIN ICE CREAM

Follow the directions for Helen McCully's Ice Cream, page 457, omitting the vanilla and using 1 cup raisins stewed in ⅓ cup rum until they are soft. Add the raisins and rum to the hot custard before cooking it.

RAISINS JUBILEE

> Serves 6
> Doubles
> Refrigerates

Marination: 1 hour
Preparation: 10 minutes
Cooking: 3 minutes

1½ cups raisins
Boiling water

(1) In a mixing bowl, pour the boiling water over the raisins to cover. Let them stand for 5 minutes, or until they are well plumped. Drain them thoroughly.

5 Tablespoons dark brown sugar
Grated rind and juice of 1 lemon
¼ cup cognac

(2) In the mixing bowl stir well these four ingredients, add the raisins and allow them to stand for 1 hour.

3 Tablespoons cognac
Vanilla ice cream

(3) Put the raisins and their marinade in a serving bowl. In a small saucepan, warm the brandy, ignite it, pour it over the raisins and, when the flame dies, spoon the raisins over firm vanilla ice cream.

RAISIN PIE

I like this raisin pie more than most because it is simply made and very fruity to the taste.

> Serving: one 9-inch pie
> Doubles
> Refrigerates

Preparation: 25 minutes*
Cooking: 40 minutes
Preheat oven: 450°

2 cups raisins
  Grated rind of 1 lemon
  Grated rind of 1 orange

(1) In a saucepan, combine the raisins and grated rinds.

4 Tablespoons flour
½ cup light brown sugar, packed
  Pinch of salt

(2) Add the flour, sugar, and salt, and stir the mixture well.

1½ cups water
⅓ cup lemon juice
½ cup orange juice

(3) Combine the three liquids. Add a little to the raisins, stirring. Over gentle heat, cook the mixture, stirring constantly; gradually add all of the liquid until it boils and the sauce is thickened and smooth. Allow the mixture to cool slightly.

Short pastry for a 9-inch pie

(4) Line a pie plate with short pastry, pour in the filling, cover it with a lattice crust. Bake the pie at 450° for 10 minutes; reduce the heat to 350° and continue to bake it for 30 minutes, or until the crust is golden brown.

* The preparation time does not include readying the pastry, page 458.

STEAMED CURRANT PUDDING

Follow the directions for Steamed Date Pudding, page 139, using, in place of the dates, 2 cups currants.

RICE PUDDING WITH RAISINS

This recipe is my mother's. She did not like pasty rice puddings
(which are more common than not) and so devised this one, which
is creamy and—I think—very good.

> Serves 6
> Doubles
> Refrigerates

Preparation: 10 minutes
Cooking: 3 hours
Preheat oven: 250°

1½ quarts whole milk
4 Tablespoons natural raw rice
¼ cup sugar
1 teaspoon vanilla
Dash of salt

(1) In a 2-quart casserole, combine these five ingredients. Bake them at 250° for 2½ hours, stirring every 20 minutes.

½ cup golden raisins

(2) Stir in the raisins and allow the pudding to cook for 30 minutes longer without being stirred.

CREAM RAISIN SAUCE

(Greek)

For broiled poultry and fish.

> Serving: 2 cups
> Doubles
> Refrigerates

Marination: 45 minutes
Preparation: 15 minutes

⅔ cup raisins
½ cup dry sherry, warmed

(1) In a mixing bowl, marinate the raisins in the sherry for 45 minutes.

2 Tablespoons butter
1½ Tablespoons flour
1 cup milk
   Salt
   Pepper

(2) In a saucepan, melt the butter and cook the flour in it over gentle heat, stirring for a few minutes. Gradually add the milk, stirring constantly until the mixture is thickened and smooth. Season the sauce to taste.

   Marinated raisins, drained
½ teaspoon cinnamon
½ teaspoon nutmeg
   Juice of ½ lemon

(3) Stir in the raisins and seasonings. Simmer the sauce, stirring, for 5 minutes.

RAISIN AND MUSTARD SAUCE

(American)

For hot tongue, boiled or baked ham, and barbecued meats.

Serving: about 2 cups
Doubles
Refrigerates

Preparation: 25 minutes

3 Tablespoons butter
2 Tablespoons flour
1 10½-oz. can condensed beef broth, plus water to equal 1½ cups

(1) In a saucepan, melt the butter and in it, over gentle heat, cook the flour for a few minutes. Gradually add the broth, stirring constantly until the mixture is thickened and smooth.

½ cup dark brown sugar, packed
1½ Tablespoons cider vinegar
⅔ cup raisins
½ teaspoon salt
¼ teaspoon pepper
¼ teaspoon ground clove
1½ teaspoons dry mustard, moistened and stirred to a smooth paste
   Grated rind and juice of ½ lemon

(2) Add the remaining ingredients, stirring until the mixture is well blended. Over gentle heat, simmer the sauce for 5 minutes. Serve it hot.

RAISIN SAUCE WITH RUM

For desserts.

> Serving: 1½ cups
> Doubles
> Refrigerates

Preparation: 20 minutes

½ **cup raisins** ¾ **cup water**	(1) In a saucepan, simmer the raisins until fully plumped and soft (about 5 minutes).
¼ **cup currant jelly** 2 **Tablespoons butter**	(2) Add the jelly and butter, stirring until both are melted.
2 **teaspoons cornstarch mixed** **with** ¼ **cup cold water** **Pinch of salt** ⅓ **cup dark rum**	(3) Add the cornstarch and cook the mixture, stirring constantly until the sauce is thickened and smooth. Stir in the salt and rum.

CURRANT STUFFING FOR BAKED FISH
(Turkish)

> Serving: about 3 cups

Preparation: 20 minutes
Cooking: 25 minutes
Preheat oven: 400°

⅓ **cup olive oil** 3 **onions, minced**	(1) In a skillet, heat the oil and cook the onion until translucent.
½ **cup pine nuts**	(2) Add the pine nuts and cook them for 3 minutes.
1 **cup breadcrumbs** ½ **teaspoon ground coriander** ¾ **teaspoon salt** ¼ **teaspoon pepper**	(3) Stir in the breadcrumbs and seasonings. Remove from the heat.
¾ **cup parsley, chopped** ¾ **cup currants**	(4) Stir in the parsley and currants.

4- to 5-lb. baking fish
Lemon slices

(5) With this mixture, stuff the fish ⅔ full. Garnish the fish with lemon slices and bake it, uncovered, in a lightly oiled baking dish at 400° for 25 minutes, or until it tests firm when pricked with a fork.

RAISIN STUFFING FOR POULTRY AND PORK

For *each* 4 cups of seasoned breadcrumbs, seasoned croutons, or packaged dressing:

2 **cups raisins, plumped for 5**
    minutes in hot water and drained
1 **small onion, grated**
6 **Tablespoons butter, melted**

If a more moist dressing is desired, toss the ingredients with a little of the raisin water.

RHUBARB

Rhubarb is not a fruit, but a vegetable. It is, however, always used as a fruit (just as tomatoes, which are fruits, are conversely used as vegetables); hence it is included here. Rhubarb was known to the ancient Greeks who, one story has it, may have named the plant: *rheon barbaron*, "wild-growing from the Rha" (now the Volga, where it grew extensively).

It was brought to England from the Volga region in 1573, but remained for 200 years only a gardener's curiosity. Its use as a food is recent; as late as 1810 a Deptford farmer sent some to market in London, but there was no buyer for it. One of the most easily grown vegetables, rhubarb is a perennial and, once established, is virtually indestructible.

Sometimes called the pie-plant, *Rheum rhaptonticum,* rhubarb produces large clumps

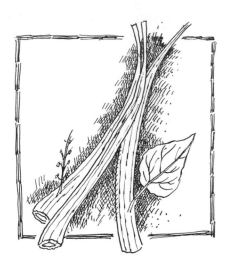

of enormous leaves, perhaps 2 feet across, on a stalk 1 inch or more in diameter and up to 2 feet long. Used in sweet dishes, preserves, and pies, the uncooked rhubarb stalk is very acid and the leaves are sometimes toxic. As a medicine, however, it is one of the oldest remedies known to man, and is still used.

RHUBARB SOUP

Serves 6
Doubles
Refrigerates

Preparation: 30 minutes
Chilling time: at least 2 hours

2 lbs. rhubarb, trimmed, rinsed, and chopped
4 cups water

(1) In a saucepan, cook the rhubarb, covered, until it is very soft (about 10 minutes). In the container of an electric blender, whirl the rhubarb on medium speed, a little at a time, until it is pureed. Return the rhubarb to the saucepan.

1 Tablespoon cornstarch mixed with 2 Tablespoons cold water
Sugar

(2) Add the cornstarch and, over moderate heat, cook the mixture, stirring constantly, until it is thickened and smooth. Season the soup with sugar, to taste. Simmer the soup, uncovered, for 5 minutes. Cool and chill it.

Whipped cream

(3) Serve the soup cold, garnished with whipped cream.

BAKED RHUBARB

An unusual accompaniment to roast lamb or pork.

Serves 6
Doubles
Refrigerates

Preparation: 15 minutes
Cooking: 15 minutes
Preheat oven: 325°

2 lbs. fresh rhubarb, trimmed, rinsed, and cut in 2-inch lengths
1 cup sugar
Pinch of salt

(1) Shake the excess rinsing water from the rhubarb. In a casserole or baking dish, arrange the rhubarb; sprinkle it with the sugar and salt.

*At this point you may stop and
continue later.*

(2) Bake the rhubarb, uncovered, at
325° for 15 minutes, or until it is
tender.

RHUBARB BROWN BETTY

(American)

Serves 6
Doubles
Refrigerates

Preparation: 15 minutes*
Cooking: 40 minutes
Preheat oven: 350°

⅓ **cup sugar**
**Grated rind of 1 lemon or 1
orange**
½ **teaspoon nutmeg**
¼ **teaspoon cinnamon**
Pinch of salt

(1) In a mixing bowl, stir together
these five ingredients.

8 **Tablespoons butter**
2 **cups breadcrumbs**

(2) In a saucepan, melt the butter
and into it, stir the breadcrumbs.
Stir in the sugar mixture.

2 **cups stewed rhubarb, page 370**

(3) Over the bottom of a buttered
baking dish, make a layer of ⅓ of
the crumbs. Over them, spoon an
even layer of 1 cup of the rhubarb.
Repeat the layers of breadcrumbs
and rhubarb. End with a layer of
breadcrumbs.

(4) Bake the dessert, covered, at
350° for 15 minutes. Remove the
cover and continue baking for 25
minutes, or until the top is golden
brown.

* The preparation time does not include readying the stewed rhubarb.

RHUBARB PUDDING

Follow the directions for Apricot Pudding, page 45, using: 4½ cups fresh rhubarb, cut in 2-inch pieces; 3 cups water; 1 cup sugar; pinch of salt; grated rind and juice of ½ lemon.

STEWED RHUBARB
(American)

This recipe is the classic for stewed rhubarb, which can be served alone or used in other dishes. The large leaves must be removed; they are toxic if eaten. One pound of fresh rhubarb yields 2 cups of stewed.

> Serving: 2 cups
> Refrigerates

Preparation: 30 minutes

1 lb. fresh rhubarb, trimmed, rinsed, and cut in 2-inch lengths
Water

(1) In a saucepan, using only sufficient water to start the cooking, stew the rhubarb for 10 minutes, or until it is just tender.

Pinch of salt
Grated rind of 1 orange (optional)
Sugar

(2) Stir in the salt and orange rind. Sweeten the rhubarb with sugar to taste. Cool and chill the rhubarb.

Variation: Stew 8 cups of prepared fresh rhubarb with 2 cups orange juice; add ¼ cup orange marmalade, 1 cup honey, the juice of 1 lemon, and ½ cup sweet sherry (optional).

RHUBARB PIE
(American)

Rhubarb pie is a classic American dessert.

> Serving: one 9-inch pie

Preparation: 20 minutes*
Cooking: 40 minutes
Preheat oven: 450°

* The preparation time does not include readying the pastry, page 458.

| 1 cup sugar | (1) In a large mixing bowl, stir |

1 cup sugar
2 Tablespoons flour
1 egg, lightly beaten
Pinch of salt
3 cups fresh rhubarb, cut in 1-inch pieces, rinsed, and drained on absorbent paper

(1) In a large mixing bowl, stir together the first four ingredients. Add the rhubarb and, using two forks, gently toss them to coat the rhubarb thoroughly.

Pastry for a two-crust pie

(2) Line a pie tin with a bottom crust. Into the pastry shell, spoon the rhubarb. Add a top crust, crimp the edges with a fork to seal them, and puncture the crust several times with a fork. Bake the pie at 450° for 40 minutes, or until the crust is golden brown.

Variation: for Sour-Cream Rhubarb Pie, mix 1 cup sugar, 2 Tablespoons of flour, and a pinch of salt with 1 cup sour cream and 3 egg yolks, lightly beaten. In the unbaked 9-inch pastry shell, arrange the rhubarb, pour the custard over it; omit the top crust. Bake the pie at 350° for 1 hour. Meanwhile, beat the remaining egg whites until frothy; add singly 6 Tablespoons sugar, beating constantly until the meringue is stiff. Spread it over the surface of the custard. Continue baking the pie at 350° for 20 minutes, or until the meringue is golden.

RHUBARB AND STRAWBERRY MOUSSE

Serves 6
Doubles
Refrigerates

Preparation: 20 minutes
Chilling time: at least 3 hours

2 cups Stewed Rhubarb, page 370
1 packet unflavored gelatin
2 Tablespoons lemon juice

(1) In a saucepan, bring the stewed rhubarb to the boil. Pour it into the container of an electric blender, cover it, and on high speed, liquidize it. While the blender is running, add the gelatin and lemon juice. Blend the mixture until the gelatin is dissolved. Allow it to cool and then chill it slightly.

(continued)

1 **pint strawberries, hulled, rinsed, halved, and drained on absorbent paper**

(2) In a mold, rinsed with cold water, arrange the strawberries, cut side up (so that the uncut side will show when the dessert is unmolded).

3 **egg whites, beaten stiff**
Whipped cream

(3) Fold a little of the rhubarb into the egg whites. Then fold all of the egg whites into the rhubarb. Spoon the mixture over the strawberries. Chill the dessert for at least 3 hours before unmolding it. Serve it garnished with whipped cream.

RHUBARB PUNCH

(Iranian)

A delightfully refreshing drink. It should be slightly tart.

> Serves 6
> Doubles
> Refrigerates

Follow the directions for Rhubarb Soup, page 368, omitting the cornstarch and whipped cream. Use the rhubarb with equal parts ice water, poured over cracked ice.

STRAW-
BERRIES

How frustrating for the strawberry to have no
connection whatsoever with straw and, indeed, to
have no relation to a berry. Indeed, botanically
speaking, the strawberry is neither a berry nor a
fruit. Rather it is the greatly enlarged stem end
of its small white blossom in which the true fruit
(the seeds of the plant) are embedded. Moreover,
the strawberry is a member of the very large
Rose Family (*Rosaceae*) which embraces some
one hundred genera and over 2,000 species,
including the hawthorne, raspberry, apple, cherry,
pear, plums, and, of course, roses. As if these
facts were not sufficiently overwhelming, the
humble strawberry seems to have no proper
private life of its own, but propagates by means of
underground runners from the "mother" plant. It
is of little comfort that strawberry shortcake (see
page 381) is, even more than apple pie, considered
the most classic of American desserts.

Never mind, little strawberry! In the sixteenth-century Dr. William Butler ate wild strawberries (*Fragaria vesca*) and wrote ecstatically, "Doubtless God could have made a better berry, but doubtless God never did." And surely there was no call for Him to do so, for the strawberry, growing low to the ground and often hiding itself under its own saw-toothed furry leaves, is one of the most delicious of Nature's gifts to man.

There are eight species of *Fragaria*, all native to temperate regions. One of these, that eaten by the good Dr. Butler, is common to America and Europe. The wild or wood strawberry, cultivated for centuries, is not considered important in today's commercial crop, however. The American strawberry we buy in the supermarket is a cross of Virginian and Chilean varieties; new hybrids are frequently developed by the United States Department of Agriculture. As for Old World strawberries, the small varieties raised in England, France, and Italy have been improved in size and succulence by the introduction of New World species. In America, there are ten June-bearing and three Fall-bearing varieties; there are also ever-bearing *fraises* imported from Europe for the home-grower.

Strawberries, which contain 90 percent water by weight, equal 90 calories per cupful and contain a large amount of vitamin C; one handful of fresh-picked berries yields the daily adult need of this vitamin, in addition to more vitamin A than there is in an equal amount of raisins.

Commercial production is directed to immediate use and to freezing, canning, or preserving. Because the fruit is very perishable, it is picked by hand and very often is grown near the centers of consumption; it requires cool, but not refrigerated, dry storage. The United States produces some 250,000 tons annually; our principal crop is from California, which yields 43 percent of the total domestic output, and where the fruit is grown under artificial irrigation. In Europe, the principal producers are Britain, France, and Italy.

In these recipes, frozen—sliced or whole—strawberries may be substituted for the fresh fruit.

STRAWBERRY SOUP

(*Russian*)

This soup may be served hot or chilled.

Serves 6
Doubles
Refrigerates

Preparation: 20 minutes

1 quart ripe strawberries, hulled and rinsed
¾ cup sugar
Pinch of salt
1 cup sour cream
1 cup dry red wine
4 cups cold water

In the container of an electric blender, combine the strawberries, sugar, salt, sour cream, and wine. Whirl them on medium speed for 15 seconds, or until the mixture is smooth. In a saucepan, combine the strawberry mixture and water. Heat the soup slowly, stirring; do not allow it to boil. If desired, chill the soup.

STRAWBERRY COBBLER

Follow the directions for Apple Cobbler, page 23, using, in place of the apple, 2 cups sliced frozen strawberries, thawed to room temperature and drained.

STRAWBERRY ICE CREAM

Follow the directions for Helen McCully's Ice Cream, page 457, adding 1 quart ripe strawberries, rinsed, hulled, drained on absorbent paper, and halved; in a mixing bowl, combine the berries with ¼ cup sugar and allow them to "bleed" for 1 hour. Sieve the berries and add the pulp to the hot custard before cooling it.

STRAWBERRIES IN ICE CREAM

(French)

"Strawberries Romanoff" would seem to be a Russian dish, but is actually a classic French dessert. A simpler version of the dish is found on page 377.

Serves 6
Freezes

Preparation: 30 minutes
Freezing time: 2 hours

1 pint vanilla ice cream, page 457
1 cup heavy cream, whipped
Juice of 1 lemon
¼ cup orange-flavored liqueur

(1) In a large mixing bowl, beat the ice cream with a fork until it is soft, but not melted. Fold in the whipped cream. Then add the lemon juice and liqueur.

2 quarts strawberries, hulled, rinsed, and drained on absorbent paper

(2) Fold in the strawberries. Spoon the dessert into a serving dish and put it in the freezer until it is used.

STRAWBERRY MOUSSE*

Serves 6
Refrigerates

Preparation: 1¼ hours
Chilling time: at least 3 hours

1 quart strawberries, rinsed, hulled, and well drained

(1) Reserving several berries for garnish, puree the remainder in an electric blender.

½ cup sugar
½ cup dry white wine

(2) Combine the sugar and wine; add the pureed berries, stirring to blend the mixture well. Chill for 30 minutes.

* This recipe is contributed by Nedda Casei, the Metropolitan Opera mezzo-soprano. Nedda, an intrepid cook herself, is an ever welcome cooking companion whose ideas are fun and tasty; indeed, I do not believe we have ever had a mutual culinary failure!

2 **packets unflavored gelatin,
softened in ½ cup cold water**
½ **cup boiling water**

(3) To the softened gelatin, add the boiling water, stirring constantly until the gelatin is dissolved. Chill for 30 minutes.

1 **cup heavy cream whipped
Reserved berries**

(4) Combine the berries and gelatin, beating the mixture until it is somewhat light and thickened. Fold in the whipped cream. Pour the mousse into a 2-quart mold and chill it for at least 3 hours. To serve the dessert, unmold it onto a large dish and garnish it with the reserved berries.

STRAWBERRIES AND ORANGE WITH WHIPPED CREAM
(French)

This simpler version of Strawberries Romanoff is still an elegant dessert.

> Serves 6
> Doubles
> Refrigerates*

Preparation: 30 minutes
Chilling time: 3 hours

1 **quart strawberries, rinsed and
hulled**
½ **cup orange-flavored liqueur**
½ **cup orange juice**

(1) In a china or silver bowl, combine the strawberries, liqueur, and juice. Refrigerate them for 3 hours, stirring gently from time to time.

1 **cup heavy cream**
2 **Tablespoons confectioner's
sugar**
½ **teaspoon vanilla**

(2) In a mixing bowl, whip the cream until it begins to thicken; add singly the 2 Tablespoonsful of sugar and then the vanilla, whipping until the cream is stiff.

At this point you may stop and continue later.

(3) At the time of serving, fold the cream into the berries. Serve immediately.

* *Note:* The strawberries and the cream will refrigerate separately; once combined, they must be served.

STRAWBERRY PUDDING I

(Finnish)

The dessert may be made with any ripe berry or, if desired, with chopped ripe peaches.

Serves 6
Refrigerates

Preparation: 30 minutes
Cooking: 35 minutes
Preheat oven: 375°
Chilling time: 3 hours

5 egg yolks
¾ cup sugar

(1) In a mixing bowl, beat the yolks until they are light yellow. Add the sugar and continue beating until the mixture is satiny.

3 cups strawberries, crushed
1 cup breadcrumbs
1 teaspoon vanilla

(2) Stir in the strawberries. Add the breadcrumbs and vanilla. Blend the mixture well.

5 egg whites
½ teaspoon salt

(3) In a mixing bowl, beat the whites until they are frothy. Add the salt and continue beating until they stand in stiff peaks. Fold them into the strawberry mixture.

Whipped cream

(4) Into a 2-quart baking dish, buttered, pour the batter. Bake the pudding at 375° for 35 minutes, or until it is firm. Allow it to cool; chill it, and serve it with whipped cream.

STRAWBERRY PUDDING II

Follow the directions for Apricot Pudding, page 45, using: 2½ pints fresh strawberries, hulled, rinsed, and well drained (*or* frozen strawberries, well drained); 2 cups water, ⅔ cup sugar; juice of ½ lemon.

STRAWBERRY PUFF

Serves 6

Marination: at least 3 hours
Preparation: 30 minutes
Cooking: 35 minutes
Preheat oven: 450°

1 quart strawberries, rinsed, hulled, drained, and halved
¼ cup sugar
¼ cup orange-flavored liqueur

(1) In a mixing bowl, combine the berries, sugar, and liqueur. Allow the mixture to sit for at least 3 hours in the refrigerator.

1 cup flour
3 Tablespoons sugar

(2) In a mixing bowl, sift together the flour and sugar.

1 cup water
½ cup butter, soft
Grated rind of 1 lemon

(3) In a saucepan, bring the water to the boil. Add the butter and rind, allowing the butter to melt.

(4) Add the flour, all at one time, stirring until the dough forms a ball. Remove from the heat and allow the dough to cool slightly.

3 eggs
2 teaspoons baking powder

(5) Into the dough, beat the eggs one at a time. It is important that the eggs be thoroughly mixed in. Beat in the baking powder.

(6) On a round, lightly buttered baking dish or tin, arrange the dough in a wreath-shape. Bake it at 450° for 10 minutes; reduce the heat to 400° and continue baking the puff for 25 minutes, or until it is golden brown. Allow it to cool. Slice it into 2 rings.

At this point you may stop and continue later.

(continued)

379

1 cup heavy cream, whipped

(7) At the time of serving, fill the bottom ring with the strawberry mixture; add the top ring, and garnish the dessert with the whipped cream. It is important that the puff rings not stand long, or they will lose their crispness.

STRAWBERRIES IN SHERRY CREAM

This dessert, rich and delicious, is good made with any fresh fruit.

Serves 6
Doubles
Refrigerates

Marination: 2 hours
Preparation: 35 minutes

3 or 4 pints strawberries, hulled, rinsed, drained, halved
¼ cup sugar

(1) Toss the berries with the sugar and allow them to "bleed" for at least 2 hours.

6 egg yolks
¾ cup sugar
1 cup cream sherry

(2) In the top of a double boiler, beat the yolks until they are thick and lemon-colored. Gradually add the sugar, beating constantly. Then stir in the sherry. Over simmering water, cook the mixture, stirring until it thickens. Remove it from the heat and allow it to cool.

At this point you may stop and continue later.

1 cup heavy cream, whipped

(3) At the time of serving, fold the whipped cream into the egg mixture and then fold the berries into the sauce.

STRAWBERRY SHORTCAKE*

(American)

Serves 6
Doubles
Freezes†

Preparation: 40 minutes
Chilling time: 1 hour
Cooking: 12 minutes
Preheat oven: 425°

1 quart firm, ripe strawberries

(1) Hull, rinse, and drain the berries. If they are medium-sized and juicy, leave them whole; if oversized and dry, halve and toss them with a little sugar to make them bleed. Chill them for 1 hour.

2 cups flour
2 teaspoons double-acting baking powder
½ teaspoon salt
1 Tablespoon sugar

(2) In a mixing bowl, sift together these four ingredients.

4 Tablespoons soft butter

(3) With a fork, work the butter into the flour mixture.

¾ cup milk

(4) Add the milk a little at a time to make a soft dough. Turn it onto a floured board and roll it out about ½-inch thick. Cut it into 4-inch rounds, arrange them on a lightly buttered cookie sheet, and bake them at 425° for 12 minutes, or until they are golden.

* My paternal grandmother's recipe for this American classic is a far cry from the sponge cake–whipped cream variety now popular. Grandmother, who insisted that her recipe was the "original," was strongly Methodist; she never cooked on Sunday and spent hours pouring over the Bible between morning and evening church services. Despite her austere Sabbath regimen, she had an irrepressible twinkle in her eye which, with Monday's arrival, expressed itself in a keen if decorous sense of fun.

† The biscuits may be frozen if protected in moisture-proof wrap. Thaw them fully before unwrapping them; heat them gently in foil just before using them.

(continued)

At this point you may stop and continue later.

Soft butter
Powdered sugar
Prepared strawberries

(5) Serve the biscuits, warm, together with the soft butter, the sugar, and the berries; each person prepares his own shortcake by: (a) splitting the biscuit with a fork and buttering it well, (b) spooning over the berries, (c) sprinkling over a generous spoonful of sugar.

STRAWBERRY TART

(French)

Tarte aux fraises is a classic dessert in French cooking.

Serving: one 8-inch tart
Refrigerates

Preparation: 30 minutes*
Chilling time: 2 hours

1 8-oz. package cream cheese, at room temperature
1 cup heavy cream
3 Tablespoons sugar
1 teaspoon vanilla

(1) In a mixing bowl, combine the cream cheese and cream and stir them together until the mixture is smooth. Add the sugar and vanilla, and blend the mixture well.

1 pastry shell, baked
1 pint strawberries, hulled, rinsed, and drained on absorbent paper

(2) Spread the baked pastry shell with the cheese and in it stand the fresh strawberries on their stem ends.

* The preparation time does not include readying the pastry, page 458.

1 **9-oz. package frozen strawberries, thawed to room
   temperature**
¾ **cup sugar**
2 **Tablespoons cornstarch**

(3) In the container of an electric blender, whirl the thawed strawberries on medium speed for 15 seconds, or until the puree is smooth. Transfer it to a saucepan. Mix the sugar with the cornstarch and add it to the puree. Over moderate heat, cook the mixture, stirring constantly, until it is thickened and smooth. Allow it to cool. Pour the sauce over the strawberries in the pie. Chill the pie for at least 2 hours before serving it.

STRAWBERRY PUNCH

A delicious, refreshing, and festive punch.

    35 servings

Marination: 3 hours
Preparation: 15 minutes

1 **quart fresh strawberries, hulled,
   rinsed, drained on absorbent
   paper, and halved lengthwise**
¾ **cup sugar**
   Dry white wine

(1) In a mixing bowl, combine the strawberries and sugar and add wine to cover. Allow the fruit to stand for 3 hours in the refrigerator.

   Block of ice
1 **cup kirschwasser, chilled**
4 **bottles dry champagne, chilled**

(2) In a punch bowl, arrange the ice. Pour the strawberry mixture over it. Add the *kirschwasser* and then the champagne. Stir the punch gently.

MIXED
FRESH
FRUIT

PART

The emphasis of this chapter is on fresh fruits used in combination. Because I know no taste fresher or more satisfying than that of fresh fruits used together—as in fresh compote, for example—I write the recipes as if fresh fruit was always used. There are times, however, when certain fresh fruits are unavailable or unreasonably costly; then, rather than forego a dish of your choice, I urge an unashamed use of either the frozen (preferable, perhaps) or canned product, thoroughly drained unless the recipe indicates otherwise.

FRESH FRUIT SOUP

This unusual fruit soup—perhaps my favorite—may be served hot or cold. A dollop of sour cream perks up the dish!

> Serves 6 generously
> Doubles
> Refrigerates

Preparation: 45 minutes

6 cups cranberry juice
4 Tablespoons quick-cooking tapioca

(1) In a large saucepan or soup kettle, combine the cranberry juice and tapioca.

1 cup sugar
1 teaspoon cinnamon
¼ teaspoon ground clove

(2) Sift together the sugar and spices. Add them to the cranberry juice. Bring the mixture to the boil, stirring; continue to cook it, stirring constantly, until it is thickened and smooth.

1 lemon, sliced paper-thin and seeded
1 orange, sliced paper-thin and seeded
18 apricot halves
1½ cups seedless grapes, stemmed, rinsed, and drained on absorbent paper
8 peaches, peeled, seeded and sliced
8 plums, halved and seeded

(3) Add the fruit, reduce the heat, and simmer the soup, covered, for 10 minutes.

FRESH FRUIT SOUP
(Israeli)

If desired, you may add peaches, pineapple, or rhubarb, or substitute any of them for the fruits indicated in the recipe.

> Serves 6
> Doubles

Refrigerates
Preparation: 30 minutes
Chilling time: at least 2 hours

1 large, ripe cantaloupe, peeled, seeded, and coarsely chopped
1 quart strawberries, hulled, rinsed, and drained on absorbent paper
½ lb. seedless grapes, stemmed, rinsed, and drained on absorbent paper
4 tart apples, peeled, cored, and chopped
⅓ cup lemon juice
⅓ cup sugar
3 cups water

(1) In a saucepan, combine these seven ingredients, bring them to the boil, reduce the heat, and simmer them, covered, for 15 minutes, or until they are tender.

(2) In the container of an electric blender, whirl the mixture, a little at a time, on medium speed until it is smooth. Pour the puree into a serving bowl.

1⅓ cups orange juice
Lemon juice
Sour cream

(3) Stir in the orange juice and add lemon juice to taste (the soup should not be sweet). Chill the soup before serving it, garnished with sour cream.

GROUND BEEF AND FRESH FRUIT

(Spanish)

Serves 6
Doubles
Refrigerates

Preparation: 25 minutes
Cooking: 1 hour

4 Tablespoons olive oil
4 onions, chopped
2 tomatoes, peeled, seeded, and chopped

(1) In a flame-proof casserole, heat the oil and in it cook the onions until translucent. Add the tomatoes and cook the mixture for 3 minutes.

(continued)

1½ lbs. ground round
1 teaspoon salt
¼ teaspoon pepper
2 Tablespoons quick-cooking
   tapioca
1 10½-oz. can condensed beef
   broth

(2) Add the meat, stirring to break it into small bits; cook it for 3 minutes. Add the salt, pepper, and tapioca. Then add the broth. Simmer the beef, covered for 45 minutes.

At this point you may stop and continue later.

2 firm ripe pears, peeled, cored,
   and sliced
2 firm ripe peaches, peeled,
   seeded, and sliced
4 purple plums, halved and
   seeded
2 tart apples, peeled cored, and
   diced (optional)
3 potatoes, peeled and diced
   (optional)
⅓ cup golden raisins
1 firm ripe banana, peeled and
   diced (for garnish)

(3) Add the fruit and, if desired, the apples and/or the potatoes. Continue to cook the dish, covered, for 15 minutes, or until the potato, if used, is tender. Remove the casserole from the heat, add the raisins and allow it to stand, covered, for 2 minutes. Before serving the dish, garnish it with the banana.

An Argentinian version uses 3 lbs. lean chuck, cut in bite-sized pieces, browned in the oil, seasoned, and removed to permit cooking the onions and tomatoes. A bay leaf and ½ teaspoon thyme are added when the meat is replaced. Then 4 Tablespoons of quick-cooking tapioca are added, together with 1½ cups dry white wine and one 10½-oz. can condensed beef broth. The meat is baked, covered, at 300° for 2 hours; then 3 medium *sweet* potatoes, diced, are stirred in for 15 minutes of cooking before the fruits are added for the final 15 minutes.

CHICKEN AND CHERRIES WITH APRICOTS*
(Italian)

Serves 6
Doubles
Refrigerates

Preparation: 30 minutes
Cooking: 1 hour
Preheat oven: 350°

Serving-pieces of chicken for 6 persons
Salt
Pepper
Oregano

(1) In a broiling pan, arrange the chicken pieces. Season them with a sprinkling of salt, pepper, and oregano. Broil the chicken, turning it once, until it is browned. Arrange the chicken in a baking dish; discard any excess fat.

1 1-lb. can pitted dark sweet cherries
1 1-lb. can apricot halves
1 onion, grated

(2) Drain the cherries and the apricot halves, reserving the juice. In a mixing bowl, combine the fruits and onion and reserve them.

Reserved cherry liquid
Reserved apricot liquid
Water
2 Tablespoons cornstarch
3 Tablespoons vinegar
¼ teaspoon sweet red pepper flakes

(3) In a saucepan, combine the juices and, if necessary, add water to equal 2 cups. Blend the cornstarch with a little of the juice mixture. Add it to the contents of the saucepan and, over high heat, cook the mixture, stirring constantly, until it is thickened and smooth; stir in the vinegar and red pepper flakes.

At this point you may stop and continue later.

(4) Pour the sauce over the chicken and bake the dish, covered, at 350° for 45 minutes.

---

* This recipe is contributed by Joseph Florestano, a close friend in New York City and an accomplished voice teacher. Joseph's mother called the dish chicken "campanelli" ("little bells"); it is a sort of Italian *poulet Montmorency,* see page 104.

(continued)

(5) Add the fruit, and continue to bake the chicken, covered, for 15 minutes, or until the chicken is tender.

CHICKEN AND PINEAPPLE WITH CRANBERRIES

Serves 6
Doubles
Refrigerates

Preparation: 30 minutes
Cooking: 1 hour
Preheat oven: 350°

Seasoned flour
2 teaspoons paprika
½ teaspoon sage
Serving-pieces of chicken for 6 persons

(1) Combine the seasoned flour, paprika, and sage. In this mixture, dredge the chicken.

2 Tablespoons butter
2 Tablespoons oil

(2) In a flame-proof casserole, heat the butter and oil and brown the chicken.

1 12-oz. can unsweetened pineapple juice
1 10½-oz. can condensed chicken broth
1 teaspoon Lea & Perrins Worcestershire Sauce

(3) Over the contents of the casserole, pour the liquids.

At this point you may stop and continue later.

1 cup fresh, ripe pineapple, grated
1 cup Whole Cranberry Sauce, page 132

(4) Bake the casserole, covered, for 40 minutes at 350°. Combine the pineapple and cranberry sauce, add the mixture to the casserole, and continue to bake the chicken, covered, for 20 minutes, or until it is tender.

390

(5) If a thicker sauce is desired, remove the chicken to a serving platter and keep it warm. To the contents of the casserole, add some of the reserved seasoned flour, mixed until smooth with a little cold water, and over high heat, cook the sauce until it is thicker and smooth. Pour the sauce over the chicken.

CHICKEN AND PINEAPPLE WITH ORANGE

Serves 6
Doubles
Refrigerates

Preparation: 30 minutes
Cooking: 1 hour
Preheat oven: 350°

2 Tablespoons butter
2 Tablespoons oil
Serving-pieces of chicken for 6 persons
Salt
Pepper

(1) In a flame-proof casserole, heat the butter and oil and brown the chicken; season it.

¾ cup toasted almonds
½ cup golden raisins
1 cup fresh pineapple, shredded
½ teaspoon cinnamon
¼ teaspoon ground clove

(2) To the contents of the casserole, add the almonds, raisins, and pineapple. Sprinkle the pineapple with the cinnamon and clove.

2 cups orange juice
2 Tablespoons cornstarch, mixed with ¼ cup cold water
1 teaspoon Lea & Perrins Worcestershire Sauce

(3) In a saucepan, combine the orange juice and cornstarch. Over high heat, cook the mixture, stirring constantly, until it is thickened and smooth. Stir in the Worcestershire sauce. Pour the orange sauce over the contents of the casserole.

At this point you may stop and continue later.

(continued)

2 oranges, sliced paper-thin and
  seeded
  Paprika

(4) Bake the casserole, covered, at 350° for 50 minutes. Add the orange sliccs in an even layer and sprinkle them with paprika. Continue cooking the chicken, covered, for 10 minutes longer, or until it is tender.

CHICKEN WITH PEACHES AND BANANAS

Serves 6
Doubles
Refrigerates

Marination: 1½ hours
Preparation: 30 minutes
Cooking: 35 minutes

1 cup light cream
2 Tablespoons turmeric

(1) In a mixing bowl, beat the turmeric and cream together until well blended.

3 chicken breasts, skinned, boned, and cut into 2-inch pieces

(2) In a shallow baking dish, arrange a layer of the chicken, pour the cream over it and allow it to stand for 1½ hours. Meanwhile, prepare the rest of the ingredients.

At this point you may stop and continue later.

3 Tablespoons butter
6 scallions, chopped, with as
  much green as possible
1 tart apple, peeled, cored, and
  diced
1½ Tablespoons flour

(3) In a large skillet with a cover, heat the butter and in it cook the scallions and apple until they are just tender. Stir in the flour.

½ teaspoon ground cardamon
¾ teaspoon ground coriander
1 teaspoon salt
½ teaspoon pepper
1 10½-oz. can condensed chicken
  broth
  Reserved marinade

(4) Add the spices. Stir in the broth and marinade. Cook the mixture, stirring constantly, until it is thickened and smooth. Add the chicken, spooning the sauce over it.

2 **bananas, peeled and sliced**
4 **peaches, peeled, seeded, and sliced**

(5) Simmer the chicken, covered, for 30 minutes, or until it is tender. Add the fruit and simmer the dish for 5 minutes longer.

CURRIED FRUIT*

Serves 6
Doubles
Refrigerates

Preparation: 40 minutes

1½ **cups dry white wine**
1 **10½-oz. can condensed chicken broth**

(1) In a saucepan, combine the wine and broth and bring the mixture to the boil.

½ **cup golden raisins**
½ **cup pine nuts**

(2) Add the raisins and pine nuts and simmer them, uncovered, for 5 minutes.

2 **Tablespoons curry powder, or to taste**
2 **Tablespoons cornstarch**
¼ **cup cold water**
Salt

(3) Mix the curry powder and cornstarch with the water and add the mixture to the contents of the saucepan; stir constantly until the sauce is thickened and smooth. Adjust the seasoning.

At this point you may stop and continue later.

3 **firm ripe bananas, peeled and sliced**
3 **firm ripe peaches, peeled, seeded and sliced**
3 **firm ripe pears, peeled, cored, and sliced**
3 **purple plums, halved and seeded**
Shredded coconut (garnish)

(4) To the hot curry sauce, add the fruits, stirring gently. Simmer the fruits, uncovered, for 5 minutes, or until they are heated through. Serve the dish over rice, topped with coconut.

* This delicious recipe is contributed by Jack Frizzelle, a close kitchen-friend of nearly twenty years. Professionally, Jack's fine hand is seen in the admirable news coverage of the Metropolitan Museum, of which he is Public Relations Director. Culinarily, his equally fine hand is found, as often as he can be lured into the country, in my kitchen, cooking such delectable dishes as this one.

(continued)

The choice of fruit is variable: 1 pint each prepared blueberries and strawberries, 1 lb. sweet cherries, pitted, the chopped flesh of 1 cantaloupe, and 3 peaches, peeled and sliced make an equally good dish.

RED CABBAGE AND FRUIT

Serves 6
Doubles
Refrigerates

Preparation: 15 minutes
Cooking: 45 minutes

3 **Tablespoons butter**
1 **medium-sized red cabbage, shredded**

(1) In a large skillet, heat the butter and in it cook the cabbage, covered, for 10 minutes, stirring often.

2 **apples, peeled, cored, and chopped**
2 **firm ripe pears, peeled, cored, and chopped**
12 **dried tenderized pitted prunes, halved**
½ **cup golden raisins**
1 **teaspoon salt**

(2) Add these five ingredients and, using two forks, toss them with the cabbage.

Water

(3) Over medium low heat, cook the vegetable, covered, for 45 minutes, or until it is tender. A little water may be added as necessary.

GRILLED FRUIT

To accompany broiled meats.

Serves 6
Doubles

Preparation: 30 minutes
Cooking: 5 minutes

1 **banana, cut in 6 pieces**
3 **ripe peaches, halved and seeded**
3 **pears, halved and cored**
½ **cantaloupe, peeled and cut in 2-inch pieces**

(1) In a mixing bowl, arrange the fruit pieces.

5 **Tablespoons butter, melted**
½ **cup port wine**
½ **teaspoon ground ginger**
  Grated rind and juice of 1 orange
  Pinch of salt

(2) In a mixing bowl, combine these six ingredients and mix them well. Pour the sauce over the fruit and allow it to stand for 10 minutes.

(3) Thread the fruit pieces onto six skewers. Arrange the skewers on a buttered cookie tin. Broil the fruit for 2½ minutes, turn it, brush it with the remaining marinade, and return it to the broiler for 2½ minutes longer.

SAUTEED BANANAS AND PINEAPPLE

This idea, contributed by Marvin Jenkins, is a versatile one, serving either as a vegetable or as a dessert. As a vegetable, it is a delectable accompaniment to roast lamb or pork. To prepare the dish as a dessert, increase the brown sugar to ¼ cup, packed. Marvin, who works in public relations and publicity, has helped to make famous various musicians and contributes to keeping in the public eye many stars whose names are known to all.

> Serves 6
> Doubles

Preparation: 15 minutes

4 **Tablespoons butter**
6 **firm ripe bananas, peeled and sliced**
1 **20-oz. can pineapple chunks, drained**
2 **Tablespoons dark brown sugar**

In a skillet, heat the butter, add the fruit, turning it gently to cover it with the butter. Sprinkle over the sugar. Allow the fruit to heat through.

CANDIED YAMS WITH FRUIT SYRUP
(American)

A dish from the southern United States. While not a "classic" fruit dish, it is a refreshing change from the more familiar yams candied in brown sugar.

>Serves 6
>Doubles
>Refrigerates

Preparation: 30 minutes
Cooking: 30 minutes
Preheat oven: 350°

6 **yams, scrubbed, cooked for 20 minutes in boiling water (or until tender), peeled, and cut in half lengthwise**

(1) Prepare the yams and arrange them in a 1½-quart casserole, buttered.

Zest and juice of 1 lemon
Zest and juice of 1 orange
2 **cups sugar**
4 **Tablespoons butter**
2 **3-inch pieces cinnamon stick**
¼ **teaspoon ground clove**

(2) Combine the two juices and add water to equal ¾ cup. In a saucepan, add the combined juices, the zests, and the remaining four ingredients, bring them to a rolling boil, and cook them, uncovered, for 5 minutes.

1 **apple, peeled, cored, and thinly sliced**
1 **lemon, sliced paper-thin and seeded**

(3) Over the yams arrange a single layer of apple slices and then of lemon slices. Over the fruit, evenly pour the syrup.

At this point you may stop and continue later.

(4) Bake the yams, uncovered, at 350° for 30 minutes, basting them frequently with the syrup. When serving, remove the zests and cinnamon sticks.

CHICKEN AND MIXED-FRUIT SALAD*

Serves 6
Doubles
Refrigerates

Preparation: 30 minutes
Chilling time: at least 2 hours

1 orange, sliced paper-thin, seeded, and cut into segments
24 seedless grapes, stemmed and halved lengthwise
1 tart apple, peeled, cored, and diced
1 banana, peeled and diced
1 8-oz. can pineapple tidbits, well drained
1 cup Orange Mayonnaise, page 262

(1) In a mixing bowl, gently toss the fruits with the mayonnaise to blend the mixture.

3 cups cooked chicken, diced
Salad greens

(2) Add the chicken, and toss the mixture again. Serve the salad, chilled, on greens of your choice.

* This recipe is contributed by Clifford Harvuot, the Metropolitan Opera baritone. Surely one of the most accomplished singing-actors on the Met's roster, Clifford has, as a consuming avocation, cooking unusual meals for musical friends. This refreshing salad is a fine dish for summer suppers.

CHRISTMAS EVE SALAD
(Mexican)

This salad is a traditional accompaniment to the Mexican Nativity feast. When cooking the beets, be sure to save their liquid!

Serves 6
Doubles
Refrigerates

Preparation: 1 hour
Chilling time: 2 hours

(continued)

2 **oranges, cut in paper-thin slices and seeded**	(1) In a mixing bowl, combine these four ingredients.
2 **limes, cut in paper-thin slices and seeded**	
4 **apples, cored and thinly sliced**	
4 **beets, cooked in water just to cover, peeled, and thinly sliced (reserve beet juice)**	
1 **Tablespoon cumin seed**	(2) In a saucepan, bring these five ingredients just to the boil. When the mixture has cooled to lukewarm, pour it over the fruit. Chill the salad.
½ **cup sugar**	
½ **teaspoon salt**	
Juice of 1 lemon	
Reserved beet juice	
Salad greens	(3) Serve the salad on shredded greens of your choice, garnished with radish slices and a sprinkling of peanuts.
6 **radishes, sliced**	
Roasted peanuts (unsalted, if available)	

FRESH FRUIT SALAD

Serves 6
Doubles
Refrigerates

Preparation: about 30 minutes, depending upon the salad of your choice

Fresh fruit salads are a seasonal pleasure. Salads made with either frozen or canned fruit do not have the same taste or quality. In an age when—we think—we have beaten the seasons at their own game, we should admit willing defeat in the area of salads made fresh from the garden! There are almost as many combinations of fruits possible for salads as there are for compotes. Fruit, like the colors in nature, seem never to clash with each other; for this reason, I suggest only a few salads which I enjoy, hoping that the reader will go on from here, making his own discoveries of what tastes good with what.

Concerning greens for fruit salads, whenever possible I use watercress. Its peppery taste is a pleasant complement to the blander flavors of the fruit. In general, the crisper-leafed lettuces provide a better bed for fruit than do the more easily wilted, delicate varieties.

1) 6 thin slices cantaloupe; 6 peaches, peeled, seeded, and sliced; 6 pears, peeled, seeded, and sliced; 6 red plums, halved and seeded.

2) 3 oranges, peeled, all white pith removed, sectioned, and seeded; 3 bananas, peeled and sliced; 1 cup seedless grapes, stemmed, rinsed, and drained on absorbent paper; ¼ cup nut meats of your choice (optional).

3) 1 grapefruit, peeled, all white pith removed, sectioned, and seeded; 2 oranges, peeled, all white pith removed, sectioned, and seeded; 1 cup seedless grapes, stemmed, rinsed, and drained on absorbent paper.

4) 3 oranges and 3 tangerines, peeled, all white pith removed, sectioned, and seeded; 1 banana, peeled and sliced; 1 small ripe pineapple, peeled, cored, and cubed.

5) 1 pint strawberries, hulled, rinsed, and drained on absorbent paper; 1 small ripe pineapple, peeled, cored, and cubed; 2 apples, peeled, cored, and cubed; 3 oranges, peeled, all white pith removed, sectioned, and seeded.

6) 4 oranges, peeled, all white pith removed, thinly sliced, and seeded; 1 small ripe pineapple, peeled, cored, and cubed; 2 red onions, peeled, thinly sliced, and separated into rings.

7) 4 oranges, 1 grapefruit, 4 tangerines, peeled, all white pith removed, sectioned, and seeded; toss the fruits with ⅓ cup fresh mint, chopped, and refrigerate them, covered, for 6 hours before dressing them.

All of these salads may be served with either Orange Mayonnaise, page 262, or Orange Dressing, page 262. Other suggested dressings:

1) ½ cup olive oil, ¼ cup lemon juice, 3 Tablespoons brandy, salt and pepper, to taste.

2) ½ cup olive oil, ¼ cup lemon juice, ¼ cup canned plum juice, 1½ teaspoons sugar, ½ teaspoon each salt and paprika.

3) In the container of an electric blender, whirl on medium speed, 2 eggs, 2 Tablespoons flour, ⅓ cup sugar, the juice of 1 lemon and 1 orange, 1 cup pineapple juice, ¼ teaspoon chili powder, and a pinch of salt; in a saucepan, cook the mixture, stirring constantly until it is thickened and smooth. Allow it to cool. Fold in ½ cup heavy cream, whipped. (This is a Mexican dressing.)

CRANBERRY-AND-ORANGE BREAD
(*American*)

Serving: one 8-inch loaf
Doubles
Refrigerates
Freezes

Preparation: 30 minutes
Cooking: 50 minutes
Preheat oven: 350°

2 cups flour
½ teaspoon salt
1½ teaspoons baking powder
½ teaspoon baking soda
1 cup sugar

(1) In a mixing bowl, sift together these dry ingredients.

1 cup fresh cranberries

(2) Rinse, drain, and chop the cranberries.

Grated rind and juice of 1 orange
2 Tablespoons butter, melted
Additional orange juice
1 egg, beaten

(3) Combine the rind, juice, and melted butter; add more juice to equal ¾ cup of liquid. Add the egg to the liquid ingredients; combine them with the cranberries.

At this point you may stop and continue later.

1 cup nut meats, chopped (optional)

(4) Combine the liquid and dry ingredients, add the nut meats, if desired, and beat the batter well.

(5) Pour the batter into a buttered 8-inch loaf pan. Bake the bread at 350° for 50 minutes, or until a knife inserted at the center comes out clean.

MIXED-FRUIT BROWN BETTY

The combination of different fruit flavors gives this classic dessert a new interest. Follow the directions for Apple Brown Betty, page 20, using 2 apples, peeled, cored, and sliced; sufficient tenderized dried pitted apricots to make 1 layer and 2 each ripe peaches and pears, peeled, seeded, and sliced. Cover the bottom of the prepared baking dish with a layer of crumbs and then make alternate layers of the fruits, and crumbs, finishing with the crumbs. Bake as directed.

FRUIT CAKE

(Turkish)

The fruit of your choice is served over the cake. The cake itself is so rich that a 2-inch wedge is a generous serving. It is improved by being made a day in advance of serving, and it keeps best if left in the cake pan.

Serving: one 10-inch cake
Refrigerates
Freezes

Preparation: 40 minutes
Cooking: 1 hour
Preheat oven: 350°

9 **egg yolks**
1 **cup sugar**
  Grated rind of 1 lemon or
1 **orange**

(1) In a mixing bowl, beat the yolks until they are light yellow. Add the sugar and grated rind and continue beating until the mixture is stiff.

9 **egg whites**
½ **teaspoon salt**

(2) In a mixing bowl, beat the whites until they are frothy. Add the salt and beat them until they stand in stiff peaks.

⅓ **cup flour**
1½ **cups farina**
6 **Tablespoons butter, melted and cooled**

(3) In a mixing bowl, sift together the flour and farina. Add the mixture to the egg yolks, stirring. Add next the egg whites. Blend the ingredients well and then stir in the butter.

(4) Into a round 10-inch cake pan, buttered, spoon the batter. Bake the cake at 350° for 1 hour.

(continued)

401

4 **cups sugar** 5 **cups water** **Zest and juice of 1 lemon or 1 orange**	(5) Meanwhile, in a saucepan, bring these ingredients to a rolling boil. Cook them, uncovered, for 15 minutes.
	(6) Remove the cake from the oven and over it gradually pour the hot syrup until it is all absorbed. Cool the cake for at least 2 hours.
Fruit of your choice (see suggestions following)	(7) Over each portion of cake, spoon some fruit and garnish the dessert with whipped cream.

1 quart berries of your choice, hulled and picked over, rinsed, drained on absorbent paper, tossed with sugar to taste, and allowed to stand in the refrigerator for 2 hours (strawberries should be halved) *or* 3 cups ripe peeled sliced peaches, tossed with sugar to taste *or* a combination of berries and sliced peaches. Whipped cream (optional).

FRUIT COMPOTES

The combinations of fresh, frozen, and canned fruits are virtually numberless, open to the inventive imagination of the cook. I would offer only one word of warning: do not combine delicately flavored fruits with strongly flavored ones—papaya and banana, for example, are incompatible because the banana overpowers the taste of papaya.

To stimulate the invention, here are several compote combinations of proven merit, together with a few suggestions for fancying them up. As in all cooking, however, the greatest satisfaction lies in one's own discoveries.

In preparing compotes, particularly of fresh fruit, it is important to use a crockery, plastic, or silver bowl; doing so avoids discoloration of utensils and prevents the fruit from taking on the "taste" of the utensil.

Unless specified, each recipe serves 6.

1) Combine 1 cup each: raspberries, blueberries, sliced peaches, melon balls, pineapple chunks, and sweet pitted cherries. Toss the fruit with ¼ cup sugar and chill it for 3 hours. Serves 10.

2) Peel, core, and cut into cubes 1 ripe pineapple, add 1 quart strawberries, hulled, rinsed, and drained. Toss the fruit with 3 Tablespoons sugar and ¼ cup orange-flavored liqueur. Chill it for 3 hours.

3) Toss 2 cups sliced peaches, 1 pint raspberries, and 1 pint blueberries with 3 Tablespoons sugar and the juice of ½ lemon. Chill it for 3 hours.

4) Peel, core, and cut into cubes 1 ripe pineapple, add 1 11-oz. can mandarin oranges and 1 pint strawberries, hulled, rinsed, and drained. Toss the fruit with 3 Tablespoons sugar and a little of the mandarin orange liquid. Chill it for 3 hours.

5) Combine 1 lb. pitted sweet cherries with one 28-oz. can apricot halves, drained. Pour over ¼ cup orange-flavored liqueur. Chill it for 3 hours.

6) Combine 1 pint raspberries, the sections of 2 grapefruit, seeded, one 11-oz. jar preserved kumquats with their liquid, and 2 apples, peeled, cored, diced, and sprinkled with fresh lemon juice. Chill it for 3 hours.

7) Combine 2 cups stewed rhubarb, page 370, 1 pint strawberries, hulled, rinsed, and drained, and 1 cup fresh pineapple cubes. Add the grated rind and juice of 1 orange; sprinkle the fruit with ginger. Chill it for 3 hours.

8) Combine 1 cup each: strawberries, hulled, rinsed, and drained, blueberries, rinsed, honeydew balls, bananas, sliced, and watermelon balls. Add 3 Tablespoons sugar and chill for 3 hours. Serves 8.

9) Combine 3 cups peeled sliced peaches, 2 cups peeled sliced pears, and 1 pint blueberries, rinsed and drained. Add ¼ cup fresh lemon juice and ½ cup sugar. Toss the fruits gently and chill it for 3 hours.

10) Combine 2 cups pineapple chunks, preferably fresh, 4 navel oranges, sectioned and coarsely chopped, 4 bananas, sliced, and 3 or 4 pieces preserved ginger, chopped. Chill it for 3 hours.

11) Combine 2 teaspoons ground ginger with ½ cup cognac. Combine 1 cup each: fresh pineapple cubes, strawberries, hulled, rinsed, and drained, and 1 banana, sliced. Pour over the cognac mixture and chill it for 3 hours.

12) Peel 2 small cantaloupes; seed them and cut the flesh into bite-sized pieces. Toss the melon with ½ teaspoon salt. Peel and slice 3 peaches. Toss the fruits with ⅓ cup sugar, the juice of 1 lemon, and 2 Tablespoons rose water. Chill it for 3 hours.

Here are three festive refinements for compotes:

1) Cover a fruit compote for 6 persons with meringue. Bake the meringue at 400° for 5 minutes, or until it is delicately browned. (*Meringue*: beat 3 egg whites until they stand in soft peaks. Add singly 4 Tablespoons sugar and then 1 teaspoon lemon juice or ½ teaspoon vanilla. Beat the meringue until it stands in stiff peaks.)

(continued)

2) Beat 3 eggs until light. Add 1½ cups milk, ⅔ cup sugar, and 1 packet unflavored gelatin. Cook the mixture, stirring constantly, until it coats the spoon. Remove it from the heat and allow it to cool. Beat 3 egg whites until stiff. Fold the whites, together with 1 apple, peeled and grated, into the custard. Chill the dessert in a lightly oiled mold for at least 3 hours. Unmold it and garnish it with the compote of your choice.

3) In the container of an electric blender, puree 1 cup of canned apricot halves, drained. Add 3 Tablespoons sugar and cook the puree until it becomes clear. Add 3 Tablespoons *kirschwasser*. Cool and chill the mixture. Use it to bind the fruits in the compote of your choice.

4) All compotes are enhanced by serving them with vanilla ice cream or a fruit sherbet. Any fruit-flavored liqueur glamorizes them (use ¼ cup for a compote serving 6 persons); akvavit is also good. If desired, 1 cup of raspberry or currant jelly, melted, may be mixed with the prepared fruits (in this case, omit any sugar). Preserved ginger, chopped, makes a pleasant accent. If desired, toasted slivered almonds may be added as a garnish.

MIXED-FRUIT COMPOTE IN PINEAPPLE SHELLS*

Serves 6
Doubles
Refrigerates

Preparation: 30 minutes
Chilling time: 2 hours

3 ripe pineapples, halved lengthwise, the core removed (with a grapefruit knife), and the flesh removed and cut into chunks (reserve the shells)
1 pint strawberries, hulled, rinsed, drained on absorbent paper, and halved lengthwise
1 pint raspberries, rinsed and drained on absorbent paper

(1) In a mixing bowl, using two forks, gently combine the pineapple chunks, strawberries, raspberries, and almonds. Sprinkle the fruit with sugar to taste and *kirschwasser*. Chill the fruit.

* This tasty and decorative compote is contributed by Antoinette Schulte, the esteemed artist, who also gives a sketch of the dessert. To visit her Paris or New York studio is to come into intimate contact with contemporary art. Her collection of paintings and drawings is unique in that each example is the work of a close friend: Laurencin, Segonzac, Despiau, Legeult, Oudot, and Cavailles.

¼ **cup blanched almonds**
  Sugar
  Kirschwasser

**Whipped cream or a few sprigs
of fresh mint**

(2) Spoon the compote into the pine-apple shells. Set the shells in bowls, so they will not spill. Garnish the dessert with either whipped cream or mint sprigs.

SAUTEED BANANAS AND PINEAPPLE

Follow the directions for Sauteed Bananas and Pineapple (a vegetable) on page 395, increasing the sugar to ¼ cup and topping each serving with whipped cream to which a little orange-flavored liqueur has been added.

CUMBERLAND SAUCE
  (English)

This very old, traditional English sauce was served cold with cold venison. It is good with any cold meat and with roast pork and baked ham.

  Serving: 2½ cups
  Doubles
  Refrigerates

Preparation: 15 minutes
Chilling time: 2 hours

1 **cup red currant jelly**
1 **small onion, chopped**
  Grated rind and juice of 1 lemon
  Grated rind and juice of 1 orange
1 **teaspoon dry mustard**
¾ **teaspoon ground ginger**
1 **cup port wine**
  Pinch of salt

(1) In the contents of an electric blender, whirl all the ingredients on medium speed for 15 seconds, or until the mixture is smooth.

(2) In a saucepan, bring the sauce to the boil, stirring; reduce the heat to very low and gently simmer the sauce for 5 minutes. Allow it to cool before chilling it.

MIXED FRUIT STUFFING I

For roast duck or goose.

> Servings: about 6 cups
> Doubles

Preparation time: 30 minutes

2 cups breadcrumbs
3 Tablespoons butter, melted

1 onion, grated
1 apple, cored and chopped
½ cup grapefruit sections, chopped
1 cup orange sections, chopped
¼ cup golden raisins
½ cup walnuts or pecans
1 teaspoon salt
½ teaspoon mace
½ cup dry white wine

(1) In a mixing bowl, using 2 forks, toss together the breadcrumbs and melted butter.

(2) Add these nine ingredients, toss the dressing well, and allow it to stand for 1 hour before stuffing the fowl.

MIXED FRUIT STUFFING II

For meats, poultry, and game.

For *each* 4 cups of seasoned breadcrumbs, seasoned croutons, or packaged dressing, prepare 2 cups of chopped fruit in a combination of your choice: apple/cherry/grape/melon/orange/peach/pear/pineapple. Toss the fruit with the breadstuff and 4 Tablespoons melted butter.

FRUIT DRESSING

For fruit salads.

> Serving: 1½ cups

½ cup salad oil
½ cup pineapple juice
1 Tablespoon lemon juice
1 ripe banana, peeled and coarsely chopped
½ orange, seeded and chopped
½ teaspoon salt
Pinch of white pepper

In the container of an electric blender, combine all the ingredients and, on high speed, whirl them until the mixture is smooth.

MIXED-FRUIT ADE

Serving: about 1½ quarts
Doubles
Refrigerates

Preparation time: 15 minutes

3 cups fresh grapefruit juice
1½ cups pineapple juice
1 cup lemon juice (lime juice may also be used)

(1) Combine these three ingredients.

⅔ cup sugar
⅔ cup water

(2) Combine the sugar and water; bring the syrup to the boil and cook it, uncovered, for 5 minutes. Add the syrup to the fruit juices and refrigerate the beverage.

Fresh mint

(3) Serve the mixed-fruit ade over cracked ice in chilled glasses, garnished with fresh mint.

FRULATTO DI FRUTTA MISTA

(Italian)

This popular Roman drink of fresh fruits and milk is, I feel, one of the most delicious of tastes and a very refreshing pick-me-up.

Serves 4
Doubles
Refrigerates

Preparation: 15 minutes

(continued)

½ banana, peeled and sliced
1 ripe peach, peeled, seeded, and coarsely chopped
½ apple, peeled, cored, and coarsely chopped
¼ cantaloupe, the flesh removed, and coarsely chopped
3 Tablespoons sugar
Pinch of salt
2 cups milk
1 cup cracked ice

In the container of an electric blender combine all the ingredients except the ice. On medium speed, whirl them for 15 seconds, or until the mixture is smooth. Add the ice and immediately turn off the blender. Serve the drink in chilled glasses.

ORANGE AND PINEAPPLE PUNCH

About 15 servings
Doubles
Refrigerates

Preparation: 15 minutes
Standing time: 3 hours

2 cups sugar
½ cup water

(1) In a saucepan, bring the sugar and water to the boil, stirring to dissolve the sugar. Cook the syrup, uncovered, for 5 minutes.

2 cups orange juice
1 cup pineapple juice
Zest and juice of 1 lemon
1½ cups water
2 Tablespoons honey
6 whole cloves
1 3-inch piece cinnamon stick

(2) Add these eight ingredients, bring the mixture to the boil, immediately remove it from the heat, and allow it to stand for 3 hours.

1 quart gingerale

(3) In a punchbowl, over a block of ice, pour the fruit mixture and add the gingerale.

SANGRIA

(Spanish)

This Spanish fruit-and-wine drink, now available bottled, is best when newly made with fresh fruit. Apple chunks, peach and pear slices, and/or melon balls may be added, as desired.

> Serves 6
> Doubles
> Refrigerates

Preparation: 20 minutes
Standing time: 2 hours

1 lemon, thinly sliced and seeded
1 lime, thinly sliced and seeded
1 orange, thinly sliced and seeded
⅓ cup sugar
½ cup brandy

(1) In a large pitcher, combine the fruit slices and sugar. Add the brandy and allow the fruit to stand for 1 hour at room temperature.

1 bottle dry red wine
Lemon juice

(2) Add the wine and lemon juice to taste. Stir the drink and let it stand for 1 hour at room temperature.

Ice
1 quart soda water, chilled

(3) When serving the sangria, add ice and the soda water.

STRAWBERRY AND APPLE PUNCH

> Serves 6
> Doubles
> Refrigerates

Preparation: 20 minutes

1 pint strawberries, hulled, rinsed, drained on absorbent paper, and coarsely crushed
1 quart apple juice
1 egg white, beaten until frothy
A few whole strawberries or fresh mint sprigs

Combine the first three ingredients, pour the mixture over crushed ice and garnish the punch with either a few strawberries or fresh mint.

DRIED FRUITS

PART

Dried fruits, when properly prepared, produce excellent dishes. Used singly or in combination, they make pleasant compotes, stuffings, meat dishes, and desserts. The recipes in this section call for dried fruits used in combination. For the convenience of the reader, the following table will show how to cook them in their simplest form, stewed dried fruit.

Fruit	Cooking time (minutes)	Amount of sugar per cup of fruit
Apples	20–30	4 Tablespoons
Apricots	20–25	3½ Tablespoons
Figs	40–45	1 Tablespoon
Mixed dried fruit	25–30	2½ Tablespoons
Peaches	30–35	3½ Tablespoons
Pears	30–35	3½ Tablespoons
Prunes	25–30	2 Tablespoons

Add water to cover the fruit by 1 inch. Add the sugar for the final 10 minutes of cooking time. The preparation time and directions for *tenderized* dried fruits are usually given on the package.

Raisins are usually plumped by pouring boiling water over them and allowing them to stand for 5 minutes before thoroughly draining them.

DRIED-FRUIT SOUP I

(*Middle Eastern*)

This hearty soup is really a one-dish meal. It is delicious served with a substantial bread and followed by salad and cheese.

Serves 6
Doubles
Refrigerates

Preparation: 40 minutes
Cooking: 2 hours

1 lb. lean stewing lamb
1 onion, chopped
1 clove garlic, chopped
2 beets, cooked and peeled
4 cups water, boiling

(1) In a large saucepan or soup kettle, combine these five ingredients. Return the water to the boil.

⅓ cup dried red beans
⅓ cup lentils
2 teaspoons curry powder, or to taste
1 teaspoon salt

(2) Stir in these four ingredients, reduce the heat, and simmer the mixture, covered, for 1 hour.

1 11-oz. package mixed dried fruit, seeded and coarsely chopped

(3) Add the fruit and continue simmering the soup, covered, for 1 hour longer.

Lemon juice

(4) Remove the lamb and dice it. Remove the beets and mash them. Return both to the soup. Season the soup with lemon juice, to taste.

DRIED-FRUIT SOUP II

(*Swedish*)

Two 11-oz. boxes of mixed dried fruit may be substituted for the suggested apples, apricots, and peaches.

Serves 6
Doubles
Refrigerates

Preparation: 15 minutes
Cooking: 1½ hours

18 prunes, pitted
⅓ cup raisins
¼ cup currants
½ cup dried apples, halved
½ cup dried apricots
½ cup dried peaches, halved
1 3-inch piece cinnamon stick
6 cups cold water

(1) In a large saucepan or soup kettle, combine the fruits, add the cinnamon stick and the water; bring the mixture to the boil, reduce the heat, and simmer, covered, for 1 hour, or until the fruit is tender.

½ cup sugar (or more, to taste)
¼ cup quick-cooking tapioca
1 lemon, sliced paper-thin and seeded
Water

(2) Add the sugar, tapioca, lemon, and, if needed, additional water; continue simmering the soup, covered, for 30 minutes, or until it thickens slightly.

Sour or whipped cream (optional)

(3) The soup may be served hot or cold, garnished, if desired, with a dollop of sour or whipped cream.

BEEF BRISKET AND MIXED DRIED FRUIT

Serves 6
Refrigerates

Preparation: 30 minutes
Cooking: 3 hours
Preheat oven: 300°

1 11-oz. package mixed dried fruits, seeded if necessary, and the larger pieces quartered
Boiling water

(1) In a mixing bowl, over the fruit, pour boiling water just to cover. Allow the fruit to stand for 15 minutes. Drain the fruit, reserving the water.

2 Tablespoons butter
2 Tablespoons oil
1 4-lb. brisket of beef

(2) In a flame-proof casserole, heat the butter and oil and brown the meat on all sides. Remove it.

2 onions, chopped
1 clove garlic, chopped

(3) In the remaining fat, cook the onions and garlic until translucent.

(continued)

413

3 **Tablespoons dark brown sugar**
2 **teaspoons salt**
½ **teaspoon pepper**
¼ **teaspoon ground clove**
1½ **cups cider or apple juice**

(4) Stir in the brown sugar and seasonings and then the cider. Replace the meat and spoon the sauce over it. Bake the casserole, covered, at 300° for 2½ hours.

At this point you may stop and continue later.

Reserved fruit
Reserved fruit water

(5) Add the reserved fruit and, if necessary, some of the fruit water. Continue to cook the beef brisket, covered, for 30 minutes, or until it and the fruit are tender.

Variations: This recipe may be made with *beef chuck*, cut in bite-sized pieces (cooking time, 2½ hours at 300°); or *lean lamb*, cut in bite-sized pieces (cooking time, 1½ hours at 350°); or *lean pork*, cut in bite-sized pieces (cooking time, 1½ hours at 350°); or serving-pieces of *chicken* for 6 persons (cooking time, 1 hour at 350°). If desired, the pan juices may be measured and thickened with 1 Tablespoon of cornstarch for each 1½ cups liquid.

GROUND LAMB WITH DRIED FRUIT AND LENTILS
(Middle Eastern)

A substantial and fairly exotic dish which, if desired, may also be made with split peas in place of the lentils.

Serves 6
Doubles
Refrigerates
Freezes

Preparation: 1 hour
Cooking: 20 minutes

1 **cup dried tenderized pitted**
prunes, chopped and soaked in
hot water for 15 minutes
1 **cup dried tenderized pitted**
apricots, chopped and soaked
in hot water for 15 minutes

(1) Prepare the fruits; drain well and reserve the water.

1½ lbs. ground lean lamb 1 onion, finely chopped 1 teaspoon salt ¼ teaspoon pepper	(2) In a mixing bowl, combine these four ingredients and blend them well. Roll the meat into 1-inch balls.
2 Tablespoons oil	(3) In a flame-proof casserole, heat the oil and in it evenly brown the meat.
½ cup lentils 1 cup reserved fruit water, boiling	(4) Add the lentils and boiling fruit water and simmer the mixture, covered, for 25 minutes, or until the lentils are just tender.
	At this point you may stop and continue later.
1 cup blanched almonds, toasted Reserved fruit Grated rind of 1 orange ½ teaspoon saffron threads, crumbled	(5) Gently stir in the toasted almonds, reserved fruit, grated rind, and saffron. Correct the seasoning and simmer the stew for 20 minutes longer.

VEAL AND DRIED-FRUIT PILAF

Delicately flavored, this dish may also be made with lamb (same cooking time) or beef (2 hours cooking at 300° before the fruit is added).

> Serves 6
> Doubles
> Refrigerates

Soaking: 2 hours
Preparation: 30 minutes
Cooking: 1¾ hours
Preheat oven: 350°

2 11-oz. packages mixed dried fruit Water	(1) In water to cover, soak the fruit for 2 hours. Drain the fruit and reserve the liquid.

(continued)

2 **Tablespoons butter**	(2) In a flame-proof casserole, heat
2 **Tablespoons oil**	the butter and oil and brown the veal;
3 **lbs. boneless veal, cut in bite-**	season it and sprinkle it with the
sized pieces	brown sugar.
Salt	
Pepper	
½ **cup dark brown sugar**	

2 **cloves garlic, pressed**
1 **teaspoon ground allspice**
1 **orange, sliced paper-thin**
  and seeded
  Reserved fruit water
½ **cup sherry**
  Chicken broth

(3) Add the garlic, allspice, and orange slices. Combine the liquids to equal 3 cups; add them to the casserole. Bake the veal at 350°, covered, for 1¼ hours.

At this point you may stop and continue later.

  Reserved fruit
1½ **cups natural raw rice**

(4) Into the casserole juices, stir the fruit and rice. Continue cooking the dish, covered, for 30 minutes, or until the veal and rice are tender and the liquid is absorbed.

DRIED-FRUIT COMPOTE

(German)

Dried-fruit compote is a classic feature of German and Austrian cooking. It is perhaps used less as a dessert and more as an accompaniment to meat dishes. The popularity of such compotes dates from times when dried fruits were a welcome change from the monotonous winter diet of cabbage and turnips.

    Serves 6
    Doubles
    Refrigerates

Preparation: 10 minutes
Cooking: 1 hour
Preheat oven: 325°
Chilling time: 3 hours

1 **11-oz. package mixed dried fruit**
1 **cup golden raisins**
3 **cups water***
⅓ **cup sugar**
   Zest of 1 lemon
   Zest of 1 orange
1 **3-inch piece cinnamon stick**
4 **whole cloves**
   Pinch of salt

In a casserole, combine all the ingredients. Bake the compote, covered, at 325° for 1 hour, or until the fruit is tender. Allow it to cool before chilling it.

* If desired, one 6-oz. can frozen orange juice concentrate, thawed, plus water to equal 3 cups, may be used in place of plain water.

NOODLES AND DRIED FRUIT
   (Israeli)

This unusual dish is served as an accompaniment to meats and poultry. It should be refrigerated only to eat as a "leftover." Served freshly made, it is light and delicate.

   Serves 6
   Doubles
   Refrigerates

Preparation: 20 minutes
Cooking: 40 minutes
Preheat oven: 350°

½ **lb. egg noodles, cooked in boiling salted water for 15 minutes (or until tender), and drained**
4 **eggs, lightly beaten**
8 **Tablespoons soft butter**
1¼ **teaspoons salt**
   Grinding of pepper
2 **apples, peeled, cored, and diced**
⅓ **cup golden raisins**
½ **cup tenderized dried apricots, chopped**

(1) In a large mixing bowl, combine all the ingredients and, using two forks, gently toss the mixture until it is well blended.

(2) Into a buttered 2-quart casserole or baking dish spoon the noodles and bake them at 350° for 40 minutes.

DRIED-FRUIT BREAD

Follow the directions for Cranberry Bread, page 124, using, in place of the cranberries, one 11-oz. package tenderized dried mixed fruit, seeded and chopped; over the fruit, pour boiling water just to cover and allow it to stand for 20 minutes. Omit the molasses, use ¾ cup of the fruit water as the liquid ingredient, to which add 2 eggs, lightly beaten.

CANDIED-FRUIT BREAD

Serving: two 8-inch loaves

Preparation: 2 hours (including rising)
Cooking: 40 minutes
Preheat oven: 375°

2 **packets dry yeast**
½ **cup warm water**

(1) Dissolve the yeast in the water.

¾ **cup unsweetened pineapple juice**
⅓ **cup sugar**
1½ **teaspoons salt**
8 **Tablespoons butter at room temperature**

(2) In a saucepan, combine these four ingredients and heat the mixture, stirring, until the butter is melted.

Grated rind of 1 lemon
1½ **cups flour**

(3) When the pineapple juice mixture is lukewarm, stir in the grated rind and flour. Beat the batter until it is smooth.

2 **eggs, lightly beaten**
Reserved yeast mixture
¾ **cup golden raisins**
1 **cup mixed candied fruit, chopped**

(4) Add the beaten eggs, then the yeast mixture, and, last, the raisins and candied fruit.

3 **to 3½ cups flour**

(5) Add, by the cupful, the flour, stirring, until the dough is moderately stiff.

(6) On a floured board, knead the dough for about 10 minutes. Place it in a greased bowl, cover it with a damp cloth, put it in a warm place, and let it rise until doubled in bulk (about 1¼ hours).

(7) Punch the dough down, shape it into two loaves, and arrange them in buttered 8-inch loaf pans. Bake the bread at 375° for 40 minutes, or until it sounds hollow when tapped with a spoon.

SPICED BREAD

(French)

Pain d'épice is a classic in French cuisine. A firm-textured bread, it keeps a long time when wrapped in foil or plastic. It is traditionally served thin-sliced with sweet butter.

Serving: one 9-inch loaf

Preparation: 30 minutes
Cooking: 1 hour
Preheat oven: 350°

1¼ cups water
1 teaspoon anise seed
1 cup honey (one 1-lb. jar)
1¼ cups sugar
3 Tablespoons butter

(1) In a saucepan, bring the water to the boil with the anise seeds. Add the honey, sugar and butter, stirring until the sugar is dissolved. Remove from the heat and let stand 10 minutes.

½ teaspoon baking soda
¼ cup brandy

(2) Sieve the liquid to remove the anise seeds, and add the baking soda and brandy.

4 cups flour
2½ teaspoons baking powder
1 teaspoon cinnamon
¼ teaspoon salt

(3) In a mixing bowl, sift together the dry ingredients. Gradually add the liquid, beating constantly until the batter is smooth.

(continued)

¼ **cup candied citron or lemon
   peel, chopped**
¼ **cup candied orange peel,
   chopped**
   Grated rind of 1 orange
¼ **cup almonds, chopped
   (optional)**

(4) Stir in the fruit and nuts.

(5) Into a 9 x 5-inch pan, buttered, turn the batter. Bake the bread at 350° for 1 hour, or until a knife inserted at the center comes out clean.

DRIED-FRUIT CREAM

Serves 6
Refrigerates

Preparation: 35 minutes
Chilling time: at least 3 hours

1 **envelope unflavored gelatin**
½ **cup sugar**
   Pinch of salt
½ **cup milk**

(1) In a saucepan, mix together the gelatin, sugar, and salt. Stir in the milk and, over gentle heat, cook the mixture, stirring constantly, until the gelatin is dissolved. Chill the mixture until it is the consistency of unbeaten egg whites.

2 **egg whites, beaten until nearly
   stiff**
½ **cup cooked prunes, pitted and
   chopped**
½ **cup tenderized pitted dates,
   chopped, or tenderized figs,
   chopped**
1 **cup heavy cream, whipped**
   Custard Sauce, page 460

(2) Fold in the egg whites, then the fruit, and, last, the whipped cream. Spoon the dessert into a 1½-quart mold and chill it for at least 3 hours. Unmold it on a serving platter and offer the Custard Sauce separately.

CHRISTMAS CAKE

(*American*)

Serving: two 8-inch loaves
Preparation: 45 minutes
Cooking: 1 hour
Preheat oven: 375°

2 cups flour
¾ cup sugar
2 teaspoons baking powder
½ teaspoon salt
¼ teaspoon ground allspice
½ teaspoon cinnamon
Pinch of ground clove

(1) In a mixing bowl, sift together these seven dry ingredients.

¼ cup currants
¼ cup golden raisins
1 cup mixed candied fruit
¼ cup nut meats, chopped

(2) Into the dry ingredients, stir the fruits and nuts.

2 eggs, lightly beaten
1 cup milk
4 Tablespoons butter, melted

(3) In a mixing bowl, blend the liquid ingredients. Add them to the flour mixture, and stir until the flour is moistened. Spoon the batter into two buttered 8-inch loaf pans. Let it rest for 30 minutes and then bake the Christmas cake at 375° for 1 hour. Allow the loaves to cool briefly in the pans before turning them out onto a rack.

ARMENIAN CHRISTMAS PUDDING

This apricot-and-raisin delicacy is contributed by Metropolitan Opera soprano, Lucine Amara, see page 453.

Serves 10
Doubles
Refrigerates

Soaking time: overnight
Preparation: 30 minutes
Cooking: 2 hours
Chilling time: 3 hours

(continued)

1 cup shelled whole grain wheat, rinsed in a colander
3 cups water
Pinch of salt

(1) In a large saucepan, combine the wheat, water, and salt. Bring the liquid to the boil. Remove the saucepan from the heat and allow the wheat to stand, covered, overnight.

(2) Over gentle heat, cook the wheat, covered, for 1½ hours, or until it is tender.

1½ cups tenderized dried apricots, quartered
1½ cups golden raisins
2 cups sugar

(3) Into the wheat, stir the fruit and sugar. Cook the pudding, covered, for 30 minutes longer. A little water may be added, if necessary.

2 Tablespoons rose water
¼ cup walnut meats
¼ cup blanched almonds

(4) Remove the dessert from the heat, stir in the rose water, and pour the pudding into a deep serving dish. While it is still warm, garnish it with the nuts. Serve the pudding cold.

MINCEMEAT

(American)

For the best mincemeat, allow it to stand in a cool place, but unrefrigerated, for 3 weeks. This mincemeat, from my great-great grandmother's handwritten recipe book of the 1840s (page 199), is more stalwart than the usual cooked variety.

Serving: 3 quarts
Refrigerates

Preparation: 30 minutes
Standing time: 3 weeks

2 lbs. beef, roasted and finely minced
½ lb. beef suet, grated
2 cups black raisins
2 cups golden raisins
2 cups currants
6 cups apples, peeled, cored, and chopped
1½ cups sugar
1 teaspoon ground allspice
1½ teaspoons cinnamon

(1) In a mixing bowl, combine these ingredients, stirring to blend them.

½ **teaspoon ground clove**
½ **teaspoon mace**

2 **cups brandy**
1 **cup dry red wine**

(2) Add the brandy and wine and stir the mincemeat well. As the liquid is absorbed while the mincemeat stands, covered, replace it, ¼ cup at a time, as needed, in a 2-to-1 brandy–wine ratio.

RICE IMPERIAL

(French)

Named for Eugénie, consort of Napoleon III, who had a special fondness for dishes made with rice, *"Riz à l'impératrice"* is a classic French dessert.

Serves 6
Refrigerates

Marination: overnight
Preparation: 1 hour
Chilling time: at least 3 hours

1 **cup mixed candied fruit**
¼ **cup brandy**

(1) In a mixing bowl, soak the fruit in the brandy overnight.

4 **cups water**
1 **cup natural raw rice**

(2) In a saucepan, bring the water to the boil, add the rice. Stir the rice once with a fork. Boil it, uncovered, for 10 minutes. Drain the rice and put it in the top of a double boiler.

1⅓ **cups milk**
¼ **teaspoon salt**

(3) To the rice, add the milk and salt. Over boiling water, cook the rice, stirring occasionally for 35 minutes, or until it is tender and the milk is absorbed. Allow the rice to cool.

1 **packet unflavored gelatin**
⅔ **cup cold water**
4 **egg yolks, lightly beaten**
1 **cup sugar**
1 **teaspoon vanilla**
 Grated rind of 1 lemon

(4) In the top of a double boiler, soften the gelatin in the water. Add the egg yolks, sugar, and vanilla and, over simmering water, cook the mixture, stirring constantly, until it is thickened and coats the spoon. Remove the custard from the hot water and stir in the lemon rind.

(continued)

423

Reserved fruit and brandy
1 cup heavy cream, whipped

(5) In a mixing bowl, gently blend the custard and the prepared rice. Stir in the fruit and brandy mixture. Fold in the whipped cream.

Raspberry Sauce, page 00

(6) In a 2-quart mold or bowl, chill the dessert for at least 3 hours, or until it is well set. Unmold the dessert on a serving platter and offer the raspberry sauce separately.

RICE PUDDING WITH DRIED FRUIT
(Chinese)

"Eight Precious Pudding," a classic of Chinese cuisine, is the Oriental cousin of "Rice Imperial," page 423.

Serves 12
Refrigerates

Preparation: 30 minutes
Cooking: 30 minutes
Preheat oven: 350°

1½ cups glutinous rice, washed and cooked in 4 cups water, very lightly salted
1 cup sugar

(1) Cook the rice for 12 minutes; do *not* drain it. Add the sugar, stirring to dissolve. Remove from heat.

8 dates, pitted and chopped
¾ cup mixed, candied peel
¾ cup almonds, blanched

(2) In a well buttered 8-inch bowl, arrange, in layers, the fruit and nuts, alternating with layers of the rice. Finish with a layer of rice.

(3) Place the bowl in a pan of hot water and bake the pudding at 350° for 30 minutes. Invert the bowl on a serving platter.

1 cup sugar
1 Tablespoon cornstarch
1 cup water
1 teaspoon orange extract

(4) While the pudding is baking, prepare the sauce: In a saucepan, mix the sugar and cornstarch, add the water, and over high heat, cook the mixture, stirring constantly, until it is thickened and smooth. Remove the sauce from the heat, stir in the orange extract and pour the sauce over the pudding.

GLÖGG

(Swedish)

A classic Scandanavian drink—very good, very warming—not very innocent!

12 servings
Doubles
Refrigerates

Preparation: 20 minutes
Standing time: overnight

1 quart claret
1 quart muscatel
½ cup sweet sherry
1 teaspoon aromatic bitters
1 cup golden raisins
¼ cup dark brown sugar, packed
1 orange, sliced paper-thin and seeded
6 cardamon seeds, bruised
5 whole cloves
¼ cup preserved ginger, chopped
2 3-inch pieces cinnamon stick
Pinch of salt

(1) In a crockery bowl, combine these twelve ingredients and allow them to stand, covered, overnight.

¾ cup akvavit (aquavit)
¾ cup sugar
1 cup whole blanched almonds (optional)

(2) Add the *akvavit* and sugar. In a large enameled saucepan, bring the *glögg* to a near-boil; remove it from the heat, add the almonds, and stir the drink to dissolve the sugar. Serve the glögg hot.

UNUSUAL CONSERVES AND RELISHES

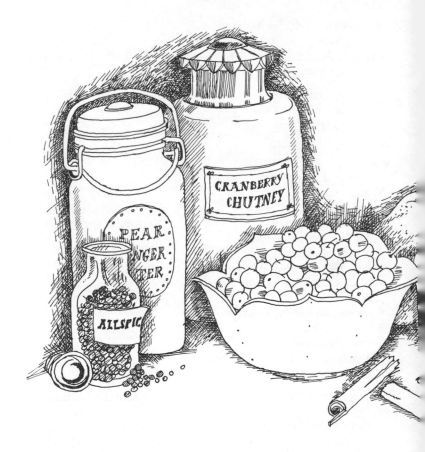

PART
IV

This chapter presents a selection of conserves and relishes which I find original and interesting. No pretense is made at "complete conserve cookery" (there is, to my best knowledge, and despite the claim of many cookbook titles, no *complete* book on any subject treating of cookery). These recipes have been chosen as compatible consorts to meat and poultry dishes and are intended to give a pleasant accent to the taste of the foods they accompany. The reader will note a predominance of relishes made with cranberries. I admit here to personal prejudice: cranberries make quick, easy, and zestful relishes, neither too sweet nor too tart, and are pleasant adjuncts to almost any meat or poultry dish.

Generally speaking, a conserve is a jam-like fruit preserve which may contain nuts, fruit rind, and other ingredients separating it from ordinary jams. Relishes are considerably spicier and may often have a sweet-and-pungent taste. Both are used as accompaniments to meat dishes.

To sterilize jars for storing conserves and relishes, wash them well and put them in a soup kettle with cold water to cover. Bring the water gradually to the boil. When ready to fill the jars, remove them and place them on a surface insulated with toweling or newspaper (to prevent their cracking). Fill the jars no more

than ½ inch from the top. To seal them, pour over their contents a small layer of melted paraffin. The conserve or relish should be completely covered and the paraffin layer should be no more than ⅛ of an inch thick; a thicker layer will not pull away from the edge of the jar. Storage is best in a cool, dark place.

APPLE BUTTER

(American)

Apple butter is a Pennsylvania Dutch classic. Among my prized
possessions is a "buttering kettle" of copper, weighing about 30 pounds
and with a 20-gallon capacity. Such a kettle, hung over hot coals,
made apple butter for a whole community.

> Serving: 6 pints
> Doubles
> Refrigerates

Preparation: 40 minutes
Cooking: 30 minutes

**4 lbs. tart apples, unpeeled,
uncored, and coarsely chopped
2 cups cider**

(1) In a soup kettle combine the
apples and cider. Bring the liquid to
the boil, reduce the heat, and simmer
the apples, covered, for 25 minutes,
or until they are soft. Stir them often
to prevent their sticking. Sieve them,
discarding the skins and seeds.
Measure the pulp.

**½ cup sugar
2 teaspoons cinnamon
1 teaspoon ground clove
Grated rind and juice of 1 lemon
Pinch of salt**

(2) For *each cup* of pulp, add the
remaining ingredients in the amounts
directed. Cook the mixture, covered,
stirring often, until the sugar is
dissolved. Remove the cover and
cook the apple butter rapidly, stirring
constantly, for 30 minutes, or until
it is thickened and smooth.

Apple butter, deriving its name from its consistency, is used as a jam, with
or without accompanying butter, on all kinds of bread stuffs. Refrigerated
and tightly sealed, it stores indefinitely.

APPLE CHUTNEY

To accompany hot or cold roast meats.

> Serving: 3 pints
> Doubles
> Refrigerates

Preparation: 30 minutes
Cooking: 1½ hours

   1 **lb. brown sugar**
1½ **cups golden raisins**
   1 **teaspoon salt**
   3 **onions, chopped**
   1 **clove garlic, chopped**
 ⅓ **cup preserved ginger, chopped**
   1 **Tablespoon mixed pickling spice**
   2 **3-inch pieces cinnamon stick**
   2 **cups cider vinegar**

(1) In a large saucepan or soup kettle, combine these nine ingredients. Over high heat, bring the mixture to the boil, stirring constantly. Reduce the heat and simmer the conserve, uncovered, for 1 hour. Stir it often.

   3 **or 4 apples, peeled, quartered, cored, and diced**

(2) Add the apples and simmer them, uncovered, for 30 minutes, or until the chutney is very thick. Stir the chutney gently but often.

(3) Store the chutney in sealed, sterilized jars in a cool place.

APRICOT RELISH

To accompany ham.

> Serving: 2 pints
> Doubles
> Refrigerates

Preparation: 30 minutes

1 lb. tenderized dried apricots
2 onions, sliced
12 whole cloves
2 3-inch pieces cinnamon stick
1 Tablespoon whole allspice
2 cups malt vinegar
Pinch of salt

2 cups sugar

(1) In a large saucepan, combine all the ingredients. Bring the liquid to the boil, reduce the heat somewhat, and cook the apricots for 5 minutes, or until they are just tender.

(2) With a slotted spoon, remove the apricots to sterilized jars. To the liquid, add the sugar. Bring the mixture to a rolling boil, stirring, and cook it for 15 minutes, or until it is syrupy. Allow it to cool somewhat before sieving it over the apricots. Seal the jars tightly.

APRICOT AND DATE CHUTNEY

For cold roast meats.

Serving: about 4 cups
Doubles
Refrigerates

Preparation: 20 minutes
Cooking: 2 hours

1 lb. tenderized dried apricots
1½ cups golden raisins
1¼ cups dates, seeded and coarsely chopped
Zest of 1 orange, cut in fine julienne
½ cup preserved ginger, chopped
1½ cups dark brown sugar, packed
4 teaspoons salt
1 teaspoon mustard seed
1 teaspoon chili powder
1½ cups white vinegar
1¼ cups water

In an enamelized iron casserole, combine all the ingredients. Bring the mixture to the boil, reduce the heat, and simmer it, covered, for 2 hours. Allow it to cool to room temperature before storing it in sterilized jars, tightly sealed.

431

CHERRIES IN BRANDY

(French)

The preparation time does not include 8 weeks of aging—the "secret ingredient" which prevents the cherries from having a sharp edge to their taste. Serve the cherries in place of a cordial after dinner.

>Serving: 4 pints
>Doubles
>Refrigerates

Preparation: 30 minutes
Marination: 8 weeks

3 lbs. ripe sweet cherries, un-stemmed, rinsed, and drained on absorbent paper
Brandy

(1) Into pint jars, sterilized, pack the cherries. Add brandy to cover them. Seal the jars and allow them to stand for 6 *weeks*.

1 cup sugar
4 whole cloves
1 3-inch pieces cinnamon stick
¼ cup water

(2) In a saucepan, combine these four ingredients, bring them to a rolling boil, stirring. Reduce the heat to low and cook the mixture, uncovered, for 10 minutes, or until it is syrupy. Drain the brandy from the cherries, add it to the syrup, and cook the liquid briefly. Pour the syrup over the cherries and seal the jars. Allow the cherries to age for at least 2 *weeks* more before serving them.

SPICED CRABAPPLES

(American)

To accompany ham or pork.

>Serving: 3 pints
>Doubles
>Refrigerates

Preparation: 30 minutes

1 cup sugar
2 cups water
24 whole cloves
6 whole allspice
2 3-inch pieces cinnamon sticks
  Pinch of salt

(1) In a large saucepan, combine these six ingredients. Bring them to a rolling boil, stirring. Cook the syrup, uncovered, for 5 minutes.

1 lb. crabapples, unstemmed, rinsed, drained on absorbent paper, and pricked with the tines of a sharp fork

(2) Add the crabapples and simmer them, uncovered, for 15 minutes, or until they are tender.

(3) With a slotted spoon, remove the crabapples to sterilized jars. Boil the syrup for 5 minutes longer, allow it to cool somewhat, and sieve it over the fruit. Seal the jars closely.

CRANBERRY AND ORANGE RELISH

Particularly good with roast duck or goose.

> Serving: 3 pints
> Doubles
> Refrigerates

Preparation: 30 minutes
Chilling time: at least 2 hours

4 cups cranberries, rinsed and drained on absorbent paper
2 oranges, quartered and seeded

(1) Through the coarse blade of a food grinder, force the cranberries and oranges.

2 cups sugar
  Pinch of salt
1/3 cup orange-flavored liqueur

(2) In a mixing bowl, combine the fruit with the remaining ingredients. Stir the mixture well and refrigerate the relish for several hours.

This recipe may be altered slightly to make Cranberry and Orange Conserve: follow the directions as given, adding, when the Relish is prepared, 1 cup golden raisins and ½ cup water; bring the mixture to the boil, reduce the heat, and simmer the conserve, uncovered, for 20 minutes; remove it from the heat, add 1 cup walnut meats, coarsely chopped; allow the conserve to cool and store it in sealed sterilized jars. (Serving: 4 pints.)

CRANBERRY AND PEAR CHUTNEY

To accompany curry dishes and roast meats.

> Serving: 2 pints
> Doubles
> Refrigerates

Preparation: 15 minutes
Cooking: 20 minutes

1 lb. cranberries, stemmed and rinsed
3 pears, peeled, quartered, cored, and diced
2 cups sugar
1 4-oz. jar candied lemon peel
1 3-inch piece cinnamon stick
Pinch of salt

(1) In a large saucepan, combine all the ingredients. Over medium heat, bring them to the boil, stirring constantly. Reduce the heat and simmer the cranberries, covered, for 5 minutes, or until their juice begins to flow. Remove the foam with a large spoon.

(2) Remove the cover and continue to simmer the chutney for 15 minutes, or until the cranberries and pears are tender.

(3) Allow the chutney to cool, uncovered. Then seal tightly and refrigerate.

GOOSEBERRY RELISH

> *(American)*

> Serving: 1½ pints
> Doubles
> Refrigerates

Preparation: 30 minutes
Cooking: 1 hour

1 pint gooseberries, stemmed and rinsed

(1) Shake only the excess water from the gooseberries. In a saucepan, simmer the berries, covered, for 20 minutes, or until they are tender. Sieve them and return the pulp to the saucepan.

1 cup walnut meats, chopped
½ cup cider vinegar
½ cup sugar
1 teaspoon salt
¼ teaspoon white pepper
1 teaspoon Lea & Perrins Worcestershire Sauce

(2) Add the remaining ingredients and gently boil the relish, uncovered, stirring often, for 1 hour, or until it is the consistency of ketchup. (If desired, the relish may be thickened with 1 teaspoon cornstarch mixed with a little cold water.)

PICKLED GRAPES

(*Syrian*)

Serving: about 3 quarts
Doubles
Refrigerates

Preparation: 40 minutes
Marination: 3 or 4 days, minimum

3 cups sugar
1 cup white vinegar
½ teaspoon ground cardamon
¾ teaspoon nutmeg
¾ teaspoon ground ginger
¾ teaspoon cinnamon
½ teaspoon basil
Zest of 1 lemon

(1) In a large saucepan, bring these eight ingredients to the boil. Over high heat, cook them, uncovered, for 5 minutes. Remove the pan from the heat and allow it to cool to room temperature.

4 lbs. firm seedless grapes, rinsed, drained on absorbent paper, and halved lengthwise

(2) Reheat the syrup until it is almost boiling, but not quite. Add the grapes, stirring once. Cook the grapes for 5 minutes; they should be tender, but still retain their firmness.

(3) Store the relish in sterilized jars with tight fitting lids. Use after several days' aging.

PRESERVED KUMQUATS

Serving: 3 pints
Doubles
Refrigerates

Preparation: 15 minutes
Cooking: 30 minutes

1¾ cups sugar
⅔ cup water
Pinch of salt

(1) In a saucepan, combine these three ingredients, bring the mixture to a rolling boil, and cook it, uncovered, for 5 minutes.

1 quart kumquats, rinsed, drained on absorbent paper, and pricked with the tines of a sharp fork

(2) Add the kumquats, return the syrup to the boil, reduce the heat, and gently cook the kumquats, uncovered, for 30 minutes, or until they are tender. Store the preserved kumquats in sealed sterilized jars.

PEAR AND GINGER BUTTER

Delicious as a spread on bread or as an accompaniment to roast lamb or pork.

Serving: 3 cups
Doubles
Refrigerates

Marination: 3 hours
Preparation: 20 minutes
Cooking: 1½ hours

3 lbs. ripe pears, peeled, cored, and thinly sliced
2 cups sugar
⅓ cup preserved ginger, finely chopped
Pinch of salt

(1) In a mixing bowl, combine these four ingredients and allow them to stand for 3 hours.

Grated rind of 1 lemon
Juice of 2 lemons
½ teaspoon nutmeg
¼ teaspoon ground clove

(2) Transfer the mixture to a saucepan. Add the lemon rind and juice and seasonings.

(3) Simmer the mixture, stirring often, for 1½ hours, or until the pears are tender. Sieve the pear butter. Bottle and seal it in sterilized jars.

SPICED PEARS

(English)

Serving: 4 pints
Doubles
Refrigerates

Preparation: 30 minutes
Cooking: 20–30 minutes

2 cups sugar
1 cup malt vinegar
2 teaspoons whole allspice
2 3-inch pieces cinnamon stick
12 whole cloves
1 piece ginger root, the size of a walnut, crushed
Zest and juice of 1 lemon
Zest and juice of 1 orange

(1) In a large saucepan, combine these ten ingredients and bring them to the boil, stirring to dissolve the sugar.

2 lbs. firm pears (such as Bosc or seckle), quartered and cored

(2) To the syrup, add the pears, return the liquid to the boil, reduce the heat, and simmer the pears, uncovered, for 20 to 30 minutes (depending upon the variety used), or until they are tender and begin to be translucent.

(3) With a slotted spoon, remove the fruit to sterilized jars. Over high heat, boil the syrup until it thickens; allow it to cool somewhat, and sieve it over the pears. Seal tightly and refrigerate.

CURRIED PINEAPPLE RELISH

To accompany roast duck and pork.

>Serving: 1½ pints
>Doubles
>Refrigerates

Preparation: 30 minutes

1 ripe pineapple, peeled, cored, and cut into small chunks (reserve the juice)

(1) Prepare the pineapple.

1 cup sugar
Reserved pineapple juice
1 cup cider vinegar
2 3-inch pieces cinnamon stick
1 teaspoon whole cloves
1 piece fresh ginger root the size of a walnut
Zest of 1 lemon

(2) In a saucepan, combine these seven ingredients, bring them to a rolling boil, and cook the mixture, uncovered, for 15 minutes.

(3) To the syrup, add the pineapple, return the syrup to the boil, reduce the heat, and simmer the fruit, uncovered, for 5 minutes.

1 Tablespoon curry powder, or to taste

(4) Remove the cinnamon sticks, cloves, and ginger root. Stir in the curry powder. Store the relish in sealed sterilized jars.

PLUM KETCHUP

>*(American)*

Plum ketchup, if not, perhaps, a "classic," is a popular relish of the northwestern United States. Good as an accompaniment to game.

>Serving: 2 pints
>Doubles
>Refrigerates

Preparation: 30 minutes
Cooking: 50 minutes

3 lbs. purple plums, halved lengthwise, stemmed, and seeded
3½ cups sugar
1 cup cider vinegar
2 3-inch pieces cinnamon stick
½ teaspoon whole cloves
½ teaspoon mace
½ teaspoon peppercorns
   Pinch of salt

(1) In a large saucepan, combine all the ingredients and bring them to the boil, stirring constantly. Reduce the heat to moderate and cook the ketchup, stirring often, for 50 minutes. Remove the foam with a large spoon.

(2) Allow the ketchup to cool and store it in sealed sterilized jars.

SPICED PLUMS

Follow the directions for Spiced Pears, page 437, using, in place of the pears, 2½ pounds firm plums, *un*stemmed, rinsed, and drained on absorbent paper.

RHUBARB CHUTNEY

Serving: 3 pints
Doubles
Refrigerates

Preparation: 20 minutes
Cooking: 35 minutes

2 lbs. rhubarb, rinsed and cut in
   2-inch lengths
4 onions, chopped
2 cups golden raisins
1 lb. dark brown sugar
1 teaspoon ground allspice
1 teaspoon ground ginger
½ teaspoon pepper
1½ cups malt vinegar

(1) In a soup kettle, combine all the ingredients, bring them to the boil, stirring constantly; reduce the heat and simmer the mixture until the sugar is dissolved.

(2) Increase the heat and boil the chutney rapidly for 8 minutes. Reduce the heat once more and simmer the mixture, uncovered, stirring often, for 25 minutes, or until it thickens.

"EXOTIC" FRUITS

PART

V

What a host of mysterious, glamorous fruits there are which, for the most part, we know only by name. Indeed, as has already been suggested in the Foreword, if we have, for example, a ripe breadfruit, papaya, or prickly pear, we would be foolhardy to chance its delicate flavor by cooking it or by combining it with other foods. For this reason, the number of recipes in this section is limited to a few which enhance these exotic fruits.

Guavas, members of the *Myrtaceae*, myrtle, Family, are big juicy berries, eaten fresh, stewed, pureed, and in jams and jellies. Native to Central America, the fruit is now found in most tropical countries. The tree, reaching a height of 30 feet, is hardy and requires little care. The round or pear-shaped guava may be 3 inches in diameter with white or salmon-pink flesh; it has many seeds and a musky, pungent odor.

Juneberry, or shadberry (the tree blossoms when this fish is spawning), is also called service berry, sarvis berry, saskatoon, and sugar berry. Members of the Rose Family and related to the apple, juneberries are dark, sweet, and about the size of a blueberry. Used by the American Indians and by the explorers and trappers of pioneer days, the fruit is occasionally cultivated for use in pies and other pastries, in jellies, and for drying. The cooked fruit tastes pleasantly of almond.

Mangoes are among the most important and widely cultivated tropical fruits. Members of the Sumac Family (which also includes poison ivy), their origin, lost in antiquity, possibly derives from the cashew nut family. Originating in eastern India and Burma, the fruit and tree are closely connected with the folklore and religion of India. Buddha was given a mango grove in which to find repose. A Chinese traveler to Hindustan, about 640 A.D., was the first to bring mangoes to the attention of other peoples. The fruit was introduced to the Western Hemisphere early in the eighteenth century, when it was planted in Brazil and the West Indies. Small as plums or weighing as much as 5 pounds, mangoes are round, oval, or kidney-shaped; some are red, some green, and some yellow. The juicy flesh is orange-yellow with a rich spicy flavor.

The papaya—also called papaw or pawpaw—grows in subtropical regions. The fruit may attain a weight of 20 pounds. The leaves of the papaya contain papin, an enzyme conducive to ripening meat, and in some countries meat is wrapped in them to tenderize. The smooth-skinned fruit, ranging from dark green to deep orange, is best when eaten raw. There are hundreds of gray-black seeds at the center of the flesh which, some say, are a digestive. The male papaya tree flowers, but bears no fruit; the female tree may produce only twelve fruits which, when unripe, may be cooked like squash.

The persimmon tree is a member of the ebony family and its fruit is a berry. Originating in China and Japan, it later spread to the Mediterranean countries. Its arrival in the United States, however, is fairly recent. The flesh of the orange-red persimmon, especially if tree-ripened, is very sweet and rich in vitamin C; the immature fruit is extremely, unpleasantly astringent. Persimmons are grown commercially on a small scale in California.

Pomegranates should be bought when thin-skinned and a bright purple-red. In Persia and Iran, where they are indigenous, they are used in soups, sauces, sweets, as well as being eaten raw. Jamaicans also use them in general cookery. The fruit consists of large, tender, easily-eaten seeds in pulpy bright red or crimson flesh. Pomegranates have been cultivated in the Orient since earliest times and share their importance only with dates, figs, and olives. When escaping Egypt, the Israelites fondly remembered pomegranates. King Solomon had an orchard of them. Muhammad said, "Eat the pomegranate for it purges the system of envy and hatred." Brought to the New World by Spanish colonists, pomegranates are now commercially produced on a modest scale in California.

The quince is generally thought to be a member of the Rose Family —albeit all botanists are not agreed on the point. The round or pear-shaped fruits are native to Iran and Anatolia. The Greeks and Romans enjoyed and cultivated them. Fragrant and astringent, they are excellent in preserves, albeit the golden-yellow fruit is edible only when cooked, at which time it turns somewhat pink. A favorite sweet of Joan of Arc was *cotignac*, a candy made of quince.

These exotic fruits are chosen because specific recipes are given for them. Thus we have omitted: custard apples (the soft pulp is eaten with a spoon—hence the name); jack fruit (which can weigh 40 pounds and tastes like banana); java plums; kiwi (the "Chinese gooseberry"); passion fruit (so-called because its blossom has become a symbol of Christ's Passion); prickly pear (the fruit of a very spiney cactus); soursop (popular in the West Indies and Malaysia, despite the fact that its pulp feels like cotton wool); star apple; tamarind (an Oriental fruit which makes a delicious syrup, available at specialty food stores); Chinese water chestnuts (yes, they are fruits!); breadfruit (in 1789, Captain Bligh of H.M.S. *Bounty* was returning to England with a cargo of breadfruit when a mutiny somewhat altered his course); olives (related to lilac, jasmine, and forsythia, cultivated by stone-age farmers, and the symbol of peace and plenty); and coconuts (the world's largest drupe—which sounds like a rude remark, but is not—requiring twelve months to ripen, used for its oil and sweet meat, and which turns up in such diverse products as oleomargarine, sun tan oil, and shaving cream).

GUAVA COBBLER

Follow the directions for Apple Cobbler, page 23, using, in place of the apple, two 2 lb.-2 oz. cans guava shells, drained on absorbent paper. To accompany the guava cobbler, make a sauce of 1½ cups of the guava liquid, reduced to 1 cup, and thickened with 1 Tablespoon cornstarch.

GUAVA AND CREAM CHEESE
(Mexican)

This dish is hardly a "recipe" in the usual sense of the word, but it is a very popular Mexican sweet, delicate and refreshing.

Serves 6

2 2 lb.-2 oz. cans guava shells, drained on absorbent paper
Cream cheese, cut in serving portions.
Reserved guava liquid

On a serving platter, arrange the guava shells and cream cheese. Serve the fruit and cheese with knife and fork and offer the guava liquid separately.

GUAVA TARTS

Serves 6
Refrigerates

Preparation: 20 minutes*
Chilling time: at least 3 hours

1 15-oz. can sliced guava shells

(1) Drain the guava shells and reserve the liquid. Dice the guava shells and reserve.

* The preparation time does not include readying the tart shells or *crème pâtissière*.

Reserved guava liquid
Water
1 Tablespoon cornstarch mixed
with 2 Tablespoons water
2 drops yellow food coloring
¼ teaspoon cinnamon
Reserved diced guava

(2) To the reserved guava liquid, add water to equal one cup. In a saucepan, bring the liquid to the boil, add the cornstarch, and cook the mixture, stirring constantly, until it is thickened and smooth. Stir in the food coloring, cinnamon, and reserved diced guava. Allow the tart filling to cool to room temperature.

6 Baked tart shells, see page 458
Crème pâtissière, page 130

(3) As evenly as possible, spread a ⅛-inch layer of *crème pâtissière* over the bottom and around the sides of the tart shells (this is made easier by having the pastries in their cooking containers).

(4) Mound the guava mixture over the *crème pâtissière*, filling the shells as full as possible. Chill the tarts for at least 3 hours to set the filling. They should, however, he served at room temperature.

JUNEBERRY CAKE

Follow the directions for Plain Cake and Berries, page 90, using, in place of the suggested berries, an equal amount of juneberries, rinsed, picked over, and drained on absorbent paper.

JUNEBERRY PIE

Follow the directions for Berry Pie, page 92, using, in place of the suggested berries, an equal amount of juneberries, rinsed, picked over, and drained on absorbent paper.

LAMB CURRY AND MELON WITH MANGO

See the recipe on page 222.

MANGO CREAM

(Mexican)

Serves 6
Doubles
Refrigerates

Preparation: 20 minutes
Chilling time: 1 hour

2 large ripe mangoes, peeled, seeded, and chopped
Juice of 1 orange
½ cup confectioner's sugar
Pinch of salt

(1) In the container of an electric blender, combine these four ingredients and, on medium speed, whirl them for 15 seconds, or until the liquid is smooth.

1 cup heavy cream, whipped

(2) In a mixing bowl, carefully fold together the mango liquid and the whipped cream. Chill the dessert before serving it. (If desired, the mango cream may be chilled in individual serving dishes.)

CURRIED CHICKEN AND PAPAYA

Elegant, exotic. Serve the papayas with rice.

Serves 6
Doubles
Refrigerates

Preparation: 45 minutes
Cooking: 10 minutes
Preheat oven: 350°

4 Tablespoons butter
1 onion, finely chopped
1 clove garlic, finely chopped
1 stalk celery, finely chopped
1 tart apple, peeled, cored, and diced

(1) In a saucepan, heat the butter and in it cook the four remaining ingredients for 10 minutes, stirring.

1 bay leaf, broken
¼ teaspoon ground clove
1 Tablespoon curry powder, or to taste
½ teaspoon dry mustard
1 teaspoon salt
3 Tablespoons flour

(2) Into the vegetable mixture, stir these six ingredients.

2 10½-oz. cans condensed chicken broth, plus water to equal 3 cups

(3) Gradually add the liquid and, stirring constantly, cook the mixture until it is thickened and smooth. Simmer it for 30 minutes.

3½ cups cooked chicken, diced
¼ cup golden raisins, plumped in hot water and drained
½ cup light cream

(4) Stir in the chicken, raisins and cream.

At this point you may stop and continue later.

3 ripe papayas, halved lengthwise and seeded

(5) Arrange the papayas, cut side up, in a baking dish. Fill the cavities with the curried chicken. Bake the papayas, uncovered, at 350° for 10 minutes, or until they are thoroughly heated.

FISH FILETS AND PAPAYA JUICE

(*Hawaiian*)

Exotic and flavorful.

Serves 6
Doubles
Refrigerates

Marination: at least 30 minutes
Preparation: 10 minutes
Cooking: 20 minutes
Preheat oven: 400°

(continued)

1 cup canned papaya juice
½ cup light cream
    Juice of 1 lemon
1 teaspoon salt
1 teaspoon Lea & Perrins
    Worcestershire Sauce
1 Tablespoon cornstarch

Fish filets for 6 persons, page xv

(1) In a saucepan combine the first five ingredients. Use a little of the liquid to mix with the cornstarch. Add the cornstarch to the contents of the saucepan and, over high heat, cook the mixture, stirring constantly, until it is thickened and smooth.

(2) In a lightly buttered baking dish, arrange the fish filets. Pour the sauce over them. Marinate the filets in the sauce for at least 30 minutes.

At this point you may stop and continue later.

(3) Bake the filets, uncovered, at 400° for 20 minutes, or until they flake easily.

RICE AND PAPAYA

(*Polynesian*)

Serves 6
Doubles

Preparation: 15 minutes
Cooking: 15 minutes

2 Tablespoons oil
1 onion, finely chopped
2 stalks celery, finely chopped
1¼ cups rice

(1) In a flame-proof casserole, heat the oil and in it cook the onion and celery until translucent. Stir in the rice and, over gentle heat, cook it for a few minutes.

2 10½-oz. cans condensed
    chicken broth
1 Tablespoon soy sauce
1 teaspoon sugar
1 teaspoon salt

(2) In a saucepan, combine the broth and seasonings, bring them to the boil, and pour them over the rice. Stir the mixture once with a fork. Simmer the rice, covered, for 10 minutes.

1 **9-oz. package frozen small peas, thawed**

2 **papayas, peeled, seeded, and sliced lengthwise**

(3) Add the peas and the papaya slices. Do not stir them in. Cook the rice, covered, for 5 minutes longer, or until it is tender and the liquid is absorbed.

PAPAYA CREAM

Follow the directions for Mango Cream, page 446, using, in place of the mangoes, 2 papayas, peeled, seeded, and chopped.

PAPAYA COMPOTE WITH PINEAPPLE AND STRAWBERRIES

A compote especially tasty served with cheese.

> Serves 6
> Doubles
> Refrigerates

Preparation: 25 minutes
Chilling time: 1 hour

1 **pint strawberries, rinsed, picked over, drained on absorbent paper, and halved**

1½ **cups fresh pineapple, diced Sugar**

(1) In a mixing bowl, combine the pineapple and strawberries; add sugar to taste and stir the fruit gently.

3 **papayas, halved lengthwise and seeded**

(2) Arrange the papayas on a serving platter. With the pineapple mixture, fill the cavities of the papayas, and chill the compote for 1 hour.

PERSIMMON PUDDING
(*American*)

Really a light cake. It is especially good split, spread with *crème pâtissière*, page 130, and reassembled.

Serves 6

Preparation: 30 minutes
Cooking: 1 hour
Preheat oven: 325°

2 cups ripe persimmon pulp, mashed and sieved
3 eggs, beaten
1¾ cups milk
4 Tablespoons butter, melted

(1) In a mixing bowl, combine these four ingredients; stir to blend them well.

2 cups flour
½ teaspoon baking soda
1½ cups sugar
1 teaspoon ground coriander

(2) In a second bowl, sift together these four ingredients.

(3) Pour the liquid ingredients over the dry and stir briefly to moisten the flour. Pour the batter into a lightly buttered shallow pan and bake the pudding at 325° for 1 hour.

1 cup heavy cream, whipped

(4) Remove the pudding from the oven, allow it to cool, cut it into squares, and serve it with the whipped cream.

DUCK AND POMEGRANATE SAUCE
(*Afghanistan*)

Serves 4
Doubles
Refrigerates

Preparation: 1 hour
Cooking: 30 minutes
Preheat oven: 400°/350°

**1 5- to 6-lb. duck, quartered,
trimmed of excess fat, and
punctured in several places with
the tines of a fork
Salt
Pepper**

(1) On the rack of a roasting pan, arrange the duck pieces, skin side up. Put them in a 400° oven; reduce the heat to 325° and bake them for 1 hour. Season them and arrange them in a single layer in a baking dish. Discard the excess fat.

**¼ cup olive oil
2 onions, coarsely chopped
¾ teaspoon turmeric**

(2) While the duck is roasting, heat the oil in a saucepan, add the onion and turmeric, and cook the onions until translucent.

**3 cups chopped walnuts
4 cups water
1 teaspoon salt**

(3) To the contents of the saucepan, add the walnuts, water, and salt. Simmer the mixture, covered, for 20 minutes. Pour the mixture over the duck after it is removed from the oven.

**⅔ cup pomegranate juice
⅔ cup orange juice
¼ cup sugar**

(4) In a saucepan, bring to the boil these ingredients and cook them, stirring, until the sugar is dissolved. This is the sauce which will be served separately later.

At this point you may stop and continue later.

(5) Bake the duck, covered, at 350° for ½ hour or until it is tender.

(6) Remove the duck to a serving platter and keep it warm; discard the pan juices; garnish the duck with the walnuts. Serve the heated sauce separately.

BEEF AND QUINCES

(Balkan)

This unusual stew may also be made with lean lamb or pork.

Serves 6
Doubles
Refrigerates

Preparation: 30 minutes
Cooking: 2½ hours
Preheat oven: 300°

2 **Tablespoons butter**
2 **Tablespoons oil**
3 **lbs. lean chuck, cut in bite-sized pieces**
   Salt
   Pepper

(1) In a flame-proof casserole, heat the butter and oil and brown the meat; season it. Remove.

2 **onions, chopped**
2 **Tablespoons flour**
2 **10½-oz. cans condensed beef broth**

(2) In the remaining fat, cook the onions until translucent. Stir in the flour and then gradually add the broth, stirring constantly until the mixture is thickened and smooth. Replace the meat.

4 **Tablespoons butter**
6 **ripe quinces, quartered, cored, and pared**

(3) In a skillet, heat the butter and in it cook the quince quarters until they are golden. Set aside and reserve them.

At this point you may stop and continue later.

(4) Bake the casserole, covered, at 300° for 1½ hours. Add the quinces and continue cooking the beef, covered, for 1 hour longer, or until it is tender.

LAMB STEW AND QUINCES*

(Armenian)

Serves 6
Doubles
Refrigerates

Preparation: 30 minutes
Cooking: 1½ hours
Preheat oven: 350°

2 Tablespoons butter
2 Tablespoons oil
3 lbs. lean lamb, cut in bite-sized pieces
Salt
Pepper
1 onion, chopped
3 Tablespoons quick-cooking tapioca

(1) In a flame-proof casserole, heat the butter and oil and brown the lamb; season it. Add the onion and tapioca.

6 quinces, rinsed, cored, and cut in eighths lengthwise
2 Tablespoons sugar
1 10½-oz. can condensed chicken broth

(2) Over the lamb, arrange the quince slices and sprinkle them with the sugar. Pour the chicken broth over the contents of the casserole.

At this point you may stop and continue later.

Pine nuts

(3) Bake the casserole, covered, at 350° for 1½ hours, or until the lamb and quinces are tender (the quinces will be slightly pink). More broth (or water) may be added, if necessary. When serving the stew, garnish it with a sprinkling of pine nuts.

* This recipe, together with that for Armenian Christmas Pudding, page 421, is contributed by Lucine Amara. One of the most highly regarded sopranos at the Metropolitan Opera, Miss Amara creates in Ellen Orford (Benjamin Britten's *Peter Grimes*) a signal example of the singer's art realized in terms of music and drama. As a companion in the kitchen, Lucine's creations are no less worthy of emulation.

FISH FILETS AND QUINCE

Serves 6
Doubles
Refrigerates

Preparation: 20 minutes
Cooking: 20 minutes
Preheat oven: 400°

Fish filets for 6 persons, page xv

(1) In a lightly buttered baking dish, arrange the filets in a single layer.

2 15-oz. cans sliced quince
1 Tablespoon cornstarch, mixed with ¼ cup cold water
2 Tablespoons soft butter
2 Tablespoons lemon juice
Salt
Pepper
1 8-oz. can bamboo shoots, drained and chopped (optional)

(2) Drain the quince slices and reserve the liquid. In a saucepan, combine the quince liquid and the cornstarch. Over high heat, cook the mixture, stirring constantly until it is thickened and smooth. Stir in the butter and lemon juice. Season the sauce to taste with salt and pepper. Stir in the bamboo shoots if desired.

Reserved quince slices

(3) Over the fish, arrange the quince slices. Pour the sauce evenly over the contents of the baking dish.

At this point you may stop and continue later.

(4) Bake the fish, uncovered, at 400° for 20 minutes, or until it flakes easily.

BAKED QUINCES

Serves 6
Doubles
Refrigerates

Preparation: 15 minutes
Cooking: 2 hours
Preheat oven: 200°

3 ripe quinces, quartered, cored, and pared
½ cup sugar
1 orange, sliced paper-thin and seeded
Water

Whipped or sour cream

(1) In a baking dish, arrange the quince quarters, sprinkle them with the sugar, and garnish them with the orange slices. Add the water to a depth of ½ inch.

(2) Bake the quinces, uncovered, adding more water as necessary, at 200° for 2 hours. Allow one-half quince per serving, topped with either whipped or sour cream.

QUINCE TARTS

Follow the directions for Guava Tarts, page 444, using, in place of the guava, one 15-oz. can sliced quince.

SOMETHING EXTRA

HELEN McCULLY'S ICE CREAM*

Of all recipes for homemade ice creams, this one, I feel, is most successful. It is not for calorie-watchers. But it is very good. It also adapts itself to treatment with various fruits.

Serving: 1½ quarts

Preparation: 1 hour
Freezing time: 4 hours

1½ cups light cream
½ cup sugar
¼ teaspoon salt

(1) In the top of a double boiler, heat the cream until a film shimmers on top of it. Add the sugar and salt, stirring until they are dissolved. Remove the mixture from the heat.

4 egg yolks, lightly beaten

(2) To the egg yolks, add a little of the hot cream, stirring constantly. Then, in a steady stream, add the egg mixture to the cream, stirring constantly.

(3) Over simmering water, cook the custard, stirring, until it coats the spoon. Remove it from the heat and allow it to cool. Then chill it.

2 teaspoons vanilla
2 cups heavy cream, two days old

(4) When the custard is cold, stir in the vanilla and the heavy cream.

(5) Pour the mixture into refrigerator trays and place them in the freezing unit. When there is a one-inch border of thick mush around the edges of the trays, rapidly spoon the mixture into a *chilled* bowl and beat it vigorously with a rotary or electric beater until it is smooth and creamy. Return the dessert to the refrigerator trays and freeze it for 4 hours, or until it is firm.

* This recipe is a gratefully appreciated contribution from Helen McCully (see p. 11).

PASTRY FOR FRUIT PIES

Serving: one 9-inch pie (top and bottom crust)

Preparation: 1½ hours (including chilling the dough)

1¾ **cups all-purpose flour** 1 **teaspoon salt**	(1) In a mixing bowl, sift together the flour and salt.
⅔ **cup butter, lard, or vegetable shortening**	(2) Add the shortening, mixing quickly with your fingers until the mixture is in crumbs the size of peas.
⅓ **cup ice water**	(3) By the tablespoonful, sprinkle the water over the flour mixture, working it in with a fork. When the dough can be handled as a ball, enough water has been added (you may not need a full ⅓ cup). Do not knead the dough.
	(4) Wrap the dough in foil and chill it thoroughly. Roll it to fit the pie plate.

If desired, the following variations may be made:

¼ cup grated cheese may be cut into the flour at the same time as the shortening is added.

⅓ cup whole wheat flour may be substituted for ⅓ cup of the all-purpose flour.

The grated rind of 1 lemon may be sifted together with the dry ingredients.

JAMES BEARD'S CHERRY TOMATO SAUCE*

Tomatoes, it is true, are fruit, and yet excluded from this book, see pages x and 2. That is, save for this recipe which is highly original and very tasty. Serve the sauce over Helen McCully's Ice Cream, page 457. Or serve it alone, as a compote, topped with sour cream.

Serving: 5 cups

Preparation: 1 hour

3 boxes firm cherry tomatoes, stemmed (but with the stem end intact)
Boiling water

(1) In a mixing bowl, cover the tomatoes with boiling water; let them stand about 3 seconds and drain them in a colander.

(2) Peel the tomatoes (yes, this is a time-consuming task, and one that must be done carefully, for the tomatoes must remain intact).

4 cups sugar
1 cup water
Pinch of salt

(3) In a saucepan, combine the sugar and water. Over medium heat, cook the mixture, stirring, until the sugar is dissolved and the syrup is clear. Bring it to the boil and simmer it, uncovered, for 5 minutes.

1 lemon, thinly sliced

(4) To the syrup, add the tomatoes and lemon slices. Reduce the heat and simmer the tomatoes gently, uncovered, for 15 minutes.

(5) Using a slotted spoon, remove the tomatoes to a serving dish and set them aside. Bring the syrup again to the boil and cook it, uncovered, until it thickens slightly. Allow it to cool somewhat; sieve it over the tomatoes, discard the lemon slices, and chill the sauce.

* James Beard, whose knowledge of food surpasses all, gave the secret of his creation to his close friend, Helen McCully. She kindly granted me permission to use it here.

CUSTARD SAUCE

For cakes, puddings, and other desserts—a very useable sauce.

Serving: about 2 cups

Preparation: 20 minutes

3 egg yolks, lightly beaten
3 Tablespoons sugar
Pinch of salt

(1) In the top of a double-boiler, combine these ingredients, stirring to mix them well.

1½ cups warm milk
½ teaspoon vanilla

(2) Gradually add the milk, stirring constantly, and, over boiling water, cook the mixture, stirring constantly, until it thickens and coats the spoon. Remove the sauce from the heat at once. Stir in the vanilla.

Cream sherry or orange-flavored liqueur (optional)

(3) If desired, add 2 or 3 Tablespoons cream sherry or orange-flavored liqueur.

LEMON SAUCE

For cakes, puddings, and other desserts. The sauce may also be made with orange or lime.

Serving: about 1½ cups
Refrigerates

Preparation: 20 minutes

½ cup sugar
1 Tablespoon cornstarch
Pinch of salt

(1) In a saucepan, combine the sugar, cornstarch, and salt; stir them well.

1 cup water
Grated rind of 1 lemon

(2) Stir in the water and grated lemon rind. Cook the mixture, stirring constantly, until it is thickened and smooth. Remove the sauce from the heat.

3 **Tablespoons soft butter**
Juice of 1 lemon
¼ **cup cognac or orange-flavored**
liqueur (optional)

(3) Stir in the butter, then the lemon juice, and, if desired, the liqueur.

The sauce will keep for a long period, tightly covered and refrigerated. If it separates, heat it, stirring constantly.

INDEX